STO

ACPL ITEM
DISCARDED

SO-BWU-822

G

1-12-78

SOCIAL SECURITY

SOCIAL SECURITY
Promise and Reality

Rita Ricardo Campbell

HOOVER INSTITUTION PRESS
Stanford University
Stanford, California 94305

Acknowledgments

I wish to thank my colleague Gerald Musgrave, Ph.D., who wrote the chapter "Savings and Capital Formation," and who also read the entire manuscript and made many excellent suggestions and helpful criticisms. My thanks also go to George Marotta, Assistant Director of the Hoover Institution, for his extensive help in compiling this volume; to Michael Edwards, who is a perceptive editor; to Mickey Hamilton, General Manager of the Hoover Institution's Publication Department; and to her assistant, Beverly Cory. I am also especially grateful to my secretary, Ilse Dignam, who has with good humor and skill typed the manuscript in the hectic atmosphere of my office during the period of construction and the selection of interior design and furnishings of the Herbert Hoover Memorial Building.

The Hoover Institution on War, Revolution and Peace, founded at Stanford University in 1919 by the late President Herbert Hoover, is an interdisciplinary research center for advanced study on domestic and international affairs in the twentieth century. The views expressed in its publications are entirely those of the authors and do not necessarily reflect the views of the staff, officers, or Board of Overseers of the Hoover Institution.

Hoover Institution Publication 179

© 1977 by the Board of Trustees of the
    Leland Stanford Junior University
All rights reserved
International Standard Book Number: 0-8179-6791-5
Library of Congress Catalog Card Number: 76-26772
Printed in the United States of America

To my husband, Glenn

1994178

CONTENTS

LIST OF DOCUMENTS

Included in this volume are numerous excerpts from selected documents, official and unofficial, grouped by chapter according to subject. Each document excerpt has been given a double number (i.e., 1.1, 1.2), the first number indicating the chapter in which it appears, and the second, the number of the excerpt.

In many cases, excerpts from a single document are included in more than one chapter. For example, the reader will find excerpts from the *Report of the Advisory Council on Social Security, March 1975,* in chapter 1 (Document 1.2), chapter 2 (Document 2.1), chapter 3 (Document 3.1), chapter 4 (Document 4.2), and so forth.

The document excerpts appear by chapter as follows:

PREFACE

This volume has been compiled because of the intense personal interest of the 33 million individuals who receive social security benefits and the over 100 million who pay social security taxes at least at some time during the year. Because the trust funds are low even for contingency pay-as-you-go trust funds,[1] and there is an error in the 1972 amendments to the Social Security Act, there will have to be federal legislation soon. The purpose of this book is not to alarm individuals, but to provide them with the facts for public debate and assessment of the anticipated legislative bills. The issues discussed here were analyzed in depth by the 1974 Quadrennial Advisory Council on Social Security. The author served as a member of that council.

Because the social security program is exceedingly complex, there is a rather lengthy introductory chapter and also annotations where they are needed to introduce the excerpts from documents and articles in this and other chapters. Additionally, there are sections of extended commentary on such topics as withdrawals from the social security system that were written by the author and in which there are few if any excerpts from official documents. Chapter 8, which deals with the effect of social security on savings, was written by Gerald Musgrave, Ph.D., Research Fellow, Hoover Institution, Stanford University. The author's own recommendations conclude the volume.

Social security is a subject of vital concern to every American, since currently over 90 percent of the work force pays social security taxes. One-half the population pays more in social security taxes than in

---

1. As of December 1976, the OASI trust fund had assets of $35 billion or approximately an amount equal to six monthly benefit payments. The disability trust fund had $5.7 billion or roughly six months "payout"; the hospital insurance trust fund had $10.6 billion or also about 9 months "payout."

federal income taxes. For most families, whether they know it or not, the promised benefits from social security represent their most important source of wealth. The total annuity value of these anticipated payments is over $2.4 trillion. For most households, social security is more valuable than the total combined worth of their auto, savings accounts, personal possessions, and their home.

Social security began in the 1930s when the nation was in the Great Depression. At that time, labor union leaders believed that if more individuals retired, there would be more jobs available for the unemployed. Administration economists believed that an excessive personal savings rate (i.e., one larger than the investment rate) was one of the obstacles in the path to full employment and economic recovery. Compulsory savings under a social security program, they reasoned, would in the future reduce voluntary private savings by reducing individual responsibility to save or otherwise provide for retirement. Less saving and thus more spending was to stimulate the economy.

Payments to the program were small in the beginning. For the first decade the maximum tax was $60 per year. In the 1940s the tax rate on covered wages, the first $3,000, was 2 percent. As of January 1977, the tax rate was 9.9 percent on the first $16,500. That amounts to over $1,600 a year, and it does not include the 1.8 percent Medicare hospital insurance. The latter brings the total to 11.7 percent, or over $1,900. It should be noted that the employee generally knows that he pays one-half of the tax and many believe the employer "pays the other half." However, the employer is concerned with total labor costs when he makes his employment decisions. The employer's half is a payroll tax. It is a cost of doing business because it increases the cost of hiring a given amount of labor. As a business cost it forces, in varying combinations, an increase in the price of the product, a reduction in earnings of the firm, a smaller increase in future wage rates, and/or a reduction in employees' work hours. In chapter 8 this issue of the incidence, or final "resting place," of the payroll tax is analyzed.

In 1940, the average monthly benefit was $23.26 and in 1975 it was $263.53. One way to evaluate the increase in the program is to adjust for the effect of inflation and compute the percentage change. The 1940 employee-employer tax is equivalent to a purchasing power of $332 in 1975. So the real growth in that part of the per capita social security tax for only the worker's retirement benefit has been 352 percent over approximately 35 years. And since the 1940 retirement benefit of a covered worker is equivalent to $89 in 1975, the growth of this one benefit alone was 196 percent over the same period.

Different measures of costs and benefits could be made, but in general the results are the same. Not only have the individual programs grown, but new programs, including many dependency and disability benefits, have been added. The social security program has had a large and growing impact on the general population. Also, the social security tax paid by an individual worker has grown one and one-half to two times faster than has the increase in the amount paid to an individual recipient. The number of persons employed by the Federal Government to administer the social security program has increased to about 85,000.

Almost all social security experts agree that the program is now more like welfare than insurance. This is because the amount of money directly taxed away from workers has less relationship to their benefits when retired than to their "presumed needs." Social security is not "funded" as are private insurance companies. The unfunded debt or obligation is larger than the gross national product. Those who now pay the tax have no legal right or claim to any benefit in the future—any more than an oil company has a legal right to a continuation of the depletion allowance, or to an investment tax credit. Social security benefits are dependent on Congress's willingness to vote funds to continue payment of benefits, which eventually means the willingness of the taxpayers to pay high enough taxes to support future benefits.

Should the assumed liability of social security be made more widely known? Should the law require the trust fund not to fall below several years of anticipated payout? As of this writing, it has only about six months of benefits payable. Should the accrued liability be fully funded? Should individuals be given more ability through lower taxes to provide for their own retirement outside of social security? How will recent Supreme Court decisions on treatment of men and women under the law affect social security? These and other questions are examined in this book.

Social security exerts an important influence on society through the redistribution of economic wealth from one group to another. The major redistributions of wealth are from the young to the old; from the working to the retired; from single individuals to families; from married working women to others; and from those persons whose incomes are generated exclusively by wages and salaries that are covered by social security to those who also have property income. That income from property does not count makes it probable that there is also redistribution, to an extent, from lower- to higher-income earners. These and related issues are analyzed throughout the book.

The social security program is under fire by some knowledgeable insiders—actuaries, economists, and others. But these criticisms are scattered within professional literature and in testimony before congressional committees. The subject has not received the careful attention it deserves from the general public. One reason for this lack of public involvement is the difficulty of obtaining information or objective analyses about social security. Predictably, the material prepared by the Social Security Administration is not designed to raise doubts about the program's soundness or long-range effects.

Additionally, the computation of benefits is so complex that individuals cannot easily estimate their own benefits. Among the documents in the Appendix is an historical summary, "Social Security Benefit Computation, 1939-1973" (Document A.2), which is followed by a table entitled "A Precise Formula for Primary Insurance Amount under Benefit Table, Effective June 1975" (Document A.3); together these may enable the reader to estimate his or her future OASDI benefit.

This book is intended to be a good starting place for those who want to know more about social security. A bibliography is therefore provided for further study. The goal of this book is to help the general public understand how the social security system operates—what it does *for* them and what it does *to* them.

RITA RICARDO CAMPBELL
March 1977

1

THE DOUBTFUL LEGACY

THE DOUBTFUL LEGACY

The purpose of this book is to present the data needed to permit an analysis of some of the major issues and problems in the current and future administration of the U.S. social security program. The objective is not to create doubts about the system, but rather to inform the public of the issues, both many and complex, that need public debate and resolution. Most of these issues were considered by the 1974 Advisory Council on Social Security, of which I served as a member. This publication includes many of the council's findings, as well as excerpts from reports by the trustees of the funds and from other official documents of the U.S. Department of Health, Education, and Welfare and the Executive Branch.

Historical Review

On August 14, 1935, the Social Security Act was signed into law and a federal Old Age Social Insurance (OASI) system was established to provide monthly benefits upon retirement for workers. Reporting on the new legislation, the *New York Times* misquoted the president as saying: "[The] act [is] designed to protect the American wage-earner against the major hazards and vicissitudes of life."[1] In the presence of thirty dignitaries, who had been chiefly responsible for directing the bill through Congress, President Roosevelt read a statement that covered Title I, or grants to the states for the needy aged; Title II, or old age social insurance benefits without a means test to selected wage and salary workers; Title III, or unemployment compensation to be financed by the states; and Title IV, or state grants for aid to dependent children and others.

---

1. *New York Times,* "How Security Bill Aids Aged and Idle," 15 August 1935, p. 4.

Although this book addresses only Title II, the Social Security program, President Roosevelt's initial statement, as distributed to the press, used the term "social security" to cover all four titles of the act and even more. Part of that statement follows.

> Today a hope of many years' standing is in large part fulfilled. The civilization of the past hundred years, with its startling industrial changes, has tended more and more to make life insecure. Young people have come to wonder what would be their lot when they came to old age. The man with a job has wondered how long the job would last.
>
> This Social Security measure gives at least some protection to 30,000,000 of our citizens who will reap direct benefits through unemployment compensation, through old-age pensions and through increased services for the protection of children and the prevention of ill health.
>
> We can never insure 100 per cent of the population against 100 per cent of the hazards and vicissitudes of life, but we have tried to frame a law which will give some measure of protection to the average citizen and to his family against the loss of a job and against poverty-ridden old age.
>
> This law, too, represents a cornerstone in a structure which is being built but is by no means complete, a structure intended to lessen the force of possible future depressions, to act as a protection to future administrations of the government against the necessity of going deeply into debt to furnish relief to the needy, a law to flatten out the peaks and valleys of deflation and of inflation—in other words, a law that will take care of human needs and at the same time provide for the United States an economic structure of vastly greater soundness.[2]

In the same exuberance of that era, the *New York Times* story stated that "the long-range provisions, such as old-age pensions and unemployment insurance, are expected to be self-financing."[3]

Clearly, President Roosevelt and his influential advisors recognized that no society can insure its residents or citizens "against the major hazards and vicissitudes of life." Nowhere in the president's message was there assurance that the system would finance itself in the long run.

The recognized authoritative early history of the act in Lewis Meriam's *Relief and Social Security,* quotes the Secretary of the

2. *New York Times,* "Social Security Bill Is Signed; Gives Pensions to Aged, Jobless," ibid., p. 1.

3. *New York Times,* "How Security Bill. . . ."

Treasury Henry Morgenthau and President Roosevelt to conclude that "the record seems to establish beyond question that both the President and the Secretary of the Treasury envisioned practically an actuarial reserve system."[4] Yet Congress has never established tax schedules to accomplish this financial goal.

The basic social security law has been repeatedly amended over the past 40 years. Dependents and survivors of workers were added as beneficiaries in 1939. Somewhat later new benefits, such as permanent disability and hospital care in 1954 and 1965 respectively, were also provided. These changes have been reflected by additions to the name of the program, so that today it is correctly called Old-Age Survivors, Disability, and Health Insurance (OASDHI).[5] There are three trust funds: old age and survivors, disability, and hospitalization. An individual cannot select to be taxed differentially; if he works in employment covered by social security, he must pay the total tax, which goes to all three funds. These benefits are paid on a current basis out of the tax monies.

The average old-age retirement benefit of workers has more than doubled in real terms even when dependent benefits are excluded. Using 1975 dollars to eliminate the effect of price increases, we find that the average monthly benefit of retired workers was $90 in 1940 and $206 in 1975. The big jump in retirement benefits has been in recent years. By the end of the first quarter of 1976, 17 million retirees, including 1.8 million under age 65, were receiving benefits. The average monthly benefit awarded to workers retiring in that quarter, some with reduced benefits because they were less than 65 years of age, was $216 per month.

The U.S. social security program is the world's largest retirement, survivors', and disability insurance program. Total 1975 beneficiaries, including dependents and survivors, were 32 million. Outlays for social security in the calendar year 1975 were $67.1 billion, and were expected to increase to $82.7 billion in the fiscal year 1977. Nearly 20 percent of total federal tax receipts are now accounted for by payroll taxes for OASDHI.

About 21 million persons aged 65 and over (about 92 percent of the

---

4. Lewis Meriam, *Relief and Social Security* (Washington, D.C.: Brookings Institution, 1946), p. 87.

5. "OASDI" is used throughout, except when Part A of Medicare, or the hospitalization benefits and financing, are being discussed. Then "OASDHI" is used. Part B of Medicare is not discussed in this book.

population of this age) receive social security payments. The system covers almost the entire labor force of the United States, and the 1976 tax rate, for employer and employee combined, is 11.7 percent on the first $15,300 of wages (1.8 percent is for Medicare hospital insurance). The taxable base will increase in coming years because it is tied to the average wages subject to payroll tax. For example, in 1977 it will be $16,500.

The reader will have noted that I speak of social security as supported by a "tax." The consistent use of "contribution" rather than "tax" by the Social Security Administration over the years has created a false image in the public's mind, especially when the word "insurance" is used in conjunction with it. Such a use also implies that the payments are voluntary rather than compulsory. It is the compulsory nature of a tax by government that most economists consider to be its defining characteristic as a tax.

Current Problems in Brief

There are several problems in the system that could grow to significant proportions if not corrected in time. The most serious problem is whether revenues are adequate, in relation to the benefits payable both in the period 1978-80 and again over the long run. In 1975 the OASDI trust funds declined by $1.5 billion because they paid out more than the total receipt of taxes and interest on assets. Because employment has been less than anticipated, revenues from payroll taxes have not increased sufficiently to make up for the increase in benefits triggered by the recent double-digit inflation.

The long-run problem is that our birth rate is falling while the percentage of older people in the population is increasing; thus there will be fewer workers to support the retired. By the year 2005, the exceptionally high number of babies born in the early 1940s as a result of World War II will be retiring, and at the same time the low number of babies born in the 1970s will be entering the labor force. Thus the ratio of beneficiaries to workers will almost certainly increase, despite the increase in number of women working. All workers are tending to retire at younger ages, especially since a reduced OASI benefit is now available at age 62 years. Also, life expectancy has been increasing, from 69.7 years at birth in 1969 to 72.5 years in 1975. These factors increase the total amount of benefits payable on one worker's earnings in the near future. Only when those born in the years with lower birth rates are retiring will the demographic pressures tend to reverse. This in turn depends on whether future birth rates continue to remain low, that is, below the replacement rate of 2.1 ultimate births per woman. The 1976 rate (provisional data) is only 1.6.

Benefit and revenue levels are projected under different assumptions as to changes in prices, wage rates, and employment. Because of an error in the 1972 amendments to the Social Security Act, the revenues in some months have been less than the benefits payable, and this draws down the contingency trust fund. In 1972, an escalator provision was enacted providing for automatic cost-of-living increases in benefits. Inflation, and especially double-digit inflation as there was in 1973 and 1974, results under reasonable assumptions of future wages, prices, and employment in future benefits increasing in a capricious fashion. There are two reasons for this. First, the weighting used to compute the benefits is uneven. Thus the formula for computing the primary benefit uses (as of June, 1975) 129.48 percent of the first $100 of average monthly earnings (AMW); 47.10 percent of the next $290 of AMW; 44.01 of the next $150 of AMW; 51.73 of the next $100; 28.77 percent of the next $100; 23.98 of the next $250—and so on. This creates a "kink" in benefit amount (figure 1.1). Additionally, double counting of the inflation means that benefit amounts that include dependency amounts, which are not taxed, will in many cases exceed

FIGURE 1.1
APPROXIMATE RELATION BETWEEN MONTHLY BENEFIT AMOUNT AND AVERAGE MONTHLY WAGE IN BENEFIT TABLE AS OF JUNE 1975

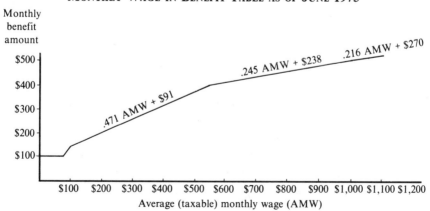

SOURCE: U.S. Department of Health, Education, and Welfare, Office of Research and Statistics, Staff Paper No. 22, *A Precise Formula for Primary Insurance Amounts,* p. 6.

recent net (i.e., after-tax) earnings, especially of low-income workers. Some low-income workers, especially married couples, one of whom works while both are 65 years of age, will have tax-free OASI benefits upon retirement that will be higher than their net incomes from recent wages after taxes. Inflation is being counted double: first, because wage rates have increased to keep pace and the benefit is computed on the basis of their inflated wages; and second, because meanwhile the benefit based on that level of wages has already been increased to compensate for the inflation. There is general agreement among economists and legislators that legislation is needed to correct this, otherwise uneasiness over the financing of OASDI will grow.

In order to understand exactly what double counting of the inflation means, consider the following hypothetical, rigid example in which no attempt is made to use actual benefit amounts. If a man earned $100 a month during year one, and subsequently in the first month of year two there was a 100 percent inflation, he would then earn $200 per month that year for identical work if his wages kept up fully with the inflation. Assume that he continues to earn $200 a month during years three, four, and five, and that there is no more inflation. His earnings for the total five-year period would be $10,800, or average monthly earnings of $180. If the man retires at the end of the fifth year, he would then receive whatever benefit at that time corresponds to $180 of average monthly earnings.

Now let us look at the benefit side. In year one, assume that average monthly earnings of $100 yield a benefit of $100 a month. Since the 1972 amendments provide that benefits rise with the cost-of-living index, in year two the $100 would become $200. It would remain there, under our assumption of no further price increases, until the end of year five, when the man retires. At this point, his average monthly earnings of $180 have already reflected the inflation, but the benefit structure reflects it too. The first $100 of average monthly earnings now yields a benefit of $200. The additional $80 earned, which in terms of a benefit in year one has been worth $60 (the weights are scaled downwards as income increments are added) is now worth $120. This adds up to an average monthly benefit of $320 upon retirement. The inflation was 100 percent, yet the individual's benefit increased far beyond that level because his wages also went up. They did so purely because of the inflation, not because of a change in job content. In general then, increases in the benefit amount awarded for those still working are "coupled" with the increases in benefit amount for retired individuals. "Decoupling" would permit benefits, once awarded, to rise with the cost of living, but the whole benefit structure used in the computation at the time of the award would not be so increased.

Another area of concern is the inequality of treatment of men and women by the system. Of particular interest is the Supreme Court decision in March 1975 (*Weinberger* v. *Wiesenfeld*). It gives a surviving male parent with child under 18 years a benefit based on his spouse's covered earnings, just as the act now provides for a similarly situated surviving female parent. Moreover, the court declared in March 1977 (*Goldfarb* v. *Califano*) that it was unconstitutional to have entitlement requirements for dependency benefits that differ by sex, for the specific category of surviving spouses, widows, and widowers. These decisions appear to set a precedent to equalize dependency benefits irrespective of sex.

There is also growing evidence that, as the tax base moves up with increases in average wages covered by social security, yearly increases in the total of payroll taxes paid are leading to reductions of benefits under private pension plans. There is an adjustment lag before firms can rearrange or renegotiate fringe benefit payments to employees. The availability of OASI retirement, plus the loss of benefits when an otherwise entitled person works, probably acts to reduce the labor supply. While there is unemployment this may not be always counted as a negative. Once our birth rate, which is falling, causes a decrease in the supply of labor, it may be so counted. Furthermore, the OASDI system may have unanticipated but important effects on savings and capital formation available for investment in business.

Despite the expansion of type and level of benefits, one hundred percent of the labor force is not covered. In 1940 about 60 percent of the labor force was covered; today, the figure is nearly 90 percent.[6] Six million workers, 70 percent of those not covered, are government workers: 2.8 million federal and 3.5 million state and local employees. If these 6 million were covered and taxes on their wages and matching payroll taxes were paid, revenues would be greatly increased because the payment of benefits to them would lag. A net revenue gain would also result, because about fifty percent of near-retirement, federal civil service employees already have entitlement to a low social security benefit through a concomitant secondary job or a prior job that was covered.

6. U.S. Treasury Department, *Budget of the United States Government, Fiscal Year 1977,* "Special Analyses" (Washington, D.C.: U.S. Government Printing Office, 1977), p. 221.

For example, in 1975, 43 percent of all retired federal employees (including those under the foreign service retirement system) were receiving social security benefits—benefits not based on their civil service employment but on minimal wages in secondary jobs covered by OASDI.[7] By paying a minimal tax for ten years on wages from secondary jobs—for example, selling one evening a week in a department store (required earnings are only $50 in a three-month period)—any such person can receive a heavily weighted minimum benefit, yielding dollar monthly benefits that are very high in relation to the taxes paid. This is because the law assumes that the very low wages from the secondary job are wage income from the primary job. As of June 1975, a 129 percent weight was used to compute benefits of very low-income workers. What is more, under the 1972 amendments this percent weight increases when the cost of living increases. Thus, although federal employees do not contribute via taxes on their regular salaries to the social redistributive purposes of the OASDI system, many of them actually receive, by taking legal advantage of the law, a social benefit intended by Congress only for very low-income workers. Additionally, they have a very favorable federal civil service retirement benefit plan. In 1975, the average monthly benefit was $550 under the Civil Service Commission and $1,152 under Foreign Service Retirement.

There are still other inequities under OASDI. For instance, either a retirement or a dependency benefit, whichever is larger, is received by a married woman who has been paying OASDI taxes, and it may be smaller than benefits received by the nonworking, married woman who has paid no OASDI taxes, but may receive a wife's and widow's benefit based on her husband's covered earnings. Similarly, single persons pay the same taxes as married persons but may have no dependents entitled to a dependency benefit. The rationale is that singles who have no children, as well as married couples without children, should from society's point of view contribute to benefits for dependent children.

The list of inequities could be continued, especially as they affect different age groups. For example, older persons in general have received and do receive a much greater return on their OASDI taxes than persons now retiring. All retired persons and survivors now receive relatively more benefits in relationship to taxes paid by them

---

7. Although about one hundred million persons pay OASDI taxes during a calendar year, many of these, being students, are not in the labor force for the whole year. The labor force in 1975 stood at 85 million.

and on their behalf. Young persons just beginning to pay into the program will probably be more affected by legislative reforms, which are needed, and can expect to receive less in relationship to taxes paid by them and on their behalf.

Additionally, many individuals complain that it is inequitable for a person who has paid into the system over a long period of years to reach age 65 and be unable to collect a retirement benefit—because he or she is earning from covered wages an amount above the allowable minimum. Meanwhile, they point out, their neighbor, who has reached age 65 and is retired from work and who receives his total social security benefit, may collect an even greater amount—in the form of rents, stock, dividends, and interest. Others, however, argue that this is not an inequity because the system is designed to pay a benefit only to persons who retire from work. In this view, social security is not planned to replace a loss of income, but only a loss of *earned* income. It is true that the system was initially promoted as one way of reducing the high unemployment rates of the 1930s; hence its emphasis on retirement. However, persons 65 years and older who continue to work resent that they too must pay OASDI taxes on earnings. This appears particularly unfair if their earnings are lower now than before they reached age 65.

In a society where the number of workers may decline as fertility rates continue to fall, the long-run effects of the OASDI program on labor supply become more crucial. It can be argued that the system should encourage individuals to work beyond their sixty-fifth year. In recent years an increasing percentage of males have been retiring earlier, and this appears to be a worldwide trend. The labor force in the United States has remained about constant because of the increasing percentage of females working. In all industrial countries with an increasing percentage of females working, the birth rate has been falling.

Finally, the system's insurance objectives, which were predominant when it was created, are often confused with its increasingly important welfare objectives, which were added in subsequent years. The confusion was actually fostered by the early social security administrators. For many years, as we have seen, the SSA has called OASDI taxes "contributions," while at the same time implying that "social insurance" has many, if not all, of the same characteristics of private insurance—for instance, the "earned right" of entitlement. By continuous use of the term "earned right," the SSA has built up the fiction that the benefits are directly related to the worker's covered earnings and taxes paid, in contrast to welfare benefits which are directly related to needs. Social security benefits have *some* relationship to social security taxes paid, but only in a capricious fashion. Thus the promise of individual equity has been eroded by successive additions of so-called social adequacy benefits.

Today we are faced with the reality that welfare-type benefits cannot be continually added to an individual equity system if the latter concept is to prevail even in a much reduced sense. The weighted, minimum benefits provided to low-income retirees is in effect a transfer of funds from higher-income participants. Going far beyond this, however, has been the addition of various assumed dependency benefits that obscure how the income transfers affect individuals at different income levels. The few clearly proven transfers of income are from the working young to the retired old; from singles to married persons with dependents; and from married women who work in covered employment to other groups.

Some younger, well-paid workers are learning that they could buy a much better annuity in the private market than the social security system provides for their tax money. Private protection against permanent disability, however, may be more costly, especially for women. During the four years 1970-74, the ratio of the median replacement rates to mean taxable monthly earnings over a working lifetime has increased from 44 to 59 for men and from 59 to 79 for women.[8] Whereas the average monthly earnings of men rose 20 percent in this period, from $320 to $390, women's rose only 12 percent from $160 to $180, which was also a much lower level to start with.

Federal Welfare Programs

Proposals to separate the welfare aspects of social security from the straight insurance concept of retirement benefits have been increasing. Since the passage of the Social Security Act, the federal, state, and local governments have established many welfare programs. These take care, in large measure, of the major social adequacy problems that

---

8. The replacement rates are defined as mean social security benefits expressed as a percentage of mean monthly earnings. See U.S. Department of Health, Education, and Welfare, Research and Statistics Note No. 18, June 15, 1976.

OASDI, as amended in 1939 and in most successive election years, has been structured to address.

There were federal cash outlays in 1975 of $14.3 billion for public assistance, including Medicaid, and $12.2 billion for unemployment insurance. When all the federal income security benefit payments in cash, including OASDHI, are included, they total $109.6 billion. Additionally, federal outlays for "in-kind" benefits—food, some medical care, as in veterans' hospitals, and housing—were $30 billion for a total federal expenditure of income security benefits in 1975 of $140 billion. This amount was estimated to rise in 1976 to $164 billion, with OASDI payments making up $81 billion of it.[9]

The new 1974 Supplemental Security Income (SSI) program should be specifically mentioned. This program in recent months has added many aged, blind, or disabled persons and dependent children to the SSI monthly rolls. These federal and state welfare payments were $6 billion in 1975, the second year after the program's inception. SSI provided on July 1, 1976, a basic monthly payment of $167.80 to an individual and $251.80 to an eligible couple. These are federally financed minimum national payments that increase with increases in the cost of living and are financed out of general revenues.

The initiation of this and other new welfare programs outside the social security system, plus the continuation of state and local public assistance in addition to Medicaid, are factors that raise the question whether social adequacy under OASDI should be as important a consideration as equity more than 40 years after inception of the program.

In the fiscal year 1950, per capita "social insurance," largely social security expenditures, including all OASDI benefits, in constant prices were $67.20; in 1960, $175.29; in 1970, $352.31; and in 1975, $567.32—an increase of 744% over 1950.[10] As the payroll taxes are increased to meet the social security expenditures, various categories of covered workers, especially those who find that their social security taxes exceed their personal income taxes, are raising questions of equity. Many of the only groups that have the option of withdrawing from the system are doing so. They are the state and local government employees. Those of San Jose, California, and New York City are examples of

---

9. U.S. Treasury, *Budget of the United States. . .1977*, p. 219.

10. *Social Security Bulletin,* January 1976, p. 10. These expenditures include *all* the benefits (i.e., they also include the so-called secondary benefits, for disability and dependency), and thus are much higher than the expenditures for workers' primary benefits alone.

groups in the late 1970s that had opted out or planned to leave the program. In the case of San Jose, much publicity was given to the fact that it had arranged for private pension plan coverage that lowered the contributions paid by city and employees while resulting in higher pension benefits. The California State Employees' Association (CSEA) had testified in favor of terminating their coverage under social security. In the case of New York City, about $180 million in taxes was expected to be saved annually.

Coverage of state employees varied greatly in 1973, from 100 percent in 11 states to less than 1 percent in Massachusetts and Ohio. In 1975 Alaska, which had 88.5 percent of its state employees covered, became the first state to give the required two-year notice of intent to withdraw all state employees. By 1977, California, Louisiana, and Texas had given notice for or actually terminated the largest number of employee groups. Some 29 states had "no terminations effective or pending," according to official figures.[11]

The Federal Legislative Process

The social security system is an exceedingly complex program because the social security program has three major parts: health, welfare, and pension components, with different entitlement rules for each type of benefit financed by taxes. It therefore comes under several congressional committees, in both the Senate and the House.[12] Additionally, the Social Security Act (section 706) requires that an Advisory Council be appointed every four years by the secretary of Health, Education, and Welfare, and that the council submit reports of its findings with recommendations to the secretary, who will then transmit them to the Speaker of the House. Also, it is customary for the secretary to send these recommendations to the president of the Senate. Thus, the reports of the various quadrennial councils play an important role in the development of new social security legislation. The work of the 1974 council is described in the headnote to document 1.2, below.

---

11. U.S. Department of Health, Education, and Welfare, *State and Local Government Employees Covered under Social Security, 1972-73,* Research and Statistics Note No. 18, September 30, 1976, p. 2.

12. This section draws heavily on the *Congressional Quarterly Weekly Report* (various issues) and the *Congressional Quarterly Annual Almanac,* 1975 and 1976.

Congressional committees

The act not only covers federal welfare and Medicare hospitalization benefits; it also involves taxes levied under the Federal Insurance Contributions Act (FICA). It concerns many congressional committees in addition to those on appropriations, budget, and oversight. In 1977 the two primary Senate committees were: (1) the new Human Resources Committee, chaired by H.A. Williams, Jr. (D., N.J.), which had a Subcommittee on Health chaired by Senator Edward Kennedy (D., Mass.) (this was apparently a new name for the Labor and Public Welfare Committee); (2) the Senate Finance Committee, chaired by Russell B. Long (D., La.), and its various subcommittees, as, for example, those on health, revenue sharing, aging, and supplemental security income (SSI). The Judiciary Committee, chaired by James Eastland (D., Miss.), had its Subcommittee on Antitrust and Monopoly hold extensive hearings in 1974 on "competition in the health services market," which involved the Medicare program.

The Senate Special Committee on Aging, with Frank Church (D., Idaho) as chairman, reports financing and makes recommendations to the Senate, but it cannot report legislation. This, then, is a weaker committee even though it has many subcommittees. From a review of the Senate committees alone it is clear that social security is so pervasive in the United States economy that there are few domestic committees without some kind of involvement in the design and operation of social security programs.

The Social Security Act was last substantially amended in 1972, after extensive hearings by the Senate Finance Committee. On the House side, corresponding hearings were conducted by the Ways and Means Committee, which controls the purse strings of the U.S. government. In January of 1975 this all-powerful committee split into six subcommittees. The three concerned with social security were: health, under Dan Rostenkowski (D., Ill.) which became very active in respect to federal health insurance for the unemployed; public assistance, whose acting chairman in 1976 was James Corman (D., Ca.); and a third on social security, chaired by James Burke (D., Mass.). There was also a Ways and Means Oversight Committee. At times even the House Interstate and Foreign Commerce Committee, through its Subcommittee on Health and the Environment, has held hearings on matters affecting the Social Security Administration. Also, the Select Committee on Aging, chaired by William J. Randall (D., Mo.), has been active in social security.

With this large number of committees and subcommittees of Congress involved in the center of and at the periphery of social security problems, there is much jockeying among the various committees for positions of influence. Generally, this results in particular subcommittees in the House and Senate gaining primary responsibility for a particular aspect of the very large program under the Social Security Act. Overall the Senate Finance Committee and the House Ways and Means Committee have the most power. This book does not discuss all the separate programs but rather concentrates on the areas of old-age retirement and survivor benefits.

Sources of information

Additional input to the congressional committees comes from the annual reports that the Social Security Act requires to be submitted by the trustees of the various trust funds established under it. There are three of these funds, and an annual report is made on each: the Old Age Survivors Insurance (OASI) Trust Fund; the Disability Trust Fund; and the Medicare Part A, or hospitalization, trust fund. Additionally, Part B of Medicare has a contingency reserve, which is inappropriately entitled the Federal Supplementary Medical Insurance Trust Fund. In practice this has always been considered to be a contingency fund. Part B of Medicare which exists primarily to pay physicians' bills, uses current "premiums" to cover an anticipated one-half or so of the program cost and general revenues to cover the other half. Initially, the OASI fund was thought of as a compromise between a private trust fund and a contingency reserve. Opinions varied as to how many years it should hold of the total annual benefits paid out; three years was an often-quoted figure. Currently, the fund has an amount that is equal to six months of benefit payments. The security of the system lies in the taxation power of the federal government.

Another very important source of information to legislators in this very complicated area is the staff of the Social Security Administration and its monthly periodical, the *Social Security Bulletin*. The latter details past experiences of the program and provides analyses that can be applied to future changes in it. Among other items recently published in the *Bulletin* are data on social security programs in foreign countries.[13] As a person who has read the *Bulletin* over the

---

13. As, for example, the article "World Developments and Trends in Social Security," in the April 1976 issue; and "Maintaining Value of Social Security Benefits: Foreign Experience," in the November 1976 issue.

years, I think it is fair to say that its articles in a sense foreshadow legislative change. The charge has been made by some that, because the articles are written, or at least approved, by the administrators of the program, it is not surprising that in general it has been a major advocate of expanding it. An example of this involving a related social issue is that for years articles in the *Bulletin* have directly and indirectly argued for comprehensive national health insurance, which as yet is not an accomplished fact. Since about 1976, however, this particular issue has been dropped. That alone is a good indicator that *comprehensive* national insurance is unlikely in the near future.

The Social Security Administration puts out two series of very valuable research papers. One consists of "staff papers," which are in-depth analyses for the specialist. For example, *Staff Paper No. 16,* published in 1975, was entitled "Reducing Social Security Contributions for Low Income Workers: Issues and Analysis." A shorter and more frequent publication is *Research and Statistics Notes;* it comes out irregularly during the year, and deals with subjects that point to issues of current debate among the well-informed. For example, the issue of July 30, 1976 (number 15) is on "Self-Employment and Retirement Age," and that of December 14, 1976 (number 24) on "Preliminary Results of the 1973 Survey of Student Beneficiaries." The first one was obviously directed towards the current debate on whether 65 was the most desirable age of entitlement to a full retirement benefit. The latter was relevant to the Ford administration's proposal to eliminate payments to children, presumed dependents of insured workers, who are eighteen to twenty years of age, unmarried, and in college eight out of twelve months in the year. The Ford administration pointed out that over a billion dollars was paid to these students in 1975, including monthly benefits for the four months of the vacation period during which they did not have to work. Indeed, most of them did not work then because if they had, they would have lost some or all of their social security benefits.

Because the social security fund was considered to be in short-run and long-run imbalance both by the annual trustees' reports and by the 1974-1975 quadrennial council's reports, and because the program is so complicated that few, including congressmen, understand it, in April 1975 a special consultant panel was appointed jointly by the Senate Finance Committee and the House Ways and Means Committee. A special report had originally been requested from the Congressional Research Service, but apparently it felt inadequate to do the

type of job that was needed. The committees therefore "engaged the
services of William C. L. Hsiao," who is both an economist and
actuary, and he in turn hired four additional persons, two economists
and two actuaries, to help him. In the course of this book their report is
referred to informally as the report of the Consultant Panel; it was
printed in August 1976.

Among other official documents quoted from are the printed
reports, dated March 10, 1975, of the 1974-75 Advisory Council; the
1976 and 1977 reports of the Council of Economic Advisers to the
president; various messages of President Ford; the U.S. Congressional
Budget Office's "Budget Options for Fiscal Year 1977"; various annual
trustees' reports of the different trust funds; the October 1975 report of
Senate Special Committee on Aging; the March 1976 report of the
U.S. Citizens' Advisory Council on the Status of Women, entitled
Women in 1975; and the December 1975 report of the House Subcommittee on Retirement and Employment.

Among unofficial documents are various articles from the *Social
Security Bulletin;* the so-called white paper, dated February 10, 1975,
by three former social security commissioners; and miscellaneous
articles and other items by members of the Social Security Administration, including memoranda to the Advisory Council, quotations from
newspapers, and other sources.

How a legislative bill becomes statutory law

There are many ways in which a federal bill, or legislation proposed
by a member of Congress, becomes a statutory law. One common
method is that an identical bill is introduced simultaneously into the
House and Senate and then immediately referred to the full committee
with jurisdiction over that bill. The latter then delegates it to the
particular subcommittee specializing in the matters involved in the bill.
The subcommittee may hold hearings and eventually submit a legislative bill to the full committee of the Senate or House as the case may be.
The full committee may then hold more hearings and revise the bill
before "reporting it out" for debate in the Senate or House. If, on the
other hand, the full committee is against the bill, it may "die in
committee."

The House Rules Committee may expedite passage resulting from
adroit floor management by the bill's major sponsor. Some bills,

especially if they are not controversial, go directly to be voted on by House members. Floor management—the art of getting a bill before the legislature at the right moment—is also important in the Senate because the Senate leadership schedules the order in which bills are taken up. A bill is usually debated; different parts of the bill may be voted on; and rather than the whole bill coming to a vote, it can then be sent back to the major Senate and House committees for "conference." The latter is a time-consuming procedure in which both Senate and House members compromise in an attempt to bring to the floor of their respective legislative bodies a bill that will have a better chance of passing.

In cases where the Senate and House have passed different bills on the same topic, the two bills will automatically go to the joint conference committee, composed of members of both legislative bodies, which will attempt to resolve the differences. If the compromise version is approved, by Senate and House, the bill then goes to the president who may sign it into law or veto it. Congress may override the veto by a two-thirds majority vote in each legislative body. The bill thus can become law without the president's signature.

After a law has been in effect for some time, congressional oversight committees and budget reviews may occur. In addition to congressional appropriation and oversight committees, the Office of Management and Budget (OMB) has in recent years increased its influence on program direction. It appeared that the Carter administration, under the "zero budgeting" concept (i.e., accounting each year for the necessity of program expenditures) would continue the trend to increase the influence of OMB, once legislation had been passed.

Document 1.1 Report of the President's Council of Economic Advisers, January 1976 [excerpt]

The old-age, survivors, and disability insurance program, generally referred to as social security, is the largest income transfer program, in terms of both funds and number of recipients. In 1975, 32 million persons received cash benefits of $67 billion, which was 19 percent of the Federal budget and 4.5 percent of GNP [table 1.1]. Growth in the program has been extraordinary during the past 5 years. The number of recipients increased by 22 percent, and after adjusting for the increase in prices over this period, the average monthly benefit for retired workers increased by 26 percent.

DOCUMENT 1.1: *Economic Report of the President: With the Annual Report of the Council of Economic Advisors* (Washington, D.C.: U.S. Government Printing Office, 1977), pp. 111-15.

The social security system has been successful in raising the income levels of a large proportion of the elderly who otherwise would have been impoverished. However, because of the sheer size of the program, there is a need to

TABLE 1.1

**BENEFICIARIES AND CASH BENEFITS IN THE OLD-AGE,
SURVIVORS, AND DISABILITY INSURANCE PROGRAM (OASDI),
SELECTED YEARS, 1950-75**

BENEFICIARY OR BENEFIT	1950	1960	1965	1970	1974	1975
Number of beneficiaries (millions)[1]:						
Total	3.5	14.8	20.9	26.2	30.9	31.9
Retired workers, dependents, and survivors	3.5	14.2	19.1	23.6	26.9	27.6
Retired workers only	1.8	8.1	11.1	13.3	16.0	16.5
Disabled workers and dependents		.7	1.7	2.7	3.9	4.3
Annual cash benefits (billions of dollars)	1.0	11.3	18.3	31.9	58.5	67.1
Average monthly benefits (dollars):						
All retired workers[1]	44	74	84	118	188	206
Maximum to men retiring at age 65[2]	45	119	132	190	[3]305	[3]342
Maximum to women retiring at age 65[2]	45	119	136	196	[3]316	[3]360
Minimum to persons retiring at age 65[2]	10	33	44	64	[3]94	[3]101

1. As of December of each year.
2. Assumes retirement at beginning of year.
3. As of June.

SOURCE: Department of Health, Education, and Welfare.

evaluate recent developments in the pattern of expenditures and of the taxes required to fund them.

PROGRAM CHARACTERISTICS

The first social security legislation of 1935 intended that the program operate on a self-financed and actuarially sound basis. Contributions from the payroll tax were to exceed benefits in the early years so that a substantial trust fund relative to annual benefit outlays could be accumulated. Individual benefits were to be closely related to each individual's prior earnings except for preferential treatment at the base (minimum) amount. The amendments of 1939 changed the character of the program by stipulating that individuals retiring early in the life of the program would receive benefits greater than the actuarial value of taxes paid, and that dependents of retired workers would also receive benefits without any additional tax payments required. The 1950 amendments moved still farther away from a fully funded trust to the "pay-as-you-go" system which prevails today, under which those currently working essentially pay for the benefits of those who are retired.

As of January 1976, OASDI benefits are funded from a tax of 9.9 percent levied on the first $15,300 of wages, the maximum taxable earnings, with the payments shared equally by employer and employees. The self-employed pay a tax of 7 percent. (An additional tax of 1.8 percent for wage and salary workers and 0.9 percent for the self-employed is for medicare hospital insurance.) Tax payments are paid into separate trust funds, one for retirement and survivors, and one for disability. About 90 percent of all wage and salary earners and the self-employed are covered by the program and subject to mandatory contributions. The major exclusions are Federal civilian employees, who are under a separate Federal retirement program, and some State and local employees. In the past, increases in benefits and taxes have been legislated by the Congress periodically. Starting in 1975, on the basis of the 1972 amendments, benefit levels were "indexed" or linked to the consumer price index so that they rise automatically depending on increases in prices. Similarly, the maximum taxable earnings base was roughly indexed to changes in average covered wages, and hence it also increases automatically over time.

Social security is designed as a replacement for earnings lost because of a worker's retirement, disability, or death. Eligibility for benefits depends on work in covered employment for a minimum period as well as on age, disability, or survivor status. Although there are no restrictions on the amount of income that may be received from property, other pensions, or any sources other than work, individual benefits may be reduced if the beneficiary has earnings from employment and is less than 72 years of age. In 1976 beneficiaries can earn $2,760 without any reduction in benefits, but for each $2 in earnings above $2,760, benefits are reduced by $1. The amount of a worker's basic monthly benefit (before any reductions) depends on the worker's record of covered earnings, averaged over a specified number of years (at present 20 years for retirement benefits). Dependents and dependent survivors receive payments tied to the benefit level of the primary beneficiary. Workers choosing to retire between ages 62 and 65 receive a permanently reduced benefit. Disabled workers under the age of 65 have been eligible for benefits since 1957.

[Table 1.2] shows the relation between the size of the benefit awarded and preretirement earnings for hypothetical male workers at different earnings levels, as calculated by one study. Examples are given for men retiring at age 65 and age 62, for single men, and for married men whose wives did not work in covered employment. The social security formula for determining benefits is scaled progressively so that benefits as a proportion of earnings fall as the benefit base rises. The benefit base, in turn, is calculated from prior earnings. For example, a male worker with a low-wage history culminating in $4,000 in annual earnings in the year before retirement would receive 55 percent of his preretirement earnings in benefits if he is single, 82 percent if he is married.

TABLE 1.2

SOCIAL SECURITY BENEFITS FOR SINGLE MEN AND FOR MARRIED MEN
WITH A DEPENDENT WIFE RETIRING AT AGE 65 YEARS AND
AGE 62 YEARS, 1974

1973 EARNINGS BEFORE TAXES AND MARITAL STATUS	MEN RETIRING AT AGE 65 YEARS		MEN RETIRING AT AGE 62 YEARS	
	AMOUNT OF TAX FREE BENEFIT (DOLLARS)	BENEFIT AS PERCENT OF 1973 EARNINGS BEFORE TAXES	AMOUNT OF TAX FREE BENEFIT (DOLLARS)	BENEFIT AS PERCENT OF 1973 EARNINGS BEFORE TAXES
$4,000:				
Single	2,197	54.9	1,758	43.9
Married	3,296	82.4	2,582	64.5
$8,000:				
Single	3,349	41.9	2,679	33.5
Married	5,024	62.8	3,935	49.2
$12,000:				
Single	3,644	30.4	2,916	24.3
Married	5,467	45.6	4,282	35.7

NOTE: Benefits are based on average amount of a worker's wages over a 19-year period. Wage histories for each category of wage earners were simulated by assuming that their wages grew at the same rate as that of the average wages of non-supervisory personnel. The wife is assumed to be same age as worker and to have no covered earnings.
SOURCE: Department of Health, Education, and Welfare (Office of Income Security Policy).

But a male worker making $12,000 before retirement would receive only 30 percent of such earnings if single and 46 percent if married. Because benefits are tax free and taxes are relatively more important at higher earnings levels, however, the decline in after-tax replacement rates as earnings rise is somewhat less than indicated here.

INCOME OF THE AGED

Social security is an important source of income for the aged. Largely because earnings decline with age, and because women are less likely to work than men, and earn less if they do, social security increases in relative importance with age and is relatively more important for households headed by a widowed woman (often single-person households). In 1973, among households headed by a widow aged 70 or older, the average annual income was $2,819, of which social security accounted for 57 percent. By contrast, among households headed by a married man aged 65 to 69, the total mean income was $9,694; social security on the average accounted for 25 percent of income, and wages and self-employment earnings accounted for 46 percent. In 1974, 23 percent of all persons 65 years old and over were women living alone, while 60 percent were married and living with a spouse.

The rapid increases in social security benefits of recent years have made a substantial contribution in improving the income status of the elderly. In 1966, 28.5 percent of those aged 65 and over were below the poverty level compared to 14.2 percent for all persons; in 1974, 15.7 percent of the elderly were in proverty compared to 11.6 percent of all persons. In addition to cash income, many of the elderly have imputed income from owner-occupied homes for which they are no longer making mortgage payments (70 percent of elderly households own their own homes). Virtually all of those aged 65 and over receive medicare and medicaid benefits, and many also finance some of their consumption out of their assets. These additional sources raise the relative level of consumption of the aged.

WORK INCENTIVES

Social security has created incentives for the aged and disabled to reduce their work during the year. The availability of the pension itself is an inducement to work less and take more leisure. In addition, the earnings test which applies up to age 72 restricts the amount that can be earned without forfeiting any benefits.

Between 1940 and 1950 only about a third of men aged 65 and over were eligible for social security benefits [table 1.3], and benefits were low and declining in real value. After 1950 there was a sharp increase in the percentage eligible for social security—to 81 percent in 1960 and 93 percent in 1975. Benefit amounts also increased sharply, even after adjusting for inflation. After remaining stable from 1940 to 1950 the labor force participation of men at 65 years of age and over declined sharply. Hours worked per week for men 65 years of age and over also fell, from 42 in 1950 to 34 in 1970.

The same relation between benefits and retirement behavior is evident for the group aged 62-64, who became eligible for retirement at reduced benefits in 1961. Although their labor force participation rate had been fairly stable until 1960, it declined markedly after benefits became available. One recent study finds that for every 10 percent increase in social security benefits relative to average wages, the number of male beneficiaries aged 62-64 increases by 2.8

TABLE 1.3
LABOR FORCE PARTICIPATION RATES AND SOCIAL SECURITY BENEFITS FOR
MEN 60 YEARS OF AGE AND OLDER, SELECTED YEARS, 1940-75

AGE GROUP	1940	1950	1960	1970	1970	1975
Percent of men in labor force:[1]						
60-64 years	79.0	79.4	77.8	73.2	75.0	65.7
60-61 years	81.7	81.8	82.0	80.3	78.7	75.2
62-64 years	77.0	77.7	74.7	67.9	69.8	58.8
65-69 years	59.4	59.7	44.0	39.3	41.6	31.7
70 years and over	28.4	28.3	21.9	16.6	17.7	15.1
70-74 years	38.4	38.7	28.7	22.5	25.2	21.2
75 years and over	18.2	18.7	15.6	12.1	12.0	10.2
Percent of men eligible for social security benefits[2]:						
62-64 years	([3])	([3])	([3])	93.8	......	96.4
65 years and over	[4]10.9	32.4	80.7	91.0	......	92.5
Average monthly primary social insurance benefit for men filing for benefits in given year:						
Current dollars	23.26	31.88	92.03	146.99	......	263.53
1975 dollars[5]	89.81	71.80	168.24	205.12	......	263.53

1. Data in the first four columns are from the "Census of Population." Data in the last two columns are from the "Current Population Survey"; they exclude institutional population and are for April.
2. Based on number of persons eligible at beginning of year.
3. Not eligible for social security benefits.
4. Data are for 1941.
5. Deflated by the consumer price index.
SOURCES: Department of Commerce (Bureau of the Census), Department of Labor (Bureau of Labor Statistics), and Department of Health, Education, and Welfare.

percent in the first quarter after the increase, and by 6.0 percent after 5 quarters.

Persons eligible for social security have also been found to adjust their work behavior to avoid losing benefits under the earnings test. Thus, following a liberalization in the earnings test during 1966, over 10 percent of the working beneficiaries raised their earnings from $1,200 to $1,500, the new ceiling. The earnings test does not apply to those aged 72 and over, who may earn any amount without forfeiting benefits. For this reason many of those with high earnings wait until age 72 to start collecting benefits.

Although social security appears to have been an important factor in the decline in employment among those of retirement age, other factors were operating as well. Increases in earnings and income over time enabled workers to save more in order to enjoy more years of leisure at older ages, and a larger proportion of the elderly now have asset holdings and private pensions. The decline in self-employment on the farm and in nonfarm industries also contributed to declining work at older ages, since the self-employed retire at a later age than employees. Studies indicate that in years of relatively high unemployment retirement is accelerated. Compulsory retirement practices may also have had an effect. However, the spread of compulsory retirement may itself have been stimulated by the availability of social security and the development of private pension systems.

There were additional incentives for the elderly to work longer, however, which have probably served to prevent labor force participation at older ages from falling even faster. Most notable may be the increase in the availability of white-collar employment, which tends to make less demand on physical strength. Increases in part-time employment opportunities have made work more feasible for those wishing a limited schedule, although the increase in part-time jobs may itself have been partly stimulated by the supply of older workers [pp. 111-15].

Document 1.2   Report of the Advisory Council on Social Security, March 1975 [excerpts]

[*Author's Note.* The Advisory Council is established every four years, and is required by section 706 of the Social Security Act. The 1974 council was appointed by HEW Secretary Weinberger on April 23 of that year, and submitted its report on March 6, 1975. The council's mandated purpose was to review the status of the four social security trust funds in relation to the long-range commitments of the social security program, the scope of coverage, the adequacy of benefits, and all other aspects of the program, including its impact on public assistance programs under the Social Security Act.

The Advisory Council of 1974 was unique in several respects. It was the first council not to include among its members any of the persons who created the system four decades ago and not to have any member who had served on an earlier council. Also, the council, which held its first meeting in May 1974, had only eight months to perform its work instead of the normal twenty months or more. It was therefore forced to limit its in-depth

DOCUMENT 1.2: U.S. Congress, House, Committee on Ways and Means, *Reports of the Quadrennial Advisory Council on Social Security,* 94th Cong., 1st sess., H.D. 94-75, March 10, 1975 (Washington, D.C.: U.S. Government Printing Office, 1975), pp. 3-5, xv-xviii, and 14.

analysis to selected portions of this complex program. The council did not discuss Medicare in any depth, but accepted the actuarial report on the adequacy of the trust fund of Part A of Medicare. The program and financing of Part B of Medicare, which has no trust fund, was not discussed. The council also refrained from exploring the interrelationships among the various federal public assistance programs, whether in or out of the social security system.

The complexity of the social security program induced the council to decide very early in its deliberations that all decisions until the last meeting would be "tentative," since its recommendations would have interlocking effects. This was especially important because of the program's financial imbalance, and because most of the recommendations would cost money, thus eventually forcing the government to weigh the costs of one recommendation against another.

The 1974 Advisory Council consisted of a chairman and twelve other members representing the general public, the self-employed, and organizations of employers and employees. The chairman was W. Allen Wallis, chancellor of the University of Rochester, and the vice-chairman Arnold R. Weber, Ph.D., dean, Graduate School of Industrial Administration, Carnegie-Mellon University. The other public members were: John W. Byrnes, attorney, former representative from Wisconsin; Rita Ricardo Campbell, Ph.D., senior fellow, Hoover Institution, Stanford University; Rudolph T. Danstedt, assistant to the president of the National Council of Senior Citizens; and Vernon E. Jordan, Jr., executive director, National Urban League (Mr. Jordan was unable to participate and was represented by Thomas E. Mitchell, deputy director, Washington Bureau, National Urban League). The three members representing labor were: Stanford D. Arnold, secretary-treasurer, Michigan State Building and Construction Trades Council, AFL-CIO; Edward J. Cleary, secretary-treasurer, New York State Building and Construction Trades Council, AFL-CIO; and Elizabeth C. Norwood, assistant research director, Eastern Conference of Teamsters. Industry members were: Edwin J. Faulkner, president, Woodmen Accident and Life Company; John J. Scanlon, executive vice-president and chief financial officer (ret.), American Telephone and Telegraph Company; J. Henry Smith, chairman of the board, Equitable Life Assurance Society of the United States; and J. W. Van Gorkom, president, Trans Union Corporation.]

A. General Comments

Social security now affects our society and economy to an unprecedented degree. It covers more than 9 out of 10 jobs. Its payroll taxes were $72 billion in 1974, about 40 percent of all Federal taxes on individuals.[14]

At the end of 1974, about $6 billion a month of benefits (including Medicare) was being paid to over 30 million people—about 1 out of every 7 of the population.

Also without precedent are current demographic trends. After a period of high fertility rates, we are now in a period of decline, and fertility rates are lower than ever before in America—in fact, at levels which, if sustained, would lead eventually to a declining population. Since social security is essentially a pay-as-you-go system, benefits to the retired, survivors, and disabled being paid from taxes collected concurrently from those still working, the ratio of workers to beneficiaries is of critical importance in determining the cost to workers. At present there are about three workers to support each beneficiary, but it is estimated that if current trends continue there will be eventually only two workers to support each beneficiary. (The resulting burden on those still working may be offset to some degree by a reduction in the number of children to be supported and educated.)

Another development now beginning to affect social security to an unprecedented degree is the changing structure of the family. Social security contributions are levied on an individual basis, but the benefits are awarded on a family basis. The program was built on an implicit assumption that most people marry and stay married to the same spouses throughout their lives, and that the man is the "head of the household" and principal source of the income on which others in the family are dependent. For half a century divorce and remarriage have become increasingly common, with not only two but three or more spouses in a lifetime becoming less unusual. In the past decade, formation and separation of families without legal sanction has appeared, as have living groups that are dissimilar to the traditional family. Even the traditional family is changing greatly in the degree of its dependence on an economically dominant male. In 1973, about 42 percent of married women participated in the labor force at any one time and over 50 percent at some time during the year, and it is estimated that 90 percent of all women participate at some time during their lives. Earnings due to "second" earners have become a substantial part of family finances.

Another recent development is that economists interested in such specialties as public finance, economic growth, welfare theory, econometrics, and accountancy have begun analyzing various aspects of social security. Some of these economists express concern that social security may have a depressing effect on productivity by reducing the flow of savings, on which depends the

---

14. The figure for payroll taxes includes employers' contributions as taxes on individuals, since many economists believe that the employers' share falls mostly on employees. If employers' contributions are not included, the proportion is 25 percent.

supply of more and better tools and machines for workers.[15]

The social security program has become complex. It is difficult for people to understand their rights and to determine the benefits they should receive unless they obtain assistance from social security employees or outside experts. Such complexity makes the system vulnerable to misinterpretation and uninformed criticism.

Increases in the complexity of the social security program have been accompanied by the assignment of administrative responsibility to the Social Security Administration for programs that are not social insurance. Supplemental Security Income, the largest and most recent of these new programs, has already been mentioned. Another example is the program of special benefits for victims of "black lung" disease. While this development has resulted at least in part from the desire to take advantage of the Social Security Administration's organization, ability, and experience, it has complicated the task of administering the social security program and made the program more difficult to understand.

Another condition without precedent is that the relationship between benefits and pre-retirement earnings now depends on fluctuations in wages and prices rather than on explicit decisions by Congress. A laudable move to apply automatic cost-of-living adjustments to benefits has inadvertently introduced instability, unpredictability, and uncontrollability into the relationship between purchasing power after retirement and purchasing power before retirement.

With the convergence of so many unprecedented developments, it is not too dramatic to say that the social security program is at a juncture of decisive importance. [pp. 3-5]

B. Major Findings and Recommendations.

Cash Benefits

PURPOSE AND PRINCIPLES

The earnings-related OASDI program should remain the Nation's primary means of providing economic security in the event of retirement, death, or disability. It should be supplemented by effective private pensions, individual insurance, savings, and other investments; and it should be undergirded by

---

15. By Mr. Arnold, Mr. Cleary, and Mrs. Norwood. The observation that social security may have a ". . .depressing effect on productivity by reducing the flow of savings. . ." is highly speculative and contradictory. Economists have observed that employers shift the cost of the social security tax to individual workers in lieu of higher wages, or pass the cost along to consumers via higher prices. To the extent this is done employer savings are not affected by the social security tax.

effective means-tested programs. Future changes in OASDI should conform to the fundamental principles of the program: universal compulsory coverage, earnings-related benefits paid without a test of need, and contributions toward the cost of the program from covered workers and employers.

BENEFIT STRUCTURE—REPLACEMENT RATES

The provisions of present law for computing average monthly earnings, on which benefits are based, and for adjusting the benefit table in the law to changes in prices may result over the long range in unintended, unpredictable, and undesirable variations in the level of benefits. The benefit structure should be revised to maintain the levels of benefits in relation to preretirement earnings levels that now prevail. Benefits for workers coming on the rolls in the future should be computed on the basis of a revised benefit formula using past earnings indexed to take account of changes during their working lives in the average earnings of all covered workers. As under present law, benefits for people on the rolls should continue to be increased as price levels increase.

RETIREMENT TEST

The provisions of the present retirement test should be modified so that beneficiaries who work can retain more of their benefits. Instead of reducing benefits by one dollar for every two dollars of earnings above the exempt amount of earnings, as under present law, one dollar of benefits should be withheld for every three dollars of earnings between the exempt amount and twice the exempt amount, and one dollar for two dollars above that level. Also, the provision under which a full benefit may be paid for any month in which a beneficiary earns less than one-twelfth of the annual exempt amount should be eliminated, except for the first year of entitlement to benefits. The test should be based on annual earnings.

TREATMENT OF MEN AND WOMEN

The requirements for entitlement to dependents' and survivors' benefits that apply to women should apply equally to men; that is, benefits should be provided for fathers and divorced men as they are for mothers and divorced women and benefits for husbands and widowers should be provided without a support test as are benefits for wives and widows. At the same time, the law should be changed, effective prospectively, so that pensions based on a person's work in employment not covered by social security will be subtracted from his social security dependents' benefits. Other provisions of the social security program which are the same for men and women but which are criticized because they appear to have different average effects on men and women (or different average effects on the married and the unmarried) should not be changed.

OTHER RECOMMENDATIONS[16]

Universal compulsory coverage.   Although social security covers over 90 percent of workers, the gaps that remain often result in unwarranted duplication of benefits. Social security coverage should be applicable to all gainful employment. Ways should be developed to extend coverage immediately to those kinds of employment, especially public employment, for which coordinated coverage under social security and existing staff-retirement systems would assure that total benefits are reasonably related to a worker's lifetime earnings and contributions.

Minimum benefit.   Partly because of the gaps in social security coverage, the minimum benefit is frequently a windfall to those, such as Federal retirees, who are already receiving a pension based on earnings in employment not covered by social security. Almost all workers who have worked in social security employment with some regularity become entitled to higher than minimum social security benefits. The minimum benefit in present law should be frozen at its level at the time the new benefit structure recommended under number 2 decoupling above goes into effect and the new system should not pay benefits exceeding 100 percent of the indexed earnings on which the benefit is based.

Definition of disability.   The definition of disability should be revised to provide disability benefits for workers aged 55 or over who cannot qualify for benefits under present law but who are so disabled that they can no longer perform jobs for which they have considerable regular experience. These benefits should be 80 percent of the benefits for those disabled workers who qualify under the present law.

Miscellaneous.   Further study is needed on three matters: the effects of the social security program on different racial and ethnic groups, ways of simplifying the social security program and its administration, and the frequency of cost-of-living adjustments in benefits. In addition, a general study of social security should be made by a full-time non-Government body, covering such matters as funding vs. pay-as-you-go, possible effects of social security on capital formation, productivity, the proper size of the trust funds, the incidence of payroll taxes, and other basic questions.

Financing

ACTUARIAL STATUS

The cash benefits program needs a comparatively small amount of additional financing immediately in order to maintain the trust funds levels.

---

16. Because the immediate problem is financing in relationship to already legislated benefits, this compilation does not include all recommendations of the Advisory Council on Social Security such as those pertaining to disability payments and the size of earnings allowed without disqualification from receiving social security benefits [author's note].

Beginning about 30 years from now, in 2005, the program faces serious deficits. Steps should be taken soon to assure the financial integrity and long-range financial soundness of the program.

TAX RATES

Employee-employer. No increase should be made, beyond those already scheduled in present law, in the total tax rates for employees and employers for cash benefits and hospital insurance. However, the OASDI tax rate should be gradually increased, as OASDI costs increase, and the increases should be met by reallocating taxes now scheduled in the law for part A (hospital insurance) of the Medicare program. Income lost to the hospital insurance program by this reallocation should be made up from the general funds of the Treasury. Hospital insurance benefits are not related to earnings, so should be phased out of support from the payroll tax.

Self-employed. The present 7% limitation on the tax rate for the self-employed should be removed. The self-employment OASDI tax rate should be the same multiple of the employee contribution rate as was fixed at the time the self-employed were first covered—150%. [pp. xv-xvii]

[FINANCING]

The Council therefore recommends that a worker's earnings should be "indexed"—that is, adjusted to reflect increases in average earnings over his working lifetime—up to retirement, and after retirement his benefits should be adjusted according to changes in the cost of living. [p. 14]

RETIREMENT AGE

The Council recognizes that under current demographic projections there will be a sharp rise in the number of people who will have reached retirement age relative to the working age population in the first several decades of the next century. Although the Council is not recommending an increase in the age of eligibility for social security retirement benefits, the Council does believe that such a change might merit consideration in the next century, when the financial burden of social security taxes on people still working may become excessive. [p. xvii]

2

COVERAGE

COVERAGE

1994178

How can we make sure that workers and their families actually get their future OASDI benefits? One helpful change would be to make the system universal by covering all the gainfully employed under OASDI. For those workers who had met the minimum covered work requirements, this would also assure continuous protection against loss of income from permanent disability and death. Meanwhile, it remains unlikely that the employees of federal, state, or local government will be made to comply, as do other workers, in paying social security taxes on their primary earned income. Many government workers, however, will become entitled to minimal benefits, which are heavily weighted in favor of low earners, by paying very small amounts in taxes on small amounts of earned income from secondary jobs.

The following extracts from the 1974-75 Advisory Council's reports provide necessary background information. The reader is reminded that the entire current social security program is known as OASDHI, but because hospitalization, part A of Medicare, is not discussed separately in this chapter, the "H" is dropped. However, individuals must pay the entire tax when working in covered employment.

Document 2.1   Report of the Advisory Council on Social Security, March 1975 [excerpts]

Over 92 percent of those now reaching age 65 are eligible for benefits. This percentage will increase in the future under present law. Also, 95 out of every 100 children under age 18 and their mothers have survivorship protection, and about 80 percent of those aged 21 to 64 have protection in the event of long-

DOCUMENT 2.1: U.S. Congress, House, *Committee on Ways and Means, Reports of the Quadrennial Advisory Council on Social Security,* 94th Cong., 1st sess., H.D. 94-75, March 10, 1975 (Washington, D.C.: U.S. Government Printing Office, 1975), pp. 9, 33-35, 54.

term disability. These percentages will increase further if coverage under social security becomes more nearly universal, as the Council recommends. [p. 9]

The social security system should be applicable to virtually all gainful employment. Therefore Congress should develop immediately ways of achieving this, giving special attention to those areas of employment in which coordinated coverage under social security and existing staff-retirement systems would assure that benefits are reasonably related to a worker's lifetime earnings and contributions.[1] [p. 33]

More than 8½ million jobs are still not covered under social security. Of these noncovered jobs, about 2½ (now 2.8) million are in Federal employment that is specifically excluded from social security coverage by Federal law because it is covered under the civil service retirement system or one of the smaller Federal staff-retirement systems. (When the social security program began, the civil services retirement system was already well established and the advantages of including Federal employees under social security as well were not then apparent.) About 3½ million of the noncovered jobs are in State and local employment and are generally covered under a State or local retirement system. (Coverage is available to State and local employees on a group-voluntary basis through agreements between the Secretary of Health, Education, and Welfare and the individual States; coverage by agreement avoids legal and other problems relating to Federal-State relationships.) Also, more than 300,000 jobs with nonprofit organizations are not covered by social security, most of which are covered by staff-retirement plans.

The Council is particularly concerned that the existing situation affords workers whose career employment is covered only by a staff-retirement system an unfair advantage over the majority of other workers, who are covered and contribute under social security throughout their working lives. Workers, such as Federal civilian workers, whose major employment is not covered under social security can, through secondary employment, become entitled to social security benefits which are in the lower benefit range but which represent a very high return on the worker's social security contributions. For example, a special study in 1969 showed that more than 40 percent of all Federal civil service retirement annuitants were also drawing social security benefits and about one-third of these dual beneficiaries received social security benefits based on the minimum primary insurance amount. Benefits in the lower benefit range are heavily weighted because they are intended for people who have had low average monthly earnings over a working lifetime. Although the wages of many workers in noncovered

---

1. Original in italics [author's note].

employment are relatively high and many such workers qualify for substantial staff-retirement benefits, these workers are likely to have artificially low average monthly earnings under social security. (This is because for social security purposes earnings are averaged over a substantial number of years and the workers in question usually have covered earnings in relatively few years.) In many instances the benefits that they qualify for under social security when combined with the benefits they qualify for under the civil service retirement system (or another system that embraces employment not covered by social security) are high in relation to their earnings and contributions; in some cases the combined monthly benefits exceed previous pay. The cost of the windfall social security benefits payable in such situations must be borne by all covered workers and their employers.

In addition, there are opportunities for windfall benefits for entire groups of State and local employees because of the special provisions for social security coverage of employment for State and local governments on a group-voluntary basis. Coverage for State and local employment may be terminated after coverage has been in effect for 7 years, and in recent years coverage has been terminated for some State and local groups. It is possible for a group to select a termination point when most of its members have qualified for continuing social security protection, including eventual eligibility for Medicare protection. Such terminations of coverage should not be permitted since they, too, impose an unfair additional cost on all who are regularly covered under social security. The Council notes that the basis for not making coverage compulsory for State and local employees is being reexamined by the Social Security Administration in light of recent legal decisions in this area concerning the immunity of the States from Federal taxation. [pp. 34-35]

Compulsory coverage of government employees. Some 90 percent of the working population is today covered by social security. By far the largest segment that remains uncovered is composed of government employees, Federal, State, and local. The Council has recommended that social security coverage of these employees be made compulsory in order to prevent the windfall benefits which they frequently receive at the expense of the social security system. [p. 54]

If all government employees were brought under social security, it is estimated that there would be a long-term reduction in the cost of the system of .25 percent of covered wages and a short-term reduction of .70 percent. These are significant amounts, but there are also significant obstacles to such compulsory coverage. A constitutional question clouds the forced coverage of employees of State and local governments. Also, although proposals for coverage of Federal employees have been considered over the years, they have not generally been supported by Federal employee groups and have not been passed by Congress. [p. 54]

Document 2.2   Report of the Consultant Panel on Social Security, August 1976 [excerpt]

[*Author's Note.* The Consultant Panel concurred with the Advisory Council on the issue of universal coverage.]

It is widely accepted that low-paid people have the greatest replacement needs. This Panel has followed the existing Social Security system in recommending that benefits relative to earnings decrease as earnings increase. This being the case, it is a serious weakness when these relatively larger benefits accrue to workers who have small earnings records only because they have worked in uncovered employment for most of their careers. It is estimated that 40 percent of persons receiving Civil Service Retirement Benefits are currently receiving benefits under Social Security.

Recommendation.   This Panel adds its voice to the widespread call for universal coverage. Particularly, government employees should be included in Social Security.

A paper prepared for the latest Advisory Council pointed out that in December, 1973, there were an estimated 8.7 million jobs not covered, 10 percent of the total. Of these, 0.4 ([*sic*] should be 2.4) were in Federal employment, and 4.2 million were in job categories for which coverage continues to be optional. The most urgent need is to remove as rapidly as possible the opportunities for people to stay out of the system while qualifying for other forms of government pension, and then, having so qualified, to enter the system for a relatively brief time, reaping the special benefit advantages that were intended for, and can be justified only for, low-paid workers. [p. 59]

Document 2.3   U.S. Social Security Administration, Staff Memorandum to Advisory Council, June 1974

IMPORTANCE OF BROAD COVERAGE

The social security program objective of preventing dependency can of course be best achieved if practically all employment in the economy is

---

DOCUMENT 2.2: U.S. Congress, Joint Committee (House Committee on Ways and Means, Senate Committee on Finance), Report of the Consultant Panel on Social Security to the Congressional Research Service, 94th Cong., 2d sess., August 1976 (Washington, D.C.: U.S. Government Printing Office, 1976), p.59.

DOCUMENT 2.3: U.S. Social Security Administration, staff memorandum to Quadrennial Advisory Council on Social Security, mimeographed, June 20, 1974 (Washington, D.C.: U.S. Department of Health, Education, and Welfare, 1974).

covered. The higher the proportion of jobs covered, the greater the likelihood that the young worker will soon acquire family survivor and disability protection and the greater the likelihood that social security protection will follow a worker as he shifts from one job to another.

With social security providing basic protection for workers and their families throughout the economy, private pension plans and staff-retirement systems could in all instances be designed with the knowledge that social security benefits would also be payable. On the other hand, where a retirement system functions independently of the social security program the movement of workers between jobs covered by social security and jobs covered only by the retirement system gives rise to gaps in protection for some workers and windfall benefits for others. Coverage of practically all regular jobs by social security would help to assure a rational relationship between total benefits and a worker's lifetime earnings and contributions.

MAJOR AREAS OF EMPLOYMENT NOT COVERED BY SOCIAL SECURITY

About 10 percent of jobs in paid employment—8.7 million out of 87 million jobs as of December 1973[2]—are not covered by the social security program. Of those jobs which are not covered, a large proportion are either jobs that are covered under other public retirement systems, or jobs which represent irregular or part-time work.

For 4.2 million of the noncovered jobs, social security coverage is permitted by Federal law, but coverage is not in effect. A very large proportion of these are State or local government jobs, almost all of which are under retirement systems. . . . The remainder are either jobs for nonprofit or religious organizations, or represent self-employed persons with little or no net earnings who have not exercised their option to elect coverage based on a percentage of their gross earnings.

About 2.4 million of the noncovered jobs are in Federal employment that is covered by civil service retirement or one of the smaller Federal staff-retirement systems, and is excluded from social security by Federal law. (A separate accompanying paper summarizes the various studies of the problems that have arisen because Federal civil service employment is excluded from social security coverage.)

Of the remaining 2.1 million noncovered jobs, about three-fourths are jobs in which people do not earn enough or work long enough in a calendar quarter or a year to meet coverage tests provided in Federal law. The main coverage tests are:

(a) domestic work for a household employer is not covered if cash wages received from that employer amount to less than $50 in a calendar quarter;

---

2. Estimates of social security coverage have generally been based on a count of jobs at a given point in time. The number of workers who engage in covered employment during the course of a year would therefore be larger than the number of jobs shown in the estimates.

    (b) farm employment. . .is not covered with respect to a particular farm
employer unless the worker is paid at least $150 in cash wages by the
employer during a calendar year or works for that employer on 20 or
more days during the year and is paid on a time basis—per hour, day,
or other time period; and

    (c) self-employment is not covered when net earnings are less than $400 in
a year (though optional coverage is available under certain conditions
when gross earnings are at least $600 in a year).

    Due to the effects of rising earnings levels these coverage tests have become
increasingly easier to meet over the years. If the tests had been kept up to date
with rising wage levels, a domestic employee would have to receive cash pay of
$159 per quarter from at least one household employer to be covered and a
farm worker would have to receive at least $337 per year from one farm
employer. For a self-employed person, the current equivalent of the $400
annual-net-earnings test would be $1,268.[3]

    Domestic employment in private homes.   Of some 1.5 million domestic
workers, it is estimated that over 400,000 do not meet the coverage test—cash
pay of $50 in a calendar quarter—with respect to any household employer. As
indicated in attachment C, "Compliance with Provisions for Reporting
Wages Covered by Social Security," compliance with social security reporting
requirements has not been as good in this area of employment as in other
areas. In view of the likelihood that broadening of the present coverage
provision—e.g., providing first-dollar coverage for domestic workers—
would exacerbate the compliance problem, proposals to broaden the present
provision have not been advanced by the Social Security Administration.

    Self-employment.   The Social Security Administration coverage esti-
mates indicate that over 700,000 of some 5.5 million nonfarm self-employed
are excluded from coverage by Federal law because they fail to meet the $400
coverage test. . . . The lack of social security coverage for these groups is not
a serious problem. In many instances, persons engaged in these very small
self-employment projects are elderly individuals who have previously built up
social security protection in some other job or are young individuals who will
subsequently acquire social security protection through covered work.

    Optional exclusion on conscientious or religious grounds.   Clergymen
and members of religious orders (who have not taken a vow of poverty) are
covered under social security under the self-employment provisions unless
they file, within a specified time, for exemption from coverage on grounds of

---

3. At the same time, it has become increasingly easy to obtain "quarters of coverage" for
purposes of becoming insured under social security. If the 1939 provision granting a "quarter of
coverage" if a worker is paid at least $50 of wages in a calendar quarter had been kept up to date
with wage levels, the $50 figure would now be about $370.

conscience. Approximately 200,000 clergymen are covered under social security, and about 20,000 are not covered either because they have elected to be exempt from coverage or because they do not have net earnings from self-employment of $400 or more in the taxable year. Coverage was made available by 1972 legislation, on a group-voluntary basis at the option of a religious order, to members of orders who have taken a vow of poverty. Up to now, religious orders have elected coverage for 70,000 out of about 197,000 members of orders. Self-employed persons who are members of recognized religious sects (mainly the Old Order Amish) which meet certain conditions may be excluded from coverage on grounds of conscience. About 13,000 individuals have been excluded from coverage under this provision.

Nonprofit organizations. Employees of nonprofit organizations exempt from income tax (such as religious, charitable, and educational organizations) who earn $50 or more in a calendar quarter are covered under social security if the organization files a certificate waiving exemption from social security employer contributions. However, persons employed at the time the organization takes this action may elect not to be covered. Over 90 percent of the 3.7 million employees of nonprofit organizations are covered under this provision. About 290,000 employees are excluded from coverage either because their employers have not filed waiver certificates or because the employees earn less than $50 in a calendar quarter.

Attachment C

[***Author's Note.***The attachment finds inequities in the coverage of domestic workers.

While there have been no recent surveys of coverage of domestic workers, the spotty data that are available indicate that of those domestic workers age 18 and over who meet the social security coverage test, almost 80 percent are being reported for social security purposes by their employer, or if they have more than one domestic employer, by at least one of their employers. Employer compliance appears to be quite high in respect to domestic employees who are at least age 25, probably in part because the workers in the older age groups are more likely to be working regularly for an employer and in part because there is greater recognition of the value of social security protection among the older workers.

Employer compliance is apparently much less good with respect to the younger employees. It is estimated that more than one-third of the workers generally classified as paid domestic employees are young people who have not reached age 18. A large proportion of these young people work as babysitters, lawncutters, snow shovelers, and at other occasional jobs.[4] The reasons for failure to report domestic wages are many and varied and may be the fault of the employee, the employer, or both. The employee may have asked that the wages not be reported, possibly because the employee does not want the earnings to come to the attention of welfare agencies or Federal or local tax authorities, or the employer may fail to report wages to avoid paying the employer share of the social security tax. Some employers are unaware of the reporting requirement; others may not want to make the effort to compute the tax due and to fill out the report form.

Coverage and Withdrawals from the Social Security System

Persons in noncovered federal government jobs, from the lowliest clerk through the upper cabinet level and congressional representatives, escape the part of social security taxes that is intended to help *(a)* the already aged and *(b)* persons with much lower-than-average monthly earnings over their lifetime. The pension benefits of persons who have the lowest average covered monthly earnings over a lifetime have a 129 percent weight. This weight, used to compute benefits, gradually and unevenly slides down to nearly 20 percent as average monthly covered earnings over a lifetime rise close to the maximum taxable base. Noncovered workers also contribute no tax money to the other programs under social security. That is to say, they contribute neither to the Medicare, Part A, trust fund, which helps provide hospitalization for those 65 years and over, nor to the fund that pays benefits to the permanently disabled.

Although participation in the social security system is mandatory for almost all nongovernment workers, Congress, as document 2.1 explains, never extended the mandate to employees of state and local governments because of doubts over the constitutional right of the federal government to tax other governments. In 1954, however, Congress decided to allow such groups of workers to join the social security program voluntarily.

About 8 million of the 12.3 million state and local government employees are covered by majority vote of the employee group.[5] This vote represents less than 70 percent of the total. (The remaining 3.5 to 4

---

4. Their "taxes" would not count for computation of social security benefits, because they are below age 21: see *Social Security Handbook,* 1973, section 704 [author's note].

5. U.S. Bureau of Labor Statistics, Historical Series.

million are uncovered.) New employees of groups that have elected coverage automatically come under the social security system.

Withdrawals

The Act provides that groups of employees of state governments and subdivisions of state governments may withdraw after participating in the system for seven years. After participating for five years, the group must give a formal two years' notice of intent to withdraw. The notice may be rescinded before date of withdrawal comes round. However, once coverage for a group has been terminated, then it may not be reinstated.

The mid-1970s saw an increase in the number of groups that had either withdrawn or given notice that they would withdraw. As of March 1976, 332 groups totaling about 46,000 employees were reported in the former category and 236 groups totaling about 430,000 employees in the latter, including employees of New York City and of the state of Alaska.[6] Alaska gave notice of withdrawal in December 1975 and was the first state to do so. The largest number of terminations had been in California, Louisiana, and Texas. As of March 1973, California and New York state each had over one million employees; 42 percent of California's and 94 percent of New York's were covered. Ohio, with 500,000 employees, had less than 1 percent covered while Pennsylvania, with a similar number of employees, had 100 percent.

Of the 332 groups that had already withdrawn, 138 jurisdictions had done so in the past two years alone, and there were almost monthly press reports of other groups that were said to be thinking of pulling out. As of August 1, 1976, 140 cities, counties, and other governmental units in California had withdrawn.

The largest local government in the United States, New York City, announced in March 1976, that it was filing to withdraw 112,000 of the city's 250,000 employees, apparently because of its precarious finances. It was estimated that withdrawal of these employees could save the city about $100 million in taxes. In many cases, no new private plan was needed; there were many city and state retirement plans covering them already, and benefits under these plans were quite generous. Additionally, a large proportion of New York City and state employees already

---

6. U.S. Department of Health, Education, and Welfare, *State and Local Government Employees Covered Under Social Security, 1972-73,* Research and Statistics Note No.18, September 30, 1976. This note states that as of March 1973 almost 8.3 million or 75 percent of 11.2 million state and local government employees were covered.

had the required ten years of coverage for "fully insured" status under OASDHI.

For example, a New York City school teacher who retired at age 65 on July 1, 1973, and who earned $14,000 in the preceding year, received a net private annuity after taxes plus a primary social security benefit from 99 to 117 percent of the $14,000. Retiring teachers with private annuity plus social security benefit and wife's social security benefit received from 112 percent to 129 percent of the $14,000.[7]

Withdrawals: pro and con

Withdrawals mean a loss to the social security system of up to nearly $2,000 per person annually.[8] Several factors appear to be fostering the trend in their favor. The negative fiscal impact on the employer, as in the case of New York City, of the increasing payroll tax and the uncertainty from year to year as to its size, is a major one. The increasing proportion of the employee's wages taxed by an increasing tax rate, the prospects of even higher taxes to be paid, and the added pressure of inflation on workers' take home pay impinge directly on disposable incomes, current and anticipated. For young, unmarried workers the private market offers about equal protection for considerably less money. Married women already are entitled to a dependency benefit based on their husband's earnings. For married women who work, then, returns on OASDI tax payments are generally limited to *(a)* protection against permanent disability and *(b)* declining term life insurance benefits for their children. In most cases, women who pay OASDI taxes are not purchasing annuity benefits greater than those that they would otherwise draw.

There are two main arguments against leaving the system: (1) other pension and disability systems are usually not as extensive as social security, particularly with regard to permanent disability benefits; (2) other systems are not as transferable from one job to another. Rare exceptions to the latter include some union plans within an industry and geographic area, and a few plans for professionals—for example, the Teachers' Insurance and Annuity Association (TIAA). The new federal legislation governing private pensions, the 1974 Employee

---

7. Robert Tilove, *Public Employee Pension Funds* (New York: Columbia University Press, 1976), p.279.

8. If the whole OASDHI tax (11.7%) is used. Once covered by social security you have to pay the whole tax, not just the part that supports an annuity or disability benefit.

Retirement Income Security Act (ERISA), requires minimal vesting rights for employees under private annuity plans. It has, therefore, greatly diminished the importance of OASDI's transferability. Such vesting refers only to the employers' contributions because the employee always, unless the company goes bankrupt, receives back what he has paid in—that is, if his seniority with a company is too brief for him to be entitled to an annuity. Private pensions are based on considerations of individual equity, not of social adequacy.

A company's newer employees, many of whom probably have low incomes, may not have been under social security long enough to qualify for benefits upon retirement. Compared to their fellow workers, then, they will have lesser total annuities. However, these persons could "moonlight" and take a minimal job covered by OASDI that yields $50 taxable income per quarter. Many government workers were doing exactly this, and so becoming entitled to the weighted minimum benefit. For example, men whose main jobs in May 1975 were in public administration (federal, state, and local government services) had, among all industrial sectors, the highest proportion of multiple jobholders—25 percent.[9] The data include agricultural workers and the self-employed; both of these classifications include many secondary jobs.

The self-employed pay less in OASDI taxes—7 percent in 1976 as compared to the 9.9 percent employer-employee OASDI tax rate.[10] The 7 percent represents somewhat less than the three-fourths of the employer-employee rate that was originally enacted for this category of employment. The major argument in favor of this rate is that the self-employed tend to postpone retirement more than those who work for others.[11] As Dr. Musgrave indicates in chapter 8, there is little justification for this reduced rate, since those who work for others bear the entire burden of the tax anyway. Although of all male workers only 6 percent hold two or more jobs, the rate is 8 percent for those whose primary job is self-employment in agriculture, and of all males holding a secondary job 18 percent had secondary work as self-employed agricultural workers (e.g., in their own vegetable gardens).[12]

---

9. U.S. Bureau of Labor Statistics, *Summary, Multiple Jobholders in 1975*, Special Labor Force Report, July 1975, table 4, p.4.

10. If the tax rate of 1.8% for Medicare, Part A, is included as under OASDHI, then the figures to be compared are 8.8% and 11.7%, respectively.

11. See chapter 7, below, for analysis of this point.

12. U.S. BLS, *Summary, Multiple Jobholders in 1975*.

It is likely that an employee group that elects out of OASDHI either already has coverage under a private plan, or will immediately purchase substitute private group insurance with employer matching contributions. For this they can use monies previously paid out as OASDHI taxes. How the private plan and the federal government system cost-benefit ratios would compare depends on the employee group's composition in terms of sex, age, and marital status.

If people find themselves paying less under a private group plan than they used to under the social security system, they can use the difference to buy a private annuity. However, the low-income person with dependents is unlikely to do this of his or her own volition because current needs are too urgent. The relatively low level of most persons' disposable income in relation to their perceived wants, not to mention the high premium rate of individual insurance as compared to group insurance, discourages such individual purchases. Moreover, younger persons tend not to have as many consumer durable goods—washing machines and dryers, for example—as older persons. They therefore place a higher value on current income and/or discount future income.

In sum, withdrawal from OASDI means reduced taxes for employees and employers, but also reduced and/or fewer benefits unless more private benefits are purchased. In many cases, employee groups, with their employers, should be able to purchase either higher pension benefits at costs equal to social security taxes or similar benefits at lower costs. For example, the city employees of San Jose, California, now contribute 3 percent less to another plan and will enjoy on the average 25 percent higher benefits. Additionally, rather than being compelled to accept a standardized package of benefits, individual groups may have a package tailored to their needs.

The withdrawal of many teacher groups indicates that private coverage is fairly extensive in this area. In particular, female teachers who are married are becoming more aware, it seems, that their monthly social security benefits as workers upon retirement will probably be less than the secondary benefit they would generally get through their deceased husbands. This is true even if they as wives have never worked and paid taxes, because as widows they stand to receive 100 percent of their husbands' primary benefits. In 1975 the annual median work income of all full-time working women was only 57 percent of that of all full-time working males, so their primary benefits on retirement will be correspondingly smaller. Although as retired working wives they would be entitled to only one-half of their

husbands' primary benefits, generally married women who leave the labor force to bear and raise children have a much lower primary benefit than their husbands, since the latter earn more and work more continuously. It is not only educators who are withdrawing, but also other state and local employees, many of whom are married women who hold low-paying clerical jobs.

Another factor that encourages withdrawal is that social security rights become fully vested after ten years. The 1974 act (ERISA), for which clarifying federal regulations were still being written in 1977, has three mandatory options on vesting: (1) after ten years of employment with one employer, an employee has a fully vested right to his accrued retirement benefit; (2) a gradual vesting plan, starting with twenty-five percent of accrued benefits after five years; (3) the more complicated "rule of forty-five" which is that whenever an employee's age and years of service total forty-five, then fifty percent vesting is attained (this percentage increases over the time that the employee continues to work).

However, the average dollar amount of monthly retirement benefits, unlike the private pension, will decline whenever more than five years—the permitted dropout from the divisor by which this average is calculated—has elapsed without covered quarters of earnings, unless that reduction is fully offset by an increase in benefits being indexed by changes in the cost of living. The number of years, from age 21 on, in which one first earns covered wages is used, minus five years of lowest earnings, to compute the average monthly earnings from the total earnings on which the benefit is based. Social security benefits are indexed to cost-of-living increases, whereas most but not all private annuity and survivor benefits are not so indexed.

If most workers in a group have coverage for ten years, some experts believe it is advantageous for them to leave the system. This is based on the fact that one is "fully insured" with ten years of coverage, and therefore entitled to all benefits although their dollar amount may decline as years pass. There is, as we have seen, an economic incentive to qualify for a minimum benefit, which is indexed to the cost of living, and then drop out. Moreover there is a greater incentive to qualify by working in covered employment for the last ten years of one's working life, when earnings are likely to be significantly higher than during the first part of one's career. About 81 percent of the state and local government employees covered by social security also have supplemental retirement plans of some sort. Many of these employees would prefer to use some of the tax money to improve their benefits under these plans.

Pat Monahan of the California State Employees' Association (CSEA) has stated in support of withdrawal:

> From the state's point of view there are significant benefits in termination. First, the increased take-home pay of each employee would yield added purchasing power which would affect the state's economy favorably. At the present tax rate, $70 million to $80 million of the employees' contributions would be converted to disposable income.
>
> Second, another $70 million to $80 million, the employer's contribution, would be available for improved benefits.
>
> Third, as time goes on social security taxes will increase. Through termination, the state would not be subject to this escalation and thus would realize savings.[13]

All of the above arguments are used by insurance companies in favor of the new private retirement plans they hope to underwrite for groups that withdraw.

Coverage and equity

Federal officials, while concerned that the trend toward withdrawal appears to be accelerating, do not seem to feel that they as federal employees should set a good example. At any rate, they have not joined or encouraged their fellow workers to join any movement urging coverage of federal government employees under social security. Both the Advisory Council's and the Consultant Panel's reports deplore the inequitable result of excluding government workers.[14] However, the December 1975 Report of the U.S. House Subcommittee on Retirement Income and Employment stated: "The Federal civil service has its own retirement system, which, unlike most private pension plans in the country, entirely replaces Social Security benefits."[15] This

---

13. *The California State Employee,* August 4, 1976, p.4.

14. U.S. Congress, Joint Committee (House Committee on Ways and Means, Senate Committee on Finance), Report of the Consultant Panel on Social Security to the Congressional Research Service, 94th Cong., 2d sess., August 1976 (Washington, D.C.: U.S. Government Printing Office, 1976): "In particular, we find no reason for the exclusion of federal government employees" (p.5).

15. U.S. Congress, House, Select Committee on Aging, Subcommittee on Retirement, *Income and Employment, Income Security for Older Women: Path to Equality,* 94th Cong., 2d sess. (Washington, D.C.: U.S. Government Printing Office, 1975), p.13.

unqualified disregard of the social adequacy concept which underlies social security makes it difficult for knowledgeable persons to accept increases in their social security taxes. Why should there be individual equity for federal government workers but not for all workers? Many of the thirty-five million persons who have coverage under their employers' private pension plans could also claim that their plans, given the chance, would "entirely replace" social security.

Although the total number of state, county, and city employees has been steadily increasing in recent years, the numbers withdrawing from the system are relatively small compared with the total still covered. Some benefits, it must be admitted, are not always included in the substituted private plans. However, survivor coverage for widows and children usually is, and permanent disability coverage can be bought by men (although not so easily by women) in the private market. Benefits for older, dependent students are not usually part of the private insurance and annuity package, nor are hospitalization benefits at age 65 years. The former may not be generally wanted, although in the first quarter of 1976 over 800,000 such benefits were awarded monthly to students aged eighteen through twenty-one. Hospitalization of the aged is a separate benefit and has a separate trust fund, but government employees, during their working life, escape its tax of 1.8 percent on their primary earnings, as it is a part of the total social security tax. Because all persons aged 65 years and over who are entitled to (but not necessarily receiving) monthly social security benefits automatically have entitlement to Medicare hospitalization, this is a benefit some government workers receive without having contributed substantially to the program. Retired federal government employees have their own employee health benefits plan, but this coverage does not prevent them from benefiting under Medicare, Part A, if they have 40 quarters of social security coverage.

Some private employer and union plans are providing medical care benefits after retirement. An advantage of private plans over government plans is that the group may select which benefits it prefers to pay for before retirement.[16] In 1974, 71 percent of the large union-negotiated heath plans provided benefits for retirees 65 years and over, and 76 percent of the plans did so for retirees under 65 years. About

---

16. No attempt is made here to discuss private health insurance versus national health insurance.

one-half of the latter provided retirees with the same benefits as working employees under 65.[17]

Many persons have noted the fact that the ordinary citizen, in contrast to local government employees, does not have the option to withdraw, while federal employees have never been included. As more jobs are covered—and just over 90 percent are today—the "social costs" of the system are being more widely distributed over the population. This, then, is a major argument for universal coverage.

Nonprofit institutions

A category that poses special problems of coverage is that of workers employed by nonprofit organizations. Originally they were barred from participation in the social security system because they were not subject to federal taxation. In 1951, a law was passed that permitted such institutions to waive tax exemptions for social security purposes only by filing a form declaring their intent to contribute to social security.

A problem arose in this regard because some employers did not file the form although they did start paying the required taxes. The Social Security Administration was willing to overlook their bureaucratic negligence and interpret actual payment as sufficient intent to be covered. However, a conflict between the Internal Revenue Service and the Social Security Administration delayed settlement of this issue, which was eventually resolved by Public Law 94-563, approved in October 1976. It provides that a nonprofit organization that has not filed, but has paid social security taxes, is to be regarded as if it had filed the required form electing coverage. However, it is not so regarded if, prior to September 9, 1976, it had requested refund of the social security taxes that it had paid.

In the mid-1970s, some nonprofit organizations were discussing withdrawal from social security. Others were planning to integrate private pensions with social security, so that any additional increases in employer taxes would be deducted from the employer's costs of the institution's private pension plan. Thus benefits under the latter would decrease. Integrated private and public pension plans of this and other types were in force in several companies and under some union contracts.

---

17. Dennis Quigley, "Changes in Selected Health Care Plans," *Monthly Labor Review,* December 1975, p.25.

Summary

It is clear that universal coverage would eliminate many inequities. It would also increase tax receipts, which would partially offset the actuarial imbalance of the system. Permitting some employee groups to withdraw enables them to avoid taxes that others are forced to pay. If the system has become in large measure a social welfare system that transfers resources in a capricious fashion, then all should bear the burden of the program.

3

SOCIAL ADEQUACY:
BENEFIT AMOUNTS

SOCIAL ADEQUACY: BENEFIT AMOUNTS

As the role of a socially adequate level of benefits has become more dominant within the social security system, while the same tax rate is applied to all, charges of inequities have increased.

An increase in inequity may be said to occur when an individual's benefit/tax ratio declines because more tax revenues are being redistributed to persons who are presumed to be in need and who pay lesser amounts of taxes. Equity, on the other hand, increases as the ratio of benefits received to taxes paid approaches equality. The concept of inequity is relative in that an individual may compare his or her benefit/tax ratio with that of others in the same age cohort. Also, young workers of today may compare themselves as they expect to be at retirement both to those in past generations who have retired, and to those who will retire in future generations. It will be obvious to them that the latter's social security tax burden relative to benefits now differs from theirs, and may possibly differ still more, in accordance with whatever new legislation happens to be passed. It is even more obvious that those who have already retired have paid less in relation to what they receive than today's young workers.

Document 3.1 Report of the Advisory Council on Social Security, March 1975 [excerpts]

While the tax rate for all employees is the same, the benefits are not equal. They are weighted in favor of lower-paid workers and those with dependents. The low-paid worker receives a benefit that is a higher percentage of his (or

DOCUMENT 3.1: U.S. Congress, House, Committee on Ways and Means, *Reports of the Quadrennial Advisory Council on Social Security,* 94th Cong., 1st sess., H.D. 94-75, March 10, 1975 (Washington, D.C.: U.S. Government Printing Office, 1975), pp. 11-12, 15, and 46.

her) average earnings than does the higher-paid employee, even though the latter receives a larger absolute amount. This weighting of the benefit schedule represents society's recognition of "adequacy" as a criterion of the plan, and is a departure from the strict principle of individual equity. Another such social concept is found in the fact that a married worker receives certain protection for his dependents without paying any more premium than a single worker who receives no such protection.[1]

The entire social security program is necessarily a blend of social goals and individual equity. Maintaining the proper blend is very important if we are to sustain the workers' support of the plan. To date, most workers feel responsible for the system because, while aware of the social weighting within the program, they still view their protection as being reasonably related to the taxes they pay. This attitude is important to the success of social security. It becomes an important factor when considering the introduction of additional welfare-type benefits or methods of financing from general revenues. [p. 46]

The concepts of social adequacy and individual equity are not easily harmonized. The social security law places a high priority on social adequacy so as to achieve the public purpose of providing a floor of protection for those whose earned income has been substantially lost because of death, disability, or retirement in old age. In this context, social adequacy means that the benefits provided will supply the eligible recipients with a certain standard of living when such benefits are supplemented by private means or undergirded by public assistance. Several elements of social security are intended to assure the social adequacy of the program:

First, full-rate benefits were provided for workers who were already near retirement age when the program was established or when their work was first covered. If the cash benefits paid in the early years of the program had been no larger than the amounts that could be financed by the contributions paid by individual beneficiaries and by their employers, the benefit amounts would have been too small to make a meaningful contribution to reducing dependency.

Second, under social security, the low-paid worker gets a benefit that is a higher proportion of past earnings than does the higher paid worker. This is accomplished through the use of a benefit formula that is weighted in favor of low-paid workers. These provisions recognize that lower paid workers and their families have less margin for reduction in income than do workers with average or above-average earnings. [p. 11]

---

1. In recent years the addition of benefits for the permanently disabled and of Medicare coverage of persons with chronic kidney disease may also be looked at from this point of view [author's note].

It has always been considered important to give assurance that even those taxed the most would "get their money's worth" from the system. This has been done, not precisely, but in a very broad way if one accepts the view that the employer's tax is not assignable to the individual employee but is pooled for the benefit of all employees. [p.12]

The continued acceptability of the present OASDI system depends importantly on maintaining OASDI benefits as an earnings-related program, not a means-tested program. The system has been presented to the American people as such. It is too little understood that today's workers and their employers pay taxes to support the currently aged, disabled, and survivors and that there is an implied social contract that future generations of workers and their employers will finance the cost of the future benefits that today's workers expect to receive.

The social adequacy and individual equity of OASDI can only be evaluated in the context of America's three-tiered structure for income maintenance. Without the undergirding of means-tested programs for those with the lowest earnings or the supplementation through private means for those who have had higher earnings, OASDI might be judged deficient for many recipients. As has been noted above, the expansion and proliferation of means-tested programs by government has diminished or eliminated the need for further emphasizing the social adequacy of OASDI benefits while rising incomes and devices for encouraging personal thrift will enhance supplementation of social security benefits through private means. What may be conceived as equitable and adequate in social security benefits may vary with time and with demographic and economic conditions, but it is essential that a balance be maintained among social security, means-tested programs, and private plans for income maintenance and capital accumulation. [p. 12]

Congress has in the past worked out a schedule relating benefits to earnings, making conscientious efforts to balance social adequacy against individual equity. Thus, benefits increase with increasing average monthly earnings, thereby recognizing the criterion of individual equity; but increases in benefits are less than proportional to increases in AME [average monthly earnings], thereby recognizing the criterion of social adequacy. In 1974, benefits were about 120 percent of the first $110 of AME, dropped to 44 percent of the next $290 and to 41 percent for the next $150, then rose to 48 percent of the next $100 of AME, then dropped to 27 percent of the next $100 and tapered off to a minimum of 20 percent of the last $100 of AME. (The highest AME possible for a man retiring at age 65 in 1974 was $511, and the maximum benefit was $305 per month.) [pp. 14-15]

Document 3.2   Report of the Consultant Panel on Social Security, August 1976 [excerpts]

[*Author's Note.* The Consultant Panel's report clarifies further the distinction between individual equity and social adequacy.]

PRINCIPLES GOVERNING THE SOCIAL SECURITY PROGRAM

Over the years, Congress has adhered to three fundamental principles to guide its social security decisions. These principles—(1) individual equity balanced with social adequacy, (2) controllability and long-run stability, and (3) economic efficiency—continue to be perceived as necessary to and consistent with the overriding goal of the system: to provide economic security to American workers and their families in the event of lost income due to retirement, disability, or death. This goal was stated in the original report of the President's Committee on Economic Security, and has been widely accepted ever since by Congress and the general public.

These three principles help to explain the nature of the legislative policy decisions through the years. Because they are the criteria by which any new legislation will be judged, they provide a frame of reference for evaluation and comparison of alternative solutions.

1. Individual equity and social adequacy.   Equity and adequacy are bound to be competing objectives. Enhancement of one tends to cause diminution in the other.

Individual equity can be identified as the degree to which an individual's benefit rights are reflected by the contributions he or she has made to purchase those rights. A program in which individual equity is the overriding goal— personal insurance, for example—requires that each individual's benefit amount be based on the actuarial value of that individual's contributions. In a program that completely disregards individual equity, benefits can be unrelated to contributions. Such a program might not even require contributions, but instead be financed from general government revenues. This is the case with the SSI program.

Social adequacy is a welfare objective in which an individual's benefit amount is determined, not by his or her contributions, but by *(a)* appropriate transfer of income from affluent to needy groups, and *(b)* a minimum standard of living beneath which society decides that no individual should fall. The Social Security Act of 1935 represented a compromise between equity and social adequacy within a system that was designed to build at least

DOCUMENT 3.2: U.S. Congress, Joint Committee (House Committee on Ways and Means, Senate Committee on Finance), *Report of the Consultant Panel on Social Security to the Congressional Research Service,* 94th Cong., 2d sess., August 1976 (Washington, D.C.: U.S. Government Printing Office, 1976), pp. 12-13.

a part of the actuarial reserve that would be necessary to fund a comparable privately operated program. But amendments to the Act steadily shifted the emphasis more in the direction of social adequacy by weakening the relationship between benefits and contributions.

Although the benefit formula emphasizes social adequacy, the benefit level, for all workers already retired and for most who will retire during a long future period, is higher than the level that could be paid from the accumulated value of lifetime contributions by and on behalf of the worker. (The exceptions are the benefits for unmarried workers whose earnings have always been close to the maximum taxable earnings base (MTEB), and the benefits for two-worker families both of whose earnings are near the maximum.) This situation has developed for two reasons: the maturing of the system, and the "pay-as-you-go" method of financing.

Any pension program, public or private, takes forty years or more to reach maturity. At the beginning of the program, it is often decided to extend full benefit rights to those who are close to retirement age, even though their contributions will have been very small. A worker reaching age 60 in the first year of such a program might be granted full benefits after only five years' contributions, while a worker reaching age 20 in the same year might be required to make 45 years of contributions to qualify for the same benefit. This condition, to a large extent, describes the OASDI program.

This discrepancy rises to its maximum under "pay-as-you-go" financing, a method in which each year's contribution rate is required to be high enough to finance only that year's current benefits. At present, the ratio of retired persons to workers is moderate, hence the required contribution rates are moderate. But this ratio will increase as demographic changes result in a greater percentage of the population at or above retirement age. Consequently, if the present system continues unchanged, the current generation will have made contributions that are less than those required to finance its future benefits.

Moreover, whenever there is growth in working population and in wage rates, the taxable wages will also be increasing. Increasing taxable wages produce greater income to the system. During a period of growth, then, a worker's contributions into a pay-as-you-go system need not be as large as will be required when the growth is no longer occurring.

All of these relationships affect the degree of inter-generation equity as well as of equity among members of each generation. Complete equity between generations demands that those different generations receive comparable benefit amounts in return for comparable contributions. Ultimate equity within a generation exists only if workers' benefits are directly proportional to the amounts of their contributions. No social insurance program can achieve ultimate equity and social adequacy. The objective can only be to do justice to both. [pp. 12-13]

[*Author's Note.* Building on studies done for and by other groups, the panel gave the following excellent brief description of five benefit principles, as follows.]

1. A flat benefit formula.   The retired worker receives an established amount regardless of need or contributions.

2. Money purchase plan.   Each contribution paid by or on behalf of a worker is used to purchase a deferred annuity. This type of benefit is frequently found in union-negotiated plans for hourly-paid workers.

3. "High-5" plan.   The benefit is a percentage of the worker's average earnings in his highest five years. The percentage would depend on the number of years the worker has contributed to the plan. This type is sometimes used in employer-sponsored pension plans. The formula tends to produce stable replacement ratios (benefits to pre-retirement wages) from year to year.

4. Wage-indexed formula.   The benefit is based on a long averaging period of each worker's history. For benefit determination the earnings of each year are adjusted proportionately to the average wages of all workers in the social insurance system for that year.

5. Price-indexed formula.   The benefit is based on a long averaging period of each worker's wage history. Those wages, however, are restated in terms of their purchasing power rather than of their value in units of the national currency.

Each benefit formula has its strengths and its weaknesses. For example, if the sole purpose of the social security program were to stabilize replacement ratios, then the "High-5" method might be the preferred choice. But, as we have seen, there is a plurality of objectives, each of which must be weighed. Thus, certain specific criteria were established by this Panel to evaluate the alternative possibilities. These were:

1. Adequacy.   Apart from the weighting of the benefit formula in favor of lower-paid workers, there are two contrasting measures of adequacy. One is the purchasing power of the benefits promised to comparable workers retiring in different years. Another is the replacement ratio, i.e., the ratio of retirement benefit to preretirement earnings. The Panel found that an unexpectedly large proportion of workers experience declining wages in the few years just before retirement. In such cases earnings in the years close to retirement may not be appropriate for calculating the replacement ratio. The purpose of a yardstick like the replacement ratio is to approximate the standard of living to which a person has become accustomed and which the retirement benefit will replace. The Panel selected as its measure of the preretirement living standard an average calculated as follows:

List the earnings subject to social security tax during the last ten years before retirement. Index each of these by the Consumer Price Index. Eliminate the figures for the one year of highest, and two years of lowest indexed earnings.[2] Divide the sum of the remaining values by seven.

2. Benefits and costs. It is a simple task to design an optimal benefit formula if one can ignore its cost. Under the current-cost financing arrangement, future benefits for each generation of workers depend entirely on the willingness of the next generation to pay the required taxes. If workers lose confidence that their benefits will be paid, a breakdown will occur. In examining the various alternatives, the Panel has considered benefits and costs as an integral whole.

3. Equity. Social security is an earnings-related program. Equity is an important consideration. The Panel examined benefit alternatives in light of three types of equity: horizontal, vertical, and inter-generational. "Horizontal" equity means that similar situations are treated similarly; "vertical" equity means that different situations[3] are treated differently.

4. Effects upon workers with varying earnings patterns. As noted [elsewhere in] this report, the Panel has noted wide variations in wage patterns. Surprisingly, few workers enjoy constant steady rise in wages over their working lifetimes. It is unsafe to assume that a benefit formula that works well for persons with steadily rising wages will be appropriate for those whose wage patterns are irregular.

5. Tendencies to influence worker behavior. A benefit formula that markedly encourages people to take unusual steps to augment their benefit amounts (e.g., by earning or reporting exceptionally large incomes at certain times) is generally less fair and desirable than a formula devoid of such features.

6. Insurance elements. Any security program, as distinct from a savings plan, should, to the extent reasonable, provide benefits upon the occurrence of contingencies (such as cessation or abnormal decline of earnings) that create need that would not otherwise exist. [pp. 15-16]

[*Author's Note.* In order to prevent inflation from being counted double, the panel favored a price-indexing rather than a wage-indexing formula. After receiving a retirement benefit, the worker sees his benefit increase with the cost of living under both systems of indexing.]

---

2. The reason for eliminating the two lowest but only the one highest was that our inspection of earnings patterns of workers above age 55 persuaded us that abnormal earnings occur much more frequently on the low than on the high side.

3. That is, at one particular time—not inter-generational.

These illustrations [i.e., figure 3.1] are displayed in a manner designed to emphasize two matters that this Panel believes to be of great importance.

The first point is that the effects of any particular formula should be studied in terms of what that formula accomplishes in each of two related but distinct measures, these being *(a)* the purchasing power of the benefit, and *(b)* the relationship of retirement benefit to income covered for Social Security just before retirement, i.e., the "replacement ratio."

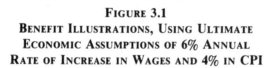

FIGURE 3.1
BENEFIT ILLUSTRATIONS, USING ULTIMATE
ECONOMIC ASSUMPTIONS OF 6% ANNUAL
RATE OF INCREASE IN WAGES AND 4% IN CPI

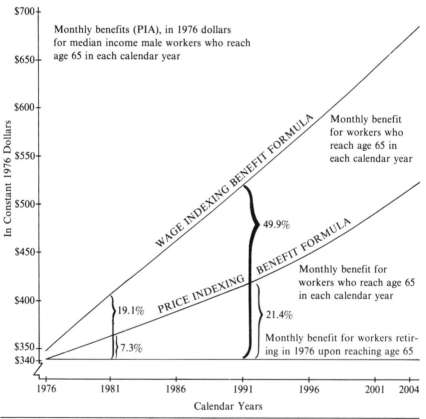

Discussion of Social Security benefit structure has concentrated heavily upon the second of these as the criterion of reasonableness. But we believe it is just as important to discover whether the proposed formula succeeds in granting nearly equal purchasing power to comparable workers who retire at different times. That is why our table [not included here] shows the results in terms of constant (1976) dollars as well as in terms of replacement ratios.

Having said this, we must also point out that the definition of "comparable workers who retire at different times" is much more elusive than seems always to be recognized. In our rapidly changing economic and social environment it is a mistake to assume that the future shape of the curve of earnings for even the median worker will be similar to that of the median worker who has already retired. This warning applies with even greater force to earnings of women in view of the changing role of women in the labor market and the widening prohibitions upon discrimination by sex.

The second point is that in studying replacement ratios as criteria of benefit suitability, errors can be made by relying upon a single post-retirement/ pre-retirement relationship. Almost no workers in this or any country enjoy a pattern of lifetime earnings that follows the national average pattern, particularly when that national average pattern combines, as is customary, wages of people at all ages. It is even true that national median wages portray a pattern that applies to relatively few people. Wage fluctuations are the rule, not the exception.

With this in mind our Panel shows two replacement ratios. . . . It is noteworthy that even for the median earnings cases these ratios show markedly different results.

The conclusion that one reaches from these considerations is that any proposed benefit formula must be subjected to a large number of tests involving different earnings patterns, different economic assumptions and different definitions of pre-retirement earnings for replacement ratio calculations. [pp. 20-21]

Document 3.3 Secretaries' and Commissioners' White Paper, February 1975 [excerpt]

[*Author's Note.* Amendments to the social security system have been moving it away from an equity basis. Momentum and pressure to convert it entirely into a means-tested, noncontributory program are feared by three former social security administrators, who agree that general revenue financing would destroy the basic foundation of the present program. An excerpt from their *White Paper* follows.]

A 100-percent noncontributory system, lacking the compact between government and contributors that is built into social security, could offer no

DOCUMENT 3.3: from "Social Security: A Sound and Durable Institution of Great Value," White-Paper [by five former secretaries of health, education, and welfare, and three former social security commissioners], mimeographed press release, February 10, 1975 (Washington, D.C.: U.S. Department of Health, Education, and Welfare, 1975).

comparable assurance to working people, or even to those already on the rolls, that the promised benefits would not be curtailed in times of budgetary stringency. Designing such a system, moreover, would raise many thorny questions in specifying who should receive benefits, how large they should be, and how, if at all, their amounts should be varied.

There is an almost infinite variety of theoretical answers to these questions but the hard reality is that a noncontributory system would almost inevitably come to rest upon a means test so that no one would receive benefits until after poverty had overtaken him. Why, the argument would run, should the general taxpayer support persons who can support themselves if they have made no contribution to their own insurance protection? The experience of public assistance (commonly known as "welfare") augurs ill for the willingness of taxpayers to help their fellow citizens who are thought, rightly or wrongly, to be able in one way or another to support themselves. It is not likely that taxpayers would be willing or that Congress would be willing to compel them to provide noncontributory benefits without a means test and at a comparable level of adequacy to the thirty million people who now receive social security benefits—the elderly, the disabled, and their dependents, the widows and the widowers, and the motherless or fatherless children.

The benefits these people now receive are earned rights based on their past work and contributions, or on those of family members, thus reflecting their previous standards of living and serving in some measure as a reward for diligence. The benefits are payable without scrutiny of individual means and needs and so permit supplementation by anything the recipients have been able to save. Because they are payable as an earned right, the benefits accord with the self-respect of people accustomed to providing for themselves. It is small wonder that Congress and the people have preferred contributory social insurance to a system benefiting only those who can show themselves to be destitute.

The working portion of our population must, in one way or another, support that portion that is not working and does not have enough resources to meet the cost of living. Most non-working wives and children are supported, in normal course, by family breadwinners. The retired and the disabled, the widows and orphans, on the other hand, commonly have neither family support nor savings sufficient to maintain them, and some governmental mechanism is essential if they are not to be allowed to go hungry. [pp. 8-9]

Document 3.4   Congressional Budget Office, March 1976 [excerpts]

[*Author's Note.* Justification for retaining a large measure of a welfare component in the social security program rests on a lack of welfare or

DOCUMENT 3.4: Congressional Budget Office, *Budget Options for Fiscal Year 1977: A Report to the Senate and House Committees on the Budget,* March 15, 1976 (Washington, D.C.: U.S. Government Printing Office, 1976), pp. 127-31 and 125-38.

noncontributory income assistance plans for the poor. The following excerpt describes the extent and level of federal income assistance programs funded from general revenues. Additionally, state and local governments have various welfare programs.]

There are two broad categories of income assistance—contributory and noncontributory programs. Contributory programs, which account for three-fourths of income assistance spending, include social security, civil service and railroad retirement, and unemployment insurance. These programs are financed by contributions or taxes from employees and employers and provide payments to workers (or their survivors or dependents) based on the employee's work history. Social security is by far the largest of these programs, accounting for about one-fifth of the federal budget and providing payments to over 31 million persons.

The noncontributory income assistance programs are directed primarily at low income persons, whose eligibility is determined by amount of income, assets and needs, and are financed from general revenues. Medicaid, food stamps, aid to families with dependent children (AFDC), and supplementary security income (SSI) are the most costly of the noncontributory programs. Some of the noncontributory programs are administered and partially financed by state and local governments.

In addition to the contributory and noncontributory programs there are 25 tax expenditures in the income assistance area. These include the nontaxable nature of the benefits provided by income assistance programs, sick pay, pension contributions and earnings, and other employee benefits. The list of income assistance tax expenditures also includes the extra exemptions provided to the aged and blind, the earned income credit, and a number of smaller tax preferences. Altogether these tax expenditures are expected to reduce federal revenues by roughly $23 billion in fiscal year 1976.

Over the past two decades federal expenditures for these income assistance programs have grown rapidly; spending has increased more than tenfold while the part of the budget devoted to such programs has increased from 15 percent in fiscal year 1956 to an estimated 37 percent in fiscal year 1976 [see table 3.1]. This rapid growth has occurred for a variety of reasons: new programs have been created, benefits of both new and existing programs have been made more generous, the populations eligible for income assistance programs have expanded and more of those who are eligible for benefits have asked to receive them. While income assistance expenditures will no doubt continue to grow, real benefit levels can be maintained under existing programs if spending grows at only a slightly faster pace than that of the current policy budget as a whole.

Because the issues raised by the contributory and noncontributory programs are fundamentally different, the two types of programs are treated separately. The discussion of contributory programs focuses exclusively on the social security program. Unemployment insurance, federal employees retirement programs, and military retirement programs are analyzed in other sections of this chapter.

Table 3.1

Income Assistance Outlays and Tax Expenditures

(Billions of dollars, fiscal years, path B)

	1956	1966	1976[c]	1981[c]
Income Security (600)				
Contributory Programs:				
Social security (601 part)	$5.6	$20.2	$72.7	$120.7
Railroad retirement (601 part)	0.6	1.2	3.4	4.2
Civil service retirement (602)	0.5	1.7	8.6	16.8
Unemployment insurance (603)	1.4	2.3	19.9	15.8
Total Contributory	**8.1**	**25.4**	**104.6**	**157.5**
Noncontributory Programs:				
AFDC (604 part)	0.4	1.2	5.8	8.6
Food stamps[a] (604 part)	0.1	0.2	5.9	10.4
SSI[a] (604 part)	1.1	1.6	5.5	8.9
Housing assistance (604 part)	[b]0.0	0.2	2.6	8.0
Child nutrition (604 part)	0.1	0.3	2.7	4.3
Total Noncontributory	**1.6**	**3.5**	**22.5**	**40.2**
Other Income Security (600)	0.2	0.1	1.1	1.5
Total Income Security (600)	**10.0**	**29.0**	**128.2**	**199.2**
Other Income Assistance for the Poor:				
Medicaid (551 part)[a]	0.1	0.8	8.3	14.0
Veterans pensions (701)	0.8	1.9	3.0	3.6
Total Income Assistance	**10.9**	**31.7**	**139.5**	**216.8**
Percent of Total Outlays	15.5%	23.6%	37.2%	38.5%
Tax Expenditures	NA	NA	$22.8	$32.5

a. For 1956 and 1976 includes commodity distribution; aid to the aged, blind and disabled; and medical vendor payments.

b. Zero due to rounding.

c. Current policy levels

NA: Not available.

Source: *Five-year Budget Projections, Fiscal Years 1977-81*, Congressional Budget Office, and the *Budget of the United States* for 1958 and 1977.

Contributory Programs: The Case of Social Security

A number of the contributory income assistance programs face a growing imbalance between projected benefit payments and expected revenues collected in their trust funds. Concern over the solvency of the social security trust funds has received the greatest amount of attention. These trust funds are financed by a payroll tax (currently 9.9 percent) on all earnings up to $15,300 in 1976. However, the amount of earnings that is taxed is scheduled to increase as average wages rise.

Benefits, which in 1975 averaged $205 a month for retired workers and $225 for the disabled are paid out of the trust funds. Benefit payments are automatically increased to reflect increases in the cost of living.

The extraordinary combination of high inflation and a deep recession experienced during 1974 and 1975 has caused the social security trust funds to accumulate reserves much more slowly than anticipated. Because of this slowdown in the accumulation of funds and because of revised estimates of future reserves based on less optimistic economic forecasts for the next several years, the trustees of the social security trust funds forecast in May of 1975 that, beginning in 1976, the funds would pay out more in benefits than they received in revenues, continuing each year until the reserves of the Old Age and Survivors Insurance (OASI) and Disabled Insurance (DI) funds would be depleted by the early 1980s. . . . More recent estimates made by both the Administration and CBO indicate that the pace of depletion will slow down and that reserves will begin to stabilize in the early 1980s. The projected stabilization of the funds does not resolve the question of whether additional action needs to be taken to build the funds up further. It is also important to note that these estimates project a loss of over one-third of the reserves in the trust funds between 1975 and 1980.

If the decision is made to build up the reserves of the funds, the effects on the long-range condition of the system must be considered. The trustees' report indicates that the trust funds are even now accumulating a future deficit that is of a different nature and far more serious than the short-run problem of year-to-year imbalances between revenues and outlays. A large part of this future deficit is the result of a feature of the benefit formula which overcompensates future beneficiaries for the effects of inflation occurring during their working years. If this feature were removed without changing the tax rate or reducing benefits, half the anticipated long-run deficit would be eliminated. [pp. 127-31]

Noncontributory Programs: Income Assistance for the Poor [4]

In recent years the noncontributory programs that provide income assistance for the poor have seemed unsatisfactory for a wide variety of reasons.

---

4. The "poor" and "low-income" families or households are used interchangeably in this section. When the "poverty level" or the aggregate number of poor families or individuals is referred to, the general definition used is the official cash income definition of the federal government which is estimated to average about $5,700 per year for a family of four in fiscal year 1977 under current policy assumptions.

First, although the number of poor has generally declined the costs of these programs have increased rapidly—some sixfold over the past decade.[5] Second, significant gaps in coverage persist. For example, many of the children living in poor families do not qualify for benefits under important public assistance programs such as AFDC and medicaid usually because they live in two-parent families. Moreover, only one in 12 low-income families receives any type of housing benefit. Third, benefit levels vary widely among those who receive benefits—largely because states administer and partially finance some income assistance programs, and the level of benefits varies from state to state. Fourth, there appears to be little coordination among the numerous programs available to an individual. Fifth, the nature of the programs may undermine long-term social goals. For example, the incentive to work may be weakened because of the cumulative loss of benefits resulting from earned income. In some instances, family stability may also be discouraged in order to meet eligibility requirements. The general dissatisfaction with existing income assistance programs for the poor has generated numerous efforts directed toward developing alternatives.

Alternative approaches for reforming income assistance for the poor can be evaluated in terms of their costs and their structures. For the purposes of this analysis, two of a number of possible approaches have been selected: (1) Adoption of individual program changes that leave the present loosely related separate cash and in-kind programs basically intact, and (2) Implementation of a highly integrated cash system, eligibility for which would be based on income, supplemented by a few in-kind programs.

Any program that transfers income from one group to another can be at a high cost or a low cost. The factors that drive up the costs are not inherent in the structure of the program. Basic policy decisions concerning who will be eligible, the benefit levels provided, and the amount by which benefits are reduced as a recipient's earnings rise will determine overall program costs regardless of how the program is structured. While structures and costs are not related, it would be difficult, for example, to initiate a comprehensive cash program without raising costs above current levels. It is unlikely that such a program using income and family size as a standard test for eligibility would cost less in the short run or would have more restrictive eligibility requirements than current programs. [p. 135]

---

5. As this book went to press, in 1977, an all-time low of about 5 percent of U.S. families were estimated by the Census's Congressional Budget Office to be in poverty. Although this may be an underestimate, CBO's testimony makes clear that the corresponding figures from HEW are overestimates. The reasons for this have often been cited: for example, downward bias by persons asked merely to recall their money income, and lack of any estimate for the value of income-in-kind, as home-grown produce or food stamps. See coverage in *National Observer,* February 19, 1977, p. 1 [author's note].

Characteristics of the Present Programs

Aid to Families with Dependent Children (AFDC) provides cash assistance to low-income female-headed families with dependent children, and to families in which the father is disabled. In some states, intact families in which the father is unemployed are also eligible. AFDC families may also receive social security, but such benefits are counted as income in determining AFDC benefits. Families eligible for AFDC are also automatically eligible for medicaid benefits. Food stamps are received by 70 percent of AFDC beneficiaries. Standards for eligibility and payment levels vary widely among states which are required to administer and bear part of the cost of the program.

Supplemental Security Income (SSI) provides cash assistance, based on need, to the aged, blind, and disabled. Dependents are not included as beneficiaries. However, children of disabled fathers may be eligible for benefits under AFDC. About half of all SSI beneficiaries receive social security benefits; one-third receive food stamps. SSI beneficiaries are not automatically eligible for medicaid although most are eligible.

The food stamp program provides needy households with a monthly allotment of coupons redeemable for the purchase of food. Households pay a portion of their net incomes for the coupons that varies according to family size and income. The difference between the total value of the coupons and the amount a household pays for them is the benefit. All households receiving federal or state public assistance are automatically eligible for food stamp benefits, while other families, including single persons, may qualify on the basis of need.

Child nutrition programs provide indirect income subsidies to both needy and non-needy children through a variety of food assistance programs. These programs include the national school lunch program, the school breakfast program, the summer feeding program, the special milk program, the child care feeding program, and the special supplemental feeding program for women, infants, and children (WIC). Federal payments to states, schools, and other sponsors of the various programs are usually based on the family income of the participating child. Children receive free lunches, suppers, and breakfasts if their family income is below 125 percent of the poverty level; meals at reduced prices are provided for children in families whose income is between 125 and 195 percent of the poverty level. In addition, all children in participating schools from families with incomes above these levels have their breakfast, lunch, and milk costs reduced by more limited payments. The national school lunch program, will serve 26 million children in fiscal year 1976. Participating schools are reimbursed according to rates that are adjusted semiannually on the basis of changing food prices.

Medicaid finances medical care to about 23 million needy people through federal/state programs. There is substantial variation from state to state both in categories of persons covered and in the benefits to which they are entitled. Almost half of medicaid recipients are under 21, while about another one-sixth are over 65. In states in which eligibility is restricted to AFDC and SSI recipients, large numbers of poor people do not qualify for medicaid support, for example, childless couples, single people between 21 and 65, the working poor, and intact families. A few states preclude coverage of the low-income aged, blind, and disabled.

Veterans' pensions are received by disabled and aged war veterans and their dependents or survivors if their incomes are below certain levels. Pensioners can receive SSI and veterans' pensions concurrently. SSI counts VA pensions as income in determining SSI eligibility, but the veterans program does not count SSI, welfare benefits, 10 percent of retirement benefits, or spouse's earnings as income when determining benefit levels. The stricter SSI eligibility requirements severely limit the number of veterans who receive SSI in addition to their veterans' pension.

Housing assistance is received by an estimated 2.3 million low-income households. This represents only 8 percent of all households that could qualify for assistance under existing law. The program is limited by the availability of suitable, low-cost housing and by the appropriations provided for the program. Unlike the other programs discussed here, it is not an entitlement program for which anyone who meets the standards can apply and receive benefits. The major types of housing assistance are public housing and programs that provide rent and mortgage payment subsidies to low-income families.

BUDGET OPTIONS

Current policy option. If no new legislation were enacted to change these programs, the costs of the current income assistance programs would almost double by 1981—from $33.8 billion in fiscal year 1976 to $57.8 billion in fiscal year 1981 (see following table). With the exception of housing assistance, these programs are all entitlements, that is, benefits must be paid to any individual meeting the eligibility requirements specified in the laws. Therefore, the costs of these programs will change according to economic conditions, growth in the eligible population, and the rate at which those eligible actually participate in the programs. Furthermore, in many cases federal costs rise as prices increase or as states decide to raise benefit levels. Deliberate changes in the amounts spent on these programs can be achieved only by altering the laws that govern the programs.

Inflation, which is assumed to average 6 percent a year, and a substantial growth in the AFDC, SSI, food stamps, and medicaid caseloads are the main factors which are increasing the costs of the current policy projections.

INCOME ASSISTANCE FOR THE LOW-INCOME POPULATION:
BUDGET OPTIONS
(Billions of dollars, fiscal years)

	1977	1978	1981
Current Policy Option	38.5	42.8	57.8
Changes From Current Policy Level			
Low Option	-7.1	-8.0	-14.4
High Option			
Outlays[a]	0.0	-2.3	-5.0
Tax Costs[b]	0.0	25.4	31.4
TOTAL	**0.0**	**23.1**	**26.4**
President's Budget	-4.9		

a. For greater detail see summary tables.

b. A composite of income tax credits and direct cash transfers which is the net effect of substituting a standard tax credit for present personal exemptions and child care deductions including higher tax liabilities for upper-income taxpayers.

An Individual Equity Approach

The concept of individual or even family equity has almost disappeared from the social security system of benefits. Initially, Title II of the Social Security Act (i.e., OASI) was intended to provide only retired workers with partial replacement of earnings. Similarly, Title I of the same act, called "Old Age Assistance," was intended to help the dependent aged. The 1939 amendments, by adding dependents and survivors, interwove the Title I aspects of welfare for the aged with the Title II concept of an "earned right" to benefits. This "right" to a benefit is derived from the statutory law; it is not a contractual right as under private insurance. Thus Congress may legislate different levels of benefits and different rules of entitlement, and has indeed done so over the years. As as a result, instead of the trust fund equaling one to three years of the dollar amount of benefits paid out, which was the original idea of Congress, it has dwindled to a level equal to about one-half of one year of benefits paid out. "Pay-as-you-go" financing was an earlier common term that correctly describes the system today, as does the now often-used term, "intergenerational transfer of funds."[6]

---

6. See, for example, Edgar K. Browning, "Social Insurance and Intergenerational Transfers," *Journal of Law and Economics,* October 1973, pp. 215-37.

Equity between similarly situated individuals who are in different age groups or cohorts is held by some to be irrelevant when discussing "fairness," and relevant only when discussing financing. Persons who subscribe to this view may restrict equity to horizontal equity, which they define as "fairness" or similar behavior (i.e., similar benefit tax ratios) toward individuals with similar earnings records in the same age groups. Thus they disregard complaints of inequity by today's younger workers who are being taxed to support the benefits of the current aged. The Consultant Panel's distinction between "horizontal" and "vertical" equity (see the remarks on equity in document 3.2) is not made here. The panel's definition of "vertical" equity is that "different situations at one point of time are treated differently." This is considered here to be merely another form of horizontal equity. "Vertical equity" is reserved solely for different treatment of like individuals who are in different age cohorts. In other words, the "fairness" of an intergenerational transfer of funds, primarily to nonworking aged from present and future working generations who are to bear the tax burden but may not necessarily vote on it, is raised as an equity issue, not merely as a financing one.

The legislative history of social security reflects the complaints that have been made over the years by those in one age cohort already under the system against allowing those in a different age cohort to enter the system on much more favorable economic terms. For example, the 1954 "new start" provision reduced to six quarters the covered employment requirement for survivor benefits for persons "who died before September 1, 1950, and after 1939," thus permitting for these persons a total, minimum-entitlement, employer-employee tax of only $9.00.[7] This was protested not only by persons in the same age cohort of the deceased worker, who already had paid more, but also by younger workers who understood that their taxes were being increased to pay for those older persons who by law would be newly entitled to benefits in the very near future. Similar "new starts" have been passed in other years.

The unfunded, accrued liability is the amount of benefits paid or promised that exceeds the taxes paid during those years when the benefits were "earned." The system's unfunded accrued liabilities are difficult to estimate today because until a person has forty covered

---

7. U.S. Congress, House, Committee on Ways and Means, *Social Security After 18 Years.* . . , staff report (Washington, D.C.: U.S. Government Printing Office, 1954), pp. 33 and 34.

quarters, there is no vested right of entitlement to the retirement benefit. Under various sets of assumptions, such liabilities have been estimated in the area of $3 trillion. The current actuarial long-run imbalance (see chapter 5) relates anticipated future payments or benefits to anticipated future receipts, taxes, and interest. The actuarial imbalance could be zero if the taxes were increased enough, but this would not change the amount of the unfunded accrued liability.

The early actuarial studies of social security financing, which were done by the Social Security Administration (SSA), present an interesting picture of the then anticipated relationship of benefits and taxes over the years. They also illustrate an intergenerational inequity of the system. For example, *Actuarial Study No. 48* states:

> The level-premium cost, after allowing for the existing fund, is 16.10 percent for present members as compared with 4.93 percent for new entrants. . . . The sum of the present value of the contributions to be paid under the present schedule by present members and the existing fund is $269 billion less than the present value of benefits to be paid to them and their dependents and survivors. . . . On the other hand, there is a "surplus" of $228 billion for new entrants.[8]

This study was prepared for the 1958 amendments and was written when Robert J. Myers was chief actuary.

Today the amount of social security taxes paid has little relationship to the amount of benefits to which the payor is entitled. The equity concept has been greatly eroded by the welfare concept. Benefits are determined in accordance with "social adequacy" at some undefined level of need, or with a standard of living below which it is considered socially unacceptable to fall. In short, the concepts of equity and social adequacy are inherently competitive.

At the end of 1976, the major groups of individuals who charged that the system was not equitable were:[9]

1. Covered workers as compared to noncovered workers

---

8. As quoted by Ray M. Peterson in "Misconceptions and Missing Perceptions of Our Social Security System (Actuarial Anesthesia)," *Transactions of the Society of Actuaries* II (1959): 815.

9. Additionally, the homemaker who does not work for pay has a more general complaint in that his or her work at home contributes to the well-being of the family, but society places no value, direct or imputed, on this work; it is not entered into the national income accounts nor, therefore, are taxes, whether social security or income, levied on it. The author views this in a different category than the claimed inequities discussed because no tax is paid for the benefit. For further discussion see chapter 4, below.

2. Women as compared to men
3. Married women who work as compared to married women who do not work
4. Working persons aged 65 to 72 years who work as compared to nonworking persons in the same age group
5. Single persons without dependents as compared to married persons with dependents
6. Young workers as compared to older workers

In all six cases the complaint is that the social security taxes paid do not bear a "fair" relationship to the benefits received. The question of equity in the first four cases is considered in some depth in other chapters of this book. The claims of inequity by singles and the young are considered here; in addition, some references are made to the claims of the other groups.

The belief that there is some "unfairness" under the social security system probably increases the system's effect on the supply of labor at the margin. This effect seems to be greatest among older persons: an increasingly large percentage of them are retiring earlier, at ages 62, 63, and 64, with an actuarially reduced benefit. Because the benefit is to replace earnings, there is an indexed limit on earnings—$3,000 annually in 1977. If earnings exceed the limit, one dollar of benefits is lost for each two dollars earned. This is called the retirement test. It is less clear for married women than for men to what degree this retirement test affects their decisions to work or not work. Availability of other retirement income and health status are important factors in deciding whether to retire or not (for further details, see chapter 7).

Fewer persons today continue to work after age 65. For some, the reason may be that they receive higher net income after taxes—social security benefits are exempt from income tax—than if they continue to work. Others, whose earnings would be close to the amount permitted without penalty or effective penalty, do not wish to earn so much that they will lose any or all of their social security benefits. They may also object to paying social security taxes on covered earnings after age 65. On the other hand, some of those who do work, because *(a)* they enjoy what they are doing, *(b)* they are not compelled by their employer to retire, *(c)* they may also be able to earn a higher income than their social security benefits would yield, actually may feel cheated out of benefits "for which they have already paid."

Since 1950, new entrants have gradually been covered by the system.

At the same time, benefits for those already in the system but retiring have been increased. These increasingly large costs have been financed primarily by coverage of more jobs, and by additions to the labor force in those sectors covered by social security.

The primary source of new workers in recent years has been women. Married women who work are already covered by social security as presumed dependents and can receive benefits based on their husband's earnings record. A married woman who has worked and paid social security taxes sufficient for entitlement to a worker's benefit receives it, or a secondary or dependent's benefit, whichever is higher. However, note that a wife who is entitled to a retirement benefit based on her own covered earnings "is entitled to a supplementary benefit only when her husband's earnings are at least three times as large as hers."[10] For the low-income, two-worker, husband-and-wife family whose

> combined earnings are below the taxable maximum for one worker (or even slightly above), the sum of the benefits to which they are entitled on their respective work record is usually smaller than one and one-half times the amount to which a man with a dependent wife would be entitled if his earnings had been equal to their combined earnings. This is not the case when their combined earnings are considerably above the taxable maximum for one worker.[11]

This is an inequity that favors higher earners over lower earners and nonworking wives over working ones.

In 1974, 7.1 million women were receiving a retirement benefit based solely on their own covered earnings. An additional 1.5 million women were receiving a secondary benefit based on their husbands' earnings. These latter women had fulfilled all requirements—forty quarters of covered earnings—for a primary benefit, but it was a smaller benefit than the one they received as dependents. Among the 7.1 million women were buried, statistically speaking, the married women entitled to a dependency benefit, but whose primary benefit exceeded it. Because the SSA does not make available the number of dually entitled women who receive a retired worker's benefit (see the right-hand column in table 3.2), it is impossible to state precisely how many of them are dually entitled, but receive only one benefit. However, it was

---

10. Lenore Bixby, "Women and Social Security in the United States," *Social Security Bulletin,* September 1972, p. 9.

11. Ibid.

probably an increasing percentage and one that represented a larger amount of total taxes paid in. I say "probably" because some of these women had been or were married, and must have earned more than retired women whose secondary retirement benefits were greater than their primary benefits.

TABLE 3.2

NUMBER OF WOMEN WHO HAVE WORKED IN COVERED EMPLOYMENT AND WHO ARE RECEIVING RETIRED WORKERS', WIVES', OR WIDOWS' BENEFITS[a]

(In millions)

	RETIRED WORKERS' BENEFITS[b] (1)	DUALLY ENTITLED[c] (2)	COLUMNS (1) & (2)	ALL DUALLY ENTITLED WOMEN[d]
1955	1.2	0.1	1.3	n.a.
1960	2.9	0.3	3.2	n.a.
1965	4.3	0.6	4.9	n.a.
1970	5.7	1.0	6.7	n.a.
1971	6.0	1.1	7.1	n.a.
1972	6.3	1.2	7.5	n.a.
1973	6.8	1.4	8.2	n.a.
1974	7.1	1.5	8.6	n.a.

a. All these women worked a length of time sufficient for entitlement to a primary benefit based on their own work record.

b. *Social Security Bulletin, Statistical Supplement 1974*, p. 113. An unknown number of these women are dually entitled.

c. *Ibid.*, p.115. Includes only those "dually entitled" whose secondary benefit is larger than their primary benefit based on their own earnings.

d. Data are not available as of March 1, 1977.

Because married women in general earn lower wages and usually work fewer years, their primary benefit is often less than half their husband's, and in almost all cases less than the 100 percent of the husband's primary benefit that the widow receives. In practice, therefore, they pay sizable amounts of payroll taxes but do not as a rule receive retirement benefits based on their own earnings. Since the percentage of women who work is expected to rise by 1990 to very high levels—75 percent of women aged 20 to 24 years, 63 percent of women 25 to 44 years, and 60 percent of women aged 45 to 54 years—it is obvious that this source of "surplus" monies cannot last forever.[12]

12. U.S. Bureau of Labor Statistics, mimeographed press release, September 15, 1976, Table I.

Moreover, if the Equal Rights Amendment passes, and/or if the U.S. Supreme Court should interpret that entitlement to benefits by sex is inequitable, then this source of surplus monies could dry up even faster.[13]

The SSA usually computes replacement-of-earnings ratios as a justification of a fair tax burden. However, these are not ratios of replacement of *total* income, but rather only of "average taxable earnings" over a lifetime. It is for this reason that the SSA's *Research and Statistics Note* of June 15, 1976 shows that 17 percent of all men receiving a social security retirement benefit in the period July-December 1974 received over 90 percent or more of their lifetime, average, covered, monthly, taxable earnings. The extent to which they had earnings that far exceeded the taxable base over their lifetime is not reflected in the computation. Neither are their earnings in non-covered employment or any of their income in the form of interest, rents, and dividends.

The SSA, using its own data, has tried to estimate the earnings beyond the tax base of men who retired in the period July-December 1974. The resulting median replacement rate of 29 percent for all male earnings is much lower than the median rate of 59 percent of their lifetime taxable social security earnings. The median replacement rate for their 3 highest years of taxable earnings in the last 10 years prior to retirement was 37 percent.

The data on replacement earnings ratios for women as a population group are similar to the data for men, but because their earnings are lower the level of benefits is also lower. However, the replacement ratios are greater because of the weights in the benefit formula, which favor low-paid persons. For women who retired in the period July-December 1974, 79 percent of median covered monthly earnings over their lifetime were replaced, but only 31 percent of their total earnings and 44 percent of their taxable earnings during the 3 highest years of the last 10 years prior to retirement. However, 42 percent of women received 90 percent or more of their lifetime average taxable earnings, as compared to only 17 percent of the men.

Higher-paid persons in later life do not receive replacement of their earnings by social security benefits to the same degree as lower-paid ones. This is, in effect, a value judgment, and a widely accepted one. It lies behind the redistributive aspects of social insurance—what I have

13. See chapter 4, below, for March 1977 decisions of Supreme Court doing just this.

called the "social adequacy" concept of the program. High earners are also more likely to have private pensions from company plans.

Women who are now retiring or who retired in 1974 generally have low average monthly earnings. Primarily, these reflect the fact that they have had many dropout years, in contrast to women at the top of the earnings scale, who have been consistently in the labor force without going in and out of it as they bear children. As the birth rate drops, there will be far more women not only in the labor force but staying in it. Their primary benefits will therefore increase, although the replacement ratios of their total taxed earnings probably will fall.

As the findings of the Task Force on Women and Social Security state:

> The likelihood of being poor is considerably greater for elderly females than for aged males. More than two out of every three poor persons in the 65-plus age category are women. In 1974 there were 2.275 million aged women in households with incomes below the poverty line[14]—or 18.3 percent of all 65-plus women. Poverty among elderly men, on the other hand, was markedly lower: 1.033 million were living in households with incomes below the poverty line in 1974, or 11.8 percent of the total male 65-plus age group. Many older persons who would be classified as poor on the basis of their own incomes live in households with total incomes above the poverty level.[15]

As the report says, older persons with low incomes tend to live with children or other close relatives with much higher incomes. This points to one of the major difficulties: How does one determine who is poor relative to others and who is only statistically poor? The statistical data, as we have seen, do not truly reflect economic status. For example, "the poor" include self-supporting students who anticipate higher incomes over their lifetime, as well as persons who have retired and no longer have income from work. The data, in short, ignore the changing pattern of income over one's life, and so overstate the total number of poor people.

Nevertheless, the data illustrate a current "social need" to raise the

---

14. The 1974 weighted poverty threshold is $2,352 for an aged individual (65 plus) and $2,958 for a two-person family with a head aged 65 and older.

15. U.S. Congress, Senate, Special Committee on Aging, *Women and Social Security: Adapting to a New Era,* A Working Paper Prepared by the Task Force on Women and Social Security, 94th Cong., 1st sess., October 1975 (Washington, D.C.: U.S. Government Printing Office, 1975), p. 37.

incomes, both monetary and in kind, of many women and some men aged 65 and over. However, it is not at all clear that the social security system should be the source of this support. In fact, the Supplemental Security Income (SSI) legislation of 1974, which paid out $5.8 billion dollars in noncontributory programs, and Medicaid, which pays medical bills for the poor and near-poor, including the aged when their Medicare benefits do not suffice, are far better sources. For SSI benefits one needs only 30 days' residence, provided one can prove need. SSI benefits to the aged, blind, and disabled in July, 1976, were running at about one-half a billion dollars, or an annual rate of about $6 billion. Of this amount, just over one-half went to some 2 million aged persons.

Retired persons with low in-kind and cash incomes probably had much higher incomes during their working years. Many own their own homes, free of mortgage, not to mention such household consumer durable goods as, for example, automobiles and refrigerators. The increasing level of education of the labor force should encourage persons who are in middle life to plan better for their later life. Divorced women with several children and uneducated minorities both male and female are probably the only groups who are poor during all or most of their lives.

The earnings base on which social security taxes are paid include only earnings up to a given level. The base does not include income from interest, rent, and dividends. The social security system, if it is to retain any semblance of equity, cannot be the primary method of redistributing income from rich to poor. By its very nature, social security is a system for redistributing income from working persons to nonworking persons, primarily ones who are older, but also to some younger dependent survivors.

Because the tax is not on all income and not even on all earned income, and because the public is told that social security benefits are earned, the system would have more viability if its welfare aspects were reduced and a determined attempt made to return it to an equity basis. If this were done, the working young would be less burdened by taxation to support the current aged. In my opinion, the secondary (i.e., dependency) benefits of a retired worker's spouse and of surviving spouses should be phased out over a 30-year and 50-year period, respectively. Otherwise, if inflation continues, the rise in the benefits, which are by the 1972 amendments tied to the cost-of-living index, may force the payroll taxes to a level at which a revolt of young taxpayers, especially young singles, may occur. This is likely even if inflation is no longer counted double.

President Carter proposed on May 9, 1977, six steps to bring about greater financial viability of the social security system. These include use of general revenues to offset the losses of tax receipts whenever the employment rate is above 6 percent, a phasing-in by 1981 of all earnings as the base on which the employer pays OASDHI taxes, and a much smaller increase in the wage base, subject to the employee tax— an additional $600 in 1979, 1981, 1983, and 1985. The financing of the system is discussed in depth in chapter five. The different treatment of taxes paid by employers and taxes paid by employees does not increase equity. The employer will shift an increase in payroll taxes back onto the employee or forward onto the consumer via higher prices. The overall effect of Carter's recommendations would be to weaken the equity concept and strengthen the social adequacy rationale for the program.

The use of general revenues does not fit SSA's insistence that these are earned benefits, not welfare or means-tested benefits. General revenue financing of social security is a subterfuge that should be avoided. If, after phasing out spouses' secondary benefits, additional aged persons were in need, it would be preferable to use the existing Supplemental Security Income program, which in the fall of 1976 was making payments to over two million aged and about two million disabled persons.

The increase in the dropout rate by nonprofit and state and local employees, while still small, does express the disaffection of young and single persons, as well as of married women who work. Although it is difficult to find a private insurance program that covers not only declining term life insurance but an annuity and permanent disability insurance as well, it is unlikely that any but the young, healthy, single person and also the married woman who works could find better total replacement buys in the private insurance market.

Many single persons believe that they are treated inequitably because they pay the same taxes but do not have dependents to collect secondary or survivor benefits. Their case is somewhat weakened by the fact that many persons still single in their twenties or thirties may marry later, but it is certainly true that other single individuals may never marry.

In partial response to the singles' case, there was added as early as 1939 a benefit for parents dependent on their children's earnings. If working, single children of such parents die before they do, some dependency benefits are generated. In general, however, single persons are not permitted to gain from their earnings record an amount anywhere near the benefits that may be collected on the basis of a married person's work record. The latter may have a spouse entitled to a retirement benefit, a dependent child, and—some years later—a surviving spouse. The degree of this difference in benefits between singles and married has recently been increased by the anticipated U.S. Supreme Court decision in *Califano* v. *Goldfarb*. On March 2, 1977, the court ruled, 5 to 4, that a widower need not prove dependency to receive a survivor's benefit based on his deceased wife's covered earnings record. This doctrine has also been extended to the current entitlement requirements for husband's benefits.

It is difficult to find a politically acceptable method of reducing or eliminating the inequity between singles and married. The Advisory Council's Subcommittee on Treatment of Men and Women considered various alternatives. They found no support for what was apparently the only viable suggestion, namely, to permit a dependency benefit for close relatives other than parents with whom the single covered person had lived for a significant number of years prior to retirement or death.

My proposal to phase out spouses' secondary dependency benefit, both in retirement and as survivors, would greatly reduce this inequity. However, this particular argument for the proposal did not then have a wide following. A more popular view was that singles should contribute especially to dependent children's benefits. Although a portion of their taxes could not easily be earmarked for that purpose, it was argued, an economic society no less than a biological one has a responsibility for continuing its existence—and, therefore, should care for its young.

Because the social security system provides a unique package of benefits, and because these benefits over the years will probably be changed, as will the tax base and rates which support them, it is impossible to make further general comparisons between social security and the private market. Social security benefits, unlike private insurance benefits, are indexed. So, too, is the earnings base, which is tied to the average of covered wages. A vested-rights equivalent under social security is equal to ten years under a private plan. However, if a person ceases to be in covered employment prior to retirement, his benefit amount, unlike one from vested private insurance, will decline as months of zero covered earnings are divided into total earnings. This decline in benefit amount is probably to some degree offset by an increase in the cost of living. Under most private plans, benefits are not indexed. It is most likely that inflation will continue. In short, social insurance cannot be compared with private insurance; there are too many legislative unknowns in addition to the unknown future level of prices and wages.

It is now over forty years since social security began. The system has had time to become fully mature. Without continual legislative reform to bring the annual receipts of benefits and interest into balance with tax revenues, the system would fail. Congress must act because of the financial imbalance. At the same time, Congress should also act to increase equity and to make the system fit within the total structure of taxation and welfare that has developed over the past forty years in the United States.

At present, social security benefits are exempt from personal income tax. Greater fairness in treatment of different people would occur if the benefits were taxed, although this should not be done retroactively. Currently, the payroll tax is a business cost deducted prior to payment of corporate income tax. The 1974 pension law permits individuals to set up retirement plans and to deduct their contributions before personal income taxes (although no credits are allowed against social security taxes). If all social security taxes, not just the part handled by companies, were so treated, and all pensions were taxed upon receipt, equity among individuals in different situations would increase. Few other countries exempt social security benefits from income taxation.

TREATMENT OF MEN AND WOMEN

TREATMENT OF MEN AND WOMEN

The Social Security Act for over forty years has treated men and women differently. It assumes that a married woman is dependent on her husband, so that when her husband retires and she reaches either 62, for an actuarially reduced benefit, or 65 for the full one, she automatically receives one-half her husband's primary benefit. A married man, on the other hand, in order to receive a retirement benefit based on his wife's earnings, must prove that he received one-half of his support from his wife.

The Supreme Court in its decision in *Goldfarb* v. *Califano,* March 2, 1977, ruled that this distinction by sex was unconstitutional in respect to surviving spouse's benefits. The court had ruled two years earlier that since under social security a mother automatically receives a parent's benefit for children under eighteen if her husband dies, it was unconstitutional for the Social Security Act not to provide a similar parent benefit for a father. The dependency requirement for entitlement to retirement benefits is identical to the one for entitlement to surviving spouse's benefits. A Supreme Court case filed on February 8, 1977 was later dismissed by request of Secretary Joseph Califano of Health, Education, and Welfare. This differentiation in Entitlement rules between men and women appeared even weaker in retirement cases than in cases of a surviving spouse.

Under social security an individual is entitled to receive only one benefit based on one earnings record at a point in time. Married women who work, therefore, receive either a primary benefit based on their own earnings record or a dependency benefit based on their husbands' earnings record. Accordingly, after working and paying social security taxes, they may receive no more than if they had never worked or paid these taxes.

A two-worker, husband-and-wife family, because of the uneven weighting in the benefit formula, may receive as a couple fewer benefits upon retirement than if only the husband had worked, earning the same income as the two of them and paying the same amount in taxes. Because this is so, married working women complain that social security is inequitable where nonworking married women are concerned. Additionally, nonworking married women receive no credits toward social security benefits from doing work in the household. Some groups consider this to be an inequity even though there is no tax paid.

Document 4.1   Dalmer Hoskins and Lenore E. Bixby, *Women and Social Security: Law and Policy in Five Countries,* 1973 [excerpts]

Complaints of discrimination against women appear to stem mainly from the provision that a married woman who has worked in employment covered under social security may draw a benefit at age 62 or later based either on her own or her husband's earnings, whichever is larger, but not two full benefits. Less clearly understood but of growing concern is the allied problem that, when both husband and wife work, the couple's benefits may be somewhat smaller than if total family earnings were the same but only the husband had worked (see below). In other words, although family protection has been emphasized in the evolution of the social security provisions, the program incorporates no direct measure of family earnings and their replacement. . . .

Benefits for working wives. The woman's benefit based on her husband's work may be larger than her own retirement benefit because the covered earnings of women, on the average, are lower than those of men. This reflects their less regular and extended employment, their greater concentration in low-paid occupations and industries, as well as any past (if not present) discrimination in pay for the same work. Thus, in many cases the working wife receives a retirement benefit no larger than the nonworking wife may receive as a dependent. This is interpreted by some as meaning that a woman's own work and her social security contribution have brought no benefit. It ignores the fact that before reaching retirement age she had insurance protection for her dependents against loss of her own earnings due to disability or death.

Married couples' benefits and contributions. When both husband and wife work, their combined retirement benefit varies somewhat with the

DOCUMENT 4.1: Dalmer Hoskins and Lenore E. Bixby, *Women and Social Security: Law and Policy in Five Countries,* U.S. Social Security Administration, Office of Research and Statistics, Research Report No. 42 (Washington, D.C.: U.S. Government Printing Office, 1973) pp. 88-95.

relative amount earned by each. If their combined earnings are below the taxable maximum for one worker (or even slightly above), the sum of the benefits to which they are entitled on their respective work records is usually smaller than 1½ times the amount to which a man with a dependent wife would be entitled if his earnings had been equal to their combined earnings.[1] This is not the case when their combined earnings are considerably above the taxable maximum for one worker. In that event, however, the couple will pay more social security taxes and get a larger benefit than if only one spouse worked and earned the same amount. Although the choice of having the husband earn as much as the combined earnings of himself and his wife is not ordinarily open to a family, the comparison nevertheless raises questions of equity.

Various proposals have been advanced to improve the retirement benefits of married couples when both spouses work. One proposal would allow each of these couples the option of having a PIA calculated on the basis of their combined earnings (up to the annual taxable maximum for one worker) with 50 percent added as the spouse's benefit and each entitled to half the sum. A form of this proposal which was considered by Congress in 1972 contains a provision applicable to couples with each spouse having had 20 years of covered employment after marriage. Unless such a provision is limited to couples with each spouse having extensive covered employment after marriage, the benefit cost would run high and administration would be complicated.

An alternative approach with particular attention to the financial difficulties of women whose marriage breaks up when they are middle-aged or younger would credit to each spouse half of their combined earnings every year during the period of marriage. It is argued that such earnings credits would yield a better retirement benefit for women with many years of low or zero earnings, and would also help if a widow or divorcee with young children becomes disabled or dies. Provision for splitting earnings credits, however, would not generally increase the retirement benefit for the couple that continues marriage, and it would have variable effects on the retirement benefits of couples with second and third marriages of either partner.

It has also been suggested that, instead of a special provision for calculating the retirement benefits of married couples, the social security tax rate might be reduced for a working wife (or for all women). Or, alternatively, some payment in excess of her own retirement benefit might be guaranteed every working wife.

Such provisions have a cost which would have to be met by tax increases for all covered workers, including those without dependents. Furthermore, all raise questions of equity in relation to the situation of the single worker.

---

1. This situation is aggravated to the extent that a wife receiving a retirement benefit is entitled to a supplementary benefit only when her husband's earnings are at least three times as large as hers. Moreover, if the wife earns more, a husband is not entitled to a secondary benefit unless he can prove his wife had provided half his support.

Noncoverage of homemaking activities. Some women are concerned that their work at home—housekeeping activities and the care of children and of older family members who are ill or disabled—is not considered employment for social security purposes. Some in the women's liberation movement believe that this attitude denigrates such activities and results in an unfavorable image of what had traditionally been considered "women's work." More important, lack of coverage means there is no benefit to help meet the real cost of providing substitute homemaking and child care services in the event of the woman's death or severe disability.

Concerning benefits earned, the time spent in homecare activities by women who work for pay during part of their lives does diminish the size of the retirement benefit to which their own earnings record entitles them. Moreover, if the young housewife becomes disabled or dies, her covered employment may not be sufficient to entitle her to disability benefits or her children to survivor benefits. Questions concerning the value to be imputed to unpaid work and, again, who should pay the "contribution" or the cost of such credits have been discussed but with many conflicting answers.

Entitlement of men dependents. The entitlement provisions for spouses differ by sex. A wife or widow who is not entitled to a retirement benefit on her own work record is automatically entitled to a benefit on her husband's earnings record when she meets age and other criteria. A husband or aged widower, on the other hand, is entitled to a benefit on the basis of his wife's earnings only if he was dependent on her for half of his support. A widower with entitled children in his care, unlike the widowed mother, is not himself entitled to a benefit for himself. Neither a divorced husband nor a surviving divorced husband aged 62 and over has even a qualified right to a type of benefit a divorced wife or surviving divorced wife may receive. Up to now, it has not seemed reasonable to most people either to assume that men generally are dependent on their wives or to require a test of dependency for wives or widows.

Earnings replacement and taxes. Certain other features of OASDHI, particularly the benefit calculation and the ceiling on taxable earnings, likewise appear to have an uneven impact on men and women workers. Any such differences, however, result not from differentiation between the sexes in the details or application of these provisions but from the operation of economic and demographic factors. [pp. 90-93]

Thus, individual retirement benefits replace a larger share of covered earnings for women than for men. The benefit formula is the same for both sexes and is weighted to replace proportionately more of low than of higher covered earnings. The higher replacement occurs, therefore, both because women earn less than men on the average and because women live about 4 years longer. [See author's note, below.]

To the extent that men are more likely than women to have earnings above the taxable maximum, the man's benefit (apart from any benefit going to his wife) replaces a smaller fraction of total preretirement earnings than does the woman's. It follows also that social security taxes represent a smaller proportion of total earnings (covered plus noncovered) for men than for women.

SUMMARY

Social insurance has an uneven impact upon women and men. In part the differences result from economic and demographic factors outside the social security system—such as women's lower earnings and longer life expectancy. In part also, they result from the diversity of women's roles as workers, wives, widows, and mothers.

Over the years. OASDHI's evolution has been significantly influenced by the necessity to accommodate these diverse and changing needs. The concept that a man is responsible for the support of his wife and children led to the creation of a broad structure of social security family protection. At the same time, the steady growth of labor-force participation by women, particularly married women, has been reflected in a phenomenal growth in the number of women entitled to benefits on the basis of their own earnings records. Complaints that the OASDHI system discriminates against women have proliferated as a result of this growth.

Various proposals have been advanced to relate the retirement benefits of married couples to their combined earnings. Whatever the form of such a provision, its costs would most likely have to be met by tax increases on all covered workers, including those without dependents. Other suggestions reflect the concern that family care and housekeeping activities performed by women are not considered employment for social security purposes. Consideration of alternative proposals for modifying the program are but part of the continuing assessment of social security in the United States. [pp. 90-95]

> [*Author's Note.* The earnings replacement rate of social security benefits treated as a percentage of life-time average (median) taxable earnings of men, increased from about 44 percent in the first half of 1970 to 59 percent in the last half of 1974. Because women workers earn less per hour, and because many work far fewer years than men during their adult life, their average monthly earnings, even with the permitted five-year dropout of low or zero earnings, are much lower than men's. Accordingly, the replacement rate of their average earnings is higher (the benefits, as we have seen, are weighted in favor of persons whose covered earnings over the years yield low average monthly earnings). Thus the replacement rate of

women's earnings during the same period, 1970-74, increased on the average (median) from 59 percent to 79 percent.[2]]

[Social Security in Great Britain]

[*Author's Note.* The example of Great Britain, as the authors Hoskins and Bixby point out, is worth considering in any discussion of how the U.S. social security system should be reformed.]

One of the most interesting countries from the standpoint of social security protection for women is Great Britain. Several countries, like Great Britain, provide retirement benefits at different ages for men and women, and some require women to pay their contributions at a different rate than men. However, the special characteristic of the British National Insurance Scheme is its distinctions regarding the level of benefits and the coverage of different risks for the employed married woman.

The British social security system may be unique in offering the employed married woman the option of paying contributions to qualify for benefits on her own insurance or electing not to pay contributions and to rely on her husband's insurance for a smaller range of benefits as a dependent. Moreover, the married woman who drops out of employment can continue to pay contributions in order to maintain her own insurance record. This provision has particularly important consequences for old-age pension rights.

The British regulations seem to offer the woman a choice between independent insurance and insurance as a dependent—a choice which is lacking in most other national systems. Nevertheless, the question is being raised whether this special treatment of the married woman is, in fact, the advantage it purports to be. When the Beveridge Plan was adopted, there was widespread acceptance of the viewpoint that most married women would, despite periods of employment, continue to be dependent on their husbands for support.

With the increasing number of married women in the labor force today, assumptions concerning the role of the wife as a dependent are being re-examined. For example, the criticism has been made that it is hardly fair for the woman who has been working for most of her adult life to wait until her husband also retires in order to receive the flat-rate pension benefit. Moreover, the right to give up independent insurance coverage can have very negative consequences, particularly with regard to pension rights for the woman in the event of divorce. The assumption that the woman is, in fact, the dependent of her husband is also reflected in the differential unemployment and cash sickness benefits for married women, a situation which is often

---

2. U.S. Department of Health, Education, and Welfare, Research and Statistics Note No. 13, June 15, 1976.

criticized as being the most obvious example of unequal treatment.

It would be misleading to say that the treatment of women under the social security system is the major social security issue in Britain today. What has been an issue there for several years is the continuing debate concerning the direction the National Insurance Scheme should take in the future in order to achieve higher benefits for all recipients. This debate involves various viewpoints on what emphasis should be placed on flat-rate benefits, earnings-related benefits, and the occupational pension schemes. The proposals made by the Labour and Conservative governments to reform the National Insurance Scheme have dealt with the status of women, but only as one of the issues in the larger question of social security reform. [pp.53-54]

If a divorced woman was entitled to child maintenance payments from her former husband at the time of his death, she may receive the child's special allowance. This allowance amounts to £2.95 a week, including the family allowance benefit, for each child.

According to the pension reform proposed by the Conservative government, arrangements are being made to extend to the divorced woman the right that a widow has to use her former husband's contribution record if this would improve her own retirement pension. [p. 67]

PROPOSALS FOR PENSION REFORM

In the background of the public debate over pension reform is the fact that an increasing number of pensioners have become dependent on the means-tested supplementary benefits program. The dilemma that has faced successive governments in Great Britain is that adequate flat-rate pensions cannot continue to be financed by flat-rate contributions without severely penalizing low-income earners. In fact, the present flat-rate benefits are financed to an increasing extent by the earnings-related contributions. The policy for several years has been to help those categories of the population most in need through the supplementary benefits program rather than increasing flat-rate benefits for the entire eligible population.

Both the Labour Party's National Superannuation proposal and the Conservative Party's "Strategy for Pensions" place a heavy emphasis on the necessity to shift from a system of flat-rate contributions to one of earnings-related contributions. Under the Labour Party's proposed reform all contributions and benefits would be related to each insured person's earnings. This means that low-paid women would pay lower contributions, but they might also, of course, receive lower benefits. The proposal did, however, include the recommendation that the pension formula should provide a higher rate of earnings replacement for low-income earners.

In the "new deal for women" proposed by the Labour Party, women would contribute on the same basis as men and earn corresponding benefits. Married women would no longer have the option not to pay full National Insurance contributions. The rates for sickness and unemployment benefits for a married woman would be the same as those for single men and women with the same earnings.

The Labour Party plan offered the married woman a choice between alternative methods of calculating her retirement pension: (1) a pension based on her own average earnings, or (2) if it would be more favorable to her, a flat-rate pension on her husband's record plus an earnings-related addition of 25 percent of her own average earnings.

The widow over age 60 would receive the same pension as her husband was receiving or had earned when he died. Nonemployed married women with no children and mothers without preschool children would be required to make contributions in order to be eligible for invalidity and retirement benefits. Retirement pensions for a couple would be calculated on the basis of the contributions which have been paid by both the husband and wife.

Since the Labour Party did not have the opportunity to enact its pension reform proposal before its election defeat in 1970, there is no indication as to how the level of contribution to be paid by the nonemployed housewife would have been fixed or how the combined husband-wife retirement pension would have been calculated.

From the standpoint of the treatment of women, the reform proposals of the present Conservative government offer far fewer changes in the existing system. As under the National Superannuation Scheme, contributions would be earnings related, but under the Conservative Party's State Basic Scheme, benefits would continue to be flat-rate. According to the government's "Strategy for Pensions," the feasibility of abandoning the contributory insurance system in favor of a tax-based scheme was examined. It was rejected, however, largely because many more women would receive higher benefits under a system not dependent on individual contribution records than under the existing system. For example, working married women who presently qualify through their husbands for a lower pension benefit would become entitled to an equal benefit. Moreover, the same married women would become eligible for unemployment and sickness benefits, which they do not presently receive if they are covered through their husband's insurance.

Thus, the government's proposal recommends that, even under an earnings-related contributory system, married women should continue to have the choice of not paying full National Insurance contributions. Widows' benefits would be payable under the same conditions as in the present system, and the flat-rate retirement benefits would continue to be paid at levels considerably lower than those for supplementary benefits.

The new scheme would terminate the graduated pension program, and major emphasis would be placed on occupational pension schemes to provide adequate incomes for retirement. [pp. 67-69]

Assumed Dependency and Required Proof of Dependency

On March 19, 1975, after the 1975 Advisory Council's report was written, the U.S. Supreme Court, in *Weinberger* v. *Wiesenfeld*, decided that a male parent, whose wife had social security coverage, was "currently insured," and died, was entitled to the same survivor parent's benefit that a widow with child would have received if her late husband had had similar coverage. The law, however, is still written in terms of a "surviving mother." This is in harmony with the concept generally accepted by the social security system, that a female is *assumed* dependent, but the male must *prove* that he receives one-half support from his wife. After the Wiesenfeld decision the Social Security Administration set guidelines to make it possible to pay a father's benefit. Nevertheless, the statutory law had not been changed.

In general, entitlement by a male to social security benefits on his spouse's work under social security and the payroll taxes she paid depends on his ability to *prove* that he received one-half of his support from his wife. A female's entitlement to social security benefits, based on her spouse's work under social security and the payroll taxes he paid, is given without any proof of dependency or need. In 1939, when the Social Security Act was amended to add dependency, it was assumed that a wife is almost always dependent on her husband.

As this book went to press, the U.S. Supreme Court ruled, as I predicted it would in my dissent to the Advisory Council's reports, that it is unconstitutional to have different rules for entitlement to secondary benefits for widowers and widows. On March 2, 1977, in *Califano* v. *Goldfarb,* the court, by a five to four vote, made it illegal to continue to deny widowers benefits based on their wives' covered earnings record when under like circumstances a benefit to a widow would be paid on her deceased husband's covered earnings. Thus the court eliminated for a surviving male spouse the required proof of dependency, namely, that one-half of his support was from his deceased wife.

The Supreme Court, on March 21, 1977, affirmed without an opinion that the Social Security Act provision 42 U.S.C. § 402(c) (1)

(C), "that requires men, but not women, seeking social security insurance benefits through spouse's benefits to show that they received at least one-half of their support from spouse violates Fifth Amendment."[3] Newspaper publicity on this important ruling was sparse. This ruling means that men will become entitled to a secondary benefit based upon their wife's earnings and will receive that benefit if it is less than their own primary benefit. Although there are relatively few men in the male population retiring each year who would probably actually receive this benefit, it was estimated by HEW in 1974 that such a ruling might cost in the neighborhood of $215 million during year one as compared to $195 million for aged widowers.[4] This latter estimate, which is relevant to the Goldfarb case, was reported in the press to be now about $500 million. Thus the effect of eliminating the one-half support test for widowers and retired males is about $1 billion in year one and additional amounts in subsequent years. As some individuals in these groups will die each year, the total amount, if there are no price increases, will eventually level off. These rulings in favor of widowers and retired men do not specify, and the court would not traditionally do so, that a private pension benefit earned in an uncovered job should be offset against a secondary dependency benefit under social security. The Advisory Council had recommended this to Congress for all secondary benefits, whether paid to men or women, because the requirement of such an offset would act as a relatively easy to enforce (though incomplete) means test.

The estimated first-year cost of implementing the Goldfarb decision was about one-half billion dollars, or 0.05 of payroll. Subsequent years will add to this cost, as only a small percentage of persons newly entitled during year one may be expected to die by the end of that year. Although a much smaller cost impact is anticipated from the Wiesenfeld decision, costs will greatly increase because the court has also ruled, in the retirement cases, that it is unconstitutional to require an aged husband of a retired wife to prove dependency. The annual costs of such a decision were estimated to be at least another one-half billion dollars in the first year of impact alone. Additionally, the costs of widowers' benefits would be higher in each successive year. Although there would be more retired husbands than widowers, the amount of the secondary retirement benefit is only one-half of the primary benefit

3. *United States Law Week* (45), March 22, 1977, p. 3626.
4. "Estimated Long-Range and First-year Costs of, and Number of People Affected by Various Changes in the Social Security Program," typed (Supplied to Advisory Council's Subcommittee on Treatment of Men and Women by SSA staff; not dated).

earned by the wife, while a survivor's benefit is equal to the entire primary benefit paid to the deceased worker.

The majority opinion in the Goldfarb case quotes from the Eastern District Court of New York's prior decision as follows:

> Whatever may have been the ratio of contribution to family expenses of the Goldfarbs while they both worked, Mrs. Goldfarb was entitled to the dignity of knowing that her social security tax would contribute to their joint welfare when the couple or one of them retired and her husband's welfare should she predecease him. She paid taxes at the same rate as men and there is not the slightest scintilla of support for the proposition that working women are less concerned about their spouses' welfare in old age than are men.[5]

Further, in footnote 5, the majority opinion states:

> The disadvantage to the woman wage earner is even more pronounced in the case of old-age benefits, to which a similarly unequal dependency requirement applies. 42 U.S.C. §§402(b), (c) (1) (C). Seen. 2, *supra*. In that situation, where the insured herself is still living, she is denied not only "the dignity of knowing [during her working career] that her social security tax would contribute to their joint welfare when the couple or one of them retired and her husband's welfare should she predecease him," *Goldfarb* v. *Secretary of Health, Education and Welfare,* 396 F. Supp. 308, 309 (EDNY 1975), but also the more tangible benefit of an increase in the income of the family unit of which she remains a part.[6]

The above and earlier references to the Wiesenfeld and Frontiero cases in the majority opinion substantiate the Supreme Court's subsequent ruling that the different entitlement requirements for a secondary retirement benefit are unconstitutional. In *Frontiero* v. *Richardson,* 411 U.S. 677 (1973), the Supreme Court ruled that it was a violation of the due process clause of the Fifth Amendment to the Constitution to deny husbands of wives serving in the armed forces the same dependency benefits (living allowances and medical and dental costs) received by wives of husbands in the armed forces. The government's defense was primarily based on high costs and administrative convenience. The court stated that "the Constitution recognizes higher values than speed and efficiency. . . ."

---

5. *United States Law Week* (45), March 1, 1977, p. 4238.
6. Ibid., p. 4239.

The dissent of Mr. Justice Rehnquist, as quoted by Mr. Justice Stevens, "demonstrates that at present only about 10% of the married women in the relevant age bracket are nondependent. . . ."[7] (45 LW 4242). It should be noted that the above, and also footnote 7 of the dissent of Mr. Justice Rehnquist, have inaccurate statistical data. The footnote correctly cites from census data that in 1974, 43 percent of wives were in the labor force. However, it does not follow that 57 percent of wives are dependent on their husbands. In 12 percent of families, no one works (as in the case of retired couples), and in 2 percent persons other than husband or wife work. A more acceptable estimate of dependent nonworking married wives, as of 1975, is 42 percent, because this is the percentage of families where either the husband alone works or he and another family member other than the wife work.[8]

Further, I do not believe that "the work habits of those [women] over 55 are most relevant for determining the actual number of widows who would be excluded by a dependence test."[9] The age group used here—an open-ended one consisting of women "over 55"—includes millions of women aged 65 to 90 or more. Although on the surface it would seem reasonable to use the labor force participation rates of women aged 55 to 64, even this is not the most precisely relevant age group. It is not necessarily true that married women within that age bracket who are 60 to 64 years of age and who do not work are dependent on their husbands. Many private pension plans permit people in these age brackets to retire. Additionally, social security benefits can be awarded on the wife's earnings, on the taxes she paid, at age 62. The logical age break, then, is not the one most easily available from the Bureau of Labor Statistics. There is also a need for information on income in the form of interest, rents, and dividends.

At the end of 1974, 46.4 percent of male workers had taken early retirement, that is, at ages 62 through 64.[10] From this one cannot conclude that these men were therefore dependent on their wives. It is true that the percentage of women aged 55 years and over who work is pertinent to the question, but these data should not include women who are aged 65 years and older. Of women aged 55 to 65 years, 42

7. Ibid., p. 4242.

8. Howard Hayghe, "Families and the Rise of Working Wives: An Overview," *Monthly Labor Review,* May 1976, p. 16.

9. *United States Law Week* (45), March 1, 1977, p. 4247, footnote 7 of Rehnquist's dissent.

10. *Social Security Bulletin, Statistical Supplement 1974,* p. 117.

percent work, and of men, 75 percent. Among both women and men aged 65 years and older, few work: 8.2 percent of women and 22 percent of men. A dependency test of widows or widowers should not include whether one is or is not working at age 65 or later, since that is the accepted and often the mandatory retirement age in our society.

Document 4.2   Report of the Advisory Council on Social Security, March 1975 [excerpts]

[*Author's Note.* The 1974-75 Advisory Council on Social Security was appointed by the Secretary of Health, Education, and Welfare as required by law. Every four years a council representing among its members the general public, the self-employed, and organizations of employers and employees, reviews the status of the four social security trust funds, scope of coverage, adequacy of benefits, and all or any portions of the Social Security Act and its interrelation with public assistance programs. The council had two subcommittees, one on financing and one on treatment of men and women. The council as a whole did not agree with all of the recommendations of the latter subcommittee. I chaired that subcommittee whose other two members were a member of the New York State Building and Construction Trades Council, AFL-CIO, Edward Cleary, and the executive vice-president and chief financial officer of American Telephone and Telegraph Company, John Scanlon, now retired. Mr. Scanlon had just gone through the experience of paying out on behalf of AT&T, as retroactive pay, $15 million to women employees who had won an anti-discrimination charge against the company. Additionally, after two years of litigation, the January 18, 1973, agreement between AT&T and three federal agencies provided for new promotion and wage policies that were anticipated to result in increases for women and minorities of an additional $23 million per year.]

The Council found the treatment of men and women under social security to be a matter of considerable current interest and controversy and directed special attention to this aspect of the program. It was reviewed in depth by a special subcommittee[11] of the Council in the light of the proposed equal rights amendment to the Constitution, recent and anticipated court actions involv-

---

DOCUMENT 4.2: U.S. Congress, House, Committee on Ways and Means, *Reports of the Quadrennial Advisory Council on Social Security,* 94th Cong., 1st sess., H.D. 94-75, March 10, 1975 (Washington, D.C.: U.S. Government Printing Office, 1975), pp. 25-32.

11. Members of the subcommittee were Edward J. Cleary and John J. Scanlon, with Rita Ricardo Campbell, Ph.D., as Chairman.

ing equal rights for men and women, and socioeconomic changes, particularly changes in family structure and earnings patterns. [p. 25]

The pending equal rights amendment to the Constitution would provide that "Equality of rights under the law shall not be denied or abridged by the United States or any State on account of sex." To date, 34 States have ratified the proposed amendment. . . . Adoption of the proposed amendment would raise serious doubts as to the constitutionality of any provision in the social security law which is different for men and women.

In the meantime, the courts are being asked in a number of cases to rule on whether various provisions of the social security law that are different for men and women are constitutional under the due process clause of the Fifth Amendment. [p.26]

In recent years Americans have been marrying later and having fewer children. Also, the service sector of the economy has been expanding at a faster rate than other sectors, thus providing an expanding number of jobs of the type that women have traditionally held.

These trends have contributed to increases in the number of working women and in the proportion of women in the labor force. In 1973, more than half of all women worked at some time during the year. About 90 percent of all women have worked in paid employment at some time during their lives.

Moreover, family structure has undergone significant changes. Married couples where only the husband works no longer comprise the majority of families. There has also been a substantial increase in numbers of one-parent families, including families headed by women who are unmarried, divorced, separated, deserted, or widowed, and an increase in households that are headed by women. In 1973, 23 percent of all households were headed by women, as compared to 18 percent in 1960.

[*Author's Note.* If "families" rather than "households" are considered, women heads were, in 1973, 12 percent of all families; in 1960, 10 percent; and in 1975, 13 percent.]

The Council gave special attention to those provisions of the social security law that are different for men and women, and to those provisions which are the same for men and women, but are targets for complaints that the program provides differential treatment based on sex or marital status. [p. 26]

In general, the provisions of the social security law that are different for men and women should be made the same for both in a way that is consistent with the purpose and principles of the social security program. Specifically, the one-half support dependency requirement in present law for entitlement to husband's and widower's benefits should be eliminated, and for any category of women entitled to secondary benefits the corresponding category of men should be entitled to the benefits on the same basis.

In light of the proposed equal rights amendment, court decisions in sex discrimination cases not involving social security, and socioeconomic changes, the Council believes it would be desirable to act now to change the provisions of the social security law that are different for men and women. These changes should be made in a way most consistent with the purposes and principles of the social security program rather than as the result of court decisions that might not offer such consistency.

To become entitled under present law to a husband's or widower's benefit based on a wife's earnings, a man must prove that he was receiving at least one-half of his support from his wife when she retired, became disabled, or died. There is no such requirement in the law for women for entitlement to a wife's or widow's benefit based on her husband's earnings.

Benefits are provided for a wife or widow without a specific test of support because it has been thought reasonable to presume that a wife or widow is dependent on her husband's earnings for support and that she loses support or a potential source of support when the husband's earnings are cut off.[12] Men, on the other hand, are not generally dependent on their wives for support, and the presumption of dependency that was thought reasonable for a wife or widow has not seemed to be reasonable for a husband or widower. Present law therefore requires a man to establish that he was actually supported by his wife in order to get benefits as her dependent.

The dependency requirements in present law for entitlement to spouses' and surviving spouses' benefits should be made the same for men and women without providing the benefits on the basis of any presumptions as to the dependency of women on men or of men on women. At the same time, the necessity of innumerable detailed investigations of personal circumstances and individual determinations of dependency for both men and women, as would be necessary if women were required to prove dependency as men now do, should be avoided. Accordingly, the Council recommends that the one-half support requirement in present law for entitlement to husband's and widower's benefits be eliminated and that secondary benefits under social security be provided for both men and women under the implied test of dependency in present law for women.

As under present law, a spouse or surviving spouse whose primary benefit as a worker equals or exceeds the secondary benefit as a dependent would be entitled only to the primary benefit. A person entitled to a primary social security benefit lower than the secondary social security benefit would

---

12. There has always been an exception to this presumption if the wife or widow is entitled on the basis of her own earnings to a benefit larger than her wife's or widow's benefit; in this situation, the wife's or widow's benefit is not payable.

continue to get the primary benefit plus the difference between it and the amount of the secondary benefit.

[*Author's Note*. Because of the potentially high costs of this recommendation by itself, the Advisory Council simultaneously recommended the following.]

The law should be changed so that a pension based on work in noncovered employment would affect entitlement to and the amount of secondary benefits under social security in the same way that a primary social security benefit does.

Under present law it is possible for a wife who works in employment not covered by social security to get a full worker's pension based on her noncovered work plus the full amount of the wife's or widow's benefit payable on the basis of her husband's earnings under social security. Generally men cannot get a spouse's or surviving spouse's social security benefit in addition to a pension from noncovered employment because they generally cannot meet the one-half support test. However, with the elimination of the one-half support requirement, as recommended by the Council, it would be possible for both men and women who were not dependent on a spouse's earnings for support and who receive benefits as workers under a pension system based on work not covered under social security to get a spouse's or surviving spouse's benefit under social security. The Council finds that the payment of spouse's and surviving spouse's benefits under such circumstances is contrary to the dependency basis for such benefits.

Accordingly, the Council recommends that the law be changed to prevent the payment of spouse's and surviving spouse's benefits in such cases. Effective prospectively, periodic payments based on a person's work in employment not covered by social security, should be subtracted from any social security dependents' or survivors' benefits for which that person may be eligible.

The Council also considered, but did not adopt, requiring women (and fathers and divorced men) to meet the one-half support test that husbands and widowers have to meet under present law. This approach, like the one recommended by the Council, would prevent the payment of spouse's and surviving spouse's benefits under social security to nondependent men and women whose primary employment was in jobs not covered by social security. The Council recognizes that adoption of the proposal to treat a pension earned in noncovered employment as though it were a primary social security benefit would reduce wife's benefits for some working wives who are approaching retirement age and who will be eligible for [other] pensions based on noncovered employment. On the other hand, application of a one-half support requirement to wives and widows could have as many or more adverse effects on people's retirement expectations.

Also, a proof-of-support requirement for women as well as men would substantially increase the administrative complexity of the program and would require large numbers of dependent women to establish dependency on the husband in order to get exactly the same benefits they can get under present law. The approach recommended by the Council would make it possible for men who are actually dependent to get dependent's or dependent survivor's benefits without making such benefits available to men and women who receive pensions from noncovered employment and who were not dependent on the insured worker.

Another approach considered by the Council was the gradual elimination of dependents' benefits or dependent's and dependent survivor's benefits for spouses; however it was not thought that socioeconomic changes warranted such a significant deliberalization in the program, and it was considered that it would be unrealistic to propose such a deliberalization. [pp. 27-29]

[*Author's Note.* Because Congress had acted in the 1972 amendments to correct prospectively, starting in 1975, an inequity in the computation of benefits of men born before 1913 as compared to women in the same age cohort, the council recommended no change. On March 21, 1977, the Supreme Court, in *Califano* v. *Webster,* held that the difference in computation for men's and women's benefits for persons born before 1913 was constitutional, because it was to compensate for past employment discrimination against women. The court stated further that the 1972 action of Congress that corrected this prospectively was not an admission that the previous policy was "invidiously discriminatory." Rather, the court continued, the action was a recognition by Congress that recent legislative reforms had lessened the economic justification.]

The benefit eligibility and computation provisions of present law are the same for men and women reaching age 62 after 1974 but are different for men and women who reached age 62 in 1954-1974. The Council does not recommend any change in these provisions since they are the same for men and women reaching age 62 now and in the future. Also, to provide the same computation for men who reached age 62 before 1975 that was provided for women would be very costly, estimated on a retrospective basis at $1.8 billion a year for the next several years, and still as much as about $1.5 billion a year even 10 years from now.

[*Author's Note.* Further this matter was considered by Congress who acted as described above to correct the inequity for all retiring after 1974 by their 1972 legislation. To suggest that Congress reconsider the 1972 action seemed, in view of the greater urgency of other matters, unwise.]

Benefit Computation for Two-Worker Families

[*Author's Note.* Retirement benefits of families where both wife and husband have worked and where their combined earnings are below the taxable base, or even slightly higher, are less than one and one-half times the retirement benefit of a husband who alone earned the same amount and whose wife did not work. If the two-worker family had considerably higher joint earnings, this discrepancy in benefits does not hold, but the family will pay considerably more in social security taxes than if only one person had earned their combined income.]

Under present law a married couple both of whom worked and paid social security taxes may get less in total benefits than a couple where only one member worked and paid taxes and whose earnings under social security were the same as the first couple. The Council's Subcommittee on the Treatment of Men and Women recommended a proposal that would assure that two-earner couples with significant attachment to the labor force would always get at least as much in benefits as single-earner couples with comparable covered earnings. Under the Subcommittee's proposal such working couples who become entitled to benefits in the future would have the option of receiving retirement benefits based on their combined earnings (with the combined earnings in any year not being permitted to exceed the maximum taxable earnings for an individual). Since higher benefits than under present law would be provided for the couples affected, the proposal could be viewed as providing a larger return on the contributions paid by a working wife with relatively low earnings whose husband also had relatively low earnings. Thus, the proposal would respond, in part, to the complaint of some married women workers that they do not get a return for their own contributions when the wife's benefit, based on the husband's earnings, exceeds her own retirement benefit.[13]

The Council does not endorse the principle of providing benefits based on a married couple's combined earnings. A basic rationale for such proposals is that couples who have paid similar contributions should get similar benefits. However, in an earnings-related social insurance system, such as social security, benefits are not directly proportional to contributions. Further, the Council notes that there is a point beyond which it is difficult to justify adding complex exceptions to the social security law in the interest of providing benefits in direct relation to contributions for special groups.

Also, proposals to base benefits on a couple's combined earnings have a

13. See dissenting statement by Dr. R.R. Campbell. The Council notes that the Subcommittee also considered and rejected a proposal to provide a married worker in all cases some or all of the spouse's or surviving spouse's benefit in addition to his or her primary benefit. The Council is in full agreement with the Subcommittee's decision. Such a change in the law would create inequities, and the very substantial increase in social security contributions that would be required to pay for the additional benefits would apply not only to married people but also to single people, who would derive no additional protection from it. (The cost of a proposal to pay a woman the full wife's or widow's benefit in addition to her own retirement benefit is estimated to be $9-10 billion above present law in the first full year; if comparable provision were made for husbands and widowers, the cost would be substantially higher.)

substantial cost—even the proposal with rather limited applicability recommended by the Subcommittee has an estimated average long-range cost of 0.20 percent of taxable payroll. (The proposal would cost about $4 million in 1976, and more in later years.) A further consideration is that combined-earnings proposals would treat married working couples more favorably than two single workers who have the same amount of covered earnings as the married couple, and, in so doing, would further increase the extent to which the value of the protection afforded married workers exceeds that of single workers. [p. 30]

Imputed Earnings for Homemaker Services

[*Author's Note.* Women who do not work for money outside the home have no social security benefit in their own right. That there is only a five-year dropout from the divisor in computing average monthly earnings over a lifetime greatly lowers the average monthly earnings of women who may work, leave the labor force to bear and raise children, and then return to the labor force. Some argue that a special credit for such women—two years for each child up to three children, for example—would help to maintain a more socially adequate level of retirement benefits for women. Others argue that either approach is contrary to the intent of the Social Security Act, namely, that benefits are to replace lost earnings. Here, there are no earnings that are lost, and no taxes, therefore, that are paid on the earnings.]

The social security law should not be changed to provide earnings credits to homemakers for work done in and around the home for which no earnings are received, or to permit people to pay social security taxes with respect to such work in order to obtain credits.

There is of course an economic value, however difficult to assess, to the work that women and men do in and around the home, and there is a loss when such work ceases. However, no wages are paid for such work, so there is no loss of earned income that occurs when the work stops, as there is when a wage earner retires, becomes disabled, or dies.

Social security is an earnings-replacement program. Its function is to replace, in part, earnings from work that are cut off by retirement in old age, disability, or death. It would be contrary to the nature of the social security program to provide for the payment of social security benefits in cases where no loss of earnings occurs, and the Council believes that it would be undesirable to change the nature and function of the social security program by providing for the payment of benefits in such cases. In addition, any proposal relating to imputed earnings raises serious questions of equity and administrative feasibility.

Change in Requirement for the Special Minimum Benefit
for the "Regular, Low-Paid Worker"

[*Author's Note.* Because women are concentrated in the low-paid service industries and often work less than full time for the convenience of the employer, the Subcommittee on Treatment of Men and Women recommended that the requirement for the special additional monthly benefit described below be changed from one-fourth of the annual tax base to one-sixth. In 1977 this would have been a reduction in required earnings from $4,125 annually to $2,750. The entitlement requirement for coverage is still only earnings of $200 a year. I suggest that $2,750, or more than ten times that amount, is a reasonable entitlement requirement for the low-paid worker, usually a woman, to benefit from this special provision.]

The Council considered a proposal recommended by the Subcommittee on the Treatment of Men and Women to reduce from one-fourth to one-sixth of the prevailing contribution and benefit base the dollar requirement for a year of coverage after 1950 for purposes of the special minimum benefit provision. (Under the law a worker may get a special minimum benefit equal to $9 multiplied by the number of his years of coverage under social security in excess of 10 and up to a maximum of 30 if that benefit exceeds his regular earnings-related benefit.) The Subcommittee report states that the recommended change was intended to "improve the protection afforded under social security to regular but low-paid workers, the majority of whom are women. . . ."

The Council recommends no change in the special minimum benefit provision. While relatively fewer women than men may be able to qualify for the higher special minimum benefits, this difference results from the fact that women in general have had lower earnings than men. To the extent that the difference in earnings between men and women is the result of discriminatory treatment in the labor market, this difference will be rectified as greater equality between the sexes in employment opportunities, pay scales, etc., is achieved.[14]

---

14. By Mrs. Campbell. I do not anticipate that this difference in earnings between men and women will be rectified in the near future. Currently the median annual wage of full-time working women is 57 percent of that of full-time working men, and this is a ratio which has been falling during the last three years from 60 percent. Although I do agree that in the long run women will increase their earnings relative to men's earnings, this will take time. Currently, and in the decade ahead, more women will wish to enter the labor force and the supply of labor is increasing relative to the demand for labor so that especially during this immediate period of unemployment, women may fare worse rather than better. Only when young women who are entering the labor force will seek occupations and gain employment in those types of work which primarily have been done in the past by males, will the ratio move in favor of women. Occupations in the United States are

Also, since special minimum benefits are not automatically adjusted to increases in prices while regular earnings-related benefits are, within a short period of time the latter will be larger in all cases than the special minimum benefits and the provision will phase out. The Subcommittee's recommendation would tend to perpetuate the special minimum benefit provision. The Council believes the provision should be allowed to phase out. This "phase out" will occur as future regular benefit levels rise—reflecting expected increases in general wage levels—and benefits for long-term regular workers under social security generally become sufficient to provide earnings replacement that is reasonably related to their preretirement standard of living.

[*Author's Note.* Words that do not imply one sex or the other should be used wherever practical. For example, "parent" is preferable to "mother" or "father."]

The Council believes that words that do not denote gender should be used in the law wherever it is practical to do so, provided no change in the intended meaning of the law would result. For example, where possible it would be preferable for the law to refer to "spouse" instead of to "wife" or "husband", and to "surviving spouse" instead of to "widow" or "widower", etc. The Council understands that there is a general principle of statutory construction that calls for interpreting words in a provision of law which denote the male sex as meaning either sex unless there is something else in the law or in the legislative history of the provision which precludes such an interpretation. The Council agrees that this should be the case where it is not practical to use words that do not denote gender (and, in fact, has followed the practice in this report of using "he" where "he or she" is meant).

---

either held primarily by men and are relatively high paying or held primarily by women and are relatively low paying.

What percent of the differential between the earnings of men and women is a residual after adjustments are made for such variables as education and interruptions over a life time in attachment to the labor force which later results in different average durations of work experience for women and men, I do not know. There is, however, considerable literature on this. I refer the interested reader to recent issues of the *American Economic Review*, Sept. 1973, their *Proceedings*, May 1974: *Journal of Political Economy,* March/April 1974, as well as to government publications, including the *1973 Report of the Council of Economic Advisors*, and Hearings before the Joint Economic Committee of Congress on "The Economic Problems of Women," July 10-30,1973, printed in three parts.

In my considered judgment, a fair summary of the literature is that the difference in earnings between women and men due to discrimination will not be corrected over any relatively short period of time. Further, many women work regularly 30 hours or less per week, as in retail stores, and although they are "permanently attached to the labor force," their total annual earnings are not sufficient to give them entitlement for this benefit, enacted in 1972 and designed to help the regular, low-paid worker. I support a reduction in the requirement that annual earnings equal ¼ of annual prevailing tax base (currently $14,100) to 1/6: that is currently from $3,525 per year to $2,350.

Document 4.3   Advisory Council, March 1975, Subcommittee on Men and Women: Recommendations [excerpt]

[*Author's Note.* The Advisory Council's Subcommittee on the Treatment of Men and Women under Social Security has an in-depth discussion with references to court cases involving sex and marital status. It is appendix B of the Council's printed report. The subcommittee's recommendations differ from the whole council's findings, as follows.]

RECOMMENDATIONS CONCERNING SOCIAL SECURITY PROVISIONS OF THE LAW THAT ARE THE SAME FOR MEN AND WOMEN

1. The retirement benefits that are payable under present law to a married working couple can under some circumstances amount to less than the benefits that are payable to a married couple with the same total earnings where only one member of the couple worked.

In view of this difference under the system with respect to the replacement of individual earnings vis-a-vis family earnings, the Subcommittee recommends that a married working couple coming on the benefit rolls in the future with each member of the couple having at least 40 quarters of coverage in the 20 years before entitlement to benefits should have the option of receiving retirement benefits based on the combined earnings of the couple. While the couple's earnings in each year would be combined, no more than the amount of the prevailing tax and benefit base in the year—the maximum amount of a worker's annual earnings that is counted in figuring social security benefits and is subject to social security taxes—could be counted in figuring benefits. Thus the proposal would benefit lower income families, that is, those in which neither worker earns as much as the prevailing tax and benefit base in a year.

Each member of the couple would get a retirement benefit based on a primary insurance amount that was equal to 75 percent of the primary insurance amount resulting from the monthly average of the combined earnings. Together the couple would get benefits based on an amount that was equal to 150 percent of the primary insurance amount resulting from the monthly average of the combined earnings, the same percent that a married couple with the same total earnings in each year would get where only one member of the couple worked.

Each member of a couple would have to have at least 40 quarters of coverage under the social security program in the 20 years before entitlement in order for the couple to elect to receive benefits based on their combined

DOCUMENT 4.3: Appendix B, "Report of the Subcommittee on the Treatment of Men and Women under Social Security (With Respect to Sex and Marital Status), pp. 133-53 in U.S. Congress, House, Committee on Ways and Means, *Reports of the Quadrennial Advisory Council on Social Security*, 94th Cong., 1st sess., H.D. 94-75, March 10, 1975 (Washington, D.C.: U.S. Government Printing.Office, 1975), pp. 147-48.

earnings, and both members of the couple would have to elect to receive benefits on this basis or neither of them could. Benefits based on combined earnings would not be payable after a divorce.

A widow or widower who is eligible for a widow's or widower's benefit could get a benefit based on the couple's combined earnings if the couple were receiving benefits based on their combined earnings when one member of the couple died, or if the deceased had 40 quarters of coverage and the survivor had 40 quarters of coverage in the 20 years before entitlement to benefits or the death of the spouse.

All other benefits based on either worker's earnings would be computed on the basis of the worker's individual earnings, as under present law.

2. To improve the protection afforded under social security to regular but low-paid workers, the majority of whom are women, the Subcommittee recommends that the dollar requirement for a year of coverage after 1950 for purposes of computing the special minimum benefit be reduced from the present one-fourth to one-sixth of the prevailing contribution and benefit base.

[*Author's Note.* The Subcommittee report goes on to explain in greater detail why they did not recommend social security credits to homemakers for work done in their own homes.]

The social security law should not be changed to provide social security earnings credits to homemakers for work done in the home for which no earnings are received, nor to permit people to pay social security taxes with respect to such or similar work in or around the home in order to obtain credits. Such a change in the law would be unwise, impractical, and very costly.

There is of course an economic value, however difficult to assess, to the work that women—and men—do in and around their homes, and an economic loss when such work ceases. However, no wages are paid for such work, so there is no loss of earned income that occurs when the work stops, as there is when a wage earner retires, becomes disabled, or dies.

Social security is an earnings-replacement program. Its function is to replace, in part, earnings from work that are cut off by retirement in old age, disability, or death. It would be contrary to the earnings-replacement nature of the social security program to provide for the payment of social security benefits in cases where no loss of earnings occurs, and the Subcommittee believes that it would be undesirable to change the nature and function of the social security program by providing for the payment of benefits under it in such cases.

Another consideration with respect to paying social security taxes to obtain earnings credits for work in and around the home is that those most able to pay such tax are nonworking wives of high-earning men. All workers, part-time, full-time, single or married, could logically feel that this option should be open to them in accordance to the degree that they do work in and around the home. To impute earnings for certain homemaker services without imputing earnings for all types of such services—for example, gardening, housepainting, etc.—would raise serious questions of equity.

Document 4.4   U.S. Senate, Special Committee on Aging, *Women and Social Security*. . . , October 1975 [excerpt]

[**Author's Note.** The recommendations of the Task Force on Women and Social Security are in total far more costly than the recommendations made by other official and semiofficial groups. Although their report stresses, as in the fourth paragraph below, that for "genuine equity" one must look at "the total impact of each proposal," nowhere in it will be found estimated costs of the individual proposals or of their total costs and of what groups will pay these costs. The document's greatest value lies in the strong case it makes for aged widows.]

Increasingly, pages of the *Congressional Record* reflect concern about Social Security treatment of women.

Some legislative proposals call for major increases in benefits paid to working couples. Others grapple with the many problems faced by homemakers who never entered the labor force.

Everywhere, the impulse seems to be for liberalization. But liberalization for some may mean increased costs for others. For example, single working women might feel aggrieved if their payroll tax contributions were increased to pay for higher retirement benefits to former working wives.

Genuine equity requires, therefore, a close look at the total impact of each proposal, not only for those who would benefit, but for those who may subsidize the improvement.

This chapter discusses major proposals now receiving attention in Congress and among advocates of change on behalf of women. It concludes with the Task Force's own recommendations.

DOCUMENT 4.4: U.S. Congress, Senate, Special Committee on Aging, *Women and Social Security: Adapting to a New Era*, A Working Paper Prepared by the Task Force on Women and Social Security, 94th Cong., 1st sess., October 1975 (Washington, D.C.: U.S. Government Printing Office, 1975), pp. 19, 39-43. Members of this Task Force were: Verda Barnes, administrative assistant to Senator Church; Herman Brotman, former assistant to the U.S. commissioner on aging; Alvin David, former assistant social security commissioner; Juanita M. Kreps, Ph.D., professor of economics and vice-president of Duke University; Dorothy McCamman, former assistant director of research, Social Security Administration; and Lawrence Smedley, director, AFL-CIO Social Security Department. The reader should note that not all of the Task Force's legislative proposals have been excerpted: for example, disability benefits are not covered here or elsewhere in this book because of the complicated nature of the subject and the rapid expansion of payments from the disability trust fund, which has yet to be explained fully by the Social Security Administration.

The Task Force recommends the following immediate and long-range proposals to strengthen Social Security protection for women and their dependents.

Benefit rights for dependents of women workers should be equalized by:

Removing the dependency test for father's benefits (including a divorced surviving father) with a child in his care. . . .

Eliminating the dependency requirement for husband's or widower's benefits. . . .

Providing divorced husband's benefits. . . .

Again in the interest of equalizing protection, the Task Force recommends that:

An age-62 computation point be made applicable for men born before 1913. This provision would provide larger benefits, not only for retired male workers, but also for older married women or widows who receive secondary benefits. . . .

In addition, the Task Force urges the following changes be made:

[*Author's Note.* These are included to indicate the size of the total costs that *all* the recommendations would impose. Disability benefits are not discussed elsewhere in this book.]

The substantial recent current work test (generally 20 out of 40 quarters) to qualify for disability insurance should be eliminated. . . .

An occupational definition of disability for workers age 55 and above should be established. . . .

Disabled widows and disabled surviving divorced wives should be eligible for Social Security without regard to age, and their benefits should not be subject to an actuarial reduction. The same would also apply for disabled widowers and disabled surviving divorced husbands. . . .

Benefits should be provided to disabled spouses of beneficiaries.

The definition of dependents should be extended to include close relatives living in the home.

The duration of marriage requirement should be reduced from 20 to 15 years for a divorced wife (or husband) to qualify for benefits on the basis of the spouse's earnings record, and the consecutive years requirement should be removed. . . .

In order to relate benefits to more current earnings, additional drop-out years should be allowed. . . .

The computation of primary benefits and wife's or husband's benefits should be adjusted to increase primary benefits for workers by approximately one-eighth and to reduce the proportion for spouses from one-half to one-third, thus maintaining the present total benefit of 150 percent for a couple, and at the same time improving the protection for single workers, working couples, and widows.[15]

The Social Security Act should be amended to eliminate separate references to men and women. [pp. 39-40]

[*Author's Note.* In a chapter elaborating on the theme "Goals—Greater Equity for Older Women," this "working paper" elaborated as follows.]

The Task Force believes that the close scrutiny currently being given to the financing of the program should include questions of equity and the treatment of women. As pointed out earlier, an important element in the long-range financial condition of the system rests on the increasing labor-force participation of married women in the years ahead.

One change now receiving serious consideration in connection with the financial integrity of the program is for indexing earnings before retirement to changes in average earnings and indexing benefits after retirement to changes in prices, thus assuring stability and predictability of replacement ratios.[16] The Task Force endorses such a change but has not included it in its special study because the impact is not primarily on women. Indexed wages could, however, be of particular value to aged widows because their benefits are frequently based on the long outdated earnings records of their deceased husbands.

Aged Widows

As a group, aged widows have traditionally been the most economically deprived of the segments of the aged population. Older women living alone, the overwhelming proportion of whom are widows, had median incomes of $2,642 in 1973 when 33.4 percent of them lived below the poverty level.

Almost all of today's aged widows were married to men born before 1913. Hence the recommendation for using the same computation point for men regardless of date of birth would raise the benefits of their widows. (See discussion in parts 2 and 3.)

Because the widow's benefit is determined by the primary insurance amount (PIA) of the deceased husband, recommendations designed to raise

---

15. Mr. Smedley feels that this proposal, because of its substantial cost and importance, requires further study.

16. Under the existing automatic provisions, when a future benefit is computed, it is a combination of the increase in the benefit for a particular average wage level—an increase which alone fully reflects the higher cost of living—plus the increase in the average itself, which results in an updating of the level of protection for those still contributing to the program. This combination is, of course, considerably more than enough to keep up with prices; it could result in a scale of benefits that over the long run exceeds preretirement wages.

The "decoupling" proposal now under consideration would index earnings to guarantee that protection for current workers be kept up at least as high as future increases in the level of earnings and thereafter, as at present, benefits once payable would be kept up to date with increases in the cost of living.

the PIA will also raise the widow's benefits. Of major importance then, are the recommendations to increase primary benefits per se and to provide for additional drop-out years in computing the benefits. The latter can be especially important for the oldest widows because it would eliminate years of very low wages earned by their husbands long ago. [This assumes retroactive computation, which is not usually done.]

Even with these improvements—and with the changes made retroactively, not just prospectively—many aged widows will still have incomes below the poverty line because they have long since exhausted any supplementary income available at the time of retirement. While the Task Force's charge was to study the impact of the Social Security system on the retirement income of women, we would be remiss if we neglected to urge simultaneous improvements in Supplemental Security Income, and specifically a raise in the guaranteed floor to at least the level needed to prevent poverty.

Single Retired Women

Single women workers without dependents pay Social Security taxes that reflect the cost of benefits for the dependents of other workers. (It is scant consolation to point out that they also pay disproportionately in other taxes.) Under a social insurance system that blends individual equity with social adequacy and which provides family protection—and these are important principles of our Social Security program that must be maintained—benefits cannot be strictly proportionate to contributions.

The value of the contributions of the single worker can, however, be increased. This is what would be achieved by the recommendation to raise the primary benefit and lower the proportion paid as a wife's benefit. Such a change is aimed also at greater equity for the working wife (see below) and is considered to be preferable to proposals for combining the wage credits of a married couple or paying more than one type of benefit. Relevant here is the fact that single workers would not be required to pay the significantly higher contribution rates that would result from these other proposals without any gain to themselves.

The Working Wife

With the recommended changes to remove the dependency test for benefits for fathers, husbands, and widowers and to provide divorced husband's benefits, the working wife's contributions will have the same value as do her husband's in purchasing family protection. Because family responsibilities may have caused her to leave the labor force temporarily, her disability protection will be greatly strengthened through elimination of the current work test.

On retirement, the average monthly wage which determines her benefit can be significantly increased through the recommendation for dropping out additional years when she had little or no earnings. Finally, the proposal to increase primary benefits and reduce the wife's percentage will almost inevitably produce a primary benefit for her that is larger than the secondary benefit paid to a nonworking wife.

The Homemaker

The Task Force struggled long and hard with the problem of the wife who either does not work at all or who has insufficient coverage to achieve insured status. Regrettably, no acceptable solution was found. While not minimizing the economic value of the homemaker's services, we question the appropriateness of using Social Security—an earnings replacement system—to provide benefits where no earnings loss has occurred.

As the Senate Committee on Aging pursues its study of "Women and Social Security," this problem area will continue to receive careful attention. These are among the questions to be faced: If a monetary value is to be placed on homemaker services, how should the value be determined? Who pays the cost? What if the homemaker is also a wage-earner? What if husband and wife share homemaking tasks? And when does the homemaker retire?

Special attention will also be given to the problems of the "displaced homemaker"—the woman with little or no work experience who is divorced or widowed without eligibility for Social Security benefits. Such a homemaker needs a source of support while undergoing job training and placement. To what extent is this a responsibility of Social Security? Of manpower? Or of other special programs?

The homemaker who is not the spouse of the wage earner—but who is nevertheless dependent on these earnings—is in a different category. There is no need here to "impute" wage credits for the value of the homemaking services. An extension of the definition of dependents to include close relatives living in the home would provide secondary benefits for these homemakers, for example, the adult daughter caring for an aged relative or an aunt who substitutes for the deceased mother.

Document 4.5   Report of the Consultant Panel on Social Security, August 1976 [excerpt]

[*Author's Note.* The "Consultant Panel" is unique in that it represents contract research done for the Congressional Research Service in response

DOCUMENT 4.5: U.S. Congress, Joint Committee (House Committee on Ways and Means, Senate Committee on Finance), *Report of the Consultant Panel on Social Security to the Congressional Research Service*, 94th Cong., 2d sess., August 1976 (Washington, D.C.: U.S. Government Printing Office, 1976), pp. 33-37.

to a request from Senator Russell B. Long, Chairman of the Senate Finance Committee, "to engage a group of outside consultants to examine the various ways in which the benefit structure could be revised to correct the problem of any overreaction to changes in price levels. . . ." (Consultant Panel, *Report,* p. 1). The Congressional Research Service hired William C.L. Hsiao, Ph.D., professor of economics, Massachusetts Institute of Technology, and he hired the other members of the panel, all of whom were either economists or actuaries.[17]]

The retired spouse of a retired worker now is granted a benefit equal to the larger of the benefit based on the spouse's own earnings record or one-half the benefit based on the worker's record (subject to reduction below age 65 and to the family maximum). Whatever the virtues of this treatment in the past, the pronounced trend toward two-worker families and the increased frequency of divorce warrant serious reconsideration of family benefits.[18] Current law does not produce a satisfactory pattern of replacement ratios for two-person families relative to one-person families and, as we have illustrated in Chapter 2, unfairly gives different benefits to two-worker families that have identical total earnings but divided differently between husband and wife.

In this section our proposal will be stated for the simplest case—that of a retired couple at age 65. Complications arising from age and retirement date differences, early retirements, and divorces will be treated in Section 6.

This Panel believes that in general the family, not the two separate individuals, should be the criterion for equity in social security. The current law seriously violates this equity principle as is indicated in the following table showing benefits arising from the same earnings shared differently. The benefit formula recommended in Chapter 3 does not in itself remedy this inequity.

This calculation ignores the temporary existing difference in averaging periods for men's and women's benefit calculations.

As the table [p. 114] indicates, the one-worker family gets the largest benefit, while benefits for two-worker families depend somewhat upon the share of income earned by each spouse. Such differences seem inequitable since these families have had approximately the same earnings histories. There follow the Panel's recommendations for remedying this.

17. Members of the Consultant Panel were: Professor William C.L. Hsiao, Ph.D., F.S.A.; Peter A. Diamond, Ph.D.; James C. Hickman, Ph.D., F.S.A.; and Actuary Ernest J. Moorhead, F.S.A.

18. In 1940, 14 percent of married women with husbands present were in the labor force; by 1950, this became 22 percent; by 1960, 31 percent; by 1970, 40 percent. In March, 1974, in 51 percent of the 36.4 million husband-wife families in which the husband was between ages 25 and 65, both worked in the paid labor force. [Sources: D. Cymrot & L. Mallan, "Wife's Earnings as a Source of Family Income," U.S. Department of Health, Education and Welfare, Social Security Administration, Office of Research and Statistics, Note N 10, April 30, 1974, p. 14, and *Current Population Reports,* Series P-60, N 97, January 1975, p. 155.]

FAMILY BENEFITS FOR A TWO-PERSON FAMILY
(With different shares of income earned by husband and wife.
Retirement in 1976. Both spouses aged 65)

	DIVISION OF EARNINGS (PERCENT)	MONTHLY BENEFIT UNDER CURRENT LAW
Low Earner (AME = $183)	50-50	$239.40
	75-25	257.90
	100- 0	264.80
Middle Earner (AME = $439)	50-50	388.00
	75-25	388.20
	100- 0	445.10
High Earner (AME = $585)	50-50	458.40
	75-25	455.60
	100- 0	546.00

PROPOSAL NO. 1 A: That upon retirement of both husband and wife, even if only one of them has insured status, they may choose between (1) averaging their two AIME's [average indexed monthly earnings] and receiving a family benefit equal to double the benefit based on the average AIME, or (2) a benefit to each spouse based on his or her own earnings record. The benefit under (1) would be divided between the spouses in proportion to the PIA's of their respective earnings records, subject to a minimum of one-third and a maximum of two-thirds. Throughout life a person would be permitted to average AIME's with only one other person. The present spouse benefit would be eliminated, and the child's and mother's or father's benefit would be revised.[19]

PROPOSAL NO. 1B: That in the event of adoption of Proposal No. 1A consideration be given to suitable revision of the factors in the basic benefit formula recommended by this Panel in Chapter 3 so that the annual disbursement will be approximately the same as would result from combining the present recommendation of Chapter 3 with the spouse benefit under present law.

ANALYSIS OF PROPOSALS NO. 1A AND NO. 1B: The Panel regards this change as desirable on either of two counts: as a solution to the problem of differing treatment of families of different sizes, or as a temporary expedient during the necessarily slow building of individual wage records for all potential beneficiaries proposed in Chapter 7. There are basically two approaches that will accomplish the objective of making family benefits

---

19. The reason why we have chosen to average the AIME's rather than the earnings records themselves is that the former seems fairer in dealing with spouses of different ages and different periods in covered employment. Admittedly, it is less satisfactory to have dropout years reflect individual rather than family earnings histories but we consider this less important than the other point.

identical whatever the division of earnings between spouses. One is our proposal—averaging earnings records *after* both spouses have retired, a method that closely parallels income tax provisions for income splitting between husband and wife. The alternative—averaging earnings records each year and granting benefits based on these two separate records—fails, for reasons stated in Chapter 7, to give suitable benefits when the spouses retire at different times. Even if it were satisfactory for the future, it involves serious transition problems not found in our proposal. It works poorly or may even be impractical for recognizing past earnings in the many divorce and remarriage situations that exist.

The following natural questions about the characteristics and implications of our Proposal No. 1 arise and are answered as stated.

Question 1. How do benefits to a couple depend upon the proportions in which their combined AIME is divided between them?

Answer. Our proposal makes the benefits completely independent of the share earned by each in the total of their AIME's.

Question 2. How do benefits to a couple with a specified total AIME compare with the benefits the couple would have received if the present spouse benefit had been retained in conjunction with our price-indexing recommendation?

Answer. This depends upon whether only Proposal No. 1A is adopted, or whether Proposal No. 1B is adopted also.

If only No. 1A is adopted, it can easily be shown that the spouse benefit in a one-worker family will never be as high as the 50 percent under present law. It is also true that the circumstances under which no spouse benefit at all will accrue are different under our proposal and present law.

In the situation in which the entire AIME is earned by one spouse, the effective spouse benefit is at its maximum, 39.1 percent, when the AIME is (currently) $400. Below $400 it declines until it is zero at AIME's of $200 or less. Above $1,200 it also declines steadily. Between $400 and $1,200 there is first a sharp decline, but then, between $600 and $1,200 a rising tendency. This pattern can easily be converted to a steady decline by moderately changing the percentage factors in the benefit formula recommended in Chapter 3. For example, if these factors were 90 percent, 36 percent, and 27 percent instead of 80 percent, 35 percent, and 25 percent, the curve beyond $400 would contain no increases. The pattern discussed here is shown in [figure 4.1].

In appraising the rationality of the pattern shown by this chart, certain matters should be recognized. First, when the AIME is low, the replacement ratio is already high without any spouse benefit. Second, when a couple is poor (e.g., has only social security benefits), the couple is eligible for SSI payments, presently $236.60 a month. A worker who has always earned the legal minimum wage through a full career in covered employment must now have an AIME of $353, which the chart shows corresponds to close to the maximum percentage spouse benefit under our proposal. Cases in which the

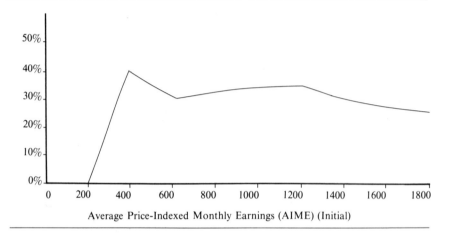

FIGURE 4.1
**PERCENTAGE EXCESS OF FAMILY BENEFIT OVER WORKER-ONLY BENEFIT
WHEN AIME's ARE IDENTICAL**
Panel's Recommended Benefit Formula and Proposed Spouse Benefit

Average Price-Indexed Monthly Earnings (AIME) (Initial)

AIME is substantially less than this and in which the SSI benefit is not payable must be cases of short periods of covered employment.

Furthermore, many two-worker families who would receive no additional benefit under present law will receive a spouse benefit under our proposal. If the spouse with the lower AIME has a PIA equal to one-half or more of the higher earner's PIA, a spouse benefit will usually emerge under our proposal as illustrated in the following table, but present law provides no spouse benefit.

All of these figures and relationships would be altered if our Proposal No. 1B for modifying the factors in the basic benefit formula so as to disburse the amounts that otherwise might be saved due to the generally lower spouse benefit were adopted. Since we have no cost estimate for this proposal, we cannot make a specific statement of the factor changes that would bring the whole benefit structure to a break-even point.

Question 3. How do benefits for a couple compare with benefits for a single worker?

Answer. The figure above shows the amount received by a couple in excess of the amount going to a single worker with the same AIME. A couple with a given AIME has had less income per person than a single worker with the same AIME. Thus it seems appropriate that the couple receive a larger benefit for the same AIME. If the costs of living were twice as high for a couple as for a single person, it would seem right to treat a couple as if they were two

FAMILY BENEFIT FOR TWO-WORKER FAMILY WHEN PIA OF LOWER EARNER IS ONE-HALF PIA OF HIGHER EARNER			
AIME		FAMILY BENEFIT	
Higher earner	*Lower earner*	*Current spouse benefits*	*Panel proposal*
$ 200	$100	$240	$240
300	122	293	328
400	144	345	370
600	188	450	456
800	243	525	545
1,000	314	600	629

persons, each with one-half of the couple's income as is done by our proposal. Since two can live for less than twice what it costs for one, our proposal is still generous to couples.

To complete our suggestions for spouse benefits, it is necessary to offer supplementary proposals for survivor benefits when one of the spouses dies.

PROPOSAL NO. 1C: That upon death of a spouse after a family benefit determined by averaging of AIME's has been awarded, the surviving spouse will receive 4/3rds of the PIA based on the averaged AIME (i.e., 2/3rds of the family benefit).

PROPOSAL NO. 1D: That upon death of a worker aged 62 or older before averaging of AIME's has been taken, the surviving spouse may choose between (a) a benefit determined by averaging the survivor's and the deceased spouse's AIME's, or (b) a benefit based on his or her own earnings record.

The basic justification for giving the survivor two-thirds of the family benefit is recognition that expenses of one are usually greater than one-half those of two. The two-thirds rule may seem too generous if the spouse is considerably younger than the deceased and will not begin receiving benefits (at age 62) until long after the death of the worker. Perhaps it would be best to scale this proposition gradually downward so that it would be as low as one-half for much younger spouses.

Under these proposals no widow or widower benefit would be available on the record of the deceased worker, except that an adjustment must be made for widows or widowers under age 62. Under current law a widow or widower receives no additional benefit from her or his own covered earnings if the AIME of the deceased worker is larger than that of the survivor. Our proposal is more generous to all surviving lower earners. On the other hand, death of the lower earner will leave some survivors with lower incomes as a consequence of having averaged their lifetime income for benefit calculation.

[*Author's Note.* The author prefers the second of the 1976 panel's two main proposals, that is, the one by which each person would as an individual receive a primary benefit based on his or her own earnings. During the 1974 and 1975 meetings of the Advisory Council, the author consistently argued that an individual who pays OASDHI taxes as an individual should receive retirement and other benefits as an individual. Moreover, this approach would eliminate the administrative difficulties inherent in the "family benefit" approach because of divorce. Today, divorces are numerous; several marriages per individual are occurring more often, and various new life styles are being openly adopted as the society becomes more permissive. The author's dissent from the Advisory Council's report states in part: "I argue for retirement benefits being paid on an individual basis, as well as OASDI taxes being collected on an individual basis" (p. 74 of printed *Reports,* March 10, 1975).

The Consultant Panel, however, favored variations of its first proposal because it believed that "in general the family not the two separate individuals, should be the criterion for equity in social security" (p. 33).

Because of this definition of equity, the panel's proposal is needlessly complicated, dealing as it does with different ages of spouses, divorces after varying years of marriage, etc. After discussing these various difficulties, the panel stated that "in the long run, the natural solution is development of individual records for all adults in our society, whether workers or not" (p. 39). It seems logical to take the first step towards this by using the individual work records now available rather than go through the subterfuge of creating the panel's "artificial record" (p. 40) to handle complications attendant on divorce and remarriage.

The Consultant Panel's recommendations about other dependency benefits are too detailed to discuss in this book. [20] The author merely notes that it recommends that

the benefit to the mother of a dependent child of a retired worker shall be available only if the child is less than 6 years old or is under a disability that began before age 18. The same benefit should be available to the father of a dependent child.

The needs that survivor and disability benefits are designed to fill are basically different from those for retirement benefits. The ages differ, frequency of presence of children differs, and needs for care differ. Hence it is not appropriate to have identical benefit structures and formulas for these quite different situations. Likewise, the different lengths of earnings records suggest a need for different benefit

---

20. These details can be found in Joint Committee, *Report of the Consultant Panel. . .*1976, chapter 5 and appendix B.

patterns and different numbers of dropout years. This Panel has concentrated on benefits for retirements, and therefore recommends a separate exploration of redesign of survivor and disability benefit programs by a selected group of authorities.[21]

Obviously the Consultant Panel has recognized the increase in number of working women, and assumes that those who have nonhandicapped children in school should enter the work force.

Document 4.6   Report of U.S. Citizens' Advisory Council on the Status of Women, March 1976 [excerpt]

[*Author's Note.* I was in the unique position of being simultaneously a member of the national Citizens' Advisory Council on the Status of Women (CACSW) and of the Advisory Council on Social Security. As such I presented to the CACSW at their September 1975 meeting the recommendations of the Advisory Council on Social Security, and also those of its Subcommittee on Treatment of Men and Women, with my own proposals. The CACSW voted as indicated in the following excerpt from their 1975 report.]

Social Security

The Citizens' Advisory Council on the Status of Women studied the *Reports of the Advisory Council on Social Security, 1975* and heard testimony on the inequities women and men face in Social Security provisions. A review of the Social Security program and a summary of recommendations concerning women made by government groups is found in Appendix J, Part VI of Women and Employee Benefit Plans. The following four recommendations were adopted by the Citizens' Advisory Council on the Status of Women at the September 1975 meeting.

The Citizens' Advisory Council on the Status of Women recommends to the Secretary of Health, Education, and Welfare the adoption of the following which is included in the *Reports of the Advisory Council on Social Security, 1975* under the "Summary of Findings and Recommendations." (Page XVI)

The requirements for entitlement to dependents' and survivors' benefits that apply to women should apply equally to men; that is, benefits

---

21. Ibid., p. 38.

DOCUMENT 4.6: Citizens' Advisory Council on the Status of Women, *Women in 1975,* Report, March 1976 (Washington, D.C.: the Council, 1976), part VI, pp. 13-14.

should be provided for fathers and divorced men as they are for mothers and divorced women and benefits for husbands and widowers should be provided without a support test as are benefits for wives and widows.[22]

The Citizens' Advisory Council on the Status of Women recommends to the Secretary of Health, Education, and Welfare that the Social Security Law should provide as recommended by the Subcommittee on the Treatment of Men and Women to the Advisory Council on Social Security, 1975, that a combined earnings approach be adopted to assure that low-income

> two-earner couples with significant attachment to the labor force would always get at least as much in benefits as single earner couples with comparable covered earnings. *(Ibid,* Page 30).

The Citizens' Advisory Council on the Status of Women recommends to the Secretary, Department of Health, Education, and Welfare the adoption of Advisory Council on Social Security's recommendation that

> Words that do not denote gender should be used in the Social Security provisions of the law whenever it is practical to do so. (*Ibid,* italics, Page 32)

The Citizens' Advisory Council on the Status of Women recommends to the Secretary, Health, Education, and Welfare that, as many amendments have made the Social Security program so complex that even well-informed citizens do not have available clear and concise information regarding their status, or benefits rightfully theirs, or how to obtain such information, that through Social Security sources readily available now, a concerted effort be made to inform the general public and especially working women, widows and still married women what their status will be under the existing Social Security Act upon retirement and not wait to give such information upon request when they apply for their retirement benefits.

The June, 1975 pamphlet of the Department of Health, Education, and Welfare, *A Woman's Guide to Social Security* (SSA 75-10127) has responded in large part to this recommendation. This Council commends this SSA effort

---

22. Dr. Rita Ricardo Campbell, a member of the Advisory Council on Social Security, 1974-75, and also of this Council, endorses this but with the *caveat* that she simultaneously endorses, because of the financial implications of the above, the sentence following the above which reads as follows: "At the same time, the law should be changed, effective prospectively, so that pensions based on a person's work in employment not covered by social security will be subtracted from his social security dependents' benefits." (p. xvi) Persons interested in reading more details about Social Security and Women should read Chapter 5 of the *Reports of the Quadrennial Advisory Council on Social Security*. . .March 10, 1975 (House Doc. No. 94-75), its Appendix B (both sections are on "treatment of men and women under Social Security"), and the dissenting statement of Dr. Campbell, pp. 73-80. This Report is available in all libraries which serve as a "government depository" and also can be obtained from Congressional Representatives or the G.P.O., Washington, D.C. 20402.

and recommends that the availability of this pamphlet be widely publicized.

For the Council's memorandum on Social Security, including the rationale for the recommendations, which is directed to citizen groups, please see [its] Appendix K.

Need for Legislation

The Task Force of the Senate Special Committee on Aging agreed with the Advisory Council's recommendation that dependents of women should be treated in the same way as dependents of men. The Supreme Court had ruled in the Wiesenfeld case that a surviving parent's benefit, based on a deceased spouse's tax credits, should be available to fathers as well as to mothers. It had also ruled similarly in respect to widower's and widow's secondary benefits and men's and women's retirement benefits. It may be construed that no social security dependency benefits will differ because of the sex of the workers, but no ruling has been issued on benefits for divorced persons.

In its *Working Paper*, the Task Force also agreed with the council's report that eliminating the one-half dependency proof for men was preferable to requiring the same proof of dependency for women as is now required for men.

The Task Force, however, did not recommend the offset of a worker's private pension against any dependency benefit to which the worker might be entitled because his or her spouse was paying OASDI taxes. In this it joined the Citizens' Advisory Council on the Status of Women in its 1975 report. Without this offset, the costs could be very high and might require a substantial increase in tax revenues. No estimate of the amounts that would be needed to implement this or any other recommendation is given in the *Working Paper*. The Supreme Court, in the above actions, has resolved the issue, at least until Congress acts, by choosing the more expensive way to equalize the dependency benefits of men and women workers. There is no provision for a private pension offset against a social security secondary benefit, as was proposed by the Advisory Council.

Additionally, the Task Force found "no acceptable solution" to the problem of providing a primary social security benefit to the home-maker, because "no earnings loss has occurred" (p. 43). Subsequently, some women have proposed that friends hire each other to do each other's housework. This would appear to have little economic appeal, except to women who do not have the ten years of coverage and are ten or twelve years away from 62 or 65 years of age. On other grounds, both practical and emotional, one would also suspect little support for this approach, originally suggested by Dr. Jessie Hartline, a Rutgers University economist.

The Task Force's *Working Paper* differs from the Advisory Council on benefits for working spouses partly because it underestimates the percentage of women who work and pay social security taxes over time. Indeed, it states that "nearly 60 percent of married women are not in the labor force" (p. 20), presumably at one point in time. It is correct, however, in emphasizing that "the likelihood of being poor is considerably greater for elderly females than for aged males. More than two out of every three poor persons in the 65-plus age category are women" (p. 37). Consistent with its interest in the economic status of older women, the Task Force's report continues:

> Women workers have not been shortchanged under the Social Security system. Taking the total of all benefits (including retirement benefits) paid on the earnings of women, the amounts are slightly greater than those paid on the earnings of men. This is true—even though male-worker accounts generate more secondary benefits—essentially for three reasons:
> 1. Women have a longer life expectancy than men;
> 2. Fewer women work beyond age 65; and
> 3. Women receive a greater advantage from the weighted benefit formula, since a much larger proportion work in low-paying employment.[23]

Another reason, of course, is that there are over 5 million more women than men receiving benefits. On a per capita basis, these findings would probably not hold true. Moreover, in 1974 the average monthly benefit awards to male workers was $215.40, but only $157.90 to females.

The following considerations, discussed in appendix 5 of the report, do not feature in its main text. The computations are based on table 4.1.

> The growth in the proportion of dually entitled women indicates that although more women have been earning enough quarters of coverage to become entitled to benefits on their own earnings records, these

---

23. Senate Special Committee on Aging, *Women and Social Security.* . .1975, p. 38.

TABLE 4.1
SOCIAL SECURITY BENEFITS—JUNE 1975

	MEN		WOMEN	
BENEFICIARY	NUMBER	AVERAGE MONTHLY BENEFIT	NUMBER	AVERAGE MONTHLY BENEFIT
Retired worker	8,981,000	$225	7,230,000	$180
Disabled worker	1,628,000	242	736,000	185
Wives of retired or disabled workers			3,257,000	100
Husbands of retired or disabled workers	8,000	96	....	
Widows			4,287,000	187
Husbands	3,000	177	....	
Parents	1,000	151	21,000	172
Disabled widows			101,000	138
Disabled widowers	200	128	....	
Special age 72	33,000	69	208,000	69
TOTAL	10,654,200	....	15,840,000	....

SOURCE: *Women and Social Security,* p. 38.

benefits are lower for many women than the benefits they would get as their husbands' dependents or survivors. Tabulations showing distributions of social security benefits by primary insurance amounts (PIA's) clearly indicate that benefit levels are lower for women retired workers—particularly those with dual entitlement—than for men retired workers.[24] At the end of 1973, for example, PIA's of less than $100 were shown for 31 percent of the women retired workers but for only 10 percent of the men retired workers. . . . However, the growth of the number of dually entitled women cannot be attributed solely to lower earnings. The increase in the benefit level for widows from 82.5 percent of the deceased husband's PIA to a possible 100 percent under certain circumstances, as authorized by the 1972 amendments to the Social Security Act, increased the likelihood of widows becoming dually entitled.[25]

24. The PIA is the amount payable to a worker on entitlement to retirement benefits at age 65 and is based on average earnings from employment covered under social security.

25. Senate Special Committee on Aging, *Women and Social Security.* . .1975, pp. 82-83.

To this it can be added that if all fathers as well as mothers are to receive the surviving parents' benefits on their working wives' earnings, and similarly for other secondary benefits, the ratio of total benefits on earnings of women to total benefits paid on earnings of men would be reversed. The Supreme Court acted in 1977 to do just this.

The Task Force's report, as I have already pointed out, gives no consideration to the cost of its various proposals, and most of these would be added to existing costs and so require increased taxes. The program is already in short- and long-run imbalance. Commissioner James Cardwell, in Senate testimony, estimated that the first-year costs of the *Working Paper's* main proposal—to increase all primary benefits by 12 1/3 percent (approximately one-eighth) and to reduce the proportion of the spouse's benefit from one-half to one-third— would be $9 billion in the first year alone. Although this would narrow somewhat the gap between couples of whom husband and wife both work and of whom only one spouse works, it would be a costly method. In any case, it does not speak directly to the working wife's major complaint, that she pays taxes and receives no more in benefits, and sometimes less, than if she had not worked and paid taxes.

In this regard Senator Percy suggested in congressional committee testimony that future increases in a wife's benefits be made only if she were truly dependent. This to my knowledge is the first time that a United States senator has seriously acknowledged the extraordinary increase in numbers of women working. The December 1976 projections of numbers of women in the labor force by 1980 are two and one-half million higher than the 1973 projections of the Bureau of Labor Statistics.[26]

---

26. H. N. Fullerton, Jr. and Paul Flaim, "New Labor Force Projections to 1990", *Monthly Labor Review,* December 1976.

5

FINANCING

DUNAGIN'S PEOPLE

DUNAGIN'S PEOPLE by Ralph Dunagin.
Reproduced through the courtesy of
Field Newspaper Syndicate.

"AT THIS RATE THE SOCIAL SECURITY SYSTEM
WILL RUN OUT OF MONEY IN 1979...AND THE
TAXPAYER WILL RUN OUT IN 1978."

FINANCING

The trust fund for the retirement and survivors' (OASI) portion of social security was not conceived as an ever-growing amount large enough to fund the program's total liabilities or even a large portion of its accrued liabilities. From time to time a fully funded approach, as in the private insurance industry, has been discussed. But it has never been adopted. The reasoning is that the federal government's power of taxation assures the future availability of funds to pay the statutory benefits.

The social security program, however, was advertised to the public as a modified form of insurance; tax payments were always referred to as "contributions" or "premiums," and benefits were described in terms of an "earned right." The Social Security Administration, during the early years of the program, implied that as more individuals were covered and the system matured, the trust fund would become larger in relation to annual payouts. It was expected to become much larger than its current level of about $40 billion, which is an amount equal to only five to eight months of total OASI benefits paid out.

Should the Program Be Fully Funded?

The 1971 Advisory Council recommended that all three major trust funds (OASI, Disability, and Part A of Medicare) should be "maintained at a level approximately equal to one year's expenditures." The 1965 Advisory Council's Report indicates that the OASI trust fund was at the end of 1955 equal to four times the annual total of benefits paid out; in 1960, about double the annual total; and in 1963, about one and one-third times. By 1967, according to the report's projections, the fund was expected to be only about equal to the annual total of benefits to be paid.[1]

The 1975 Advisory Council discussed at length whether to recommend that the OASI trust fund should be maintained at a level equal to eighteen months of benefits paid out. Among the consultants, Martin Feldstein of Harvard University has advocated in the economic literature and elsewhere that the current pay-as-you-go concept should be abandoned, and a large trust fund accumulated and invested by the federal government.[2] However, Professor Feldstein believes that to make a direct comparison of social security with private pension programs in regard to their financial solvency is "totally misleading." He advocates that the annual taxes collected should substantially exceed the annual benefits paid out, not because it is financially unwise in an actuarial sense if the taxes fail to do so, but because private savings in general are declining. The "forced savings" under the social security system have reduced personal savings, so that private capital formation is declining in the United States. This, Feldstein states, is resulting in a redistribution of income from wage earners to owners of capital. The interest rates obtainable on money from a pay-as-you-go fund are low as compared to interest rates on money that can be used for investment in such capital goods as industrial plants and machinery. Feldstein's argument is analyzed in chapter 8, below, by my colleague Gerald Musgrave.

Feldstein's approach supports the contention that a large reserve fund is not needed, even for reasons of actuarial soundness. The U.S. government, it is claimed, may increase taxes to make up any deficit and pay the promised benefits. This assumes, of course, that future generations will be willing to pay increasing taxes as the ratio of retired aged persons to working persons increases. I object to full funding. Not only is it impractical—even the Social Security Administration estimates that the actuarial imbalance is in the order of $2.4 trillion—but it would generate "excess" monies that Congress, I believe, would then legislate away, as it has always done, in the form of increased kinds and amounts of benefits. To avoid this, I favor a fund equal to about only four years of benefit payments. Currently, this would be about $300

---

1. Quadrennial Advisory Council on Social Security, 1965, *The Status of the Social Security Program and Recommendations for its Improvement* (Washington, D.C.: U.S. Government Printing Office, 1965), p.109.

2. Martin Feldstein, "Toward a Reform of Social Security," *Public Interest,* Summer 1975, pp. 75-95.

billion, or nearly one-third of a trillion dollars. The money could be invested in government securities and could be considered primarily as a safety valve in case of higher unemployment, when the taxable payroll base and thus the tax revenues would fall. Additionally, the level of taxation needed to fund the program fully is so high that it alone would have a very depressing effect on the economy.

Because the social security tax, when considered apart from the benefits, is regressive, and because many young people do not wish to forego today's consumption of goods and services for promised returns in their old age, increases in payroll taxes are politically unpopular. Young, unmarried persons, as well as married women, are expected to increase their opposition to future increases in OASDI tax rates. A trust fund with four years of benefit payments would also provide some leeway whenever Supreme Court decisions require increases in equity. In the month of October 1976, about $5 billion was paid out to OASDI beneficiaries, while the two trust funds had about $42 billion in assets. The 1976 annual report by the trustees of the combined OASDI trust funds noted that, under their intermediate or middle set of assumptions, by 1981, under current law, these two funds would have only $9 billion.[3]

Inflation counted twice

The 1972 amendments, as we have seen, permit double counting of an inflation, and since 1965 the annual rate of inflation has been considerably higher than it was before. The inflation is reflected both in computation of the primary benefit, which is based on inflated earnings, and additionally in the level of benefits over time for those already retired, because that level has already risen with the cost-of-living index. This double count creates sizable short-run deficits. It will result, if uncorrected, in OASI benefits, which are not taxed upon receipt, eventually becoming higher for some retired workers and their dependents than their previous earnings were after taxes. In the terminology used by the Social Security Administration, the replacement ratio of benefits to recent and especially to recent net earnings will exceed 100 percent. Moreover, future replacement ratios, partly because of uneven weighting and the variability of price and wage rate

---

3. U.S. Trustees of the Federal Old-Age Survivors Insurance and Disability Insurance Trust Funds, *1976 Annual Report,* mimeographed (Washington, D.C.: U.S. Government Printing Office, 1976), p. 74.

increases, are far from being logical or predictable.

Double-digit inflation has created a situation in which the double counting of inflation will soon result in social security benefits being greater than recent earnings after social security and income taxes. This will occur first among low- and even some middle-income earners, whose benefits are more heavily weighted. For example, if wages rise at 7 percent annually and consumer prices at 6 percent (which are lower rates than in 1974 and 1975), the income replacement ratios automatically determined by the present formula become:

YEAR OF RETIREMENT	RATIO OF PRIMARY BENEFIT TO EARNINGS LEVEL IN YEAR BEFORE RETIREMENT		
	Earnings Level		
	Maximum	Median	Low
1975	.301	.436	.624
2000	.484	.675	1.031
2025	.676	.997	1.782
2050	.824	1.254	2.399

SOURCE: Geoffrey N. Calvert, "Statement," mimeographed (Society of Actuaries, Social Security, United States, Bal Harbour, Florida, October 22, 1975), p. 2.

Meantime the tax rates required to support these fantastic and obviously impossible benefits would have to rise progressively to 43 percent of the covered payroll by the end of the period shown. Because social security benefits are exempt from taxation—as were the employers' payroll taxes that partially provide them—post-retirement disposable income will exceed pre-retirement by an even greater margin. It would thus be possible to have a higher standard of living after retirement than while still working, even if one's income replacement ratio were less than one.

Under other assumptions—for instance, if wage rates were to increase by 5 percent and prices by 2 percent, which would be deflation—replacement ratios of OASDI benefits to earnings would fall. Clearly, this is an irrational, unpredictable system of benefits that depends on relative changes in wages and prices. It needs to be corrected so that predictable, stable replacement ratios occur.

It is estimated that the average long-run cost of the current OASDI system is almost 19 percent of taxable payroll while the average tax revenues are only about 11 percent. The resulting deficit, then, is about

8 percent. The amount of interest earned on assets decreases as the trust funds decrease. In practice, these are contingency funds, and revenues from interest are minimal. The Ford administration's decoupling proposals (H.R. 14480), which were developed by the Advisory Council and are also supported by President Carter, would reduce the long-run 8 percent deficit by about 4 percent or by one-half. The topic is discussed further in document 5.1 by William E. Simon, former secretary of the treasury.

Difficulties of predicting

The working population has been growing rapidly as the so-called postwar babies have entered the work force, and this effect will continue for some years. The result is a relatively large number of people who are paying the benefits of a relatively small number of people. For this reason, the costs per worker will not rise substantially in the immediate future even with automatic increases in benefits. However, after all the postwar babies have entered the work force, costs per worker will rise more. The rate of increase will climb after the relatively small number of depression babies, who will have been drawing benefits, are gradually replaced by the larger number of retirees from the baby boom years. The effect will be aggravated by the impact of a declining birth rate on the labor force.

The 1976 trustees' annual report on the OASDI trust funds wisely recognizes the impossibility of accurately predicting such components of economic growth as prices, wage rates, and employment several years hence. The report therefore offers three alternative sets of assumptions: low, high, and intermediate. The "intermediate" assumptions in the 1976 report correspond to the "central" assumptions in the 1975 report, as follows:

INTERMEDIATE/CENTRAL ASSUMED ANNUAL GROWTH RATES, 1982-2050 [4]		
	1976 Report ("Intermediate")	*1975 Report* ("Central")
Wages	5.75%	6 %
CPI	4 %	4 %
Real Wages	1.75%	2 %
Fertility Rate (ultimate)	1.9 %	2.1%

4. OASDI Trustees, *1976 Annual Report,* p. 149.

The assumptions made by the trustees in their 1975 report yield much lower long-run costs than the newer 1976 assumptions, which result in an average annual deficit, over the period 1976-2050, of 7.96 percent of taxable payroll.[5] In the short run, under the 1976 assumptions and without any corrective action, the assets of the old-age and survivors' insurance trust would be exhausted in 1984, and the disability insurance trust fund would be exhausted in 1979.

Document 5.1   William E. Simon on Social Security

As chief financial officer of the U.S. government, I am required to assess the soundness of the Social Security system. My assessment covers both the system's current financial position, and its ongoing viability. I have been shocked by what I have learned. Even though I am sure there is no immediate danger, the future prospects of the system as we know it are grim.

The worst of the problem lies some four years from now, but the squeeze is going to be severe enough that all of us will feel its approach much sooner. In fact, the tip of the iceberg is already with us. Social Security today is paying out each year $4.5 billion more than it is taking in. Obviously, this is not healthy for a program that is supposed to pay for itself.

What has gone wrong? And why is the problem expected to get so much worse in the future?

Since 1935, when the Social Security Act became law, the government has tinkered with the program. Bit by bit the soundness of its financing has been undermined. It was originally understood, at least in the way the program was presented to the public, that the premiums contributed (Social Security tax payments) would be accumulated in a reserve account, just like the pension fund of a business firm or labor union. This fund was supposed to grow steadily, earning interest, until it reached an amount large enough to meet its commitments. The contributors themselves would own the assets in the fund, for which the government would serve merely as trustee. The members' economic security in old age would be fully protected by this ownership. They would never have to depend on anyone else's charity for their livelihood.

A LIFELINE NEEDED

Today, Social Security actually operates in a very different fashion. The reserve account (later relabeled the Trust Fund) has not been allowed to grow

5. Ibid.

DOCUMENT 5.1: William E. Simon, "How to Rescue Social Security," *Wall Street Journal,* Wednesday, November 3, 1976, p. 16. Reprinted with permission of *The Wall Street Journal,* © Dow Jones & Company, Inc., 1976. All Rights Reserved.

to more than a fraction of the required size. Instead, the government has used much of the money contributed by wage earners to pay increased benefits to people whose contributions were not enough to warrant those benefits. The government has also failed to raise taxes commensurately with benefit increases. As a result, the Trust Fund is so meager that it is barely enough to keep the program going for six months. Current taxes and the fund combined are only sufficient to keep the program above water for another six years.

There is really nothing we can do about the insufficiency of the Trust Fund. It is far too late to rebuild it to the required size. For that an astonishing amount of money would be needed—by official estimates, more than two full years of our entire GNP! That is not practical, and it would not be desirable even if it were practical. Our past mistakes are behind us, and all we can do is to avoid repeating them in the future.

In any event, today's contributors have not been building a fund at all. The taxes they are paying into Social Security are being merely handed over as benefits to other people. In turn, when the current workers retire, they will be completely dependent upon future workers for their benefits. Their position is even more vulnerable should anything go wrong with this delicate balance. Each generation has the power through the elective process to refuse to pay. If the next generation were to refuse to pay, the retired population would be helpless.

Thanks to the "baby boom" of the 1950s, and the low birth rates of the 1960s and early '70s, there is going to be an unprecedented increase in the ratio of retired persons to workers. By the year 2020, you can expect the number of Social Security claimants to double, while the labor force will increase by only about one third. Since most of these beneficiaries have already been born, an imbalance of great magnitude is practically guaranteed. If the beneficiaries are to be paid the amounts to which they are legally entitled, Social Security tax rates are projected to have to increase by between 50% and 200%.

Future taxpayers are not likely to accept such tax increases passively, especially since the plight of their elders will not be of their making. Furthermore, future taxpayers cannot expect extra benefits in return if they do pay higher taxes. I don't think there is any practical way to force future workers to pay substantially higher taxes under these conditions. Actually, no Congress can bind its successors in the future to impose an obviously undeserved penalty on the majority of the electorate.

To put the point bluntly, I can see no way in which the government's current promises can be kept. For the problem is even worse than official projections suggest. High taxes are bad for the economy. By taking a big slice of the reward from human economic effort, they reduce the incentive to undertake the effort. As tax rates rise, the base upon which they depend therefore contracts. To counteract this shrinkage of the tax base, tax rates are forced higher still, causing the tax base to contract even further. Eventually we can visualize a situation where tax rates get so high that it is impossible to generate more revenue.

What should we do about this prospect? First of all, we must analyze the problem objectively and not allow the issue to become an emotional one. It is counterproductive to divide public opinion into those who are "for" Social Security and those who are "against" it. Social Security is strengthened when we diagnose its problems and develop ways of dealing with them.

If we do not reduce the growth rate of Social Security benefits, an eventual financial crisis is inescapable. Unlike other such crises, this one will be too big to solve using other sources of money to bail out the program. The country's GNP is just not large enough to support the tax increases that I think would be necessary to bail the program out in the middle of a crisis. Large and perhaps sudden cuts in benefits to the aged, bereaved and disabled members of our population would be unavoidable. In my opinion, that is the worst possible outcome.

Since there is nothing we can do to rebuild the Trust Fund, we should concentrate on realistic improvements that can be made in the system. The President has already made a substantive proposal to the Congress to get rid of "coupling," which became law in 1973 when its long-ranging consequences were not foreseen. The effect of "coupling" is to increase the benefits ultimately paid to retirees by more than the increase in the cost of living. In fact, in the long run, benefits would be adjusted upward at twice the rate of inflation. This happens because benefits are already tied to wages, and on the average whenever the cost of living goes up, wages go up too. There is no justification for a double adjustment for inflation.

But this is only an essential first step toward making the Social Security system sound. Even if the plan were enacted immediately, enormous future deficits 40 or 50 years from now would remain to be dealt with.

THREE POSSIBILITIES

I can think of three possible ways of dealing with the deficits. None of them will be popular. We can change the way in which the program pays increased benefits as wages go up, so that benefits no longer rise quite as fast. This is not as radical as some people think. Wage-earners' capacity to provide for their own old age through saving and private retirement insurance will grow as the general level of wages continues its historical upward trend. Social Security is designed to provide an income floor to the aged—it was never intended to be a welfare program providing the entire means of support for everyone in old age.

This is still not enough, however, to ensure financial soundness under all projections. We will probably have to fall back on another economy measure that a number of economists have recently suggested: to increase the age at which people can claim their retirements—gradually from 65 today to, say, 67 eventually. It would be essential to phase in such a change slowly so that people today nearing retirement would not find their plans disrupted.

A third economy measure may still be needed in addition to the other two. That would be to make Social Security benefits taxable in the same way that other pension benefits are. Closing this tax loophole would be a significant economy for the system, and it would not hurt the aged poor who are below the personal income tax threshold. The tax receipts obtained could, if necessary, be earmarked for deposit into the Social Security Trust Fund. I favor this kind of tax increase and oppose others mainly because, unlike most other taxes, it would have only limited negative effects on economic incentives.

Whether we like it or not, a lot of changes are in store for Social Security. If we make the changes early and in a concerted and deliberate way, we can avoid the disruptions that would be precipitated by sudden actions resulting from crisis. But it will take a great educational effort on the part of the government to put across to the public what is necessary. I will do whatever I can to contribute to that task.

Document 5.2 Report of the Advisory Council on Social Security, March 1975 [excerpts]

[*Author's Note.* This section of the Advisory Council's report is included to clarify the complexity of the several issues involved in financing indexed benefits.]

The Council recommends that until retirement all earnings should be "indexed". . . . Until 1972, social security payments were computed on the basis of a fixed relationship between benefits and an individual's average monthly earnings[6] in covered employment. . . . Congress in 1972 enacted automatic cost-of-living increases in social security benefits. Automatic cost-of-living increases in benefits are an important improvement in social security. The method by which they are made, however, needs basic changes, particularly because it has an apparently unintended erratic effect on the future relationship between benefits and the earnings they replace. [p. 13]

The effects of inflation while a worker is still earning should be allowed for explicitly, and by a different method from that used to allow for the effects of

---

DOCUMENT 5.2: U.S. Congress, House, Committee on Ways and Means, *Reports of the Quadrennial Advisory Council on Social Security,* 94th Cong., 1st sess., H.D. 94-75, March 10, 1975 (Washington, D.C.: U.S. Government Printing Office, 1975), pp. 13-14, 45-50.

6. Throughout this report "earnings" refers to earnings only up to the maximum amount subject to the social security tax.

inflation after a worker begins to draw benefits.

The Council therefore recommends that a worker's earnings should be "indexed"—that is, adjusted to reflect increases in average earnings over his working lifetime—up to retirement, and after retirement his benefits should be adjusted according to changes in the cost of living. [p. 14]

The financing of the OASDI system is based on the "current cost" [pay-as-you-go] method. Under this approach, no fund is created during the life of a worker from which his benefits are ultimately paid. Instead the social security taxes he pays are immediately paid out by the government to persons who are already beneficiaries. His own benefits will be paid from taxes that are collected in the future from persons who are then working. The tax rate is set so as to provide tax receipts that approximate current expenditures. In essence, the plan transfers money from one generation to another with the amount taken from the one generation being measured by the other generation's benefit requirements.

The current cost method would be unacceptable for a private pension plan, but it is a sound alternative for OASDI, because the government has the continuing power to tax future workers in order to pay benefits in the future to those who are not working. If OASDI were funded, in the actuarial sense, by creating a fund of one or two trillion dollars, that fund would have to be invested.[7] The largest part would almost certainly go into government bonds because they are considered to be the safest investment. The value of such bonds, however, depends on the power of the government to tax in the future. There would be, therefore, no really greater security behind the system than there is today, but the funding would have a very real effect on capital formation in this country.

In fact, even with the current cost method, the OASDI system has affected the capital formation of the country and will continue to affect it in ways that are not clearly understood at this time. Since the formation of adequate capital for the nation's needs is a currently pressing problem, the Council strongly recommends that a study of the relationship between the financing of the social security system and capital formation be made at the earliest possible time.

---

7. By comparison, the Federal debt outstanding at the end of fiscal year 1975. . . held by the public is estimated to be about $360 billion. [At the end of calendar year 1975 it was $538.5 billion. The net national debt at the end of calendar year 1974 was $360.8 billion publicly held, and $76.4 billion held by federal agencies—a total of $437.2 billion in fiscal year 1975. The gross national debt was $544 billion, of which $397 billion was held by the public. The assets of the Old Age and Survivors Insurance trust fund held in government securities amounted to $39.9 billion in fiscal year 1975. In fiscal year 1976 they fell to $37.5 billion: See *Survey of Current Business* and *Social Security Bulletin,* November 1976 (author's note).]

MEASURING LONG-RANGE COSTS

In discussing the "cost" of the OASDI system, the use of numbers in absolute dollars is of little help, because there are constant changes in the number of workers, beneficiaries, wage and benefit levels and other factors. Throughout this report, therefore, we will be expressing "cost" as a percentage of total covered earnings, meaning earnings subject to the OASDI tax. This is the measure of cost that will be used herein because it focuses attention on the size of the burden to be borne by each individual taxpayer and employer.[8] As an example, the cost of the system in 1974 was 10.67 percent of covered earnings. Since total covered earnings in 1974 approximated $600 billion, absolute cost of the system in that year was around $64 billion.

OASDI TAX RATES

The current tax rate for OASDI is 9.9 percent, payable on all earnings up to $14,100.[9] (In 1977, the same tax rate is payable on a $16,500 earnings base.) The total tax is split equally between the employer and employee, with each paying 4.95 percent.[10] (To this is added .9 percent for hospital insurance making a total social security tax of 5.85 percent borne by each.) The cash benefits tax rate for the self-employed was originally established at a level of 150 percent of the employee's tax. However, in recent years it has been frozen at 7 percent. [pp.45-46]

Automatic Adjustment to Inflation

In the 40 years since the program was created, Congress has voted many raises in benefits. Whenever such raises were enacted, the tax rate was usually also increased to help cover the additional cost. The maximum amount of wages subject to tax has likewise been raised from time to time.

In 1972, Congress made a basic change in the system. It modified the *ad hoc* approach and provided that thereafter benefits would increase automatically in accordance with changes in the cost of living, without any action by Congress. The cost of living is to be measured by the Consumer Price Index (CPI). The first such automatic increase is now scheduled to take place for the month of June 1975, with the increase in benefits to be payable in early July.

---

8. In chapter 8 of this book the issue of who actually pays this tax is discussed [author's note].

9. The $14,100 applies to earnings of 1975. The amount rises each year in accordance with the increase in average wages in covered employment. The 9.9 percent includes tax rate for disability, but not the additional 1.8 percent for Medicare, Part A (Hospitalization) [author's note].

10. The reference here to payment should be considered as the payment mechanism rather than the actual burden of the tax. In chapter 8 of this book, it is shown that the employee bears the burden of the payroll tax, and that it is not in fact shared by the employer.

[*Author's Note.* The July 1975 cost-of-living increase was 8.7 percent and cost about $5.7 billion for 12 months. The 1976 automatic increase effective as of July 1st is 6.4 percent and will cost $5.3 billion for the next fiscal year.]

TAXES

Congress is relying on the fact that, as prices increase, wages will also increase, thereby raising the total wage base and providing the needed additional revenue to cover the automatic increase in benefits. The social security law provides that whenever benefits are automatically increased, the base for the following year is raised by the amount of the increase in wages in covered employment.

EFFECT OF WAGE AND PRICE INCREASES ON COST ESTIMATES

Adoption of this automatic method had made the future cost of the system dependent upon future changes in prices and in wages. The cost can no longer be determined on the basis of today's benefit schedule, because it will move up automatically with changes in the CPI. In determining the   long-range financial soundness of the system, therefore, estimates of the movements of prices and wages are made for a 75-year valuation period. This long period of time is used because the inter-generational transfers and the impact of the controlling factors are best reflected when measured over a very long time frame.

1974 Trustees' Report on the Financial Condition of OASDI

ASSUMPTIONS

In the first part of 1974, the trustees of the OASDI system made their regular actuarial review of the plan and projected its cost over the period beginning with 1974 and ending with the year 2048. Their projections were based on four major assumptions:

1. Wages will increase over the 75-year period at an average rate of 5 percent;
2. The CPI will increase at an average rate of 3 percent;
3. Real wages[11] will increase at an average rate of 2 percent;
4. The total fertility rate[12] will rise from 1.9 in 1974 to 2.1 by 1985 and remain there. [p. 47]

---

11. Real wages are wages adjusted for changes in the Consumer Price Index. This factor actually expresses the relationship between the first two assumptions, but it is set out separately because of its importance, the cost of OASDI being very sensitive to this relationship.

12. The total fertility rate is the average number of babies born per woman during her lifetime.

The difference between the costs and the tax rates above represent a financing deficit of 2.98 percent.

PATTERN OF THE DEFICIT

It is not enough, however, to say that the long-term deficit is 2.98 percent. The "shape" of that deficit is very important. It is clear. . .that the deficit does not occur evenly over the period. This is a vital factor in determining future tax rates, and it is even more evident in [figure 5.1].

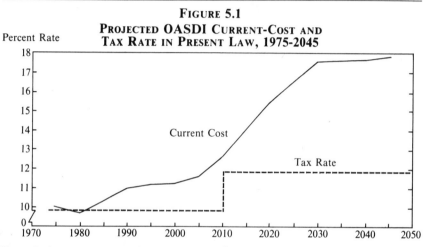

FIGURE 5.1
PROJECTED OASDI CURRENT-COST AND TAX RATE IN PRESENT LAW, 1975-2045

NOTE: Both rates are expressed as a percentage of covered earnings.
SOURCE: U.S. Congress, House, *Reports of the Quadrennial Advisory Council on Social Security . . .* 1975, p. 48.

The deficit is the spread between the tax and cost curves. [Figure 5.1] shows that a relatively small amount of the deficit occurs in the next 30 years, but thereafter the deficit increases rapidly. [pp.48-49]

[*Author's Note.* I found unbelievable the council's assumption that the fertility rate would rise to 2.1 children per woman by 1985 and stabilize there. The majority of the council's members struck from the draft report of the whole council, but not from the reports of the subcommittees, that there had been a change in the commonly used method of contraception. Only in my dissent occurs the thought, however, that because of this change in technology "it is the woman, and not the man, who decides for the first time in history the number of children a woman will bear,"[13] and that, therefore, historical trend lines were not applicable. Most members of the

13. House Committee on Ways and Means, *Reports of the Quadrennial Advisory Council . . .* 1975, p.79.

council, and some members of the subcommittee on finance, preferred to state that, historically, such a reversal of birth rates had been the pattern and that the pattern would be repeated.

I recognize that because the number of women aged 20 to 30 years will still be increasing until 1980 that total fertility rates may rise until 1980. It is in this younger age group where fertility rates are the highest. After 1980, however, the trend line of fertility rates and births per 1,000 population should reflect the decline in ultimate fertility per woman.

There continues to be a decline in the number of births to a woman after she has had two children. Whereas in 1974 there were 9.6 births per 1,000 women where the birth was a third child, in 1965 this figure was 16.6 births and in 1960 22.8 births per 1,000. In 1974, decreases for the fourth and higher-order births range from 8 percent to 25 percent.[14]]

The most important reason for this shape of the deficit is demographic. Relatively few people were born during the great depression of the '30s. After the war, the total fertility rate rose sharply to a peak of 3.77 in 1957. Thereafter it began to decline and it has recently reached the very low rate of 1.9 which is below the population replacement rate. The trustees have estimated that this rate will gradually rise to 2.1, which is the rate at which the population will eventually stabilize itself, and will remain there indefinitely.

It is this historic birth rate pattern that largely shapes the deficit. [p. 49]

Starting about 2005, however, the process reverses itself. Then the war babies begin to draw social security benefits in ever larger numbers, while the work force is not increasing at a commensurate rate because of the low fertility rate now existing and forecasted for the future.

These demographic changes are reflected in two important statistics:
1. Today there are 30 beneficiaries for every 100 workers.
2. In the year 2030 it is estimated that there will be 45 beneficiaries for each 100 workers. [p. 49]

Obviously the demographic projection has an almost overwhelming effect on the costs of the system. This can be seen in the table below where the 2.98-

---

14. U.S. National Center for Health Statistics, *Monthly Vital Statistics Report* 24:11 (February 13, 1976), supplement, p.8. The use of a semi-log scale in the monthly *Vital Statistics Report's* graphs, which are commonly used and circulated within the government, masks the degree of the drop for the younger women that occurred in the boom years of the 1960s and early 1970s (measured by continuously increasing gross national product). It is the young women who bear most of the children.

The precipitous decline in birth rates in the 1920s reflected the recession of the early 1920s and foreshadowed and later reflected the depression of the thirties during which GNP was halved. GNP dropped considerably from 1920 to 1923, but has not done so during the later period of oral-contraceptive usage. A precipitous drop in the birth rates has never before occurred in the United States in years of prosperity.

percent deficit has been broken down into its components:

	Percent of Taxable Payroll
Actuarial balance of OASDI estimated in late 1973	-.51
Effect of subsequent changes in:	
Population assumptions	-1.87
Economic assumptions	-.19
Disability rates	-.21
All other assumptions	-.20
	-2.47
New actuarial balance	-2.98

The change in population assumptions accounts for 63 percent of the total deficit and 76 percent of the increase in the deficit since the last actuarial review.

APPRAISAL OF ASSUMPTIONS USED IN THE TRUSTEES' REPORT

The Subcommittee on Finance reviewed the four basic assumptions used by the trustees in arriving at their conclusion of a 2.98 percent deficit [and] found reasonable support for the trustees' conclusion, but were of the firm opinion that the deficit is more likely to be higher than lower. The consultants also reviewed the trustees' four basic assumptions. While not unanimous in their opinions on individual factors, they stated that "we find the Trustees' conclusion is a reasonable indicator of future experience."[15] [p. 50]

Document 5.3 Author's Dissent to Finance Subcommittee Report, March 1975

[*Author's Note.* My dissent was general in nature. Prior to this point, it covered several other matters, as for example: *(a)* entitlement rules for secondary benefits which differ by sex; and *(b)* the anomaly of a two-worker, husband-and-wife family having in total the same covered earnings as a one-worker family, and the former family receiving a smaller monthly retirement benefit than the latter.]

Because only a single set of assumptions, covering projected birth rates and price and wage increases, were presented by the Finance Subcommittee to the Council (and these are the same as in the 1974 Trustees' Report) rather than is

---

15. At this point the report refers the reader to the dissenting statement of "Mrs. Campbell" [sic], here reprinted in part as document 5.3 [author's note].

DOCUMENT 5.3: "Supplementary Statement by Rita Ricardo Campbell," in House Committee on Ways and Means, *Reports of the Quadrennial Advisory Council. . .1975*, pp. 78-79.

more customary, a range of low, medium and high estimates, and the single set of assumptions was accepted by the Council as "reasonable," the underlying assumptions of the long-run projected deficit should be examined critically.

The three assumptions are: (1) an annual 5-percent increase in average money wages, (2) an annual 3-percent average increase in the Consumer Price Index and thus a 2-percent average rate of increase in real wages, and (3) a 2.1 fertility rate by 1985, which will remain constant at that level for the remainder of the 75 years.

If, however, 1.9 births per woman were the average fertility rate for the whole 75 years, the 2.98 percent actuarial imbalance would be 3.73 percent of taxable payroll. Additionally, without decoupling the system but with a steady annual rate of growth in real wages of only 1 percent, based on wages increasing at 5 percent and prices increasing at 4 percent, the long-run deficit may be as high as about 10 percent of taxable payroll.[16]

It is noted in the Finance Subcommittee Report of February 3, p. 98, and also in Chapter 7 of the Council Report (Sec. 3.3), that ". . .the demographic projection has an almost overwhelming effect on the costs of the system. . . . The change [by the Trustees of the funds in their 1974 Report] in population assumptions accounts for 63 percent of the total deficit and 76 percent of the increase in the deficit since the last actuarial review." (p. 98. "Deficit" is the long-run actuarial imbalance.)

The argument to support an assumption of 1.9 births rather than 2.1 births per female over the 75 years period follows. Because of the change in technology in respect to birth control, it is the woman, and not the man, who decides for the first time in history the number of children a woman will bear. Because of this factor, it is impossible to predict on the basis of experience, future birth rates, and the statistical data available appear to support this conclusion.

I attach as [figure 5.2a] a graph which gives birth rates by age of mother, 1945-1973, originally drawn on a "semi-log" scale [figure 5.2b], but redrawn here on the normal scale to which most persons are accustomed and which does not compress the extreme drop, but rather makes clear the size of the drop from 1960 on in birth rates by age of mother. There is clearly a precipitous decline in birth rates for each of the five-year age brackets which the compression of the original chart tends to minimize.

Additionally, the February 1975, Census Bureau's *Population Estimates and Projections*[17] includes a range of estimated birth rates through the year 2025, one of which, Ser. III, is only 1.7 births per woman, in order "to provide a reasonable range in projections of future births." (p.3) [pp.78-79]

---

16. Office of the Actuary, SSA.
17. Ser. P-25, No. 541.

Author's Update of Original Dissent

Figures released since my dissent was written have served only to strengthen my initial position.

Birth rate

Birth and fertility rates have continued to fall steadily. During the first five months of 1976, the birth rate was 14.1 per 1,000 population as compared to 14.5 in the same period of 1975. The birth rate in 1970 was 18.4 per 1,000 population, and has been falling steadily since.

Figure 5.2a, which uses the more usual, arithmetic scale clearly indicates the importance of the drastic drop in births among women aged 20-24, 25-29, and even 30-34 years. It is these age groups that generally bear the largest percentage of children in a year, not the groups aged 35-39 and 40-44 which the semilogarithmic chart dispro-portionally emphasizes.

In 1960, 50 percent of then-married women were using some form of contraception; in 1973, 65 percent.[18] The proportion of couples who use what are considered to be the more effective modern methods rose from about 37 percent in 1965 to almost 70 percent in 1973.[19]

Although the effect of these matters was not reflected in the Advisory Council's majority recommendations, the council did predict that "the 1975 trustees' report will almost certainly show a significantly higher long-term deficit than is currently projected" (p. 50). As the economy improves, some increase in the fertility rate is anticipated, but not to as high a level as 2.1 births per woman in her lifetime.

Labor force rate

More recent predictions of the future size of the labor force bear out my own predictions as to a higher participation by women in the labor force than was assumed in 1974 by the Social Security Administration. However, because of the continuing high rate of unemployment—above 7 percent—this higher labor force participation rate has not been fully reflected by a higher employment rate of women workers.

The most important factor in long-run financing of deficits is the projected narrowing ratio between workers and beneficiaries. Future trends in the ratio of workers to retirees depend on many demographic factors, including age at entrance to the labor force and age when

---

18. U.S. National Center for Health Statistics, *Monthly Vital Statistics Report,* October 4, 1976, Supplement, p.25.

19. Ibid.

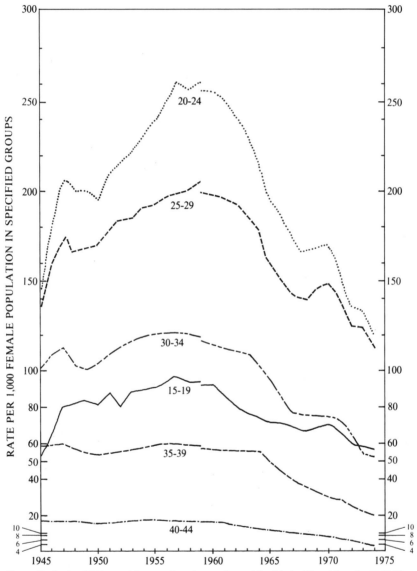

FIGURE 5.2A
BIRTH RATES BY AGE OF MOTHER, UNITED STATES, 1945-74

NOTE: Beginning 1959, trend lines are based on registered live births. Trend lines for 1945-59 are based on live births adjusted for underregistration.

SOURCE: Private communication, based on U.S. Census data.

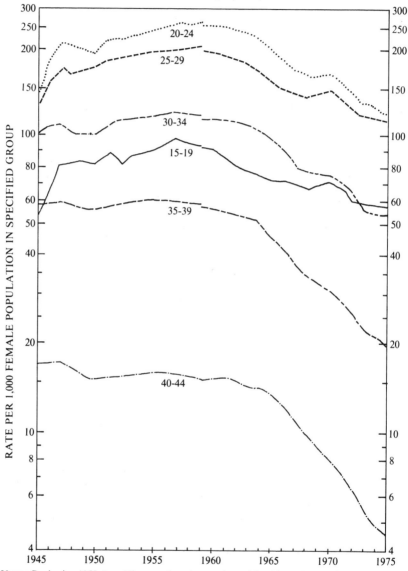

FIGURE 5.2B
BIRTH RATES BY AGE OF MOTHER, UNITED STATES, 1945-75
(Semi-Log. Scale)

NOTE: Beginning 1959, trend lines are based on registered live births. Trend lines for 1945-59 are based on live births adjusted for underregistration.

SOURCE: U.S. Department of Health, Education, and Welfare, *Monthly Vital Statistics Report* 25:10 (December 30, 1976), p. 3.

retirement begins. Since the early 1900s, there has been a reduction in labor force participation rates for men at both the beginning and the end of worklife. Their delayed entry has been due to longer periods of schooling. At the same time, women have entered the labor force at a rate sufficient to offset almost exactly this downward pressure on overall labor force participation. The current women's labor force participation rate gives promise of future rates of increase that will exceed the slower, continuing decrease in the men's rate.

In 1977, the most recently projected overall (men and women) labor force participation rate was, by 1990, 64 percent compared to the actual rate of 61 percent in 1975. By 1990, 60 to 65 percent of women aged 25 through 54 years were anticipated to be in the labor force, while only 55 percent of women belonging to that group were in the labor force in 1975. The men's labor force participation rate was expected to continue to decline to 77 percent for all males aged 16 years and over by 1990, and the comparable female rate to rise to about 51 percent.

If this latter increase can be absorbed by the economy, and the rate of unemployment falls to more normal levels, it will help financing of OASDI until about 1990. The years after 1990 will probably witness a smaller work force than in 1975, probably one that is declining as a percentage of the population as a whole. By 2005, an absolute decrease in the relative number of social security taxpayers will be occurring. By that year, however, the post World War II baby boom will have increased the number of aged eligible for social security benefits.

Because of the falling birth rates during recent years, the size of the labor force aged 16 to 24 years will be about 1.3 million persons fewer in 1990 than it was in 1975. However, because more women are expected to join the labor force—at least 12 million more in all by 1990 than were in the labor force in 1975—recent estimates are that the total labor force by 1990 will be over 113 million people. These estimates of the labor force participation rates for women working in 1990 are higher than the ones assumed in the 1974 OASI trustees' report—the same ones that were used by the Quadrennial Advisory Council. The following table compares these 1974 SSA projections with the Department of Labor's new 1976 projections of the percentage of women in the labor force by 1990.

It is possible that the decidedly higher rate at which the labor force participation of women workers is increasing may for a short period overtake the rate at which males are retiring early. Because of the

FEMALE LABOR FORCE 1990, AS PERCENTAGE OF ALL WOMEN
IN GIVEN AGE BRACKETS

Ages	1974 Projections (SSA[a])	1976 Projections (BLS[b])
20-24	67%	75%
25-29	56	64
30-34	55	
35-39	58	63
40-44	59	
45-49	59	60%
50-54	58%	

a. SSA, Office of the Actuary, 1 page, mimeo; sent to author 6/30/74.
b. BLS, press release, September 15, 1976, table 1, "Civilian Labor Force."

number of variables involved, I have no firm confidence in predictions regarding the financing of OASI, beyond a fifteen-year period. In fact, I have considerable reservations about the reliability of predictions even for that shorter period of time.

There has been, for example, little exploration of the impact, both on the economy and on various institutional arrangements, of the tremendous increase in the number of families in which both husband and wife work.[20] For example, the total labor supply is currently increasing faster than employment, so that we have the phenomenon of increasing employment and also increasing unemployment. Additionally, husband-and-wife working families probably affect personal savings and consumption patterns, and also the intensity with which persons who are unemployed, fired, or temporarily laid off, may look for work. To ignore the impact of such demographic phenomena is foolhardy.

The increase in the numbers of married women working has enabled OASDI to increase benefits more than it otherwise could have done without incurring substantial current, "pay-as-you-go" deficits. The dramatic increase in the percentage of married women who work, and who pay the same OASDI taxes as all other individuals in covered employment, permits their OASDI taxes to be available, at least in large part, to support the expanding level of retirement benefit

20. Myra Strober, "Wives' Labor Force Behavior of Family Consumption Patterns," *American Economic Review* 67:410-17.

amounts. Eventually, the percentage of married women working will level out and this annual, additional source of revenues will dry up, because married working women who retire will collect only one benefit.[21]

The rapidly rising total expenditures for social security benefits have in the past been financed by a combination of *(a)* increases in the tax rate and *(b)* the increasing employment level of a growing population. The leveling off of the numbers of married women who work, with an increasingly high ratio of beneficiaries to workers, points either to much higher OASDI taxes, or to lesser benefits, or to the necessity to tap other forms of tax revenues and earmark them for social security benefits.

General-revenue financing

Traditionally, general revenues are used for military expenditures and other forms of public goods, as well as for welfare benefits designed to redistribute income from rich to poor. Entitlement to the latter depends on a means test. Welfare expenditures, because of new programs and recent high unemployment levels, have been growing rapidly in the United States. There appears to be an increasing redistribution of income from higher- to lower-income persons. In general, it is easier politically to increase benefits than to increase taxes

The Committee on Economic Security in 1935 recommended that social security be financed by a three-way taxing mechanism, that is, by *(a)* taxes to be paid by employees, *(b)* taxes to be paid by employers, and *(c)* the federal government's general revenues. However, the law, as it was passed, provided that only payroll taxes would support social security benefits. Then, in 1943, a provision was written into the law to provide for use of federal general revenues if ever needed. This provision was deleted from the law in 1950, and actually general revenues have never been used to support a category of benefits paid by the system. From time to time, however, funding of social security benefits for specific groups in the population has come from general revenues. Thus general revenues have been used to cover, on a transitional basis, uninsured persons age 72 and over; to provide payroll credits for persons in military service; and to do likewise for persons of Japanese ancestry who had been interned during World

---

21. A primary benefit based on their own earnings, or a dependency benefit equal to one-half their husband's primary, and if a surviving widow, equal to his total primary amount.

War II. These were all very special cases.

A major argument against the existing payroll tax structure is that, considered apart from the benefit structure, it is regressive. The tax rate is proportional on an earnings base, now at $16,500, but there is no social security tax imposed on earnings above the base. Accordingly, the rate of tax on total earnings for a person earning, for example, $40,000 in 1977 is much less than the rate of tax for a person earning $16,000 in that year. The system considered as an entity, that is with benefits included, appears to be, however, progressive in nature because persons with covered, low average monthly earnings over a life-time receive a heavily weighted benefit. As of June 1975, this benefit was as high as 129 percent of the first $110 of average monthly wages, and fell off for additional increments to a low of 22 percent.

Many proponents of general revenue financing believe in expanding the type and level of benefits. Financing from general revenues could greatly increase available funds. The 1974-75 Advisory Council's major recommendation was to make up the immediate short-run deficit in the OASI funds by use of Part A (hospitalization) of the Medicare program's trust fund, because "there does not seem to be any real reason for funding such costs by a tax on wages. Hospital insurance expenditures would seem to be more properly funded from general revenues, and the Council recommends such a proposal to the Congress" (see document 5.4).

Four members of the council dissented from this recommendation. As one of the members who dissented, my concern was that this recommendation pointed any congressional consideration of federal legislation for national health insurance towards support from general revenue funding. It is noted that the council's report correctly reflects that the majority of the council's members voted "against the use of additional general revenue financing in the social security cash benefits program. The Council believes that the deficit can and should be dealt with through the conventional system of ear-marked payroll contributions."[22] Indeed, the majority of the council's members believed that general-revenue financing in a social security system should be limited to very special cases, like the ones cited above.

---

22. House Committee on Ways and Means, *Reports of the Quadrennial Advisory Council . . .* 1975, p. 61.

Document 5.4   Report of the Advisory Council on Social Security, March 1975 [excerpt]

The OASDI program is financed from taxes on covered earnings, because the benefits of the program are always related to the earnings of a worker-taxpayer. This is true even when the beneficiary is a spouse or dependent survivor. The same principle does *not* apply to benefits under part A of the Medicare program. There the amount of the benefits is determined by the hospital and related health care costs of a particular person, and bear no relationship whatsoever to his wages or those of anyone else.

Under such circumstances there does not seem to be any real reason for funding such costs by a tax on wages. Hospital insurance expenditures would seem to be more properly funded from general revenues, and the Council recommends such a proposal to the Congress.[23] [p. 55]

The Medicare program is the Nation's basic method of providing insurance to help meet the costs of health care for the aged and the severely disabled.

The hospital insurance program (part A of Medicare) helps beneficiaries to meet the costs of inpatient hospital care and related services. It is available to persons age 65 and over who are entitled to monthly social security or railroad retirement benefits, to severely disabled persons under age 65 who are entitled to monthly social security or railroad retirement benefits on the basis of their disability, and to persons under age 65 who suffer from chronic kidney disease.

Benefits under part A are, like social security cash benefits, financed mainly through taxes based on covered earnings. When the program began, provision was made for meeting from general revenues the cost of part A benefits for people age 65 or older who had not had sufficient covered work under the program to become entitled to monthly benefits and who could not be expected to pay hospital insurance taxes. Also, provision has been made (under the 1972 amendments) for aged people who are not eligible for social security cash benefits to enroll voluntarily in part A upon payment of a monthly fee—now $36, and scheduled to rise to $40 in July 1975, and to rise thereafter as hospital-care costs rise.

The voluntary supplementary medical insurance program (part B of Medicare) complements the hospital insurance program by insuring enrollees against the costs of physicians' services and certain medical services not covered under the part A program. Part B of Medicare is available to hospital insurance beneficiaries and to virtually all people age 65 and over. This

DOCUMENT 5.4: House Committee on Ways and Means, *Reports of the Quadrennial Advisory Council* . . . 1975, pp. 55, 67-68.

23. See dissenting statement of Rita R. Campbell, Edwin J. Faulkner, John J. Scanlon, and J. Henry Smith.

program is financed through the monthly premiums paid by those who enroll in the program and contributions from the Federal Government.

The Council has not recommended any changes in the benefit structure of the Medicare program. Throughout the period during which the Council met, a number of proposals for national health insurance, including the Administration's Comprehensive Health Insurance Program, were under consideration in the Congress and were the subject of widespread public discussion and comment. Most of the major proposals would change in some manner the benefit structure of Medicare. The Council reasoned that any recommendations it might make to change the benefit package provided under the Medicare program might soon be outdated by broader modifications of Medicare within a national health insurance framework. For this reason, and because of the limited time available for its study, the Council decided to concentrate its efforts primarily on the social security cash benefits program.

However, the Council has examined the financial structure of the Medicare program and recommends that the method of financing part A of Medicare be changed. The Council's recommendation calls for a gradual reallocation of the contributions scheduled in the law for part A to the cash benefits program. Eventually, general revenues would be the sole source of funding for part A. The Council has concluded that the changeover from payroll tax to general revenue financing of part A is warranted because part A benefits are not earnings-related, as are cash benefits. [pp. 67-68]

The Council finds the part A program to be actuarially sound.[24] If the present financing schedule is unchanged it would be adequate to provide for payment of expenditures anticipated over the period for which estimates are made. Of course, it should be noted again that the Council is recommending that the financing schedule be changed by gradually decreasing the payroll tax for part A and replacing the income lost thereby with general revenues.

The part B program is financed on a current basis. In testing the actuarial soundness of the part B program, it is appropriate to look at the period for which the premium rate and the level of general revenue financing have been established. The Council finds that for fiscal years 1975 and 1976, part B premiums, along with anticipated Federal general revenue contributions, are adequate to finance total program costs for those years. [p. 68]

---

24. *By Mr. Smith.* I do not believe the Council sufficiently investigated the Medicare program and probable costs thereunder to be justified in making the unequivocal statement that Part A is actuarially sound.

Document 5.5   Dissent by Four Council Members on Use of Medicare Trust Fund Monies

The Council has recommended that Medicare Part A payroll tax contributions be diverted to meet impending deficits in OASDI financing and that the government fill in the Medicare loss with funds from the general Treasury revenues.

While this device would meet the early funding problems of OASDI (but not the long range one), it does not seem to us to be an appropriate solution to the problem. It would shift the deficit from one social insurance plan to another, but it would not solve the basic problem of under funding. The Treasury is not an inexhaustible source of funds. The cost would still have to be met and resort to general revenue financing would mark a serious retreat from the principle of payroll tax financing that the Council has endorsed elsewhere in this Report. Also, additional large expenditures from general revenues, unless financed by new taxes, carry the great risk of contributing further to inflation.

The argument that Medicare benefits are not wage related and, therefore, it is appropriate to support them by general revenues, is more a rationalization than a principle. There is no more valid reason now for funding Medicare from general revenues than there was initially. Medicare is now looked upon truly as a social insurance program, and it is just as desirable to support it with joint employer-worker contributions as it is for OASDI. General revenue financing would mask the cost of the program and weaken even further the control over it. Furthermore, it would jeopardize Medicare by placing it in competition with all other government programs financed by general revenues; and it would make it more like a welfare plan which perhaps should involve a means test.

It's our preference, therefore, to approach the problem of the OASDI deficit directly by raising the FICA tax rates in the near future. During the next several years only a limited increase (about a half percent for employees and employer each) would be needed. And certainly, in view of the increasing benefits being provided by the plan, this added contribution is not an unreasonable price to ask. It is likely that in the long run the cost of the OASDI system will rise to levels that will require additional taxation, and we might as well continue to exercise the discipline of balancing benefits and taxes just as we have in the past. In this way the philosophy, integrity and general understanding of the system will be preserved. [pp. 72-73]

DOCUMENT 5.5: "Statement of R. Campbell (senior fellow, Hoover Institution), Edwin J. Faulkner (president, Woodman Accident and Life Company), John J. Scanlon (executive vice-president, AT&T), and J. Henry Smith (chairman of the board, Equitable Life Assurance Society)," House Committee on Ways and Means, *Reports of the Quadrennial Advisory Council . . .* 1975, pp. 72-73.

Document 5.6   Trustees' Report on Medicare, Part A, 1976 [excerpt]

[*Author's Note.* This section is included to increase the understanding of
the reader as to the meaning of the council's recommendation to use the
trust fund of Part A of Medicare to make up the short-run deficit of OASI,
and then to obtain the funding for the payment of hospital bills under
Medicare from general revenues. In effect, this would open the door to
national health insurance financed out of general revenues.]

Actuarial Status of the Trust Fund

Acting on the recommendation of the 1971 Advisory Council, the Board of
Trustees has adopted the general principle that the hospital insurance
program should be financed in such a way that annual income to the program
should be approximately equal to annual outlays of the program plus an
amount to maintain a balance in the trust fund approximately equal to one
year's expenditures. This principle reflects the view that there is a need for a
sizeable fund for the contingency that future income and outgo may differ
substantially from projections, but that it is unnecessary and impractical to
fully fund the future benefits of workers as they accrue the right to those future
benefits. [p. 27]

The ratio of expenditures to taxable payroll has increased from 0.95 percent
in 1967 to an estimated 1.73 percent in 1975, reflecting both the higher rate of
increase in hospital costs than in earnings subject to hospital insurance taxes
and the extension of hospital insurance benefits to disabled beneficiaries and
persons suffering from chronic renal disease. Further increases in this ratio to
2.26 percent in 1980 and to 4.93 percent in the year 2000 result from the
assumed continuation of increases in the cost of institutional health care at a
higher rate than increases in taxable earnings. [ibid.]

The adequacy of the financing of the hospital insurance program under
current law is measured by comparing on a year to year basis the actual tax
rates specified by law with the corresponding total costs of the program,
expressed as percentages of taxable payroll. If these two items are exactly
equal in each year of the 25-year projection period and all projection
assumptions are realized, tax revenues along with interest income will be
sufficient to provide for benefit and administrative expenses for insured
persons and to gradually build the trust fund to the level of a year's outgo by
the end of the period. In practice, however, tax rate schedules generally are
designed with rate changes occurring only at several-year intervals, rather

Document 5.6: U.S. Trustees of the Federal Hospital Insurance Trust Fund, *1976 Annual
Report* (Washington, D.C.: U.S. Government Printing Office, 1976), pp. 34-39.

than with continual year by year increases to match exactly with projected cost increases. To the extent that small differences between the yearly costs of the program and the corresponding tax rates for short periods of time are offset by subsequent differences in the reverse direction, the financing objectives will be approximately met.

The projected total costs of the program, expressed as percentages of taxable payroll, and the tax rates scheduled under current law are shown in [Table 5.1: compare table 5.2] for selected years over the 25-year period 1976-2000. The total cost of the program, including expenditures plus trust fund

TABLE 5.1
ACTUARIAL BALANCE OF THE HOSPITAL INSURANCE PROGRAM, EXPRESSED AS A PERCENT OF TAXABLE PAYROLL

Average contribution rate, scheduled under present law[a]	2.75%
Average cost of the program:[a]	
Expenditures, for benefit payments and administrative costs for insured beneficiaries	3.31
Building and maintaining the trust fund, at the level of one year's expenditures	0.08
Total cost of the program	3.39
Actuarial balance	-0.64%

a. Average for the 25-year period 1976-2000.
SOURCE: Federal Hospital Insurance Trust Fund, Board of Trustees, *1976 Annual Report*, p. 35.

building and maintenance, exceeds the tax rate in nearly every year of the projection. In addition, expenditures for benefits and administrative expenses alone exceed the corresponding tax rates for all future years, beginning in the late 1980's. [pp. 28-29]

The present financing schedule for the hospital insurance program is not adequate to provide the expenditures anticipated over the entire 25-year valuation period, if the assumptions underlying the estimates prove to be realistic. The tax schedule is sufficient to provide for program expenditures over the next 10 years. However, it is not sufficient, under current assumptions, to provide for any growth in the trust fund—relative to annual disbursements—toward the level of a full year's disbursements recommended by the 1971 Advisory Council. The financing for the last half of the 25-year period is not sufficient even to provide for projected benefits and administrative expenses.

The trust fund balance at the beginning of 1976 is 77 percent of the projected disbursements for 1976, somewhat below the level of a full year's disbursements. The ratio of fund to disbursements is projected to drop slightly

TABLE 5.2
ACTUARIAL BALANCE OF THE HOSPITAL INSURANCE PROGRAM, UNDER ALTERNATIVE SETS OF ASSUMPTIONS

	ALTERNATIVE I [low-cost]	ALTERNATIVE II [intermediate]	ALTERNATIVE III [high-cost]
Average contribution rate, scheduled under present law[1]	2.75%	2.75%	2.75%
Average cost of the program, for expenditures and for trust fund building and maintenance[2]	2.59	3.39	4.39
Actuarial balance	+0.16%	-0.64%	-1.64%

1. Average for the 25-year period 1976-2000.

2. Average for the 25-year period 1976-2000, expressed as a percent of taxable payroll.

SOURCE: Federal Hospital Insurance Trust Fund, Board of Trustees, *1976 Annual Report*, p. 37.

during the next 5 years and then to return to a level of approximately 75 percent during the early 1980's. After 1985, the trust fund is projected to decline steadily, until it is completely exhausted in the early 1990's.

The Board recommends that the financing of the hospital insurance program be strengthened to remove the average 25-year deficit of 0.64 percent of taxable payroll. Most of the increased financing is required after 1985. [pp. 38-39]

Document 5.7   Trustees' Report on OASDI Funds, 1976 [excerpt]

Conclusion

The short-range actuarial cost estimates indicate that the assets of the old-age and survivors insurance and disability insurance trust funds will decline during the period 1976-1981, under each of the three alternative sets of assumptions [low, intermediate, high] presented in this report. Without legislation to provide additional financing, the assets of the disability insurance trust fund will be exhausted in 1979 under all three alternative sets of assumptions. Similarly, the assets of the old-age and survivors insurance trust fund will be exhausted in 1981 under the most pessimistic set of alternatives, in 1984 under the intermediate set, and sometime after 1984 under the most optimistic set of assumptions.

The Board recommends that prompt action be taken to strengthen the financing of the old-age, survivors, and disability insurance system over the near term by means of appropriate increases in the tax rates. The Board opposes the use of additional general revenue financing for the old-age, survivors, and disability insurance program. The Board recommends against an increase in the taxable earnings base, other than increases which will occur automatically as average wages in covered employment increase, as a means of producing additional income because of the effect this would have on increased benefits and expenditures in future years.

The long-range actuarial cost estimates indicate that for every year in the future, under present law, the estimated expenditures will exceed the estimated income from taxes. This excess increases with time and is estimated to average about 1.9 percent of taxable payroll over the next 25-year period (1976-2000) based upon the intermediate cost estimates. Under more optimistic assumptions this excess of expenditures over income is projected to average 1.0 percent of taxable payroll, and under more pessimistic assumptions this excess is projected to average 2.9 percent of taxable payroll. Therefore, all alternative long-range cost estimates presented in this report indicate that over the remainder of this century the old-age, survivors, and

DOCUMENT 5.7: OASDI Trustees, *1976 Annual Report,* pp.116-18.

disability insurance program will require additional revenues.

The long-range cost of the old-age, survivors, and disability insurance program projected to occur after the turn of the century will substantially exceed the taxes scheduled in present law. Although those projected costs are highly sensitive to variations in the demographic and economic assumptions, all reasonable assumptions indicate that there will be significant excesses of expenditures over income. Estimates have been presented in this report under three alternative sets of assumptions indicating a broad range within which actual future experience may fall; however, no assurance can be given that these estimates define the broadest possible range of variation in the long-range cost estimates.

The Board recognized in the 1975 annual report, as it does in this report, that the high cost of the old-age, survivors, and disability insurance program projected to occur after the turn of the century is partially due to unintended results of the automatic benefit adjustment provisions enacted in 1972. These provisions, under the economic assumptions currently being utilized in making projections, cause future projected benefits to increase substantially from the levels of wage replacement established by benefits currently paid under the program, resulting in unreasonably high benefits for persons first becoming eligible for benefits in the next century. Accordingly, the costs which are projected to occur after the turn of the century should be interpreted with caution and in light of the likelihood that legislation will be enacted to prevent these projected benefit levels from materializing. The Board is in full concurrence with the intent of the 1975 Advisory Council on Social Security that the benefit structure be revised in a responsible manner. The Board recommends the adoption of a specific plan as soon as possible in order to improve the predictability of future benefit levels and to reduce the long-range cost of the system.

The Board also recommends that the development of additional plans to further strengthen the long-range financing of the old-age, survivors, and disability insurance program be given high priority. [pp. 116-118]

Document 5.8 Report of the Consultant Panel on Social Security, August 1976 [excerpts]

Major Recommendations

In arriving at its recommendations, the Panel has been acutely aware of the financial needs of retired persons, both now and in the future. But we

DOCUMENT 5.8: U.S. Congress, Joint Committee (House Committee on Ways and Means, Senate Committee on Finance), *Report of the Consultant Panel on Social Security to the Congressional Research Service*, 94th Cong., 2d sess., August 1976 (Washington, D.C.: U.S. Government Printing Office, 1976), pp. 3-5 and 7-9.

recognize that every increase in benefits must be financed by an increase in taxes—whether from payroll or from general government revenue. We have tried, therefore, to strike a reasonable balance between benefits and the costs of providing them.

The Panel was guided also by the long-established principles that Congress has set for the earnings-related OASDI: namely, the principles of social adequacy and individual equity applying to both benefits and the supporting taxes. Furthermore, we recognize that the social security system has created strong expectations among its participants that they will receive retirement benefits that are reasonably related to their lifetime earnings. The OASDI must seek to fulfill these expectations.

A worker's willingness to pay the required taxes depends largely on his belief that his expectations will be realized. Yet, if these benefit expectations are unreasonably high, then the program will encounter financial difficulty. To operate the system successfully in the face of unpredictable social, demographic, and economic changes, requires flexibility that the system now lacks.

1. Benefit formula. The Panel recommends that:

(a) as under present law, retirement benefits continue to be increased automatically after retirement in proportion to the Consumer Price Index;

(b) benefits for future retirees be computed using earnings that have been indexed in proportion to the change in price levels during the earnings-averaging period;

(c) the progressively lengthening averaging period of present law be retained;

(d) the minimum benefit provision under OASDI be eliminated; and

(e) future Congresses determine the extent to which benefits can be increased beyond the levels reached automatically, in the light of needs of the beneficiaries and willingness of the workers to pay the necessary taxes.

The effect of these recommendations would be:

— Benefits to workers already retired would be protected against erosion from inflation.

— The purchasing power of benefits for future retirees would tend to increase even without future congressional action and can be further increased by congressional action. However, in the absence of such action, the benefit measured in relation to workers' pre-retirement earnings would decline. [pp. 3-4]

2. Financing. The Panel recommends that:

(a) the system continue to be financed by payroll taxes, not from general government revenues;
(b) the ceiling on wages subject to payroll tax be moderately increased, and then maintained at a point at which the entire earnings of approximately 90 percent of all workers are covered. In 1977, the estimated maximum would be $18,900 instead of the $16,500 expected under present law. This maximum would continue to increase automatically in proportion to increases in covered wages, subject to revisions from time to time to maintain the 90 percent benchmark;
(c) the combined employer and employee payroll tax rate be increased by 0.4 percent (i.e. 0.2 percent each); and
(d) the tax rate for the self-employed, for both OASDI and HI, be increased to 75 percent of the combined rate for employees and employers.

The effect of these financing recommendations, in conjunction with the benefit structure recommendations, would be:

— Under economic and demographic assumptions that appear to be within a reasonable range, the tax rates needed to finance promised benefits would remain close to those initially recommended by this Panel. (Tables at the end of this chapter illustrate these rates.)[25]
— Congress would have leeway to finance additional benefits out of acceptable tax increases.
— The tax rate for the self-employed would return to the level relative to the combined employer-employee tax rate that existed in the past.

The emphasis of this Panel's proposal is upon congressional control rather than upon maintenance of approximately today's tax rate. Even if Congress believes that workers at the turn of the century will be willing to pay a combined payroll tax rate substantially higher than the current tax rate, we consider it undesirable to incorporate that belief into the system at the present time, thereby causing rigidity. As time passes Congress can raise benefit levels and the corresponding taxes at its discretion.

The Panel has concluded that the use of general government revenue to finance the OASDI program is inappropriate. Our reasons are:

— General revenues are more properly used to support needs-related old-age income programs and general tax relief to low-income workers.
— Needs of elderly persons other than for income maintenance—such as housing, long-term care, and social services—appear to have more urgent claims on general revenues.

---

25. This assumes that productivity, or real growth per year, is maintained at 2 percent, and that the fertility rate returns to replacement level by the year 2000 [author's note].

— General-revenue financing of the OASDI program would weaken the earnings-related nature of the program. It could even jeopardize the long-range stability of the entire social security system, thwarting citizen expectations of retirement income protection.

3. *Spouse's benefit.* The Panel recommends abandonment of the present schedule of spouse benefits for future retired workers. We recommend instead averaging the earnings of the husband and wife for determining benefits to members of both one-worker and two-worker families. This procedure would result in more equitable treatment in relating benefits to contributions. [pp. 4-5]

A COMPARISON OF THE PANEL'S RECOMMENDED PRICE-INDEXING AND WAGE-INDEXING METHOD PROPOSED BY PRESIDENT FORD IN JUNE 1976

There is widespread agreement that the present overindexing of benefits must be corrected. Two major alternatives have been proposed: the price-indexing method recommended by the Panel and the wage-indexing method proposed by President Ford. These grant identical treatment to those already receiving benefits, both guarantee that benefits will keep pace with increases in the Consumer Price Index.

However these two approaches differ in the computation of initial benefits for workers who retire in the future. The Panel's price-indexing method would protect future retirees against inflation through automatic adjustments in the benefit formula used to compute initial retirement benefits. In other words, the benefits for workers retiring in the future years would be automatically increased to keep pace with inflation. In addition, their initial benefits would tend to increase even further when real wages increase. However, the initial benefits, measured as a percent of immediate pre-retirement earnings would decline in the absence of legislated increases.

On the other hand, the wage-indexing method proposed by President Ford would provide an initial retirement benefit that replaces approximately the same ratio of each workers's pre-retirement wages as applies for a worker who retires in 1976.

The two different approaches of correcting the overindexing produce very different outcomes in:

1. *Flexibility and congressional control.* These two methods produce different promises of benefits to workers retiring in the future. The price-indexing method guarantees a moderate benefit that compares favorably with that for a worker who has previously retired and preserves a greater degree of control and flexibility for Congress to increase the benefit in the future. The price-indexing method would guarantee a benefit amount that is protected against inflation. Moreover, the benefits for future retirees would tend to increase even without future congressional action because of the rise in workers' productivity. Congress can further raise the benefits in light of the needs of retired people and the economic, social, and demographic conditions prevailing at that time.

The wage-indexing method, on the other hand, would make benefit levels fully automatic. These automatic adjustment provisions establish benefits at a higher level and thus leave less financial flexibility for congressional control. Belief in the achievability of these promised higher levels of benefits without large tax increases requires a strong faith in the reliability of forecasts about future economic and demographic conditions.

In [table 5.3] are shown cost comparisons using the intermediate assumptions of the 1976 Trustees Report. The price-indexing method produces expenditures that are relatively level as a percentage of taxable payroll. But the wage-indexing method produces expenditures that require substantially greater tax payments from future generations of workers.

TABLE 5.3
COMPARISON OF OASDI LONG-RANGE COST
(In percent)

	EXPENDITURES AS PERCENT OF TAXABLE PAYROLL[1]	
	PRICE-INDEXING METHOD USING THE PANEL'S FORMULA	WAGE-INDEXING METHOD USING PRESIDENT FORD'S FORMULA
1976	10.8	10.8
1980	10.6	10.7
1990	10.5	11.8
2000	10.0	12.4
2010	10.0	13.4
2020	11.5	16.5
2030	12.5	18.9
2040	11.9	18.9
2050	11.3	18.8

1. One percent of taxable payroll equals $8 billion in 1977.

3. Unequal treatment of people retiring at different times. The price-indexing formula provides that retirement benefits will be protected against inflation. It leaves financial flexibility for Congress to give whatever periodic general benefit increases that appear reasonable from time to time for everyone: currently retired people and workers retiring in the future. [pp. 7-9]

Document 5.9   Congressional Budget Office, Options, March 1967

ALTERNATIVES FOR THE SHORT RUN

The basic issue is whether there is an immediate need for remedial action or whether there is time to develop a remedy adequate to solve both the short- and long-term problems. Here are some of the alternatives that could be considered.

Any action could be delayed for a year or two. Arguments for this approach include the fact that current estimates indicate a substantial, although significantly diminished, reserve at the end of fiscal year 1981. In addition it is possible that any tax increase in fiscal year 1977 would tend to retard economic recovery. . . . However, should the current estimates prove too optimistic, tax and benefit adjustments could still be made in a year or two without endangering the future stability of the funds. A delay would also provide time for a better assessment of the short-term financial condition of the funds and for the development of a short-term plan that would be consistent with long-term considerations. In the end this could be a better way to restore public confidence than numerous short-run adjustments.

Limited changes could be made in the tax structure to eliminate the trust funds' short-term deficits. Arguments which favor an increase in taxes now include the fact that current economic assumptions may be too optimistic and that public confidence would be improved if action were taken now to increase the reserve fund above currently projected levels. In addition there may be unforeseen outlay increases from the trust funds for which no contingency has been made. Increasing the tax *rate* would distribute the burden to all taxpayers proportionately.[26] Any increase in the tax rate of roughly .25 percent or more would balance the reserves in the funds over the period 1976-81. An argument against tax rate increases now, in addition to those cited in favor of a delay, is that taxes are already high and an increase would fall most heavily on lower-income working families.

An alternative to higher tax rates would be an increase in the wage base, i.e., the maximum wage subject to social security taxes. The short-term deficit could be eliminated if the wage base were raised higher than the currently scheduled increases. This alternative would redistribute the tax burden towards higher-income workers. One could argue that higher-income workers

---

DOCUMENT 5.9: Congressional Budget Office, *Budget Options for Fiscal Year 1977: A Report to the Senate and House Committees,* March 15, 1976 (Washington, D.C.: U.S. Government Printing Office, 1976).

26. Only if *all* wages were covered would the increase distribute the burden proportionately. The proposed increase would make the tax more regressive, or the total program less progressive [author's note].

can more easily bear this additional burden, which would be at no greater rate than that paid by lower-income workers and which would relieve lower-income individuals of any additional deductions from their wages. On the other hand, the higher wage base would generate higher benefits in the future because benefits are tied to taxable wages. Therefore, increasing the wage base would increase the long-term deficit because future costs would be greater than future revenues. The possibility that this alternative could have adverse effects on private investment markets and on private capital formation should also be considered.

Selective reductions in benefit levels represent another means of dealing with the short-term deficit. What is contemplated here are prospective reductions, not reductions in benefit levels to current beneficiaries nor limiting or "capping" cost-of-living increases. These reductions could include *(a)* requiring a test for financial dependence as a condition for benefits to spouses and survivors; and, *(b)* limiting minimum benefits to current-dollar levels. These changes would reduce social security outlays by $300 million in fiscal year 1977 and $1.2 billion in fiscal year 1981. As a short-term measure selective benefit reductions would not provide sufficient savings unless the reductions were very substantial. Furthermore, this course of action could create hardships among future beneficiaries.

A grant from general revenues offers still another approach for dealing with fund deficits. This alternative would not require any shift in the tax rate or additional shifts in the wage base; nor would it require increases or decreases in benefit levels. On the other hand, it might be difficult to ensure that general revenue grants would be only a temporary measure; if they became a permanent fixture, a basic change would have occurred in the heretofore self-financing structure of the social security program.

Borrowing authority from the general fund. To the extent that the crisis is only short term, a limited authorization to cover temporary deficits without using long-term measures could be provided to the trustees of the funds to borrow funds from the Treasury. Since such borrowing would be used only in the event of actual depletion, it would permit the system to retain its self-financing structure. Given the current situation, this alternative could be retained as a safety valve to be used if needed. In the meantime a sound program of long-range changes in the benefit and tax structures could be developed.

THE PRESIDENT'S BUDGET

The President's budget contains a number of proposed changes in the social security system that are aimed primarily at eliminating the short-term deficit in the trust fund. Foremost among these changes is an increase in the social security (OASDI) tax from 9.9 percent to 10.5 percent. Individuals earning median wages would pay $36 more in 1977 than they would pay under current law. This tax increase would add $3.5 billion in income to the funds in 1977, and $9.9 billion in 1981. Rather than falling to $30 billion or 25 percent of outlays, the reserves in the OASDI funds would rise from $45 billion in 1976 to $72.7 billion or 60 percent of outlays by 1981.

The President also proposes phasing out, over a four-year period, the benefits that since 1965 have been accorded to beneficiaries' children, 18 to 22, who are attending school. Similar provisions of the veterans benefit program, railroad retirement, and other programs would not be affected. This change would affect 581,000 beneficiaries. The savings to the trust funds from this change have been estimated by the Administration to be $283 million in the first year rising to $1.4 billion the fourth year. The President's budget message also proposes changing the formula by which benefits are computed to correct overcompensation of future beneficiaries for inflation, but the details of the proposal have not yet been provided.

The budgetary impact of the President's proposals are summarized below [figures represent billions of dollars, fiscal years]:

	1977	1978	1979	1980	1981
Additional income from taxes	3.5	5.6	6.9	8.2	9.9
Savings from benefit reductions	0.8	1.5	1.8	2.1	2.6
Increase to funds	4.4	7.1	8.7	10.3	12.5

Indexing of Benefits

The Advisory Council recommended correcting the 1972 error of counting double any inflation in computing benefits of future retirees by wage indexing. The Consultant Panel recommended using only price indexing. The two sets of recommendations agreed that benefits of persons once retired should be automatically increased as the Consumer Price Index increases. A concise objection to this latter procedure was written by Gabriel Hauge, an economist, in his dissent to the 1971 Advisory Council's recommendations:

> The Council's recommendation that social security cash benefit levels be automatically adjusted upward to keep pace with the cost of living

leaves me with deep concern, because such automatic adjustment would make the control of price inflation even more difficult than it already is.

One-eighth of the total population of the Nation, and fully 21 percent of the voting age population, receive retirement, survivors, or disability insurance benefits. To insulate so large a group from the cost of inflation with respect to their social security benefits would surely undermine the public's willingness to support the self-restraint and sometimes painful policies that are necessary to curb inflation. Of even more importance is the virtual certainty that the adoption of an "escalator clause" for social security benefit payments would give additional support to the already insistent demands for inflation protection through escalation in a whole range of other private contracts. I do not see how we, as a Nation, can wage a successful battle against inflation by automatically adjusting to it.

If the issue were simply that of protecting those who cannot protect themselves from the consequences of inflation, escalation of benefits would be the easy answer. But there are other considerations. First, the record of the past twenty years is that the Congress has not only adjusted benefits to compensate for changes in the cost of living, it has much more than compensated for price increases. There is no reason to believe that the Congress will be less responsible in the future. Second, the ironic fact is that those least able to protect themselves—precisely the groups receiving social security benefits— are the people most hurt by the acceptance of inflation as a fact of life. Approximately four million retired workers are presently getting benefits under private pension plans, equal to about 30 percent of the retired workers receiving social security benefits; many more retired people have supplemental income in the form of fixed income investments; and a very large number of disabled persons and widows and children have similar sources of fixed income. The hardship that inflation imposes upon these people, in my opinion, far outweighs the marginal benefits that automatic adjustment to inflation would confer upon other social security beneficiaries.

But most important is the pervasive effect that acceptance of inflation through income escalation would have upon our society. With the passage of time, more and more of the self-imposed disciplines that have made possible our unique social, political, and economic structure seem to be eroding. I regard it as a great mistake to accelerate that process.[27]

---

27. Gabriel Hauge, *1971 Advisory Council on Social Security: Reports on the Old-Age, Survivors, and Disability Insurance and Medicare Programs* (Washington, D.C.: U.S. Government Printing Office, 1973), p. 104.

To this, I add that if all social security benefits are increased as the cost of living rises, then the non-indexed majority of the labor force bears both a higher inflation and higher social security taxes to support these benefits.

Under the Consultant Panel's proposal to use a price-index method and not a wage-index method, replacement ratios of retirement benefits to average earnings would tend to decline whenever increases in wage rates are greater than increases in prices or, in other words, when there is a real wage gain or increase in productivity. Under the Advisory Council's wage-index proposal, replacement ratios in these circumstances would be constant.

Thus, the Consultant Panel's proposal would permit some uncommitted monies to accumulate over several years of growth in the real national income. Congress could then legislate an increase in benefits without having to increase the taxes, or it could maintain the trust fund at a higher level in anticipation of the demographic squeeze as the birth rate falls. The panel's proposal lets Congress remain in control of the redistribution of any increase in real national income. In contrast, the wage-indexing would produce an automatic redistribution, in order to maintain the existing replacement ratios of retirement benefits to earnings at different income levels.

Taxation of Benefits

The part of earned income that is automatically removed from an individual's paycheck and sent to the government for payment of one-half of social security taxes is taxed when earned, while deductions from payroll for private pensions are not taxed when earned but taxed upon receipt. The latter is also true of the matching payroll social security tax paid by the employer. The statutory law does not state that social security benefits, or any part of the benefits, are exempt from income taxes. This is apparently an administrative interpretation.

If all social security tax payments were exempt from income taxation when earned, and all social security benefits taxed upon receipt of benefits in the same fashion as private pensions, several benefits would ensue. Younger individuals would enjoy a slight lessening of tax burdens, and older persons would be encouraged to work beyond early retirement ages. Low-income aged would not have to pay additional taxes upon receipt of benefits, but those with higher incomes would. This would increase the equity of the system.

Document 5.10   Advisory Council on Social Security, Subcommittee on Financing, Minutes, September 1974 [excerpt]

The consultants[28] were asked to comment on the idea of a substantial general revenue contribution to the cash benefits program, possibly to help finance those aspects of the program that might be considered to be primarily designed for social adequacy ("welfare") purposes. Mr. Trowbridge said that the consultants had discussed the question of a general revenue contribution as a way of dealing with the actuarial deficit but that none of them is prepared to make such a recommendation solely on technical or economic grounds and that some are strongly opposed to it.

The Subcommittee considered the possibility that the Council as a whole might want to deal with the question of a general revenue contribution and the broad social and political aspects of the question. The consultants were asked if any of them wished to suggest economic or technical reasons why they did not advocate the broad use of general revenues in the OASDI program. Mr. Feldstein said that one reason for this view was that it was felt that whatever economic problems that were thought to arise because of the payroll tax might best be dealt with as a matter of general tax policy through the income tax system. It was noted that proposals to use general revenues to help finance OASDI are frequently linked with proposals to make the social security tax less regressive or to eliminate it for low-paid workers or for everyone. It was thought that the question of tax burden should be addressed through the income tax system, including—at least in theory—a negative income tax. Similarly any effect the payroll tax might have with regard to the relative value of capital and labor income might best be handled as a matter of general tax policy. [p. 3]

Document 5.11   Martin B. Tracy on Financing Social Security in Other Countries [excerpts]

In 1973, a total of 105 countries had some kind of old-age, survivors, and invalidity insurance program. The scope and organization, size of benefits, and type of financing are far from uniform among them. In the major earnings-related pension plans, the source of funds is primarily or exclusively the payroll tax for the regular pension. In addition a government subsidy may make up for deficits or more often help pay for means-tested benefits, for exemption of low-income earners from the payroll tax, and for other special categories. [p. 3]

DOCUMENT 5.10: Quadrennial Advisory Council on Social Security, 1975, Subcommittee on Financing, *Minutes,* September 4, 1974, p. 3.

28. Economists and actuaries.

DOCUMENT 5.11: Martin B. Tracy, "Payroll Taxes under Social Security Programs: Cross-National Survey," *Social Security Bulletin* (38), December 1975.

Countries with a unified national system that covers almost the entire labor force are in the minority. They include Israel, Japan, the Netherlands, Switzerland, the United Kingdom, and the United States. [p. 4]

Most social security programs are financed primarily by payroll tax deductions. A survey that focused on the payroll tax characteristics of all social security programs in five industrial countries and on old-age, invalidity, and survivors insurance in seven industrial countries found that combined employee-employer contributions range from about 10 percent of covered earnings to a high of more than 70 percent. The wide disparity reflects differences in social objectives and benefit levels and a variety of program and payroll tax patterns. [p. 3; original in italics]

The term 'social security' itself has no universal definition but usually includes five major types of programs: old-age, invalidity, and survivors insurance; sickness and maternity insurance (medical and hospital insurance, cash sickness payments for temporary disability, and cash maternity benefits); work-injury compensation; unemployment insurance; and family allowances (cash payments for families with children).[29] A national social security system may include a combination of some or all of these programs. The revenue source for the programs varies from country to country, with the method of financing depending on the system's approach to the providing of benefits— that is, whether they are employment-related, universal, or means-tested.

The focus of the article, however, is basically on old-age, invalidity, and survivors insurance.

"Social security" refers here to programs established by government statutes that insure individuals against interruption or loss of earning power and for certain special expenditures arising from marriage, birth, or death. Of the three broad approaches used in providing social security benefits, the employment-related is most dependent upon the payroll tax for financing and that will be discussed here primarily.

Employment-related systems base eligibility for pensions and other periodic payments directly or indirectly on length of employment or self-employment, or, for family allowances and work injury insurance, on existence of the employment relationship itself. The amount of individual benefit is usually related to the level of earnings before any of these contingencies caused the earnings to cease. Such programs are financed entirely or largely from the payroll tax by employers, employees, or both, and are usually compulsory for expressly defined employee and employer categories. Such systems are generally referred to as social insurance systems.

---

29. Social Security Administration, Office of Research and Statistics, *Social Security Programs Throughout the World, 1974*, Research Report No. 44, 1973 (Washington, D.C.: U.S. Government Printing Office, 1973). Data in this article are based largely on the 1973 edition.

The differing benefit levels are also important to consider in comparing payroll tax rates. The pension may vary from 20 percent of final earnings in one system to almost 70 percent in another.

The wide variety of programs from country to country produces great variation in payroll taxes [table 5.4]. Several of the European systems have a combined employee-employer payroll tax that goes as high as 50 percent of earnings. Some developing countries may also approach this level (Chile and Uruguay). At the other end of the scale is Canada, with a total average contribution rate of about 10 percent of earnings. The combined total employee-employer payroll tax in the United States is 14.60 percent for all social security programs.

It should be pointed out that to say that one country has a 10-percent payroll tax and another has a 70-percent rate may have little meaning, unless the programs financed by the taxes are equivalent. Each country may have a different mix of programs. One system, for example, may have a costly family allowance program and national health insurance; another may not have these programs but includes an extensive national program of means-tested benefits in its social security system.

The relative size of the total payroll tax, whether in the upper or lower range, depends basically on how many programs a country has and how extensive they are. The systems of five countries—Italy, Japan, the Netherlands, Spain, and Switzerland—are examined here to show program differences and the payroll tax structure [table 5.5].

The payroll tax rates for old-age, invalidity, and survivors insurance programs are closely related to the extent and amount of benefits provided. The modest portion of previous earnings replaced by pensions in Switzerland and Japan, for example, is paralleled by a low tax in both countries.

In Switzerland, reliance on private pensions to provide benefits to supplement those of the Federal program led to relatively low social security benefits and correspondingly low payroll tax rates. In Japan, private pension programs also play a role in compensating for the low level of the benefits payable under the national programs; specifically, they take care of the interim period between 55—the traditional retirement age—and age 60 when Federal pensions become payable.[30]

Higher tax rates are usually found in systems where benefit amounts are designed to replace a high proportion of previous earnings. In Italy, for example, because of the relatively low wages the program provides ultimately for an income-replacement rate that goes as high as 74 percent of the average earnings of the highest 3 of the latest 5 years worked. A high payroll tax rate is necessary, in turn, to meet the cost of the replacement rate in the absence of other major sources of revenue.

---

30. Paul Fisher, "Major Social Issues: Japan, 1972," *Social Security Bulletin,* March 1973, pp. 3-15.

TABLE 5.4
EMPLOYEE-EMPLOYER PAYROLL TAX RATES (PERCENT) BY TYPE OF PROGRAM, SELECTED COUNTRIES, 1973

Country	For All Social Security Programs			For Old-Age, Invalidity, and Survivors Insurance[1]		
	TOTAL	EMPLOYEE	EMPLOYER	TOTAL	EMPLOYEE	EMPLOYER
Austria	34.80	13.40	21.40	17.70	8.75	8.75
Belgium	39.85	10.40	29.45	14.00	6.00	8.00
Canada	10.00	4.70	5.30	3.60	1.80	1.80
Federal Republic of Germany	31.20	14.35	16.85	18.00	9.00	9.00
France	39.15	6.64	32.51	8.75	3.00	5.75
Italy	54.16	7.05	47.11	20.65	6.90	13.75
Japan[2]	17.59	7.35	10.24	6.40	3.20	3.20
Netherlands	51.40	24.00	27.40	19.80	14.55	5.25
Norway[3]	25.90	9.20	16.70	25.90	9.20	16.70
Spain	70.82	10.05	60.77	19.00	5.00	14.00
Sweden[2]	23.70	9.65	14.05	16.18	5.68	10.50
Switzerland	24.32	6.75	17.57	8.60	4.30	4.30
United Kingdom[2]	13.46	6.57	6.89	12.47	6.00	6.47
United States	14.60	5.85	8.75	9.70	4.85	4.85

1. Includes financing for some programs in addition to old-age, invalidity, and survivors insurance in the Netherlands, Norway, Spain, and the United Kingdom. Excludes financing for certain programs in Belgium and France that are covered by separate taxes under other programs.

2. Includes rates based on a percentage of average earnings in manufacturing.

3. Includes 3.8-percent tax on income and 5.47 percent of pension-producing income.

SOURCE: Based on *Social Security Programs Throughout the World, 1973* (U.S. Department of Health, Education, and Welfare, Social Security Administration, 1973); and *Yearbook of Labour Statistics* (Geneva: International Labor Organization, 1973), pp. 482-83 and 577-82.

TABLE 5.5

**MAXIMUM EMPLOYEE-EMPLOYER PAYROLL TAX RATES (PERCENT),
BY TYPE OF PROGRAM, FIVE COUNTRIES, 1973**

COUNTRY AND PROGRAM	PAYROLL TAX RATES		
	TOTAL	EMPLOYEE	EMPLOYER
Spain	70.82	10.05	60.77
Old-age, invalidity, and survivors insurance	19.00	5.00	14.00
Sickness and maternity	20.65	4.00	16.65
Italy	54.16	7.05	47.11
Old-age, invalidity, and survivors insurance	20.65	6.90	13.75
Sickness and maternity	14.61	0.15	14.46
Netherlands	51.40	24.00	27.40
Old-age, invalidity, and survivors insurance[1]	19.80	14.55	5.25
Sickness and maternity	18.60	5.45	13.15
Switzerland	24.32	6.75	17.57
Old-age, invalidity, and survivors insurance	8.60	4.30	4.30
Sickness and maternity[2]	2.00	2.00	0.00
Japan	17.59	7.35	10.24
Old-age, invalidity, and survivors insurance	6.40	3.20	3.20
Sickness and maternity	7.00	3.50	3.50

1. Employees contribute 12.00 percent of wages for old-age and survivors benefits and 2.55 percent for invalidity benefits. Employers contribute 5.25 percent of payroll only towards invalidity benefits.

2. Estimated average rate; actual rates vary with insurance fund.

Another major reason for high payroll tax rates is the use of old-age, invalidity, and survivors insurance contributions to finance the sickness, work-injury, or other benefits. This practice is common in systems where cash benefits for disability resulting from work-related or non-work-related accidents or illness are lumped together, as in the Netherlands and Spain. In some cases the size of the payroll tax rate is also affected by the use of Government subsidies to help finance all or various provisions of the program.

Payroll-tax variations are greater in the health area than in any other. The list of possible differences is long. In most industrial countries the major component of sickness and maternity programs is national health care that covers the cost of medical services and hospitalization. Where health care is provided directly through Government-owned-and-operated hospital facilities and salaried medical practitioners, the rates tend to be high, generally because this type of system is funded entirely (Spain) or primarily (Italy) by payroll taxes. Where the program is financed chiefly through Government subsidies, low payroll taxes prevail.

When most or all hospital and medical care fees are covered by federally controlled, semi-independent insurance funds, the size of the tax varies with the degree of Government subsidization. That is, in countries financing comprehensive health care programs almost exclusively through compulsory contributions (the Netherlands), the tax rate is high. In Switzerland the sickness insurance funds are heavily subsidized and, in general, do not assess a high premium from their members.

The payroll tax rate is also related to the degree to which health care costs are shared by the patients and the insurance program. Italy, the Netherlands, and Spain—the countries requiring the least amount of cost sharing (coinsurance) by the patient—have the highest tax rates. To increase revenue intake and help reduce program expenditures by discouraging overuse of available services, Japan and Switzerland require the patient to pay most or some of the services covered. Such cost sharing is usually in the form of a fee for service or a percentage of the actual cost for medicines, appliances, or laboratory tests.

The type and extent of medical services covered by a program also affect the size of the tax rate. Countries that pay for full dental care, health-spa treatment, or drugs require additional revenue to cover their cost. Conversely, excluding such items as laboratory tests, appliances, or transportation to medical facilities reduces the cost of the program and the need for revenue.

An additional factor in the size of the payroll tax may be the use of the tax revenue to fund other programs. A significant portion of the tax revenue under the sickness and maternity program in the Netherlands and Spain, for example, is used to finance short-term work-injury payments.

The duration of the benefits, both for health care and the cash allowances, must also be considered. Health care coverage ranges from 6 months in Italy to no limit at all in the Netherlands, Japan, and Switzerland. Cash sickness benefits range from 6 months in Italy and Japan to 24 months in Switzerland for some of the insurance funds. The duration of cash maternity benefits ranges from 10 weeks in Switzerland to 31 weeks in Italy.

[Table 5.5] reflects these various factors. The data show that Switzerland and Italy, both of whom have been debating for some years the need to reorganize their health care benefits into a unified national system, are the only countries in which the payroll tax rate for sickness and maternity programs is lower than that for old-age, invalidity, and survivors insurance. The rates in the other three countries, which do have national systems of health care, are highest in this field, followed by those for old-age, invalidity, and death.

Document 5.12   Social Security Administration, *Social Security Programs Throughout the World*, 1975 [excerpts]

Financing

In general, payroll tax rates were increased between 1973 and 1975 to cover the cost of higher benefit amounts and additional programs. During this period, the payroll tax rate went up for one or more programs in 33 countries. More taxes also became payable where the ceiling amount of earnings subject to payroll contributions was raised or eliminated in 27 countries.

General revenue financing was introduced for the first time in a number of countries to cover increased expenditures for particular programs. This includes new government contributions to the unemployment program in Chile; old-age, sickness, and maternity programs in Egypt; and the work-injury program in Egypt and Thailand. [p. xii]

There are normally three sources of revenue for financing old-age, disability, and survivor programs—a percentage of covered wages or salaries paid by the worker, a percentage of covered payroll paid by the employer, and in many countries a government contribution.

Almost all pension programs under social insurance (as distinct from provident fund or universal systems) are financed from at least two of these sources. Slightly more than half of them have tripartite financing, deriving their funds from all three sources. Among those with bipartite financing, employer-employee contributions are the norm. These contributions are usually related to earnings, the amount levied being determined by applying a fixed percentage to the salaries or wages of covered individuals up to a certain maximum. This percentage may be the same for both, although in most countries the employer pays a larger share. A few countries, notably in Eastern Europe, provide for employer contributions but do not require employees to contribute, except insofar as they pay taxes which support the government's general revenue contribution to social insurance.

The government's contribution may be derived from general revenue or, less frequently, from special earmarked or excise taxes (e.g., on tobacco, gasoline, or alcoholic beverages). It may be used in different ways—to defray

DOCUMENT 5.12: U.S. Department of Health, Education, and Welfare, Social Security Administration, *Social Security Programs Throughout the World, 1975*, Research Report No. 48 (Washington, D.C.: U.S. Government Printing Office, 1974), pp. xii, xiii, and xiv.

a portion of all expenditures such as the cost of administration, to make up deficits, or even to finance the whole cost of a program. Subsidies may be provided in the form of a lump sum or an amount to make up the difference between receipts from employer-employee contributions and the total cost of the system. A number of countries with social insurance systems reduce or, in some cases, eliminate contributions for the lowest wage earners, their benefits being financed entirely from general revenue or sometimes by the employer.

The rate of contribution as apportioned between the sources of financing may be identical or progressive, increasing with the size of the wage, or according to wage class. In countries where universal and earnings-related systems exist side by side, and the demogrant or universal benefit is not financed entirely by the government, separate rates may exist for each program. Other countries levy flat-rate contributions in the form of fixed monetary amounts per week to finance basic pension insurance programs. These amounts are uniform for all insured workers of the same age and sex, regardless of their earnings level. Often a distinction is made with respect to the self-employed by requiring that they contribute at a higher rate than wage and salary workers, thereby making up for the employer's share. For administrative purposes, a number of countries assess a single overall social insurance contribution covering several contingencies. Not only pensions, but also other types of social security benefits are financed from this contribution, such as sickness, work-injury, unemployment, or family allowances.

General revenue financing as the sole source of income is found in some universal systems. Other universal systems are partly financed by contributions of the insured. The contribution of the resident or citizen is often expressed as a specified percentage of taxable income under the national tax program. General revenue finances all or part of the means-tested supplementary benefits in many countries. [pp. xiii-xiv]

Summary

President Carter's message to congress on May 9, 1977, was on financing of social security (see chapter nine). The Senate's Subcommittee on Social Security held hearings starting June 15, 1977. There was agreement on the need for legislative action, but disagreement as to the best course to ensure the financial integrity of the program without unduly increasing the tax burden.

6

DISSENTING STATEMENTS TO ADVISORY COUNCIL'S REPORT

STATEMENTS DISSENTING FROM
ADVISORY COUNCIL'S REPORTS

This chapter contains selected dissenting statements of members of the Advisory Council. Those which are included appear because of their subject. Omitted is a statement by Messrs. Byrnes, Faulkner, Scanlon and Smith on "disability benefits," which is complex and involves solely issues not covered specifically in this book. For the dissent involving use of the Medicare, Part A, trust fund, see document 5.5. For the dissent against liberalization of the retirement test, see document 7.2. All quoted statements are given in their entirety, even though this may involve some duplication.

Document 6.1   Supplementary Statement by Rita Ricardo Campbell

[*Author's Note.* Although this statement also addresses the different effects of the Social Security Act on men and women, it is quoted here in its entirety (as it was in the Council's printed Report) because its main thrust is towards a solution of the financial problems.]

During the several meetings of this Council, I have felt that we are tinkering at the edges of what was originally, in 1935, a rather simple program, but which has grown because of its many amendments so complex that even the well-informed citizen does not understand it. Additionally, over the 40 years since the initial passage of the Social Security Act, tremendous socio-economic changes have taken place, a whole new welfare system of benefits has been enacted, and other tax laws with which OASDI taxes interrelate have been amended.

Although I view any change in OASDI benefits which add to present costs as undesirable in view of the short-run and especially the long-run actuarial

DOCUMENT 6.1: U.S. Congress, House, Committee on Ways and Means, *Reports of the Quadrennial Advisory Council on Social Security,* 94th Cong., 1st sess., H.D. 94-75, March 10, 1975 (Washington, D.C.: U.S. Government Printing Office, 1975), pp. 73-80.

imbalance, which is based on what I believe to be over-optimistic assumptions,[1] I have voted as a Council member to recommend some changes in benefits which, relative to the system as a whole, have minor cost impact. My reason in one instance was to eliminate an inequity which exists because of differences in entitlement between dependents of men workers for secondary benefits and dependents of women workers. My reason in another instance was to improve the social adequacy of the system by making less stringent entitlement to long-term permanent disability benefits for those persons 55 years and over.

[Treatment of Married Women Who Work]

The Council's refusal to recommend "fairer" tax treatment of the twenty-two millions of married women who work and many of whom earn little and yet pay OASDI taxes on what are low earnings[2] is an example of the dangers in "tinkering" rather than restructuring Social Security into a logical part of the U.S. total system of taxes and social benefits. There are hundreds of thousands of couples, the precise numbers are not known, where both the husband and wife work, earn relatively low wages and pay a tax on those wages and who when they retire at age 65 receive not more but *less* than other couples where the husband has worked and earned the equal of the two-worker family wages and his wife has not worked. For example, as stated in the Report of the Subcommittee on the Treatment of Men and Women, a husband with average, annual earnings of $4,000 and a wife with average, annual earnings of $4,000, each receive $228.50 a month on retirement at age 65, or a monthly total of $457.00, which is $17.50 less than $474.50 or one and one-half the monthly primary benefit payable to a married worker with average, annual earnings of $8,000 and a spouse who has not worked in covered employment. Further, this situation also exists for comparable families with average annual earnings of $6,000.

[INEQUITIES IN RETIREMENT BENEFITS.]

To cite a more general example, consider the difference in benefits upon retirement for two families: Family A, where the wife works and earns 40% each year of the family income, the husband 60%; and Family B, where the wife does not work. Since the social security program began, the annual earnings of the two families are equal and year-by-year are equal to the maximum, annual earnings tax base which is also used to compute benefits. If it is assumed that all four individuals are 65 during the first six months of

1. See elaboration of this point on [p.183 ff.]

2. In 1973, the median earnings of full-time working women were 57% of the median earnings of full-time working men. (U.S. Census. CPS. P-60, No. 93, July 1974, p.2.)

1975, the husband in Family A would receive $226.50 monthly benefit and the wife, whose earnings were considerably less, $179.60 for a total monthly retirement benefit of $406.10. In Family B, where the husband alone has worked, he and his wife would receive a much greater monthly retirement benefit, the husband's primary of $316.30 plus one-half of this amount ("rounded") or $158.20, (a secondary benefit) for his "presumed dependent" wife, or $474.50 in total. For each year that Family B receives retirement benefits, it would receive $820.80 more (before automatic adjustments to take account of cost-of-living increases) than the two-worker family, Family A.

It is largely because of such anomalies as these which are inherent in the benefit structure that I argue for retirement benefits being paid on an individual basis, as well as OASDI taxes being collected on an individual basis. To argue that working, married women should not only contribute in large measure to the "social" benefits under social insurance, but should also actually in a family unit receive less than if she had never worked at all [and the identical total family income were earned by the husband] and paid substantial taxes is to me ethically unacceptable.

[WHO AMONG WORKING MARRIED WOMEN ARE A "SPECIAL GROUP"?]

The Council members fail to recognize the impact of the dramatic continuing increase in the numbers of married women who work, generally for low wages, and pay OASDI taxes on those wages, sometimes in preference to going on welfare or anticipating, when they are older, going on welfare. Many of these women pay higher OASDI taxes than income taxes. Many of the twenty-two million married working women (and generally also their husbands) are highly critical of the OASDI program because they know that they will not receive upon retirement or widowhood any more benefits than if they had not worked and paid taxes during their lifetime. They may know that they have protection for dependent children and for long-term disability, but feel that these tax payments are high "premiums" for such insurance. Since the vast majority of these women bear and raise children, they contribute to society in ways beyond what the usual single person does.

In those families where both husband and wife worked in 1973, the *differentials* in annual median income compared to families where only the husband worked, by age of head of household, were as [shown in Table 6.1].Obviously, married women contribute substantially to the family earnings. The life styles of their families are based on combined earnings, and it is the replacement ratio of combined family earnings, at least of low-paid workers, which the social security system should consider in determining replacement ratios (percentages of earnings replaced by social security benefits upon retirement) if it is claimed to have made some adaptation to the rapid socio-economic changes of the last 40 years.

TABLE 6.1
MEDIAN INCOME OF U.S. FAMILIES, 1973, WITH WORKING
AND NON-WORKING WIVES, BY HUSBAND'S AGE AND RACE

AGE, BY AGE OF HUSBAND	HUSBAND & WIFE	HUSBAND ONLY	DIFFERENCE IN FAMILY INCOME
Whites:			
25-34	$14,186	$11,967	$2,219
35-44	17,056	13,653	3,403
45-54	18,418	12,609	5,809
55-64	16,819	11,918	4,901
Negroes:			
25-34	$12,509	$8,528	$3,981
35-44	13,082	7,872	5,210
45-54	13,867	8,280	5,587
55-64	11,526	5,853	5,673

SOURCE: U.S. Census, P-60, No. 97, January 1975, table 74, p. 156.

The argument of the Council's majority that to give more individual equity to working married women is wrong because it would favor a "special group" (Report of the Council, Chapter 5, Sec. 3.1) indicates to me a surprising lack of awareness of today's socio-economic world—a world in which the majority of married women work.[3] [By March 1975, the largest percentage, 41 percent, of the 46 million husband-wife families had both husband and wife in the labor force. In 34 percent of these families only the husband was in the labor force. In 12 percent, no member was in the labor force, and in 8 percent the husband and another member of the family, and in 3 percent only the wife was in the labor force. The remaining 2 percent of families had persons in the labor force other than husband or wife.[4]]

There are other special groups which are smaller in number and for whom the Council has recommended that their benefits be liberalized, e.g., those over age 65 and under 72 who continue to work.

If among married women there is currently a special group, it may be that it is those non-working married women who become entitled in 1975 and later, to only secondary benefits often sizeable and based only on their husband's earnings. These women have not accumulated enough, or any, earnings credits to obtain a primary benefit based on their own earnings and many of

---

3. Mrs. Norwood concurs with the portion of this statement beginning with paragraph 3 and ending with this paragraph.

4. *Monthly Labor Review,* May 1976, p. 16.

them may have husbands who had high earnings from which savings were accumulated and also these women may enjoy other sizeable income as interest, rents and dividends. As the years go by, the number of women who have never worked in covered employment will decline. Of all aged wives of retired worker beneficiaries, the group entitled only to a secondary benefit, that is, one-half of their husband's primary retirement benefit because they are "presumed dependent," is estimated by SSA to fall to about 30-35% by 2020.[5] However, by 1970, 68% of women, ages 45-49, had already earned enough quarters of covered work to be insured for their own primary benefit. SSA's projection that 30-35% of aged wives of retired worker beneficiaries will be entitled to only secondary benefits by 2020 rather than earlier, as in 1990 or 1995, when women ages 45-49 would be old enough to be entitled to and be drawing benefits, depends on two major assumptions. These are the rate at which women already receiving a secondary benefit leave the rolls by death or other disqualification and the labor force participation rate of women in future years by marital status.

SSA actuaries, in projecting future costs of the system, assumed an increase for women by age groups of their labor force participation rate. For example, the percent of women in the labor force by selected age groups in 1970 (actual) and 1995 (estimated) is:[6]

Ages	1970 Actual	1995
45-59	55%	59%
50-54	54	58
55-59	49	53

In every case there is an estimated increase. [But the increase is not as great as the one actually observed for 1975. See chapter 5, above, section headed "Author's Update of Original Dissent."]

It is possible, depending on the assumptions used, that women who are entitled only to a secondary benefit—that is they did not work even intermittently and/or part-time to acquire 40 quarters of coverage, the equivalent of 10 years in covered employment— may be 30% or even less of all aged women whose husbands are receiving old-age benefits some years before 2020.

For example, an article in the *Social Security Bulletin*[7] states that, "More than half the women between ages 60 and 64 in 1970 were insured for benefits in their own right. Among women in their forties and early fifties in 1970, 2 in 3 were earning insured status at a rate that would qualify them for benefits when they reached retirement age."

---

5. Office of the Actuary, Social Security Administration.

6. Developed by the Office of the Actuary, Social Security Administration, for use in long-range cost estimates in the 1974 trustees' report (unpublished data).

7. Virginia Reno, "Women Newly Entitled to Retired-Worker Benefits. . . ," *Social Security Bulletin,* April 1973, p. 4.

[Two Interrelated Proposals]

My proposal is two-fold. The first part was supported by the Subcommittee on the Treatment of Men and Women (see Report Appendix B, pp. 147-148), but the second part was not. The proposal is (1) to help low-earning, married men and low-earning, married women by permitting a couple coming on the benefit rolls in the future an option in computing their retirement benefits to combine their earnings up to the taxable base (thus helping only low earners) when each of them has paid taxes on 10 years (40 quarters) of covered earnings during the last 20 years prior to retirement at a long-run cost of .20% of taxable payroll; and (2) to phase out gradually over a 30-year period (see Subcommittee Report, p. 146 for details) secondary, retirement benefits of an aged spouse (wife or husband). The secondary benefits of surviving spouses and children would be retained. The second part of the proposal would result in an estimated long-run savings of .39% of payroll. This estimate assumes that the following three recommendations initially made by the Council will be enacted and effective immediately.[8]

(1) The same rules of entitlement to secondary benefits would apply to men and women; (2) immediate universal coverage and (3) for those coming on the rolls in the future an immediate offset of a private pension earned in uncovered employment against secondary, retirement and survivor benefits of social security based on earnings of a spouse in covered employment. If either of the latter two recommendations are not enacted and the first one is enacted—as is likely to be the case, as note the finalized version of Chapter 7 of the Council's report points out that universal coverage will face many obstacles—then the savings would be somewhat greater than 0.39% of payroll. Actuarial data are not available covering the cases when all or some of these assumptions are dropped.

There are among the 8.8 million workers who are not currently covered, 3.6 million persons who work for state and local government, where legal problems probably would interfere with their rapid, compulsory coverage under social security.

The Council voted to recommend, without any phase-out period but merely prospectively, to treat as an offset against both the retirement and survivor's secondary benefits, based on the spouse's covered earnings, any pension earned by the other member of the couple which derives from work in non-covered employment. This recommendation would create a new inequity primarily to a particular class of married, working women and that is those wives whose husbands work in covered employment while they work in non-covered employment as in civil service or in many states as school teachers. The lack of a phase-out period gives virtually no time for these couples, some

---

8. Office of the Actuary, Social Security Administration.

of whom may be within ten or less years before retirement, to attempt to make up or recapture the proposed sudden loss in secondary benefits to the wife and benefits on which their retirement plans have been based.[9] This is an example of what "tinkering" with benefits, rather than restructuring the system to pay retirement benefits on an individual basis, may do.

[PHASING OUT SECONDARY RETIREMENT BENEFITS]

The second part of my proposal has a phase-out period of thirty years to avoid a comparable inequity to non-working, married women and it applies only to retired couples, not to the surviving spouse.

Under my proposal the secondary benefits to aged wives and/or husbands, without a dependent child in their care would be phased out at the end of 30 years. Thus, the largest savings impact would occur at a most favorable time to coincide with the timing, the year 2005, when the double impact of high costs of total benefits due to the relatively large number of World War II babies who will be retiring and collecting OASDI benefits, and concomitantly of fewer workers to pay these benefits as the relatively fewer births during the past several years enter the labor force, occurs.

The Finance Subcommittee and the Council's Reports reflect the estimate used in the 1974 Report of the Board of Trustees that the fertility rate will return to 2.1 babies per woman, the population replacement rate, by 1985. It is anticipated that the double impact of more beneficiaries and relatively fewer workers will increase the number of social security beneficiaries from 30 beneficiaries for every 100 workers to 45 beneficiaries for every 100 workers by 2025. In 1950 the ratio was 6 beneficiaries for every 100 workers.[10] If a fertility rate of 2.1 is not achieved by 1985, and there are good reasons to anticipate this, then the long-run actuarial imbalance will be considerably greater.

Because only a single set of assumptions, covering projected birth rates and price and wage increases, were presented by the Finance Subcommittee to the Council (and these are the same as in the 1974 Trustees' Report) rather than is more customary, a range of low, medium and high estimates, and the single set of assumptions was accepted by the Council as "reasonable," the underlying assumptions of the long-run projected deficit should be examined critically.

The three assumptions are: (1) an annual 5% increase in average money wages, (2) an annual 3% average increase in the Consumer Price Index and thus a 2% average rate of increase in real wages and (3) a 2.1 fertility rate by

---

9. Mrs. Norwood also concurs with the portion of this statement beginning with paragraph [3] on page [182] and ending with this sentence.

10. Subcommittee on Finance Report, February 3, 1975, U.S. Congress, House, *Reports of the Quadrennial Advisory Council. . .1975*, Appendix A, p. 98.

1985, which will remain constant at that level for the remainder of the 75 years.

If, however, 1.9 births per woman were the average fertility rate for the whole 75 years, the 2.98% actuarial imbalance would be 3.73% of taxable payroll. Additionally, without decoupling the system but with a steady annual rate of growth in real wages of only 1%, based on wages increasing at 5% and prices increasing at 4%, the long-run deficit may be as high as about 10% of taxable payroll.[11]

It is noted in the Finance Subcommittee Report of February 3, p.98, and also in Chapter 7 of the Council Report (Sec. 3.3) that, ". . .the demographic projection has an almost overwhelming effect on the costs of the system. . . . The change [by the Trustees of the funds in their 1974 Report] in population assumptions accounts for 63% of the total deficit and 76% of the increase in the deficit since the last actuarial review." (p. 98, "Deficit" is the long-run actuarial imbalance.)

The argument to support an assumption of 1.9 births rather than 2.1 births per female over the 75 year period follows. Because of the change in technology in respect to birth control, it is the woman, and not the man, who decides for the first time in history the number of children a woman will bear. Because of this factor, it is impossible to predict on the basis of experience, future birth rates, and the statistical data available appear to support this conclusion.

I attach as Exhibit A, a graph which gives birth rates by age of mother, 1945-1973, originally drawn on a "semi-log" scale,[12] but redrawn here on the normal scale to which most persons are accustomed and which does not compress the extreme drop, but rather makes clear the size of the drop from 1960 on in birth rates by age of mother. There is clearly a precipitous decline in birth rates for each of the five-year age brackets which the compression of the original chart tends to minimize.

Additionally, the February 1975, U.S. Census Bureau's *Population Estimates and Projections*[13] includes a range of estimated birth rates through the year 2025, one of which, Ser. III, is only 1.7 births per woman, in order "to provide a reasonable range in projections of future births." (p. 3)

My proposal supports the philosophy of a replacement ratio of earnings lost by retirement, but interpreted as replacement ratio of *family* earnings. Two-worker families gear their style of living to two incomes. The replacement of "head of household" earnings with an allowance for his dependents does not fit the facts of family structure in 1975. Married couples with only the

---

11. Office of the Actuary, Social Security Administration.
12. *Monthly Vital Statistics Report* 23 (1975), no. 11 (January 30), Supplement, p. 3.
13. Series P-25, no. 541.

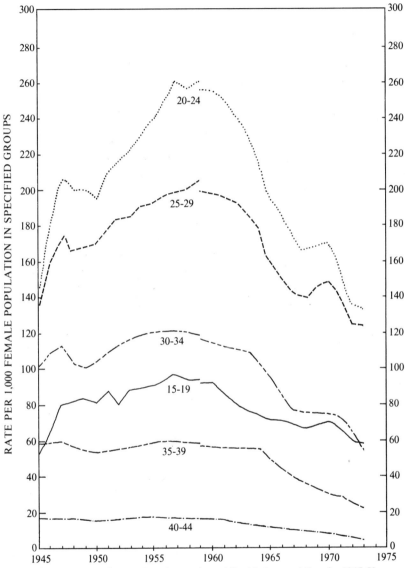

EXHIBIT A:
BIRTH RATES BY AGE OF MOTHER, UNITED STATES, 1945-73

RATE PER 1,000 FEMALE POPULATION IN SPECIFIED GROUPS

20-24

25-29

30-34

15-19

35-39

40-44

(Beginning 1959, trend lines are based on registered live births; trend lines for 1945-59 are based on live births adjusted for underregistration.)

husband working no longer comprise the majority of families in those age brackets where it is usual to work.

The advantages of the two proposals as a package would be to give greater equity to married women who work and eventually, as the phase-out is completed, greater equity to singles who work, pay the same tax and have no dependents. It is my belief that because of the continuing trends in the increasing labor force participation rate of women, the declining labor force participation rate of men, the increase in divorce and decrease in marriages, and the decline in the birth rate, it is advisable to begin now to restructure the social security system to adapt to these socio-economic changes rather than wait for dissatisfaction with the system to so increase as to force hurriedly changes which may be undesirable.

The current system, coupled with federal income taxes, discourages women from working outside of the home and also discourages private savings which provide the financing for investment needed for growth of national real income. As the ratio of beneficiaries to workers increases, it will create a need for more revenues to finance social security benefits, but from taxes on relatively fewer workers or producers. Then the undesirable effect of the loss of economic product to society because of penalties imposed by the tax system, and especially by OASDI taxes on married women, will become more obvious. It may be in the area of inducing a higher labor force participation rate by women, rather than in attempting to extend normal retirement age to 68 years, that long-run solutions may be successfully sought.

Document 6.2   Statement of Rudolph T. Danstedt

The Council has made three major findings and recommendations and several minor ones:

1. I strongly support the statement on the philosophy and objectives of social security in which the Council unanimously endorsed the major principles of the contributory, wage-related social security program.

2. I support the Council's recommendation that the method of computing social security benefits be changed to a system guaranteeing that the protection for current workers is kept up-to-date automatically at least as high as future increases in the level of earnings and that, as in the present system, benefits once payable would be kept up-to-date with increases in prices. I support this recommendation, however, with the understanding that the "wage replacement ratios" established under the new system will be those pertaining under present law after the updating of benefits in June of 1975.

DOCUMENT 6.2: U.S. Congress, House, *Reports of the Quadrennial Advisory Council* . . . 1975, pp. 80-87.

3. I strongly disagree with the Council's recommendation that the hospitalization insurance part of Medicare be changed from a program of contributory social insurance to one which would be entirely supported by general revenues and that the contributions now earmarked for hospital insurance be shifted to the support of the cash benefit program.

The Council made several other recommendations which, however, compared with the above recommendations are of lesser significance.

While agreeing that the definition of disability for older workers (55-64) should be liberalized, the Council's liberalization of the disability definition does not address itself adequately to the older disabled worker in a job market that discriminates against the older worker. I support a definition under which older workers should be able to qualify for disability benefits if they are occupationally disabled, that is, if they can no longer engage in substantial gainful activity in their last regular occupation. These older occupationally disabled people are in a situation similar to that in which many people find themselves at age 65 when, because of their age, they cannot find job opportunities, and are in effect superannuated.

I disagree with further loosening up of the retirement test. Basically I strongly support the concept of social security as retirement insurance. The present retirement test with its automatic adjustment for an increase as wages rise is a liberal one. It allows individuals to have more in total income—social security benefits plus earnings—the more an individual works and earns. Under present law some people earning as much as $8,000 or $9,000 a year may still be eligible for partial social security benefits.

I see no good reason to incur extra costs for the program to favor further those who are fortunate enough to be able to continue at work, particularly the self-employed and professional people and higher-paid salary and wage workers who frequently do not encounter the same age barriers to gainful activity as other members of the labor force.

Abolishing Medicare as an Earned Right

I want to indicate in detail why we strongly disagree with the Council's recommendation to change the hospitalization part of Medicare from a program of contributory social insurance to one which would be entirely supported by general revenues, and shift the contribution now earmarked for hospital insurance to the support of the cash benefit program.

The charge to the Council from the Congress specified an examination of "The scope of coverage and adequacy of benefits and other aspects of the Program" including Title XVIII—Medicare. However, at an early stage of the Council's deliberations, the lateness of the Council's appointment which allowed only nine months for its study, and the extensive study presumably underway of national health insurance proposals, were presented as reasons for this Council excluding an examination of Medicare.

I agreed reluctantly with this decision because I believed that the Medicare program for older and disabled people should be improved in several important respects. I was and am now concerned with the financial burden on low and middle-income social security recipients of the $6.70 per month premium payment of Part B of Medicare which reduces their cash benefits approximately 5%. I support for financing purposes elimination of this premium by combining Part A (Hospital Insurance) and Part B (Supplementary Medical Insurance)—now financed through premiums and general revenues—of Medicare and the financing of Medicare by one-third contribution from employers, one-third contribution from employees, and one-third from the general revenues. Such a recommendation was endorsed by the 1970-1971 Advisory Council.

In spite of the fact that the Council has not studied the Medicare program, at its very last meeting the Council voted to fundamentally change the nature of the hospital insurance part of Medicare from a contributory social insurance system to a system which would be one entirely supported by general revenues. In contrast to the careful work of the Council and its staff on the cash benefit part of social security, the reasoning put forth in support of this recommendation shows a lack of serious attention and analysis. The notion that hospital insurance should be paid for entirely by general revenues because the medical benefits provided by the hospital insurance program vary according to the medical needs of the insured individual seems to be based on a misunderstanding of the nature of health insurance. What people are paying for under the Medicare program is "protection against a risk." The fact that some people may draw much more in the way of benefits than others is no more a reason to drop the contributory concept than it would be to drop the contributory concept in the case of the life insurance part of the program where the amount actually paid differs according to the age of the individual at death, the number of dependents, etc.

Moreover, the fact that the amount of protection under hospital insurance (as distinct from the value of benefits actually paid) does not vary by past earnings does not seem to us a significant reason for dropping the contributory principle. In hospital insurance it is the fact that those who earn more pay somewhat more for the same protection and the fact that more of the employer's contribution is used for the protection of the lower paid that introduces progressive principles into the program. In the cash benefit program this result is accomplished by the combination of a flat percentage contribution rate but a weighted benefit formula. In the Medicare program the progressive element is established by having the low-wage earner pay less for comparable protection.

I am greatly concerned that changing Medicare from a contributory social insurance program to one supported entirely by general revenues could well lead to the loss of the concept of earned right and to the possible introduction of an income or means test into the program.

Workers contribute toward hospital insurance with the clear understanding—amounting to a social compact with their government—that when retired or disabled with income down and the incidence of illness up—their hospital insurance costs will be paid as a matter of right.

It needs to be underlined that when Medicare was enacted the representatives of large groups of organized employees—the AFL — CIO and a wide range of international unions—supported the payroll contributions for hospital insurance as a guarantee that hospital insurance shall be an earned right. This continues to be their position.

If Medicare is to be supported entirely by the general taxpayer rather than in significant part by earmarked contributions from those who are to benefit from the protection, the question in the future will inevitably arise as to why general funds should go to pay for the hospitalization and physicians' bills of a selected group in the population—the elderly and disabled—regardless of whether or not a particular elderly or disabled person is entirely able to pay for the services on his own. Thus I fear that the recommendations of the majority could over time transform the Medicare social insurance program into a relief program. There is enough experience with the income-tested Medicaid program to predict what the implications of such a transformation would be for the perpetuation of a two-class system of medicine and in terms of undermining the dignity of the recipient.

If the protection that is now afforded the hospital insurance program by its contributory nature is destroyed, it is likely that it would become much easier to reduce the protection provided. In times of budgetary restriction it would be easier to propose and harder to restrict such money-saving proposals. Even today, this Administration is seeking to reduce the deficits in the unified budget by requiring the elderly and disabled to bear more of the cost of Medicare through cost-sharing. Thus I fear that the proposal to finance Medicare out of general revenues so as to use the hospital insurance contributions for the cash benefit program could easily result over time in the elderly being asked, in effect, to make up for the deficits in the cash benefits program through reduction in their health insurance protection.

Although the Council had not considered these matters or any other matters concerning the Medicare program, and operating under the pressure to conclude its affairs on its final meeting day, the Council seized on the hospital insurance contributions to finance the deficit in the OASDI program.

Recommendations for Improving the Financing Base for the Cash Benefit Program

Instead of sacrificing the Medicare program in order to improve the financing base for the cash benefit, I propose that the financing problems of the cash benefit program be faced directly.

That the outgo of the cash benefit programs should exceed income in the immediate future is not a cause for concern. The $46 billion in trust fund assets available to the OASDI program exist for just this purpose. The reserves should be drawn on in a period of recession like the present. What this means is that social security beneficiaries get more money to spend than is being deducted from worker's earnings as social security contributions, and today that is good for the economy.

The annual deficit, however, cannot be allowed to continue. To meet this deficit I propose first, that beginning in calendar year 1977 the maximum amount counted for the computation of benefits and for contributions—the wage base—should be raised above the approximately $16,800 that can be expected to be in effect in 1977 under present law. The economic impact of such an increase would not be felt until the fall of 1977 because it is not until then that any significant number of workers would have earnings that exceed the $16,800 figure that would be in effect in any event. The exact amount of the increase in the earnings base should be determined by whether it is to be done in one step or in several steps. One alternative is to increase the amount to $24,000 in 1977 and have it rise automatically from this figure as wages increase. Another possibility is to provide for more gradual increases, that is, a lesser increase for 1977, compensated for by larger increases later. It is of interest to note that the AFL—CIO Executive Council has endorsed moving the wage base up to $28,000 over a period of years.[14]

I propose, further, a tax on the employer's full payroll. A maximum on the benefit and contribution base for individual workers is appropriate since the amount that people pay and the amount that is credited to their record for benefit purposes should be tied together, and it would seem unreasonable under social insurance to compute benefits on the very high salaries earned by the top 2 percent or 3 percent of the wage-earning portion of the population. There is no similar need for a limitation on employer's payroll. The tax on employer's payroll is less now than contemplated in the original Social Security Act. There was then provided an ultimate combined employer tax rate for social security and unemployment compensation totalling 6 percent. Because of the lower proportion of wages now covered under the experience rating of unemployment compensation and the increased tax deductible advantages now available through corporate tax laws, the tax burden on employers is now significantly less than provided by the original law.

With a higher benefit and contribution base, the contribution schedule in present law would substantially over-finance the Medicare hospital insurance program for many years into the future. Consequently, it would be possible to allocate the 1978 scheduled increase of 0.2 percent of payroll to employees, and a like amount on employers, to the cash benefit program rather than to

---

14. Mrs Norwood concurs with this paragraph.

the hospital program. I propose that this be done.

The increase in the wage base I am proposing would return the system, partly, but not all the way, to the original program intent. In 1938, the first year for which there is adequate social security data (the social security system began to collect contributions in 1937), 97 percent of all the workers in the system had their full wages counted toward social security. Today, only 85 percent of the workers covered by the system have all of their earnings counted. To get back to the situations that existed at the time the program first went into effect would require an earnings base substantially in excess of what I propose, probably an earnings base in 1977 in excess of $30,000.

Although the Council adopted an increase in the tax base to $24,000 at its next to last meeting, because of a concern that an increase in the maximum earnings base would invade an area of protection which it was argued should be left to private pensions and individual savings, the Council at its last meeting rescinded this earlier decision. It was my view then and is now that an increase in the earnings base such as I have proposed would still leave substantial room for supplementation by private pension plans and savings. The replacement rate for the worker earning at the $24,000 maximum would be only about 35 percent.

Moreover, such a higher wage base obviates the necessity for an increase in the contribution rate—a position which I strongly favor—and imposes no additional cost on the middle level and lower paid workers, while providing increased protection for those who pay more. It is important to emphasize that the social security program provides a unique protection which offers the workers absolute assurance as to vesting, portability and receipt of benefits when they are due. Raising the maximum earnings base increases benefit protection for workers as well as contributes to the improved financing of the program. For example, if the maximum earnings base were increased to $24,000, a 55 year old worker earning the maximum amount would get nearly $125 a month more when he retired at 65 than he would if the earnings base were left as in present law. If he were 60 when the increased earnings base went into effect, he would get benefits at 65 of somewhat more than $50 a month above present law.

I share the Council's commitment to income programs supplementary to social security, effective private pensions (as well as individual insurance, savings and other investments) but I hold that we must also keep in mind that less than one-third of all older people now have supplementation from private pensions and even in the long run it is doubtful whether the proportion would exceed 50 percent. Maintaining the financial integrity and protection of the social security system is thus of paramount concern.

These steps that I propose—the increase in the maximum earnings base, a tax on the employer's total payroll and the reallocation of the 1978 contribution increase from hospital insurance to the cash benefit program—would solve what the Council has described as the short-run financing problem of the cash benefit program and carry the cash benefit program on a self-sufficient basis well into the late 1980's.

However, depending on what happens to wage and cost of living rates, a limited contribution may be required from the general revenues in the last decade of the century.

I propose, therefore, to meet this possible contingency by restoring to the Social Security law the provision for general revenue financing that existed from 1944–1950 as follows: "There is also authorized to be appropriated to the Trust Fund such additional sums as may be required to finance the benefits and payments provided for in this title."

The financing problem in the next century growing out of the likelihood of an increasing proportion of older people as compared to those of working age, will require a gradual introduction of a government contribution.

As I have indicated, I am opposed to solving the financial problems in social security through an increase in the contribution rates beyond those provided in present law. In place of further contribution rate increases beyond those presently scheduled, I believe that the government, as in other countries, should make a contribution to the social security program, not just for the hospital insurance part of Medicare but for the cash benefit program as well. Thus, in the long run, I see a social security system covering both cash benefits and health insurance financed partly by employer contributions, partly by employee contributions, and partly by contributions from the government in recognition of society's stake in a well-functioning social insurance program. While preserving the values inherent in contributory social insurance, such a tri-partite approach will make the financing of the system more progressive.

To recapitulate—I seek to deal responsibly with the OASDI deficit in the proposals we have presented, introducing at a later time the use of the general revenues when this is indicated. The Council's proposal does not only undermine the Medicare program, but adds $7–8 billion now to the government's deficit when this deficit is at an all time high. I believe this proposal is the more fiscally responsible one.

Social Security in the 21st Century

Whether or not there are financing problems for social security in the next century depends, under present law, not only on the future course of fertility rates but on what happens to wage and price increases over the next 75 years. I do not believe it is wise to place substantial reliance on any particular set of assumptions concerning the movement of wages and prices. The assumptions made in the 1974 Report of the Board of Trustees of an average increase of 5 percent in wages and an average increase of 3 percent in consumers' prices produces one level of deficit in the funds after the year 2000. An assumption of a 5 percent increase in wages and a 2 percent increase in the cost of living, on the other hand, would eliminate the deficit even with the fertility assumptions used in the Trustees' Report. Higher assumptions, such as an average increase of 6 percent in wages and 4 percent for the cost of living, as assumed in a recent study by a group of consultants to the Senate Finance Committee, produces still larger deficits than those shown in the 1974 Trustees' Report. Under these assumptions, retirement benefits at award would have increased under present law by the year 2045 by 56 percent more than the increase in earnings. It also produces unreasonably high increases in wage replacement rates. In my judgment, such benefit results would never be allowed to take place and would call for legislative correction. Consequently, I consider the cost results of such assumptions to be highly unrealistic.

Fortunately, the Council's recommendation for basing benefit computation on a system of wage indexing largely removes these uncertainties, making the level of protection more certain and the cost-estimating job more reliable. Pending this change in the benefit system, a change which I support, I see no need to provide, on the basis of a highly speculative set of assumptions concerning the movement of wages and prices, a set of contribution rates in the next century that are any higher than those required to support the program over the next few decades, and have recommended that it would be more reasonable now to provide specifically for contribution income to finance the present program over such a period, and at the same time to restore to the social security law the provision for general revenue financing that was contained in the law from 1944 to 1950.

The predicted change in the age composition of the population does not present any major increase in the burden of supporting non-workers. The very assumptions that lead to an increasing proportion of older people to those of working age leads [sic] to a smaller number of children per person of working age. Taking the two non-working parts of the population together—the retired aged and children—there is little change in the ratio of dependents to workers. Thus the resources now required for the upbringing and education of children can under these population assumptions be directed toward providing for older people, at least in part, without any increased burden on current workers. Under such circumstances there is little doubt also but that the labor force participation of older people would increase. Cost savings to social security would, of course, result from such increased labor force participation by older people. It is not necessary to change the legal age at which an individual becomes eligible for benefits, as discussed in the Council. With greater opportunity for employment, the cost savings will come about automatically. The proposal to change the legal age of entitlement not only violates the agreement between the social security payee and his government, but penalizes the person who chooses to retire or has to retire because of health or employment circumstances.

It is also possible that costs in the next century measured as a percentage of covered payroll will be smaller than indicated by current estimates because of greater labor force participation by women. With smaller families such a result would seem to be quite likely. Most fundamental, of course, is the long-range trend of productivity increases. Although as indicated earlier, the long-range actuarial deficit of the system is 3% of payroll with an assumption of 5% increases in wages and 3% increases in prices, and a 6% of payroll deficit on a long-range assumption of a 6% increase in wages and a 4% increase in prices, an assumption of a 5% increase in wages and a 2% increase in prices shows the present program to be fully financed! Thus, whether or not there really is a long-range financing problem for social security depends on a highly speculative set of assumptions about fertility rates, labor force participation rates, and long-range movement of wages and prices and the productivity of the labor force.

Conclusion

I share the firm conviction contained in the title of the recently issued White Paper, endorsed by *five* former HEW Secretaries and three former Social Security Commissioners, "Social Security: A Sound and Durable Institution of Great Value," that (1) the short-term financial problems of the system are clearly manageable without radical change, and (2) that any long-range problems in financing can and will be met in a way to fully redeem the promises made to social security contributors.

Document 6.3   Statement of Stanford D. Arnold, Edward J. Cleary, and Elizabeth C. Norwood

While there is much in this report with which we agree, we feel the need to make a separate statement for two reasons; first, for the purpose of clarification and second, to draw attention to those areas in which the Council failed to make any recommendations.

The Adequacy of Benefit Levels

In the "Purpose and Principles" section of this report, it is pointed out that income protection among the aged is made up of three parts; social insurance, private insurance and means-tested programs. Social Security benefits are believed to make up only a part of the income of retired workers. It is assumed

---

DOCUMENT 6.3: U.S. Congress, House, *Reports of the Quadrennial Advisory Council . . .* 1975, pp. 68-70.

that pension incomes or welfare money supplement the retirees' Social Security benefit. This belief in the existence of other sources of income, helps to explain the very low Social Security benefits received by the retired population. Currently, benefits for a single retiree averages [sic] about $2,220 per year (about $185 per month); the same figure for a retired couple is $3,720 per year ($310 per month); and for a widow, $2,124 per year ($177 per month).

What is ignored is the fact that for many of the aged, Social Security represents their only source of income. It is generally estimated that about half of all retired persons have no other regular retirement income apart from their monthly Social Security checks.

Our concern then, is that it is unrealistic to reaffirm belief in a tripartite system of income protection for the aged, when only one part—Social Security benefits— provides most of the support. Assessments of the adequacy of benefit levels must no longer assume that other outside incomes are making up the difference between a benefit level and what it costs to maintain a decent standard of living.

In keeping its attention riveted on cost factors and the hypothetical tripartite system of income protection, the Council has given inadequate attention to the social adequacy of benefit levels and the need to raise benefits. Until benefits are raised, the true purpose of Social Security—to prevent poverty among the aged—will not be realized.

General Revenue Financing

We consider the single most important achievement of this Council was its recommendation to move Medicare under general revenue financing. The present Medicare tax paid under Social Security would stay as part of Social Security revenue. This switch of Medicare financing anticipates a national health insurance program and, to some extent, may facilitate this development.

The move to general revenue financing has been debated for many years by past Councils and in the Congress. Economic changes and demands on the system today, however, give this recommendation a new importance. The Social Security trust fund is declining relative to expenditures, and sources of new funds must be found in order to insure stability and confidence in the system. Further, it is no longer acceptable to expect the lowest paid sector to continue to shoulder the expense of the regressive Social Security tax. The move to general revenue shifts the burden towards the better paid.

A remarkable, and in our view regrettable, oversight in this report is the systematic failure to give adequate emphasis to the recommendation to fund Medicare under general revenue which this Council endorsed. We feel this recommendation is the most important one to be made to Congress.

Further, we note in the financing sections of this report, that considerable

attention is given to the necessity of increasing the Social Security tax rate. At
no time, in our recollection of Council meetings, did this financing alternative
receive majority support. In fact, the final Council vote on financing was
clearly drawn between the choice for a Social Security tax rate increase and
the use of general revenue financing for Medicare. The majority voted against
the tax rate increase and for general revenue financing. The sections on
financing do not convey this explicit Council decision.

Rather, the opposite impression is given, that is, that the Council supports a
Social Security tax rate increase. At no time did we support such a proposal
and we emphatically dissociate ourselves from it.

Another funding alternative discussed was increasing the taxable income
base upon which the Social Security tax is levied. Though this proposal was
not adopted, we supported this change and certainly consider it preferable to
any tax rate increases at this time.

Financing Medicare (Part A) from General Revenue

In making the recommendation for reducing the Medicare payroll tax, the
Council is not recommending any reduction in the intent of the proposal on
Medicare benefits. The intent of the proposal is that sufficient funds be made
available from general revenue to continue the Medicare benefits just as if no
change in financing occurred.

Disability

Although the Council is recommending a change in the definition of
disability as it applies to workers 55 and over, we feel that the change is not
comprehensive enough. Simply stated, disability should be strictly related to a
worker's last regular occupation. In our view, any alternative definitions
which fall short of this, provide insufficient protection to older disabled
workers, a group particularly disadvantaged when competing for jobs outside
their regular occupation.

Indexing Wages (Decoupling)

Another important policy recommendation of this Council concerned the
issue of "decoupling." Without attempting to paraphrase a description of the
subject already covered at some length in this report, we would like to make
certain points for clarification. In our opinion, the crucial factor in the
argument for the proposed "indexed" system for determining benefit levels,
was not the alleged flaws in the present system. The advantages of an indexed
system are twofold. First, by stabilizing replacement ratios (i.e., the relationship between a worker's monthly benefit and the monthly wage they earned

just before they retired) through a technical formula, Congress might better focus attention on the adequacy of replacement ratio levels. In our view, this is the real merit of the indexing system. A system which predicts benefits according to a set formula, will provide a specific replacement ratio for the working population. Instead of not knowing what a replacement ratio will be, attention could focus on the social adequacy of benefits produced by the formula. When higher benefits are needed, the indexing formula can be adjusted to produce such benefits.

Second, the proposed change has the advantage of updating wages earned many years ago. Wages earned early in a career are reassessed upwards to make them comparable to today's higher salaries. We consider that this change provides more equitable treatment to these wages.

Final Comment

A controlling factor on this Council's deliberations was the strict time limitation imposed (8 months). The Social Security staff was often called upon to give rough cost estimates on very important financial implications of different courses of action. This led to some confusion and the need to revise "off the cuff" estimates. Council deliberations, based upon partial, misleading or erroneous assumptions, were inevitable. Future Councils simply must be given a more adequate time period for making recommendations of such general social importance.[15]

---

15. [Dr.] Campbell concurs with this [sentence].

7

RETIREMENT TEST

RETIREMENT TEST

Definition and Rationale

The existing law states that if a beneficiary is under 72 and earns more than the annual exempt amount, which was $3,000 in 1977, then dollar amounts are withheld, at the rate of $1 in benefits for each $2 in earnings above that amount.[1] The 1975 Advisory Council on Social Security received more letters protesting this so-called retirement test, which amounts to a 50 percent tax on the earnings of persons 65 and older, than any other aspect of social security. Although before 1954 noncovered earnings were not counted for the retirement test, the 1954 amendments make all income from work subject to it. Finally, at 72, retirement benefits are paid irrespective of the recipient's earnings.

Under current law, an individual may receive his full benefit amount for any month in which he neither earns more than one-twelfth of the annual exempt amount nor performs any "substantial" service in self-employment during that month. Thus a writer, a member of a board of directors, or anyone else with irregular earnings, may receive in one month of a year a lump sum far exceeding the one-twelfth of the annual exempt amount and then, for all other months during which he or she does not exceed this limitation nor perform substantial work, receive a full social security benefit.

No wonder, then, that the very existence of the retirement test, as well as its annual rather than monthly application, has been highly controversial. Indeed, it probably is the most political of all the issues being discussed currently in respect to reform of the social security system. For example the arbitrary selection of 72 as a cutoff in applying the test was a compromise in response to pressures for changes, but there is no logic in selecting 72 rather than 75 or 70 years.

---

1. The exempt amount now automatically increases with the annual increase in average earnings.

The rationale for awarding benefits at a given age irrespective of earnings depends on the concept of individual equity. On the other hand, the existence of the test itself reflects the concept of social adequacy.

In regard to most other issues, as, for example, short-run and long-run financing, there is at least agreement on some of the needed changes, such as the need to stop counting inflation double. On the retirement test, however, even among those individuals who fully understand that the social security system was originally intended to replace loss of earnings, and not loss of income, the arguments are heated. Over one hundred legislative bills were introduced in the 1975 Congress on this topic alone.

The rationale for the retirement test is two-fold: if older persons retire earlier then, it is argued, there will be more jobs for younger ones. This has never been proven as an overall effect. Unemployment rates in the United States do not appear to substantiate it. In 1975, only 21 percent of white males and 22 percent of nonwhite males, aged 65 years and over, were in the labor force. The unemployment rate for males 20 years and over was 9 percent. In 1950, 45 percent of white males and 50 percent of black males aged 65 years and over were in the labor force, but the unemployment rate for males 20 years and over was only 5 percent. Moreover, the supposed relationship between early retirement and low unemployment cannot be proven theoretically. The second argument is that only a welfare-type program, supported by general revenues, can replace loss of income, and that the level of a person's standard of living depends on earnings, not other income. The latter simply is not true: *all* one's income, not just earnings, affects a person's standard of living. For example, a nonworking widow—one, in fact, who has never worked outside of her home—may have substantial income in the form of rents, interest, dividends, or some combination of these.

Probably the major reason for the intensity of the disagreement is the lack of up-to-date data on why people retire, and on the effect of the social security act itself on the age at which they retire. It is interesting that the 1976 Consultant Panel on Social Security, in its 119-page report, devoted only a few pages to this subject. The panel did conclude, however, with the recommendation "that Congress fund a 'social experiment' financed by the OASI trust fund to examine responses of older workers to different earnings tests, different sizes of actuarial reduction for early retirement, different delayed retirement increments, and variations in other benefit provisions that may influence retirement decisions."[2]

Whatever the age is at which workers become entitled to the full social security benefit, that age receives an unofficial stamp of approval as the acceptable age of retirement. Sixty-five was arbitrarily selected in 1935. Additionally 62, the age at which workers may retire with an actuarially reduced benefit, was also arbitrarily selected. Sixty-two has become accepted as a suitable and desirable age to retire by both men and women. Women became entitled to a reduced retirement benefit at 62 in 1956; men in 1961; and both widows and dependent widowers at 60 to a reduced dependency benefit in 1965 and 1972 respectively.

There has been in recent years a great increase in persons retiring earlier. The labor force participation rate for white males aged 55-64 years has dropped from 90 percent in 1948 to 78 percent in 1974; for nonwhite males, it has dropped from 89 percent to 70 percent. On the other hand, for white females aged 55-64 years the labor force participation rate has increased from 23 percent in 1948 to 40 percent in 1974, and for nonwhite women from 38 percent to 44 percent during the same period. The percentage increase for women starts from a lower base, and thus the absolute number of individuals retiring earlier is still increasing. This imposes a heavier load on those who are still working. All these events are taking place at a time when medical improvements are extending life beyond age 62 and the birth rate is dropping dramatically.

In 1975, males aged 60-65 had an average life expectancy of another 16.8 years and females aged 60-65 of another 21.8—exactly 5 years more than the males.[3] A downward trend in deaths from diseases of the heart began in 1963 and from cerebrovascular disease in the 1920s. Additionally, during 1973, the 55-mile speed limit and fewer miles driven per capita, as gasoline prices increased, are usually cited as the major causes for the subsequent 2.3 percent drop in age-adjusted death rates from automobile accidents. Thus, although for many years increases in life expectancy at birth have gradually increased by sizable

---

2. U.S. Congress, Joint Committee (House Committee on Ways and Means, Senate Committee on Finance), *Report of the Consultant Panel on Social Security to the Congressional Research Service,* 94th Cong., 2d sess., August 1976 (Washington, D.C.: U.S. Government Printing Office, 1976), p. 57.

3. U.S. National Center for Health Statistics, *Monthly Vital Statistics Report* 25 (1977), no. 11 (February 11), supplement, p. 7.

amounts, in very recent years life expectancy of older persons has also begun to increase, although by comparatively smaller amounts.

Demographic changes in our society give importance to the continually decreasing age at which people are retiring. Although men at age 65 have only a slightly higher life expectancy than in earlier years, women at 65 may anticipate about 3 more years of life than they could anticipate in 1930.[4]

It is difficult for professional persons who enjoy their work to understand the pressures to retire early on persons doing work that is more physically demanding, boring, or both. Many persons in retail trade, in some service industries, workers on the assembly line and industrial workers in general have usually started to work much earlier, at 18 as compared to other persons who work after graduating from college at 21 or 22. The professional may start to work at 24 or even later. The data indicate that it is those who start to work early in jobs requiring more physical effort and leaving less opportunity for creativity who retire early. Professional workers, politicians, some managers, and—usually—the self-employed continue to work beyond 65.

The self-employed, of course, are not forced by company rules to retire, and also have the opportunity to reduce their work load gradually. A recent study of 1973 OASI data on the ages at which self-employed persons retire indicates that, of those persons aged 65 years and over in 1973 (by age cohorts) and with "more than 5 years of OASI-covered self-employment between 1951 and the year in which a person attained age 62," a greater percentage through age 70, as compared to "strictly wage-salary workers," did not collect social security retirement benefits. The study concludes that "for the age-65, age-66 and age-67 cohorts, those with substantial self-employment are more than 1¼ times as likely to forego benefits as are hired workers. The difference is smaller for the next three age cohorts."[5] The difference between ages 68 and 69 and between 70 and 71 may be explained largely by the exclusion of self-employed clergymen and physicians, who were not required to be covered until 1968 and 1965, respectively. It is probable, therefore, that some percentage of employed persons would prefer not to retire from their customary job at the age of 65, which is mandatory in most companies. But that decision is not one the

4. Metropolitan Life Insurance Co., *Statistical Bulletin,* May 1976, p. 4.

5. U.S. Department of Health, Education, and Welfare, *Self Employment and Retirement,* Research and Statistics Note No. 15, July 30, 1976.

employee can make. Many persons who are forced to retire may eventually become self-employed. This self-selection affects the above data.

As early as 1971, over 90 percent of active workers (about 21 million) were covered by a private pension plan that had some form of an early retirement option. Communication and public utility workers, as well as workers in finance and real estate, have early retirement options that are generally phrased in terms of a specified age and required years of work on the job, as, for example, 55 to 60 years and ten years of service.

By 1973, many trade union contracts had early retirement clauses that permitted persons at age 55 years and ten years of service (e.g., San Francisco, Plumbers Local 3) or age 55 and 15 years of service (e.g., New York City, Carpenters) to retire with a reduced benefit. Some also provide disability benefits with no age requirement, but after 15 years of service. These are common contracts in the various building trades. The August 1975, United Steel Workers' contracts provide for early retirement at age 60 years and 15 years of service, as do United Automobile Workers' contracts. In these industries especially, jobs may be physically demanding and in the automobile industry involve a large amount of assembly-line work.

The generally accepted retirement age is important because it affects the national supply of hours of labor and therefore the potential size of the country's gross national product. Also, as the birth rate continues to fall, the age of entrance to the labor force continues to rise, and older persons continue to retire earlier, those who are working will be taxed more heavily to pay for the promised social security benefits. Various groups have proposed a phasing-in of 67 or 68 years for entitlement to a full social security retirement benefit, and of 65 years for a reduced benefit. In 1974, 64 percent of retired workers receiving newly awarded benefits were persons under 65 years. This compares to 56 percent in 1970, 49 percent in 1965, and 21 percent in 1960. Therefore, a later retirement age under social security does not appear to be politically viable, even if phased in over a very long period. It would mean that, at some future year, persons who retired at 62-64 years would not receive their anticipated benefit. Persons near retirement are unlikely to vote for this, and younger persons cannot be assured of lower taxes if they postpone their retirement. Only if the labor supply becomes very tight, so that money returns to workers or their shares of national income greatly increase, would later retirement appear to become popular.

The retirement age under private plans tends to be the same as the entitlement age for full benefits under social security. If the latter age were increased from 65 to 67 years and there were a lag—as there probably would be under private plans, since their benefits are a contractual right—and if the transitional period were not well planned, it is possible that some persons might need welfare benefits when otherwise they would not have. They should be a very small percentage, however, comprising mostly those who had been ill or are ill.

Exploration of alternative, later retirement ages, such as may have existed in other countries, and/or alternative work-leisure arrangements over an individual's lifetime may in the long-run become very important. Many countries in the early years of their "social security" plans had higher age requirements for entitlement to a retirement benefit. However, by 1975, the only country still requiring age 70 for full benefits was Israel. Recently, Ireland lowered its age of entitlement to 68 years (to 65 years under some circumstances), and age 67 was the age of entitlement for a full pension benefit in Sweden until July 1976. Some countries require both a certain age and a certain number of years of coverage. This dual requirement tends to help those who start to work earlier and pay in for longer periods.

Initially, the U.S. Social Security Act was passed to strengthen the inducement to retire, so that vacated jobs could be filled by the unemployed. Current unemployment levels are such that arguments in favor of postponing retirement are likely to have little political impact. However, if employment increases, as it probably will now that the market has begun to absorb the extraordinary increase in the supply of women workers during the period 1974-76, then shortages of some types of labor will eventually encourage later retirement.

Studies of isolated societies that have long average life expectancies indicate that these are agricultural societies, usually at high altitudes, where persons work hard physically even into their seventies or later and also eat frugally. The tensions of industrialized society may reduce longevity, but life expectancy at age 65 is increasing in the United States. There are those who claim that quitting work early may actually reduce longevity. Status in many groups depends on one's job. Because of the many variables, data are as yet inconclusive on the effect of retirement. However, data on why people have been retiring earlier in recent years in the United States are conclusive: it is not because of an increase in sickness, but rather because some business firms find it advantageous, and because liberal pension and social security benefits make it financially possible for many to retire early. Sometimes an individual's combined private and government benefits net of income taxes are greater than recent earnings net of such taxes.

The medical literature clearly points to an improvement in the level of health of older persons as compared to forty and even twenty years ago. Some business executives may believe that innovative approaches are less likely to come from elderly managers than from more vigorous, younger persons, while other firms believe that wisdom of experience and maturity of judgment offset this. Heavy manual labor is declining in importance. Individuals do age at different rates. These are arguments for retirement at a later age and also for a nonmandatory retirement age personalized to an individual's capabilities and the demands of his job.

Among older women, there are many who would prefer to work part time or not at all while their children are small. Many mothers of school-age children would prefer to work shorter work weeks and have more vacation days over their lifetime, perhaps retiring at a later age. Women do live longer than men. These alternatives are open today only to the self-employed or to persons with an unusual combination of initiative, training, and luck that enables them to put together this favorable package over a lifetime. Yet, a preference for timing work-loads to dovetail with family demands may exist among women of all ages. For example, healthy widows who may live alone and who have not worked for pay during a good part of their lives, may prefer to work beyond age 65. Women at birth live on the average almost 8 more years than men do. Although by age 45, the differential is 6 years and at age 65, only 4 years, women at 65 years have on the average a life expectancy of 18 more years and men of 14 more years.

For those older persons who remain healthy, an alternative choice of later retirement and higher benefits during retirement should be available. If one continues to work past age 65, one's social security benefit, which is computed at 65, will under current law automatically increase by 1 percent per year and possibly by more if earnings after 65 are greater than the average of earlier earnings. However, this potential gain is an extremely small fraction of the benefits foregone by working. It seems to be a very small relative gain when maximum primary benefits can be as high as $387.30 a month and maximum family benefits as high as $1,010.70 a month.[6] Additionally, persons who

---

6. Effective June 1976, $387.30 is the woman's maximum primary benefit; the man's is $378.80 because of the discrepancy in computation prior to its correction (but not retroactively) by the 1972 amendments. The family benefits cited here are for male worker, wife, and one child. *Social Security Bulletin,* July 1976, pp. 41-42.

work in covered employment after age 65 years must continue to pay social security taxes, now almost 12 percent in all. For the year 1977, it is estimated that this tax rate will be on a base of $16,500, which means that each employee may directly pay social security taxes up to $965.25 a year and indirectly—primarily via lower wages—an equal amount, for a total of $1,930.50.

Without a government plan offering a choice of later retirement with a lesser penalty than now exists, individuals are unlikely to seek new work beyond age 65 and employers are loathe to retain them or hire them as new employees beyond age 65. Yet many persons in the so-called young-aged group—say, 65-69 years—are today far healthier and more capable of working than persons under 65 some forty years ago when the Social Security Act was first passed. To some persons in the young-aged group, the fact that they have to go on paying social security taxes on earnings after 65 is the final insult. If they are entitled to a full benefit at 65 and do not take it because of the way the law is worded, why, they ask, should they also be forced to pay social security taxes on their earnings, and therefore have lower wages than if their employer did not have to pay the matching payroll tax? These older persons are contributing to the national income and additionally paying a personal income tax on their earnings, while the social security benefits that they have foregone would have been free of income tax. As one of my colleagues has so well expressed it: "I agree with the resentment about a failure to collect at age 65 and seethe with indignation at having to continue to pay social security taxes beyond that date."[7]

From an individual equity point of view, taxation of social security on income from work after age 65 is inequitable. Because social security benefits are paid without taking into account other income receipts by the aged, as from interest, rent, and dividends, and because persons over 65 have an automatic double exemption, taxation of social security benefits would affect only the middle- and higher-income groups of aged. Exemption of all social security benefits from income tax favors higher-income over lower-income aged. Social security taxation of earnings of persons 65 years and older penalizes the person who contributes to society, as compared to like individuals who do not.

---

7. Dan Throop Smith, special assistant and deputy to the secretary of the Treasury, 1953-59, memo to author, August 13, 1974.

Document 7.1 Report of the Advisory Council on Social Security, March 1975 [excerpt]

[Author's Note. The Advisory Council's recommendations were worked out to aid only those low wage earners whose annual earnings were less than or equal to two times the "exempt" amount. The recommendation to use only an annual test would penalize primarily persons with higher earnings.]

The social security retirement test, under which benefits are not paid in full to a beneficiary under age 72 who has substantial income from work, should be changed. The rate at which benefits are withheld for earnings above the exempt amount should be liberalized. In addition, the retirement test should be changed from a combined annual-monthly test to an annual test only.[8]

PRESENT LAW

Under the social security retirement test, if a beneficiary under age 72 earns more than the annual exempt amount ($2,400 in 1974, $2,520 in 1975, and adjusted with rising average earnings thereafter), benefits are withheld at the rate of $1 in benefits for each $2 in earnings above that amount. Regardless of his annual earnings, a beneficiary may receive full benefits for any month in which he neither earns more than the monthly measure (1/12 of the annual exempt amount—$200 in 1974, $210 in 1975) nor performs substantial services in self-employment.

The retirement test is controversial, and is widely regarded as inequitable. The Council has received many letters urging the liberalization or elimination of the retirement test.

DOCUMENT 7.1: U.S. Congress, Committee on Ways and Means, *Reports of the Quadrennial Advisory Council on Social Security,* 94th Cong., 1st sess., H.D. 94-75, March 10, 1975 (Washington, D.C.: U.S. Government Printing Office, 1975), pp. 21-24.

8. By Mr. Mitchell. A relaxation of the retirement test proceeds from one or both of the following assumptions: *(a)* it is irrational and *(b)* it imposes a hardship on those receiving low benefits, no other retirement income, and an ability to participate in the labor force to at least a limited degree. My agreement to relax the test flowed from the latter sentiment for the most part. In adopting the proposal outlined in this report, we implicitly recommended a high cost for increased benefits to a group with entirely sufficient retirement income. My alternative to the current proposal would be to exempt from the retirement test those earnings of a beneficiary which, when added to the individual's PIA, did not result in a retirement income greater than the maximum PIA permissible under the law. Because of the lack of universality of Social Security, I would probably include other sources of retirement income such as Federal retirement benefits in calculating the retirement test disregard. Under my alternative, I would retain the present retirement test "tax rate" over the level described. In other words, I would prefer to alter the retirement test in a fashion which focuses on the needy without giving anything to the more affluent retirees.

BASIC PURPOSE

The Council has reviewed the provisions of the retirement test and believes that the test is consistent with the basic purpose and principles of social security: to replace, in part, earnings lost because of retirement in old age, disability, or death. Complete elimination of the retirement test is inadvisable.

The retirement test has been criticized because it does not take into account a beneficiary's income from such nonwork sources as dividends, rents, or pension payments. If the test took account of income other than earnings from work, it would no longer be a retirement test but an income test. If it became an income test, the fundamental idea that social security benefits are intended as a partial replacement of earnings from work would be diluted or lost.

The most frequently discussed alternative to the retirement test would be to pay social security benefits to all beneficiaries who reach age 65, independent of their employment status at that age. The Council agreed that this annuity concept, in which individuals would receive their "retirement" benefits while still gainfully employed, perhaps at high salaries and wages, is counter to the basic philosophy of social security. In addition, such a recommendation would add a significant cost to the system at a time when future costs are already a matter of concern. Therefore, the Council recommends that a retirement test be retained.

LIBERALIZE PROVISIONS OF THE RETIREMENT TEST

Despite basic agreement with the concept of the retirement test, the Council recognizes that negative consequences arise from its application. Under the present $1-for-$2 withholding rate for earnings above the exempt amount, the additional earnings a beneficiary receives over the exempt amount may result in little additional net income to the worker when allowance is made for the additional effects of Federal income, OASDHI, State, and local taxes, in addition to work-related expenses. Thus, the retirement test discourages work by healthy and able individuals aged 65-71. At the moment there is much concern over unemployment, but recent and current low birth rates will soon cause a decline in the rate of increase in the labor force. The Council is, therefore, concerned with provisions of the law which may act to discourage participation in the labor force.

In addition, the burden of the retirement test probably falls most heavily on low-income individuals who do not have access to private insurance, pension plans, savings, or other sources of nonwork income to supplement their social security retirement benefits. Such individuals are most likely to be dependent on additional income from gainful employment to supplement social security benefits after "retirement."

The Council believes that the most appropriate means for mitigating the disincentive effects of the retirement test and the heavy burden it imposes on low-income workers aged 65-71 is to reduce the withholding rate on earnings which are just above the exempt amount. The Council proposes to establish three levels of earnings that would be subject to different reductions in benefits.

The first level would include earnings up to the annual exempt amount as defined in the present law ($2,520 in 1975). As under the present law, no benefits would be withheld from earnings within the first level.

The second level would include earnings between the annual exempt amount under the present law and twice this annual exempt amount ($2,520 to $5,040 in 1975). Earnings within this level would be subject to a withholding rate of $1 in benefits for each $3 earned, instead of the present withholding rate of $1 for every $2 earned.

The third level would include all earnings in excess of twice the annual exempt amount under the present law (i.e., $5,040 in 1975). The withholding rate at this level would be, as under present law, $1 in benefits for each $2 of earnings.

The provision of the law which automatically adjusts the exempt amount assures that the second level of earnings, to which the $1-for-$3 withholding rate is applied, will increase in the future as general levels of earnings rise.

The main effect of this liberalization would be a significant reduction in the benefits withheld from individuals who earn between one and two times the annual exempt amount. For example, under present law, a worker who earned $5,040 in 1975 would have $1,260 of social security benefits withheld. Under the Council's proposal, this individual would have only $840 withheld, corresponding to a 1/3 reduction in the burden of the retirement test. The table below illustrates the effect in 1975 of the proposed reduction in withholding rates for earnings in the second level. The percentage reduction in the amount withheld is greatest at the lower level of earnings, where the needs of social security benefit recipients may be presumed to be greater.

Annual Earnings	Withholding under Present Law	Withholding under Proposed Liberalization	Percentage Reduction in Amount Withheld
$2,520	0	0	....
$5,040	$1,260	$ 840	33.3
$7,560	2,520	2,100	16.7
$10,080	3,780	3,360	11.1

It is estimated by actuaries of the Social Security Administration that this liberalization of the withholding rate would increase the cost of the program by an average of 0.04 percent of taxable payroll over the next 75 years (about $0.6 billion for months in 1976, the first full calendar year).

ELIMINATE MONTHLY MEASURE OF RETIREMENT

The Council recommends that the monthly measure of retirement be eliminated so that the retirement test would be based solely on annual earnings. The monthly measure should be retained, however, for the first year for which a cash benefit is received so that a beneficiary (as now) can receive benefits beginning with the first month of retirement, regardless of his annual earnings prior to retirement.

Elimination of the monthly measure from the retirement test would result in savings estimated at 0.02 percent of taxable payroll (about $0.2 billion for months in 1976, the first full calendar year).

The present test, with a combined annual-monthly measure of earnings, creates an anomaly by permitting the payment of benefits in some situations where payment is difficult to justify. For example, a beneficiary who earns, say, $15,000 a year and who works regularly throughout the year has all benefits withheld. A beneficiary, however, who earns the same amount, but works only part of the year, say 8 months, can receive benefits for the remaining 4 months. Also, people who customarily work less than a full 12 months each year (e.g., in seasonal employment) can, upon reaching the age of eligibility for benefits, receive some social security benefits during the year even though their work patterns have not changed and their annual earnings are substantial.

The two changes that the Council has recommended in the retirement test, when taken together, would increase the cost of the program by 0.02 percent of taxable payroll (about $0.4 billion for months in 1976, the first full calendar year).

UPPER AGE LIMIT FOR THE RETIREMENT TEST

Under current law, the retirement test is not applied to individuals over the age of 72. One possibility for liberalizing the impact of the retirement test would be to lower the age at which the retirement test no longer applies. The Council felt that this feature of the law, which represented special considerations, should not be extended by using it as a basis for policy or proposed liberalization of the existing retirement test. Any liberalization of the retirement test should be accomplished by direct changes in the provisions of the test, not by exemptions from the test. Therefore, the Council does not recommend any change in the age at which the retirement test no longer applies.

TAXES ON EARNINGS AFTER AGE 65

The Council considered suggestions for reducing or eliminating social security taxes on earnings of individuals aged 65 and older. Contrary to common impressions, such workers do receive some benefits from these taxes.

Earnings after age 65 can be substituted for lower earnings of earlier years in calculating the average monthly earnings on which benefits are based, thereby increasing the primary insurance amount of the worker when he does retire. (This effect will be lessened if earnings before retirement are indexed as the Council recommends in chapter 3.) Also, some workers may use work after age 65 in covered employment to qualify for social security benefits to which they would not otherwise be entitled. Finally, insured workers receive a 1-percent increase in benefits for each year of delayed retirement after the age of 65. In view of these offsetting factors and of the significant loss of income resulting from eliminating the tax for workers aged 65 and over, the Council decided not to recommend exemption from the payroll tax for workers over 65. However, the Council does believe that these offsetting factors are not widely known and that the Social Security Administration should make efforts to publicize them more effectively. [pp. 21-24]

Economic Incentives and Retirement Decisions

The Advisory Council's proposals on the retirement test were developed out of "bargaining" among its members. Many close votes (e.g., 6 to 5, 7 to 4) were taken at the October 22, 1974, meeting when these matters were discussed in depth.

At its September 22 meeting, the council tentatively decided to recommend exemption of workers, including the self-employed, from payment of social security taxes after age 65.[9] The council argued that after forty years the social security system was "mature," and earnings after age 65 were probably relatively unimportant in determining individual future benefits. Moreover, employers would thus be encouraged not to retire automatically persons aged 65 and over. The latter could enjoy, if they wished, current consumption of the part of their earnings that was being taxed by social security, instead of being forced by taxes to delay consumption and/or savings.

The staff memorandum dated November 1, 1974, stressed, however, that if the portion of the tax paid by the employer were eliminated, it would tend to discourage employment of those over 65 because it would "increase the administrative complexity of employer payroll operations and record keeping." No mention was made of an offset of

9. The Advisory Council members very early decided that all decisions involving expenditures would be tentative so that the council could at the end of its deliberations consciously weigh the costs of one recommendation against the costs of another.

savings because of the decreased amount of taxes paid by the employer. Rather, the memorandum stressed that

> if earnings after age 65 were not counted for benefit purposes, the resulting significant deliberalization in present law would disadvantage many people. On the other hand, if post-65 earnings were not subject to social security contributions, it would be possible, for example, for a person who had spent most of his working life in noncovered employment to work in covered employment after age 65 and to become eligible for social security benefits and hospital insurance without paying any contributions.

The memorandum fails to point out, however, that the latter provision would become moot if coverage were universal; that this could be clarified simultaneously by a simple change in the law; and that already nearly one-half of uncovered federal employees have become entitled to social security benefits, often from a very secondary job with a very small total payment of social security taxes. The numbers of covered persons who might be adversely affected by losing their annual increase in benefits of 1 percent would probably be far better off overall because their social security taxes while they were working would be reduced by a much greater amount.

An estimate of the cost of eliminating employee-only and self-employed taxes for workers 65 years and older, effective January 1, 1975, was made for the first year of enactment by SSA actuaries, who came up with a figure of about $0.8 billion. The long-range costs were estimated at 0.11 percent of payroll covered by the OASDI program and 0.02 percent for the hospitalization program. This would be more than offset, however, by a long-run gain of 0.13 percent if the delayed retirement credits of 1 percent per year were not allowed in recomputing benefits and, additionally, if earnings after 65 years were not credited toward benefit eligibility,[10] nor higher earnings after 65 years allowed in recomputation of retirement benefit purposes. Thus the net effect could be a saving, not a loss, of 0.02 percent of taxable payroll under the OASDI program, and would exactly balance if the hospital insurance part of the tax were included.[11]

---

10. This would affect mostly the aforementioned windfall groups — federal government workers, for example.

11. Quadrennial Advisory Council on Social Security, "Minutes," meeting of November 3, 1974, p. 6.

It was after consideration of such data, without any of the interrelated data on anticipated higher revenues from personal income tax or other concomitant effects outside the social security system, that the Advisory Council reversed its original tentative recommendation to exempt earnings of persons 65 and over from the social security tax. The council also suggested that consideration be given gradually to increase the age of entitlement to full benefits from 65 to 68 years, and the age of entitlement to reduced benefits from 62 to 65 years. This would greatly reduce the number of years during which the retirement test would be effective.

Persuading the public to accept postponement of retirement was deemed difficult. In 1975, 49 percent of men and 66 percent of women retiring that year took early retirement with a reduced benefit. Reduced benefits at 62 have been available for men since 1961 and for women since 1956. Although the data show that both men and women are retiring earlier, the increase in men so doing is a recent development; a substantial number of working women had traditionally retired earlier. In 1955, almost 60 percent of males aged 65 to 69 were in the labor force, but by 1974 only 33 percent. For all males over 65 years, the figure was only 22 percent. For women aged 65 to 69 the corresponding figures were just under 20 percent in 1955 and about 14 percent in 1974.

In 1974, 74 percent of males and 40 percent of women aged 62 to 64 reported some work experience. Today "roughly one-half the men and at least two-thirds of the women starting to draw cash benefits since the early-retirement provision was enacted have done so before age 65. The proportions have been even higher since 1972."[12]

It has been argued, but without reliable supporting data, that most persons, especially males, retire early because of health reasons. In 1977, it was just becoming known to what degree early retirement, that is, retirement before age 65 and also retirement between 65 and 69, were because of perceived ill health, and to what degree for other reasons. Among the latter were such economic incentives as the availability of private pensions and anticipated benefits, and the impact of the high implicit marginal tax rate on earnings via reduction of the potential OASI benefits (if one earned more than the amount permitted for entitlement). To eliminate the latter entirely, that is, the retirement test's $2.00 earnings offset against $1.00 of OASI benefits,

---

12. *Social Security Bulletin,* August 1976, p. 6.

would be very costly. Moreover, the comparative importance of health and economic incentives in retirement decisions appeared to be the reverse of what the SSA had believed. Recent studies of UAW members and federal civil servants had shown that availability of OASI benefits plus the second pension was the major factor for many persons in these groups who chose early retirement. Although some retrospective data supported poor health as the major factor, no prospective data did.

It appears that an individual's perception of the state of his or her health as "poor" involves subjective evaluation, which may be positively correlated with other factors. Thus "poor health" without availability of retirement benefits might play a less decisive role in an individual's decision whether or not to retire. There are many persons whose health, when self-evaluated, may become a "borderline" factor, so that they consider themselves well enough to work if retirement income is not sufficient. Cross tabulations with the National Center for Health Statistics morbidity data, if this is possible, would throw light on this area.

Today over 90 percent of private pension plans offer an option of early retirement. Employers like this flexibility during layoff periods. Because the usual age of early retirement under union contract plans is 55, it is anticipated that union leaders will continue to press for lowering OASI's age levels of entitlement. About 30 million employees are covered by private pension plans.

Document 7.2   Statement of John W. Byrnes, Rudolph T. Danstedt, and Edwin J. Faulkner

Dissent to Liberalization of the Retirement Test

Much of the dissatisfaction over the Retirement Test stems from a misconception of the nature of the benefits established by the Social Security Act. The old age benefit is not a right to an annuity but rather is "earned income insurance" providing at least partial replacement of formerly earned income lost upon retirement from the work force. The measure of whether the loss indemnified has occurred is the amount of the recipient's earned income, if any, at and after the age of eligibility. Whether Congress should have

---

DOCUMENT 7.2: U.S. Congress, House, *Reports of the Quadrennial Advisory Council on Social Security . . .* 1975, p. 71.

established an annuity benefit rather than an earned income replacement benefit is beside the point. The Social Security taxes paid have been calculated to finance only the more restricted insurance benefit. Elimination of the Retirement Test for recipients age 72 and older was a political concession to the self-employed who frequently never retire (or more truly think they will never retire), but one that had small financial impact on the system. The annual exempt amount was established and has been increased from time to time to permit benefit recipients to earn some income from employment not conceived as their regular work or of substantial amount, thus somewhat reducing pressures for OASDI benefits.

While the Council's recommendation for liberalization of the Retirement Test is much less onerous and costly than would be the elimination of the Retirement Test, at a time when the system is confronted with long-range financial problems, the additional liabilities involved in liberalization should be avoided. Liberalization of the Retirement Test would intensify the "transfer payments" complexion of OASDI and would encourage retirement at the earliest date of eligibility for Social Security benefits. [It] is believed the liberalization of the Retirement Test would be advantageous to only a small minority of recipients since many recipients cannot continue in regular employment because of health reasons, non-availability of jobs, or because they do not want to continue to work. The present Retirement Test provides ample opportunity for those who can and wish to continue to work to earn a reasonable amount without forfeiting all of the OASDI benefits. The exempt amount, under the automatic adjustment provisions of the present law, will be kept up to date with changing levels of earnings in the future. It is estimated the exempt amount will increase to at least $3,000 by 1977 as a result of this provision. The Act already provides eligible recipients who wish to continue in covered employment with incentives for so doing. A 1% annual increment in benefits for each year of work is provided those who continue to work after age 65. The higher earnings characteristic of employment in recent years permits the older worker to increase his wage history and thus to enjoy a higher average wage on which benefits are computed.

We believe that the Retirement Test as presently constituted should not be liberalized.

Document 7.3   Report of the House Subcommittee on Retirement Income and Employment, December 1975 [excerpt]

[*Author's Note.* An SSA memorandum of June 7, 1974, to the Advisory Council estimated that the long-range cost of making the annual exempt

DOCUMENT 7.3: U.S. Congress, House, Select Committee on Aging, Subcommittee on Retirement Income and Employment, *Report . . . .,* December 1975 (Washington, D.C.: U.S. Government Printing Office, 1975).

amount $3,900 in 1975 was 0.28 percent of payroll, making it $4,200 was 0.32 percent, and removing the limit was 0.56 percent.[13]]

Recommendation: Liberalization of the Retirement Test

The Social Security Act should be amended by raising the ceiling on the earnings limitation to $4,000 to permit retired persons to earn more income without reduction of their benefits.

Document 7.4   The Social Security Administration Views the Retirement Test, June 1974

[*Author's Note.* Tables 7.1 and 7.2 (originally unnumbered) are from a memorandum, dated June 17, 1974, that was prepared by the Social Security Administration and handed to the members of the Advisory Council at their meeting of November 3-4, 1974. The memorandum describes the retirement test as "the principal measure provided in the law" for determining if the "loss insured against" — i.e., the loss of income

TABLE 7.1
BENEFICIARIES AGED 65 AND OVER
AFFECTED BY THE SOCIAL SECURITY RETIREMENT TEST

	NUMBER OF PERSONS (MILLIONS) AND PERCENTAGE	
People aged 65 and over,[a] eligible for OASI benefits, 1/1/74[b]	22.0	(100%)
People with earnings above exempt amount ($2,400) with some or all benefits withheld	1.4	(6.4%)
Some benefits withheld	0.9	(4.1%)
All benefits withheld	0.5	(2.3%)

a. The vast majority of the beneficiaries affected by the retirement test (i.e., earning over $2,400) are 65 and over.

b. Includes dependents under age 65 of workers aged 65 and over.

---

13. Social Security Administration, memo from Francisco Bayo, deputy chief actuary, to James E. Marquis, acting assistant commissioner, on "Revised Long-Range Cost Estimate for Proposals to Change the OASDI Earnings Test," June 7, 1974, distributed as "Attachment C" to document 7.4, below.

DOCUMENT 7.4: Social Security Administration, "The Social Security Retirement Test," anonymous memo, mimeographed, distributed to members of Quadrennial Advisory Council on Social Security at their meeting of November 3-4, 1974, in Washington, D.C.

TABLE 7.2.
LEGISLATIVE HISTORY OF THE SOCIAL SECURITY RETIREMENT TEST

ACT[a]	BENEFICIARIES EXEMPT	EARNINGS SUBJECT TO TEST	AMOUNT PERMITTED WITHOUT REDUCTION IN BENEFITS		REDUCTION IN MONTHLY BENEFITS
			Annual Earnings	Monthly[b] Wages	
1935		Covered			Full monthly benefit
1939				$14.99	
1950	Aged 75 and over		[c]$600	$50	
1952			[c]$900	$75	
1954	Aged 72 and over	[d]All	$1,200	$80	One month's benefit for each $80 or fraction thereof.
1956	Disabled				
1958				$100	
1960					$1 for each $2 of earnings from $1,201 to $1,500. $1 for each $1 of earnings over $1,500.
1961					$1 for each $2 of earnings from $1,201 to $1,700. $1 for each $1 of earnings over $1,700.
1965			$1,500	$125	$1 for each $2 of earnings from $1,501 to $2,700. $1 for each $1 of earnings over $2,700.
1967			$1,680	$140	$1 for each $2 of earnings from $1,681 to $2,880. $1 for each $1 of earnings over $2,880.
1972	Excludes earnings after attainment of age 72		[e]$2,100	$175	$1 for each $2 of earnings over $2,100.
1973			$2,400	$200	$1 for each $2 of earnings over $2,400.

a. The years shown below are years of legislative change; usually the change was effective the following calendar year.
b. Monthly test for self-employment income is defined in terms of substantial services.
c. Applied to self-employment income only.
d. Special provisions for earnings in noncovered employment outside United States.
e. Subject to automatic provisions.

consequent upon retirement, disability, or death — has actually occurred. Table 7.1 has the following remarks appended to it:

> There are, of course, some beneficiaries who hold their earnings below the retirement test annual exempt amount, and who would, if the retirement test were eliminated or liberalized, earn more. However, the number is small—no more than about 3 percent of the eligible aged—since most beneficiaries do not have the option of setting the amount of time they can work. When these people are added to the number of beneficiaries directly affected by the test, the total number of eligible people age 65 and older who could be affected would be about 10 percent.

Table 7.2 shows how the concept of the retirement test has been elaborated over the years. The data except for 1973 appear also in SSA's *History of the Provisions of OASDHI, 1935-1972*, February 1973, p. 6.]

Document 7.5 Report of the Consultant Panel on Social Security, August 1976 [excerpt]

[*Author's Note.* At the time that the Consultant Panel was writing its report, little research documentation emanating from outside SSA was available. This lack of what would be more objective data and analyses than the in-house SSA reports was so obvious that the panel made the following recommendation.]

Retirement test. Effects created by the retirement test are largely unknown; so are the forces responsible for the present large number of early retirements. The Panel recommends that Congress use OASDI Trust Funds to finance a study of the economic impact of the retirement test. The study would apply different retirement tests to different samples of workers. Resulting increased knowledge of the factors affecting retirement decisions could aid Congress in making sound changes.

This Panel supports in the interim the removal of the monthly earnings test as part of the retirement test. [p. 5]

[Elaboration of that proposal follows.] Revealing the effects of strengthening or weakening particular present benefit provisions would be the first task of the social experiment. In addition, however, it affords opportunity to test alternate designs. Possibilities include the following: Consequences of providing part of benefits without any earnings-test limitation could be discovered. Responses to taxation of all or part of retirement benefits could be ascer-

DOCUMENT 7.5: U.S. Congress, Joint Committee, *Report of the Consultant Panel. . .* 1976, pp. 5 and 57-58.

tained. Another possible experiment would be replacing the present abrupt removal of the earnings test at age 72 by a gradual easing of the test during the ten years through which it now operates. The benefit might be related to the size of the decline in earnings as well as to their level.

This Panel concurs in the recommendation of the latest Advisory Council that the earnings test should be annual, not monthly. We believe that the purposes served by the monthly test are insufficient to offset the unfairness that arises because some people have greater opportunities than others to time their earnings to their own advantage. We note also that useful administrative simplicity can be accomplished by the recommended change.

A pair of different questions about the early retirement adjustment are *(a)* whether the "5/9 of 1 percent per month" actuarial reduction ratio needs to be changed, and *(b)* how a cost-of-living increase should be computed for people whose benefits have been subjected to the actuarial reduction. The Panel has looked at both these questions.

With respect to *(a)*, we recognize that there are philosophical and mathematical considerations involved. We propose that the former be explored through the social experiment and that the latter be examined in conjunction therewith.

As to *(b)*, it seems to us that a change in the present method of granting cost-of-living benefit increases to people whose benefits began before age 65 is desirable on equitable grounds and in the interests of simplicity. The present rule is that the original benefit before actuarial reduction is increased proportionately to the increase in CPI, and then the original *amount* of actuarial reduction is subtracted. We propose instead that the original reduced benefit be increased proportionately to the increase in CPI, an arrangement consistent with the Panel's general recommendation that purchasing power of benefits be maintained. [pp. 57-58]

Some Unresolved Problems

The way in which the social security system creates problems of inequity can be illustrated by data already referred to in this chapter. When the system assumed incorrect reasons for early retirement (poor health) and constructed a fallacious economic argument in favor of early retirement (i.e., that it would provide more jobs for younger people), it developed an emotionally appealing rationalization for early retirement on which to base its benefits policy. Ignored, until the mid-1970s, was the inequity of making those who work beyond age

62 or 65 pay social security taxes. While they gave up substantial money income, others, often in good health, received substantial benefits without working and paid no income taxes on them.

Social security's effect on labor supply

Men have been retiring from the labor force at an increasing rate. This is due to several factors: the availability of social security benefits, the increasing level of the benefit amounts, and the increase in private pensions. Although there has been a concomitant improvement in health of the aged, that development has not reduced the number of pensions. In contrast, the SSA usually maintains that retrospective studies show the declining health of the aged to be the most important reason for retirement. When retirement is planned, however, its timing is related to anticipated income, and the data do not appear to support the hypothesis that many retirees, especially the young aged, are too ill to work. The retirement test, as well as potential benefits and social security taxes, influence labor supply decisions more than does health status. According to one author, who studied the effects of the retirement test,

> our results suggest that a decrease in the implicit tax rate on earnings from one-half to one-third would reduce the annual probability of retirement by about fifty percent! Applying the coefficient estimates to time series data on the labor force participation of the elderly implies that the social security system has been the major factor in the explosion in earlier retirement.[14]

The above is based primarily on data about white males, and is modestly qualified. It does, however, appear to debunk SSA's rationalization that illness is the major cause of retirement.

> In light of the conjecture reported above that poor health is the primary cause of retirement, it is interesting to note that for those people in the sample who retired, the average hours of illness the year prior to retirement was 59.2; for the entire sample of work years, the average was 84.5![15]

It is true that compulsory retirement is increasingly mandated by business firms, and that this interacts with the influence of anticipated

---

14. Michael Boskin, "Social Security and Retirement Decisions," *Economic Inquiry,* January 1977, p. 1.

15. Ibid., p. 10.

retirement incomes. However, the SSA's 1976 report, *Reaching Retirement Age,* states that "failing health is the most important reason described by over half the men claiming reduced benefits."[16] This retrospective analysis, in contradiction to prospective studies, appears to reflect the usual defensive response offered by persons who rationalize an earlier decision to retire by pleading ill health because it is the reason most acceptable to society. Among other reasons commonly given are that their businesses were doing poorly, or that they had reached the compulsory retirement age.

The supply of labor at the margin is the part of labor supply that is most affected by the retirement test, which acts as a very heavy marginal tax on earnings exceeding the amount—$3,000 in 1976—that carries no penalty or loss in benefits.

For married women, health reasons appear to be less important in their retirement decisions. During retrospective interviews, they even answer, for the most part, that they retire early because of "the impact of household responsibilities." The effects of a worker's husband's or wife's employment, earnings, and retirement appear to need more analysis, both in total and at the margin.

An information gap: social security and "Catch 22"

Many married women do not know that if a married woman elects to take a reduced benefit based on her own earnings record, at early retirement (that is, at 62 through 64), then any social security benefit to which she may become entitled later—for example, a secondary wife's benefit based on her husband's earnings record—will also be reduced. In June 1975, in response to the Advisory Council's concern about this, the Social Security Administration published a pamphlet, "A Woman's Guide to Social Security." On page 6 of that pamphlet we find that a woman who once elects to receive a reduced benefit on her own wage record will then always receive a reduced benefit even though it may be based on her husband's record.

Despite this publication many women are still ignorant of this fact and act in ignorance of it. Having retired early on their own earnings record, they find out too late that when they are widowed they cannot transfer to the "unreduced" amount of the secondary benefit, which is 100 percent of their husband's primary benefit. The latter benefit is

---

16. Virginia Reno, "Why Men Stop Working Before Age 65," in U.S. Department of Health, Education, and Welfare, *Reaching Retirement Age,* Report No. 47, p. 43.

reduced by the same percentage as the primary benefit based on their own earnings was reduced. I believe that their ignorance of this point is due to the lack of logic behind this ruling, and I find it incredible from an equity point of view. Men who also elect to take a reduced benefit based on their own earnings are subject to the same rule.

On the other hand, a married woman who elects a wife's reduced benefit (because it is larger than her own primary benefit or because she has no primary benefit) may receive, if she outlives her husband, 100 percent of his primary benefit.[17] Such a regulation is truly a "Catch-22."

---

17. *Social Security Handbook,* 1973, p.131. This also applies to a husband's (widower's) benefits.

—————— 8 ——————

SAVING AND CAPITAL FORMATION

By Gerald Musgrave

SAVING AND CAPITAL FORMATION

Does the U.S. social security system have an important influence on the nation's saving and capital formation? This is a critical question, since economic growth, productivity, and prosperity all depend in the long run on capital accumulation, both present and future. If a government program reduces saving, and thus both investment and capital growth, we must expect to have slower economic development.

A favorite topic among economists in the mid-1970s was the capital shortage widely predicted for the next decade. Because the American economy's capital stock results from investment generated by saving, economists had renewed their interest in the economics of saving. One important motivation to save is future retirement. An important element in retirement is the loss of all or a major part of the person's annual work income. Expected loss of work income during retirement is therefore likely to influence workers' present economic decisions. Since social security taxes are a major deduction from most workers' pay and the "benefits" a major component of retirees' income, social security could indeed have an important influence on personal savings.

In 1976 more money was collected in social security payroll taxes than in corporate income tax. This made the social security payroll tax second only to individual income tax as a source of tax revenue. As compared with the personal income tax, 53 percent of the work force was paying more in social security taxes than in income taxes.

Recognizing the importance of these issues, the Quadrennial Advisory Council on Social Security recommended that a nongovernmental body study the "possible effects of social security on capital formation

---

Chapter 8 is by Dr. Gerald Musgrave, Research Fellow, the Hoover Institution.

. . . [and] the incidence of [social security] payroll taxes."[1] This chapter reviews the current understanding of the relation between saving, capital formation, and social security.

In the sections that follow, the question of who pays for social security is considered first. Economists call this the "incidence" of the tax. It is important to start here because we can determine the program's economic influence only if we know who pays for it. Then three effects of social security on saving are considered. First, because social security taxes reduce disposable income, the program thus reduces the aggregate saving rate of workers. Second, social security benefits are an asset of the individual and these increase household wealth. This additional wealth also causes families to save less. Third, because social security has influenced individuals to retire at an earlier age, additional savings are needed to provide retirement income over the additional retirement years. This effect would cause persons to save more. The last section is an explanation of how these three forces are resolved.

Incidence of Social Security Taxes

The influence of the social security tax on individuals has been the subject of some discussion since its payment mechanism is different from that of other taxes. Half the tax, supposedly, is paid by the employee and the other half by the employer. I say "supposedly" because the worker sees the deduction of his tax in his payroll record; the employer's payment is not shown. The payment mechanism causes some persons to believe incorrectly that the tax's final resting place— what economists call its burden—must necessarily reflect the 50/50 payment arrangement. Unfortunately, for policy makers it is not easy to focus the burden of the tax by the payment mechanism. A good way to begin analyzing the influence of social security on saving and capital formation is to see who pays for it.

Social security benefits are paid according to a flat rate tax of 11.7 percent on wage income up to a maximum of $16,500. The maximum tax of $1,930.50 (16,500 × 0.117) is composed of three parts: $1,443.75 for so-called old-age and survivors "insurance;" $189.75 for disability insurance; and $297.00 for Medicare. Table 8.1 presents the maximum rates for Old-Age and Survivors, Disability, and Health Insurance (OASDHI) from 1937 to 1977. The growth in both the tax rate and the

1. U.S. Congress, House, Committee on Ways and Means, *Reports of the Quadrennial Advisory Council on Social Security*, 94th Cong., 1st sess., H.D. 94-75, March 10, 1975 (Washington, D.C.: Government Printing Office, 1975), p.xvi.

TABLE 8.1
OASDHI TAX RATES AND MAXIMUM TAXABLE EARNINGS

YEARS	EARNINGS TAX OASDHI	MAXIMUM TAXABLE EARNINGS ($)	MAXIMUM TAX PAID ($)	ADJUSTED FOR CONSUMER PRICE INDEX (1967 DOLLARS)[a]
1937 through 1949	2.0%	3,000	60.00	84.03 (1949)[b]
1950	3.0	3,000	90.00	124.83
1951	3.0	3,600	108.00	138.82
1952	3.0	3,600	108.00	135.85
1953	3.0	3,600	108.00	134.83
1954	4.0	3,600	144.00	178.88
1955	4.0	4,200	168.00	209.48
1956	4.0	4,200	168.00	206.39
1957	4.5	4,200	189.00	224.20
1958	4.5	4,200	189.00	218.25
1959	4.5	4,800	216.00	247.42
1960	6.0	4,800	288.00	324.69
1961	6.0	4,800	288.00	321.43
1962	6.25	4,800	300.00	331.13
1963	7.25	4,800	348.00	379.50
1964	7.25	4,800	348.00	374.60
1965	7.25	4,800	348.00	368.25
1966	7.7	6,600	508.20	522.84
1967	7.8	6,600	514.80	514.80
1968	7.8	7,800	608.40	583.88
1969	8.4	7,800	655.20	596.72
1970	8.4	7,800	655.20	563.37
1971	9.2	7,800	717.50	591.51
1972	9.2	9,000	828.00	660.81
1973	9.7	10,800	1,047.60	787.08
1974	9.9	13,200	1,306.90	884.83
1975	9.9	14,100	1,395.90	865.94
1976	9.9	15,300	1,514.70	886.31
1977	9.9%	16,500	1,633.50	901.99

a. Assuming a 6% price increase in 1977.

b. 1939 = $154.64 (table B-42, U.S. Department of Labor, Bureau of Labor Statistics).

SOURCE: Adapted from *Social Security Bulletin,* "Annual Statistical Supplement 1974," (Washington, D.C.: U.S. Government Printing Office, 1976) p. 32. Includes Old-Age and Survivors Insurance, and Disability Insurance; excludes Medicare and Unemployment Insurance.

maximum earnings level is impressive. The last column is an attempt to present the growth of the program in perspective. The maximum tax paid has been converted to 1967 dollars in order to account for inflation ($60.00 in 1949 had the purchasing power of $84.03 in 1967).

The real growth of the program, after the effect of inflation is removed, amounts to a compound rate of 7.32 percent per year from 1950 to 1977, or nearly 11 times its original amount. The maximum social security tax on self-employed persons rose from $1,208.70 (7.9 percent of $15,300) in 1976 to $1,303.50 (7.9 percent of $16,500) in 1977. Under current law, the rate will grow to 12.1 percent in January 1978 and the wage base to about $17,700. The total payment would then be $2,141.70. However, the Senate Finance Committee wants to raise social security tax revenue by more than $1 billion starting in January 1978. If, as seems likely, the additional revenue is generated by a rate increase, the new rate would be 12.3 percent. This rate would yield a maximum payment of $2,177.10 per year. Thus the program is a large and growing part of every worker's economic life.

The original intent of Congress was to distribute the burden of the tax between employers and employees, a goal that was to be accomplished by having the employer pay half and the employee pay the remaining half. This describes the "statutory tax incidence" or division of legal responsibility for writing the check to the government. However, the payment mechanism of a tax does not, in general, determine who bears its economic impact. After the tax is levied, each taxpayer will attempt to pass the economic burden of paying it to someone else

Market and institutional factors in most cases determine the success of such efforts. In some cases, the relative bargaining strength of economic units determines who actually pays the tax. Eventually, however, every tax is paid by individuals. A tax can be levied on business but it must be paid by individual citizens. The tax may have differential effects on citizens who are sole proprietors, shareowners (directly or through private pension funds), employees, bondholders, consumers, renters, etc. How could a payroll tax levied on business be shifted to labor?

The most reasonable position for any business manager is to consider total cost of labor when making personnel decisions. For a moment, consider a hypothetical law requiring each married employee to receive two pay checks, one check payable to the employee for half the salary and the other half to the spouse. This law would increase administrative costs and require more data processing than a single check to the married worker, but the economics of the employment situation, other things being equal, would not change. The employer does not care if the check is given to the employee, the spouse, or a financial manager. In every case, the payment mechanism is just a formality. The reality is the trading of the worker's labor for money income. The same thing is true if the employer has to write a check for 4.95 percent of the worker's wage and send it to the government.[2] Any influence of the tax on business would be independent of the payment mechanism. So we must determine the economic incidence of the tax without regard to its statutory incidence.

Imposition of the payroll tax could lead the firm to try avoiding it in a number of ways. As a direct action, the firm might cut wages by the amount of the tax. In a world of inflation and institutions that make wage reductions impractical, the result would be to make wages grow at a slower rate than productivity and price increases—until real wages were reduced by the amount of the tax.

In the sections that follow, it is understood that such adjustments can and do occur, and that the focus will be on the real economic effects. The first response of the firm is most likely to reduce (real) wages paid to the worker by the whole amount of the tax and leave (real) labor costs unchanged. The result is that 95.05 percent of the earnings are paid to the employee and 4.95 percent to the employee's "hidden partner," the Social Security Administration. Other possible responses are:

1. The firm could attempt to increase the price of its product. Because it had higher labor costs, it might reduce the supply of its product (i.e., reduce the quantity supplied at any given cost level), and thus the price of the product increases.
2. The firm could substitute labor-saving capital for the now more expensive labor (it is assumed that the cost of capital goods will not increase in the same proportion as has labor).
3. The firm could substitute skilled for unskilled workers if the earnings of its skilled workers were greater than the tax base, currently $16,500. The idea here is that if the employer pays tax on the first $16,500 of earnings, he would rather hire one worker than two provided the one worker produces as much as the two together. The reason for this is the employer would "pay" $816.75 for the one worker and $1,633.50 for the two workers. In most firms this would be impossible; it is unlikely that one highly skilled worker would be twice as productive as two less-skilled workers. Usually, productivity increases are achieved by

---

2. Income taxes can become important. In this case, the worker does not have to pay income tax on the 4.95% of his earnings that is sent to the government.

       dividing the job into several lesser tasks or by adding capital
equipment.

4. Two final possibilities have been proposed that are less plausible
   than the ones listed above.[3] First, firms would reduce nonlabor
   costs. Supposedly, these new social security tax pressures would
   cause the firm to be more cost conscious. The argument is that
   the firm would attempt to engage in new cost reduction plans,
   such as energy conservation or more economical inventory
   policies.

5. The second possibility is that the firm could accept a lower profit
   rate. The presumption here is that the firm determines its own
   profit rate.

Each of these actions would be met in turn with reactions from the
intended recipient. Most firms would consider a combination of
responses unique to the firm's production and marketing conditions.

If the statutory taxpayer were successful in shifting all or part of the
tax to someone else, that person would also attempt to shift the tax to
another individual. Figures 8.1 and 8.2, adapted from work done by
the Tax Foundation, give an impression of how the shifting process
might work and what are some of the alleged barriers to it.[4] The figures
describe only some of the things that could take place. The list is not
intended to include all the complexities involved. Two things are clear:
first, the tax must be borne by individuals; and second, the statutory
incidence of the tax is not the same as its true or economic incidence.
So far, we have viewed the burden of the social security tax from the
perspective of the individual taxpayer. It is also true that this tax, like
every other, has an *excess* economic burden. This excess burden is in
addition to the economic burden previously discussed. The burden
comes from the fact that the tax distorts the allocation of resources and
causes the economic system to operate less efficiently. The excess
burden, or "dead weight loss" as it is sometimes called, results from the
distortion of economic decisions, especially in the choice between work
and leisure, present versus future consumption, and relative factor
costs.

The true or economic incidence, then, is not necessarily the same as
the statutory incidence, while the total burden is larger than the tax

---

3. Tax Foundation, Inc., *Economic Aspects of the Social Security Tax,* Research Publication
No. 5 (New York: the Foundation, 1966), pp. 32-41.

4. Ibid.

FIGURE 8.1

EMPLOYER'S ATTEMPT TO SHIFT PAYROLL TAX

SHIFTING ACTIONS	POSSIBLE FORMS OF RESISTANCE TO THESE ACTIONS	TAX "BEARER" IF TAX SHIFTED	REACTIONS BY THE NEW BEARER
1. Reduce employees' direct compensation by the amount of tax. Maintain labor cost to the firm constant.	Changes in existing labor contract prohibited; union opposition; labor shortages; worker opposition because workers may believe that the tax-based benefits are not equal to the costs.	Employees.	See figure 8.2.
2. Increase product price because labor costs have increased.	Company may fear such action will lead to large reduction in profits; fear of loss of market position; fear of reaction by various regulatory authorities.	Consumers of the product and workers, to the extent that employment is reduced.	Purchase less of the product; form consumer pressure groups; workers form unions and lobby for nonlabor legislation.
3. Substitute · capital for labor because relative prices have changed.	Capital goods may not be available; technical production problems; financing difficulties; large startup costs; capital goods may increase in price.	Workers who lose jobs or must retrain.	Form unions with restrictive work rules; lobby for legislation limiting employers' rights.
4. Substitute more-skilled for less-skilled labor because taxes have an upper limit.	Upper limit too large to allow much advantage; cost of skilled labor; production methods not available for such substitution.	Unskilled or less-skilled employees.	Same as item 3, above.
5. Reduce all other costs to compensate for increased labor costs.	Firm may not be able to economize on resource use; costs of efficiency program larger than reduction in costs; resistance to change of management.	Uncertain.	——
6. Accept lower profit rate.	Profit level not under the control of management; the firm cannot administer the price and cost levels; shareholders not willing to accept lower return.	Shareowners; pension funds and beneficiaries; other trusts that hold the securities; sole proprietors and partners.	Sell securities; hold wealth in other forms (jewels, gold, art); invest in other nations; venture capital for new firms and products reduced.

FIGURE 8.2
EMPLOYEE'S REACTION TO WAGE TAX

SHIFTING ACTIONS	POSSIBLE FORMS OF RESISTANCE TO THESE ACTIONS	TAX "BEARER" IF TAX SHIFTED
1. Reduce saving.	Employees have a target saving level or rate; employees have no savings; workers have a fixed ratio of consumption to saving.	Borrowers; national economy, if growth is reduced.
2. Reduce consumption.	Workers have fixed financial obligations; workers unwilling to reduce real or psychological consumption level.	Sellers of the products; workers in these industries who receive lower wages or are unemployed.
3. Seek work that is not covered by the tax.	Restricted entry in noncovered areas; large capital requirements needed to make change; most jobs covered by the law.	Avoiding the tax by moving from covered to noncovered jobs would place higher burdens on the remaining workers.
4. Seek additional work or overtime.	Workers unwilling to consume less leisure; institutional restrictions on part-time employment; lack of job opportunities at wage level.	Other workers who would have been employed.
5. Argue for a wage increase to compensate for reduction in after-tax income.	Low bargaining power of the employee; workers' current salary at the going wage level; employer threatens to automate.	Employee or consumers of the product.

revenues. The next step is to look at the evidence and see who does in fact pay for social security.

Paying for social security: the facts

Each economic agent will, in his own self-interest, attempt to shift the burden of the tax to others. The tax's final resting place depends on the ability of individuals to make others bear the burden of it. Where individuals are sensitive to price or wage changes, the tax is likely to be shifted. The burden thus falls on individuals who cannot respond to changing economic conditions, or on those who have few alternative ways of reacting to price or wage changes.

The empirical analysis of data concerning the incidence of the social security tax is a relatively new undertaking by economists. The social security system is important because of its large size and its potential impact on the economy. Both the techniques and the data are available for econometric analysis of the tax incidence.

The most important issue is, who pays the employer's part of the tax? It seems clear that if in the long run labor pays for the employer's share, labor probably pays the employee's share too. Another way to look at it is that if labor cannot avoid the burden being shifted from the employer, it could not shift its own burden. So it is clear that one should study who bears the burden at the most fundamental level— that of labor and capital.

First, we will briefly consider the two most important and most recent time series studies, one by Brittain and the other by Deran.[5] These two studies are similar in that each uses time series data from the same country, the United States. However, they reach opposite conclusions.

Brittain's analysis, which covered the period 1947-65, found support for the hypothesis that the employer tax is completely shifted to the employee. His model was an adaption of one developed by Ronald McKinnon, with the addition of payroll tax and cyclical variables.[6] Evidence from 18 of 27 two-digit SIC code industries seemed to confirm the total shifting of the tax from the employer to the employee, while evidence from 9 favored no shifting. When Brittain used another model, data from 21 industries supported shifting and evidence from 6 supported no shifting. Unfortunately, these statistical procedures do not yield impressive results.

The Deran study is unique in that it found the burden of the social security tax not to be borne by labor.[7] Deran used time series data from Puerto Rico — an interesting choice, since residents of Puerto Rico were first taxed in 1951. Deran attempted to compare pretax with posttax factor shares on a national income accounts basis. For the period 1948-55, she attempted to detect any year-to-year changes in the proportion of national income that went respectively to labor, rental income, interest, and profits. In 1952, labor's share of income rose to

5. John A. Brittain, *The Payroll Tax for Social Security* (Washington, D.C.: Brookings Institution, 1972); Elizabeth Deran, "Changes in Factor Income Shares Under the Social Security Tax," *Review of Economics and Statistics,* November 1967, pp.627-30.

6. Ronald I. McKinnon, "Wages, Capital Costs, and Employment in Manufacturing: A Model Applied to 1947-58 U.S. Data," *Econometrica,* July 1962, pp. 501-21.

7. Deran, "Changes . . . ."

66.7 percent from the 1951 level of 64.8 percent, when the tax was first introduced. From 1947 to 1951, before social security was introduced to Puerto Rico, labor's share of national income averaged 63.7 percent; after social security, from 1952 to 1955, it averaged 66.1 percent. Deran's interpretation was that labor's share increased at the expense of business profits and, to a lesser extent, of rental income and net interest.

A statistical error in Deran's work was discovered by Dr. Ronald Hoffman of the Office of Research and Statistics of the Social Security Administration: when the data were examined using Hoffman's method, the yearly changes were not statistically significant.[8] He also pointed to a number of other problems, one of which was that the years 1951, 1952, and 1953 had been years when changes in the labor share resulted "in no small part from changes in compensation paid by the United States Federal Government." This "Federal Compensation," he added, was not covered under the social security system, so that when it was extracted from both income and labor, the values of the statistics in question were "not significant."[9] The Deran study was the only one I could locate that purports to show that the burden of social security was borne by any group other than workers. We must conclude that it does not provide convincing evidence that the payroll tax falls on capital rather than on labor.

However, when we consider these time-series results in conjunction with other cross-country studies, a more compelling result emerges. These other studies are cross-country analyses of social security. They differ from time series studies in that they permit more variation in tax rates. Also, it is generally agreed that cross section regressions tend to yield long-run relations.[10]

An interesting study of social security using cross-country data appeared in the *American Economic Review* for 1971.[11] Statistical estimates of production functions were undertaken to measure the effect of different social security tax rates. Such econometric estimates measure how average wage rates vary across countries in response to

---

8. Ronald F. Hoffman, "Factor Shares and the Payroll Tax: A Comment," *Review of Economics and Statistics,* November 1968, pp. 506-8.

9. Ibid., p. 508.

10. Lawrence Klein, *An Introduction to Econometrics* (Englewood Cliffs, N.J.: Prentice-Hall, 1962).

11. John A. Brittain, "The Incidence of Social Security Payroll Taxes," *American Economic Review,* March 1971, pp. 110-25

different tax rates. Economists agree that many factors influence wage rates; the most important are productivity of labor, value of output produced, and supply of labor. In practice economists use value added in U.S. dollars as a measure of output produced, and labor in man-years as a measure of the quantity of labor supplied. Productivity of labor is measured by dividing value added by the amount of labor employed. Wage rates are basic earnings in U.S. dollars excluding the employer's social insurance tax. The tax rate is measured as the percentage of workers' base earnings taxed by the social insurance agency. With econometric methods, these influences can be held constant, and the effect of changes in the tax rate can be measured. In these studies the attempt is to measure the final impact of the employers' part of the tax. The presumption is that if the employees bear the employer's share, via reduced wages, it is unlikely that they would be able to transfer their share of the tax to others. That is, if the employees cannot avoid the shifting action of the employers, they will be unable to shift the tax to other individuals.

If it is found that wages are not sensitive to changes in the social security tax rate, the conclusion would be that employees do not bear the employers' share of the tax. This would mean that in countries with a high social security tax as in countries with a low one, all the influences mentioned above (productivity, value of production, supply of labor) would explain the various wage rates. If, on the other hand, wages tended to be lower in the high-tax nations and higher in the low-tax ones, we would know, after taking into account the other factors, that the employees bear a part of the employers' social security tax. Where taxes are high, the employer would be reducing the wage paid to the employee to compensate for the wage tax paid to the Social Security Administration or its equivalent. Fortunately, the economic models that are used to analyze these wage patterns across countries are accurate. Accuracy in this context means that between 90 and 95 percent of the sample variation in wage rates can be attributed to the estimated effect of variation in productivity, value added, labor supply, and social security tax rates.

Let us assume that only one of the following two possibilities can occur: (1) employers shift all of the social security tax to employees via reduced wages; (2) employers shift none of the tax to their employees. Which is more likely? This was the first question studied; data were for the period 1952 to 1959, and were drawn from samples of 64, 44, and 30 industrial nations. It was found that in all these cases the employees were paying the employers' share of the tax.[12] Since the monetary values of these nations were converted to U.S. dollars, and since such conversion involves a number of complex issues, the conversion methods may have influenced the results. In this study, however, two conversion formulae, i.e., purchasing power parity and official exchange rates, did not produce different results; in all cases, the employers' share was shifted to the employees.[13]

A more complex measurement was undertaken with the same data to see how much of the social security tax was shifted. Six separate equations were estimated; both currency conversion methods were used; various samples consisting of 64, 44, and 30 countries were taken. These equations were also found reliable in a statistical sense: over 93 percent of the variance in wage levels was explained by variations in the explanatory variables, including the social security tax rate. The result was that the employers' part of the social security tax was shifted to the employees.[14] In fact, the results indicated that in most cases more than the whole amount was shifted. One explanation might be that firms added the administrative expense of the paper work connected with social security, and then removed this amount from the employees' take-home pay in addition to the social security wage tax.

The ability of an employer to shift the burden of the tax to his employees might vary from industry to industry. As a final test of the proposition that employers shift the burden in some industries, the data were disaggregated into separate industries: food, clothing, chemicals, metals, textiles, wood products, paper products, printing and publishing, leather and leather products, rubber products, nonmetallic mineral products, basic metals, metal products, and a category know as "other manufacturing." A separate equation was estimated for each industry; because of data availability, the number of countries in each industry varied from 25 to 36. In only two industries, leather and nonmetallic mineral products, did it appear that the burden of the tax was not shifted to the employees.[15] In the 11 remaining industries the tax was shifted to the employees.

----

12. Ibid., p. 119.

13. Ibid., p. 120.

14. Brittain, *Payroll Tax,* table 3-3, p. 70.

15. Although in these cases the statistical justification was not strong, the shifting coefficient was not statistically significant.

All these studies lead to the general conclusion that the burden of social security is most likely borne by workers. Employers are able to shift their portion of the tax to employees. Employee earnings are reduced from what they would be in the absence of the social security system. Such reductions in workers' disposable income have important influences on their present and future economic behavior—for example, on their consumption and saving decisions. Also, we would expect the influence of the tax on the economic process to be somewhat different than it would be either if the tax were paid by employers from rents, interests, and profits, or if it were paid by consumers via increases in product prices.

Because the payment mechanism does not influence the economic consequences of the tax, the Social Security Administration should include both "halves" of the tax when estimating the cost-benefit ratios of different parts of the program. The employee pays income tax on the earnings out of which the employee tax comes, but not on the earnings foregone in the form of the employer's payroll tax. This is consistent with the fiction that it is the employer who really pays the employer tax. Thus current income tax is inconsistent with economic reality, which is that the employee pays all the social security tax. The tax treatment of both parts of the tax should therefore be the same.

I recommend that both parts be excluded from current income tax, just as voluntary contributions to private pension plans are excluded. This might help to save the concept that social security is social "insurance." After retirement, social security benefits should then be fully taxed as ordinary income. This recommendation would decrease the burden of the tax during working years. It would not hurt low-income retirees because their income after retirement would be (with double exemption at age 65) too small to be taxed, or at least taxed at lower rates than during their working years.[16]

Social Security and Saving

Economists do not know what effect social security has on the saving rate and capital formation. Recent research has attempted to measure

---

16. Brittain, *Payroll Tax*, pp. 79-81, lists a number of other implications concerning income distribution, international competitive positions, collective bargaining, and economic stabilization. These are of secondary importance to our study but demonstrate the pervasive impact of the results.

the effect of social security on saving; however, each study has been strongly criticized. Many studies of social security are now underway, and in the next few years we may see a consensus among economists. One important reason why consensus will be difficult to achieve is that the study of social security revolves around some of the most controversial issues in economics.

The cause of our uncertainty about social security's effect on saving is that we do not fully understand the economics of saving itself. One of the important features of the economic landscape is the secular constancy of the proportion of total disposable income saved. The ratio of aggregate saving to disposable income has fluctuated around 0.09 since the turn of the century. Personal saving has averaged 6.5 percent of personal disposable income since 1950, the only major changes being very high rates during the world wars and very low rates in depressions. At one time it was believed that the saving rate would increase as the income of the nation grew. The following quote illustrates the Keynesian notion of consumption, accepted by many economists until the mid-1950s.[17]

> The fundamental psychological law, upon which we are entitled to depend with great confidence both *a priori* from our knowledge of human nature and from the detailed facts of experience, is that men are disposed, as a rule and on the average, to increase their consumption as their income increases, but not by as much as the increase in their income.
>
> This is especially the case where we have short periods in view, as in the case of the so-called cyclical fluctuations of employment during which habits, as distinct from more permanent psychological propensities, are not given time enough to adapt themselves to changed objective circumstances. For a man's habitual standard of life usually has the first claim on his income, and he is apt to save the difference which discovers itself between his actual income and the expense of his habitual standard; or, if he does adjust his expenditure to changes in his income, he will, over short periods, do so imperfectly. Thus a rising income will often be accompanied by increased saving, and a falling income by decreased saving, on a greater scale at first than subsequently.
>
> But apart from short-period *changes* in the level of income, it is also obvious that a higher absolute level of income will tend, as a rule, to

---

17. A.C. Pigou, in his *Employment and Equilibrium* (London: Macmillan, 1941), indicates that Alfred Marshall recognized this relationship many years earlier than did Keynes.

widen the gap between income and consumption. For the satisfaction of the immediate primary needs of a man and his family is usually a stronger motive than the motives towards accumulation, which only acquire effective sway when a margin of comfort has been attained. These reasons will lead, as a rule, to a greater *proportion* of income being saved as real income increases. But whether or not a greater proportion is saved, we take it as a fundamental psychological rule of any modern community that, when its real income is increased, it will not increase its consumption by an equal *absolute* amount, so that a greater absolute amount must be saved, unless a large and unusual change is occurring at the same time in other factors.[18]

However, subsequent long-range studies found no evidence supporting the hypothesis that saving would increase relative to income as income grew. The underestimation of post-World War II spending by Keynesian economists, who proceeded to extrapolate the prewar data, proved embarrassing. They used equations like $C = a + bY$, where C was consumption, Y was income, and a, b, were parameters, estimated from 1930-40 data. These estimates were too low to substantiate the Keynesian hypothesis. Ad hoc explanations were brought in to save the day. It was time to reevaluate the basic Keynesian idea.

Since then, two new ideas have revolutionized economists' thinking about consumption and saving: the "permanent income hypothesis," developed by Milton Friedman; and the "life-cycle hypothesis," contributed by Franco Modigliani.[19] Both base their analyses on work done by Irving Fisher, and indeed the two hypotheses have much in common.[20] The noneconomist should understand that theories about consumption are theories about saving too. In other words, income has only two uses, to be saved or spent. When economists talk about saving, they mean—nonspending. This is different from other ideas about saving, as when people think of their stocks or bonds, consumer durables, or art and jewels as "saving" or maybe an "investment." To an economist, these personal possessions are wealth. As such, they are

18. J.M. Keynes, *The General Theory of Employment, Interest, and Money* (London: Macmillan, 1936), pp. 96-97.

19. Friedman, *A Theory of the Consumption Function* (Princeton, N.J.: National Bureau of Economic Research, 1957); Modigliani and Richard Brumberg, "Utility Analysis and the Consumption Function," in Kenneth Kurihara, ed., *Post Keynesian Economics* (New Brunswick, N.J.: Rutgers University Press, 1954); Modigliani and Albert Ando, "The 'Life Cycle' Hypothesis of Saving: Aggregate Implications and Tests," *American Economic Review*, March 1963.

20. Irving Fisher, *The Theory of Interest* (New York: Macmillan 1930).

a stock of resources that can be sold to provide consumption, but purchasing them is not saving.

Saving, then, is the absence of consuming. Unspent income can be held in cash or a bank account. This money can be loaned to business. When business firms purchase capital equipment, it is called investment. Economists would not consider the purchase of existing securities as investment but rather a transfer of financial assets from one stockholder to another. Economists traditionally use saving to refer to the annual flow of disposable income not consumed. Saving is thus a rate. In contrast, savings is the term used to represent the stock of accumulated saving. The terms are used correctly when we say that a person who is saving $100 per year will have $1,000 of savings at the end of 10 years (that is, if the money is being stuffed under the floorboards instead of deposited in a savings bank). The final point on nomenclature is that gross private saving is composed of personal saving. In addition, gross private saving includes corporate saving in the form of increases in retained earnings, capital consumption allowance or depreciation, and increases in business inventories.

In this chapter, except where noted, personal saving is the kind of saving that is being discussed. Neither Friedman nor Modigliani bases his analysis on psychological propensities to consume or save. Both analyses are based on the rational decision-making process of the household. Since analyses of social security have been based on the life-cycle hypothesis, the following discussion concentrates on this idea. One should expect that the new research on social security will investigate saving with the help of consumption functions based on the permanent income hypothesis.

The life-cycle hypothesis

The basic idea of the life-cycle hypothesis is that decisions about saving are made in the same way as all other economic decisions, namely, by an individual who has constraints placed on his behavior, and is attempting to maximize his well-being within those constraints. In this case, the worker begins his working career earning a relatively low income and saving little. As he gains experience and knowledge, his wages increase. So do his savings. At retirement, those savings become the source of his consumption. When he spends his previous savings, it is called dissaving. Thus savings are used to smooth the consumption stream over the life cycle of the individual. Figure 8.3 is representative of the individual's earning, consuming, and saving history.

FIGURE 8.3
LIFE CYCLE HYPOTHESIS

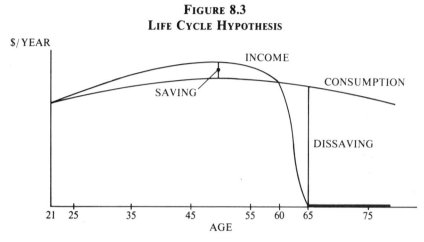

Figure 8.3 shows the time path of a worker's earnings. The first twenty years of this person's life have been excluded; however, we could have begun at any time. After this person's twenty-first birthday, he works for forty-four years and retires at 65. In fact, our worker actually began to dissave after his sixtieth year, primarily because his earnings fell. So the savings during his first working years are used to smooth out his consumption expenditures over his lifetime. This is only one of many patterns that could emerge. A more typical pattern might be one in which the income grows less rapidly and peaks in the late forties to early fifties, decreasing slowly to age 65, then falling to zero at retirement. Of course, these elements vary across occupations and by sex. The important fact is that during one's working years consumption is less than income. Consumption is relatively smooth through the life cycle even though wage income falls to zero. Individuals may differ in their life spending patterns, for example, when a son or daughter enters college or when an uninsured medical expense occurs. The expenditure patterns under discussion are for the economy as a whole, and individual exceptions will not alter the analysis.

This smooth consumption path for the economy is maintained through dissaving. The analysis could be expanded to include provision of estate accumulation for one's heirs. In our stylized case, we have no net saving in the sense that saving by workers is exactly counteracted by dissaving of those on retirement. This result, of course, requires a number of assumptions about the age distribution of the population, their plans for retirement and the productivity of the workers. We mention this last point since the result over the life cycle has some of the features of the "pay-as-you-go" social security system.

The analysis of social security would be straightforward if its only effect was to transfer wage taxes from workers to retirees (that is, if people included neither the reduction in current income nor the expected future payments in their decisions to save). The result would be proportional reductions in consumption and saving of workers and proportional increases in consumption and saving of the retired. The plan would have differential effects on workers and retirees because of differences in income. Suppose, for instance, that workers on an average spend about 91 cents of each additional dollar of take-home pay and retirees spend the whole dollar of social security benefits. Then an additional dollar of social security tax would reduce saving by 9 cents. If social security taxes were $90 billion, that would reduce saving by $8.1 billion per year. With personal saving amounting to $80 billion a year, this would amount to a 10 percent reduction in saving.

However, if the workers think of social security as forced saving replacing voluntary saving, the story is very different. A person who earns $16,500 annually and wants to save 9 percent of his income for his old age, presuming no social security, would save $1,485 per year. This is less than the $1,930 now withheld from his wage. Such a person need not save, because the compulsory program does his saving for him, so to speak. A person with twice the income, $33,000, who also wants to save 9 percent would save $2,970 in the absence of social security. The program would still provide $1,930 of forced saving, leaving only $1,040 to be voluntarily saved, not $2,970. Accordingly, if social security were a forced replacement of personal saving, it would have a large effect on total savings.

In 1976, $92.7 billion was collected in social security taxes.[21] Personal saving in the same year amounted to $77.8 billion.[22] The $92.7 billion can be seen as a direct reduction in personal saving, which would have totaled $170.5 billion. Personal saving has been reduced from its "potential" amount of $170.5 billion to $77.8 billion — a reduction of 54.4 percent, i.e., of $(170.5-77.8)/170.5$. Reducing "poten-

---

21. *Economic Report of the President: With the Annual Report of the Council of Economic Advisors* (Washington, D.C.: U.S. Government Printing Office, 1977), p. 267.

22. Ibid., p. 212.

tial" saving by this magnitude would have an important impact on the economy in addition to the impact of transferring income from current workers to current retirees.

The reader who wants to concentrate on the intergenerational transfer of resources should consult an important paper by Edgar Browning.[23] He finds these transfers to be analogous to debt-financed shifting of costs to future generations. However, his model does not allow for the effects of changes in saving and capital formation—effects that are the central concern of this chapter.

Some quantitative studies

Much of what we suspected but didn't know about social security was developed in the mid-1960s from two studies that dealt with private pension plans. The first study was by George Katona at the University of Michigan. His study, published in 1965, dealt with data collected in the period 1962-63 by the organization he heads, the University of Michigan Survey Research Center.[24] The center conducted interviews from a total of approximately 5,000 family units and the report covered 1,853 cases from families with incomes over $3,000. He found that individuals covered by private pension plans saved more than those not so covered. This was explained by what was called "level of aspirations"; supposedly, the worker raised his retirement needs and put more effort into saving. Also, the worker was presumed to have "goal feasibility," that is, his private pension plan made his retirement goals possible.

The second study had a similar result in that individuals covered by pension plans were found to save more than those who did not have a private plan. The study by Phillip Cagan of Columbia University, drew on the responses of more than 15,000 subjects who subscribed to *Consumer Reports;*[25] the data were collected from 1958 and 1959. Cagan, like Katona, found that participation in private pension plans increased the person's saving rate. He attributed this increase to a "recognition effect" that called attention to future retirement needs.

Cagan and Katona imply that participation in private pension plans somehow changes employees preferences in favor of future over

---

23. Edgar Browning, "Social Insurance and Intergeneration Transfers," *Journal of Law and Economics,* October 1973, pp. 215-37.

24. George Katona, *Private Pensions and Individual Saving,* University of Michigan Survey Research Center Monograph No. 40 (Ann Arbor, Michigan: the Center, 1965).

25. Phillip Cagan, *The Effect of Pension Plans on Aggregate Saving* (Princeton, N.J.: National Bureau of Economic Research, 1965).

present income. Nothing is said in their studies about the possibility
that people with these preferences might be self-selected into the
covered jobs. Also, we do not have data showing how a family actually
changes its decisions about saving over time. But in any event, these
results, which seem questionable, were assumed to apply to social
security. The conclusion was that social security actually caused people
to save more, presumably because they knew their retirement goals
were now possible: they recognized the need for such saving, and could
aspire to the good retirement life.

Recent studies of social security have yielded dramatically different
results. First, since they are the most controversial ones, we will
consider the series of studies by Martin Feldstein of Harvard.[26] They
are controversial because they indicate social security has had a large
and damaging effect on saving and capital formation. Rather than
look at social security taxes, Feldstein analyzed the process from the
perspective of the benefits. Some individuals might view the expected
benefits as an obligation of the government to provide an annuity. In
this way, the individual has an asset, the government annuity, that
increases his wealth. It is well known that changes in wealth alter
consumption patterns, so that social security may influence the saving
decision in this way.

This returns us to the basic Fisherian analysis.[27] Accordingly, Feldstein was able to introduce a wealth variable in an aggregate life cycle
consumption function. The hypothesis was that the addition of wealth
provided by the social security benefit would offset the individual's
private wealth accumulation. One of the main tasks in the study was to
compute the value of social security wealth for the American economy.
The size of such wealth depends on the number of individuals entitled
to benefits, their ages, the rate at which their income is expected to
grow, the discount rate that is used to measure the present value of
these future benefits, and the age-specific mortality rates of the covered
workers and spouses. These data were calculated for the period 1929-
71.

In 1971, social security wealth amounted to $2.029 trillion.[28] Social
security wealth is 60 percent of household wealth. This estimate implies

26. Martin Feldstein, "Social Security, Induced Retirement, and Aggregate Capital Accumulation," *Journal of Political Economy,* September-October 1974, pp. 905-26.

27. In the sense that Fisher, *Theory of Interest,* indicated that individuals make rational
decisions to purchase savings as they would other goods.

28. Feldstein, "Social Security . . .," pp. 911-16.

that social security may have reduced the stock of private wealth by 40 percent from $5 trillion to $3 trillion. Feldstein believes that this reduction is "remarkably close to the estimate obtained by looking at the reduction in personal savings that would occur if households viewed Social Security taxes as an alternative to savings."[29] As confirming evidence, Feldstein points to the U.S. Treasury estimate of $2.4 trillion as the unfunded liability of the social security system. But in our context, the financial liability is not the major issue; this astronomic amount is important as an indication of the program's huge effect on household wealth.

A trillion dollars is a large amount. A stack of silver dollars a mile high would amount to less than a million dollars. If the stack were a thousand miles high it would amount to less than a billion dollars. And remember, a trillion is a thousand billion. We would need seven stacks of silver dollars from the earth to the moon to make a trillion dollars.[30]

We have already seen that social security would reduce private capital accumulation if expected social security benefits were substituted for private savings. This would be an important effect. However, we do not know whether such a substitution has taken place.

The question was investigated with an aggregate life cycle consumption function. Based on data from 1929 to 1971 (the war years of 1941 to 1946 were excluded), the estimated equation was:

$$C_t = 228.0 + 0.530\, Y_t + 0.120\, Y_{t-1} + 0.356\, RE_t + $$
$$0.014\, W_{t-1} + 0.021\, SSW_t$$

The equation was estimated by the method of least-squares regression. Here, C is per capita consumer expenditure in 1958 dollars; Y is per capita disposable personal income in 1958 dollars; RE is per capita retained earnings; W is per capita non-social security wealth, in 1958 dollars; and t is the observation year.

Standard statistical tests were performed on the equation. It passed all of them. The interpretation is that the marginal propensity to consume disposable income is 0.650.[31] This indicates that as per capita

29. Martin Feldstein, "Toward a Reform of Social Security," *Public Interest*, Summer 1975, p. 84.

30. We thank Mr. Geoffrey Calvert, for many years director of the Consulting Actuarial Division of Alexander and Alexander, Inc., for this example. An illuminating discussion of the magnitudes involved in social security policy can be found in his paper, "Will a Trillion Dollars Satisfy the Wolf?", in *Thinking About the Future* (New York: Alexander and Alexander, 1975).

31. The "marginal propensity" is the additional consumption that is generated by an additional dollar of disposable income.

disposable income increased 1 dollar, persons on an average increased their consumption by 65 cents and their savings by 35 cents. Economists familiar with these data might suspect that the 0.650 figure is too low. However, it should be remembered that the equation contains both wealth and retained earnings; if these were not included, the value would increase. Current and lagged disposable income are included as representative of expected future income.[32] The marginal propensity to consume retained earnings is 0.36, which is consistent with earlier work of Feldstein. The value of the non-social security household wealth coefficient is 0.014.

The most important result is that the marginal propensity to consume social security wealth is 0.021. Out of each additional dollar of social security wealth, 2 cents are consumed. This means that at each level of disposable income, 2 cents are not saved that would have been saved in the absence of social security. Remember the only two choices we have are to spend or to save. Two cents does not seem like much except when we recall that social security wealth is $2,029 billion. The resulting reduction in saving is 2,029 x 0.021 = $42.609 billion. Also, the social security wage taxes reduced disposable income by $51.0 billion, which indicates a reduction of (1.0 - 0.650) x 51.0 = $17.85 billion in personal savings. The total reduction in savings is $60.459 billion. Personal savings as a whole are estimated to be about one-half of what they would be without social security.[33] This means that social security greatly reduces capital formation and the level of GNP. Personal saving amounts to about 60 percent of total private saving, the principal addition being corporate retained earnings. Social security reduces total private saving by 38 percent. So, in the long run, the private capital stock of the nation would be reduced by 38 percent. This is the figure most quoted.

With other definitions for social security wealth and with various time periods, similar estimates of the reduction in the saving rate were obtained. These estimates ranged from $44 to $63 billion. Also, attempts were made to see what effects the introduction of an unemployment variable, or the use of a so-called permanent income variable would have on the result.[34] These changes had some effect on the social

---

32. See Modigliani and Ando, "The 'Life Cycle' Hypothesis . . .," for a justification of this procedure.

33. The actual level of personal saving in 1971 was $57.3 billion and in 1976 it was $77.8 billion. See *Economic Report of the President 1977*, p. 212.

34. Researchers often use an exponentially weighted moving average of past income as an approximation of permanent income. The purpose is to obtain a number that would be equivalent to the value of the earnings an individual anticipates.

security coefficients, but did not change the basic conclusion: social security has had a large and depressing effect on saving and capital formation in our economy.

One way to measure the impact of these estimated reductions is to determine how much higher our national income would have been in the absence of the social security program. For the past 30 years, economists have measured capital and labor utilization, and estimated the economic output that results. The mathematical formula used to estimate this relation is called the Cobb-Douglas production function. The formula is Output (GNP) = (Capital) $^{0.3}$ × (Labor) $^{0.7}$. In our example, capital would be increased by 40 percent with the elimination of the social security tax.

Using the estimated values for the economic parameters, Feldstein estimates GNP would be 10.62 percent higher in the absence of social security. Feldstein says a 40 percent reduction in the capital stock would be a conservative estimate. The computation would be $(1.4)^{0.3}$ × $(1.0)^{0.7}$ = 1.1062. GNP in 1972 would have increased by more than $124 billion.[35] In 1976 GNP would have increased from $1.692 trillion to $1.872 trillion, an increase of $179 billion. According to Feldstein's estimates, over the past five years the economy has lost over $750 billion of GNP because of the social security program.

Private pension plans and social security

It is possible to reconcile the Feldstein result of a large aggregate reduction in personal saving (compared to what it would have been without social security) with the Cagan-Katona result of more saving under private pension plans. Workers who are covered by private pension plans have an economic incentive to retire earlier than they would otherwise. But when they retire, their income will drop and they must save more to cover the additional years of retirement. So it is possible to have two effects: (1) the substitution of social security benefits or wealth for private saving; (2) the early retirement of beneficiaries. The first effect decreases the amount of private saving; the second increases saving. The net effect depends on the relative importance of these two counteracting forces.

A number of studies by economists outside the Social Security Administration have found OASDHI to be an important factor in causing people to retire. Analysis of census and manpower data confirms the view that social security has encouraged retirement at

35. Feldstein, "Social Security . . .," p. 923.

younger ages than would otherwise have occurred. An interesting paper by Colin and Rosemary Campbell reviews the apparent dichotomy between research done at the Social Security Administration and research by independent scholars.[36] They found that the studies performed by the SSA from the 1940s onwards, using personal interviews, rejected the idea that social security influences the retirement decision. Instead, these studies cite such involuntary reasons for retirement as ill health, mandatory age limits, and failing or poor business conditions. In contrast, the independent studies, which used other sources of statistical data, found social security to be an important influence on the retirement decision. The Campbells cite over twenty studies in which social security does seem to have an impact on the age at which one retires.

Since age of retirement might be a factor in the decision on saving, it seems appropriate to consider it in the aggregate saving analysis. This is primarily what Alicia Munnell did in her doctoral dissertation.[37] She investigated the impact of the two offsetting forces under discussion. The first, of course, is the effect of the social security benefit acting as an asset that substitutes for private savings. The second we need to remember at this point, is early retirement which generates a need for more savings to last over the increased retirement years.

Munnell's work confirms the hypothesis that social security benefits have been a substitute for private savings. The result of this influence alone is to reduce the saving rate. Another of her findings is that people save for a variety of reasons. She finds the most important ones to be emergencies, retirement, and childrens' college education. Other reasons considered by Munnell included bequests and saving for equity positions in long-lived consumer durables. Her statistical analysis confirms the hypothesis that social security has exerted a stimulating but indirect influence on the saving rate by increasing the number of retirement years.

When Munnell reviewed the Cagan study, she rejected his idea that the net effect of pensions was to increase the saving rate. In her view, two major economic factors are at work and each has counteracted the other, leaving the saving rate relatively constant over the last twenty years. But she reminds us that this balance is unlikely to continue

36. Campbell and Campbell, "Conflicting Views on the Effect of Old-Age Survivors' Insurance on Retirement," *Economic Inquiry,* September 1976, pp. 369-88.

37. Alicia Munnell, *The Effect of Social Security on Personal Saving* (Cambridge, Mass.: Ballinger, 1974).

because the decline in the labor force participation rate of males over fifty has slowed. Also, benefits are expected to grow, and this will lead to a greater wealth substitution effect. She concludes that, if all other factors are held constant, "the net effect of Social Security in the future may be a serious decline in the saving rate. . . ."[38]

Feldstein, too, acknowledges the impact of social security on retirement.[39] He agrees with Munnell that social security has decreased the retirement age of people over 65 years. In other words, a person over 65 and eligible for benefits is more likely to retire than if there were no program. It is a time of life to recover the forced savings, and the social adequacy (welfare) provision of the program places a high marginal tax rate on earned income from the age of 65 to 72. This influence on saving means that more personal savings are necessary for the additional retirement years. It is, however, an influence that has been negated by the asset substitution effect of social security wealth.[40] Social security's forced saving effect has overpowered the early retirement effect.

The studies by Feldstein and Munnell are consistent in that one can say the saving *rate* has been relatively constant, with the early retirement effect offsetting the asset substitution effect. And, at the same time, private saving would have been higher without social security. Both authors agree that the asset substitution effect which depresses private saving, will be the dominant factor in the future.[41]

There seems to be no such thing as a noncontroversial study of social security. A particularly interesting critique of our present understanding of the relation between social security and saving was made by Selig Lesnoy and John Hambor, who are researchers at the SSA.[42] Their interests went farther than the simple impact of social security on saving; they also wanted to know whether the reduction in saving was necessarily bad, and if it was desirable to increase capital formation and economic development. Moreover, they considered what policies could be undertaken to promote economic growth without altering the social security system.

---

38. Ibid., p. 99.

39. Feldstein, "Social Security . . .," p. 921.

40. Ibid., p. 920.

41. Martin Feldstein, "Social Insurance" (Paper presented at the Conference on Income Distribution, American Enterprise Institute, May 20, 1976).

42. Lesnoy and Hambor, "Social Security, Saving, and Capital Formation," *Social Security Bulletin,* July 1975.

Although their remarks were directed at Feldstein, Lesnoy and Hambor made two key points about the regression studies that apply no less to Munnell. First, the quantitative results of such studies are sensitive to the structural form of the model and the selection of time periods. This implies that we should be careful in interpreting the magnitude of the relation between savings and social security. Second, the studies rely on variables whose construction makes them sensitive to alternative assumptions. Also, these constructed variables for social security wealth may in fact be serving as a proxy for other economic effects. It may be that unemployment insurance, private retirement programs, Medicare, and other social programs have been the real driving forces in the economy, and that the constructed variables are really measures of their influence. Lesnoy and Hambor also indicate that the ratio of the total dependent population (young and old) to the working population has increased as has educational expenditure, which is investment in human capital. These factors may have influenced saving decisions.[43]

Finally, it may be that interest rates should be included in the consumption function. One reason that they have not been included is that interest rates are included in the computation of the social security wealth variable. Another reason for the exclusion of interest rates is that, although an *a priori* case can be made that these rates would influence a rational saver, the statistical evidence does not substantiate it. It is known that changes in interest rates affect the form of saving, e.g., savings in banks as opposed to savings in savings and loan associations or in the form of government securities, and this effect is called disintermediation. However, the effect of interest rates on aggregate saving is not clear.[44]

Summary

Much more analysis needs to be done before we have a complete understanding of how social security alters saving. Evidence suggests that social security has had a detrimental effect on aggregate saving in the U.S. economy. But the quantitative estimates of the social security effect and the specification of appropriate economic analysis are both

---

43. Ibid., p. 12.

44. The classic study on family budget analysis of saving is: George Katona, *The Powerful Consumer* (New York: McGraw-Hill, 1960).

still at issue. Some of the difficulties stem from our lack of understanding about the process of saving and capital formation. We need to refine our econometric analysis so that the retirement decision is an integral part of the economic analysis. We need to investigate the influence that changing labor force participation rates of men and women have on savings decisions. Until these things are done, we cannot be confident about our conclusions.

The burden of the social security tax is born by workers. Administratively, the payments mechanism makes the statutory incidence appear to fall equally on the employer and employee. In reality, both economic theory and empirical analysis lead us to believe that the employers' share of the tax is shifted to the employees.

The present state of knowledge suggests that two counteracting forces connected with social security influence saving and capital formation. Individuals retire at a younger age because of social security. They must, therefore, save more during their working years. However, the expected benefits from social security act as an annuity of the individual. Since beneficiaries have this large expected asset, they need save less. The wealth effect created in this way reduces private saving and capital formation. The net effect has left the saving rate relatively unchanged over time, but has also greatly reduced saving and capital formation from what they would have been without social security.

9

LEGISLATIVE PROPOSALS AND EXECUTIVE RECOMMENDATIONS

LEGISLATIVE PROPOSALS AND
EXECUTIVE RECOMMENDATIONS

Major Agreements and Disagreements

Over the years, many official bodies have analyzed the social security system. A substantial number of the 1974 through 1976 groups agreed on several recommendations. Foremost among these is the need to assure the public that the program can be changed or amended to ensure payment of future benefits. There is agreement across the political spectrum that the double indexing of the inflation must be corrected prospectively. There is also agreement that the system must be made more equitable, and that to reach this goal universal coverage and equal entitlement to benefits regardless of sex are necessities. Additionally, all groups have pointed out the need for more data and most commonly for data on the social security system's effect on savings and private capital formation.

Major disagreements exist, however, on how best to correct the double indexing error of the 1972 amendments. There also are diverse opinions which surround the questions of equity. Should a substantial degree of individual equity in the system be restored? Should family equity take precedence over individual equity? How can more equity best be given to the two-worker (husband and wife) families and at the same time to single persons?

The most immediate problem is, however, how to correct the actuarial imbalance of the trust funds. Although decoupling would decrease substantially the long-run actuarial deficit, it would make little impact on the immediate short-run deficit. There are many changes which would improve both the short-run and the long-run imbalance of the trust funds. Each of the following methods has its proponents: 1) enacting higher tax rates, 2) increasing the tax base, 3) using general revenues, 4) phasing out some benefits, and 5) enacting a later retirement age for eligibility to benefits. Because of the size of the imbalance, most persons recommend some combination of the five above ways. There is also disagreement about whether to change the retirement test.

Document 9.1   Report of the Advisory Council on Social Security, March 1975 [excerpts]

[*Author's Note.* The immediate problem facing the social security system was financing in relation to benefits already legislated. The following excerpt, then, excludes some of the Advisory Council's recommendations, such as those relating to disability payments.

Future changes in OASDI should conform to the fundamental principles of the program: universal compulsory coverage, earnings-related benefits paid without a test of need, and contributions toward the cost of the program from covered workers and employers. [p. xv]

The benefit structure should be revised to maintain the levels of benefits in relation to preretirement earnings levels that now prevail. Benefits for workers coming on the rolls in the future should be computed on the basis of a revised benefit formula using past earnings indexed to take account of changes during their working lives in the average earnings of all covered workers. As under present law, benefits for people on the rolls should continue to be increased as price levels increase.

Retirement Test

The provisions of the present retirement test should be modified so that beneficiaries who work can retain more of their benefits. . . . The test should be based on annual earnings.

Treatment of Men and Women

The requirements for entitlement to dependents' and survivors' benefits that apply to women should apply equally to men. . . . At the same time, the law should be changed, effective prospectively, so that pensions based on a person's work in employment not covered by social security will be subtracted from his social security dependent's benefits [that is, from any secondary or dependency benefit that he or she may receive based on another person's (spouse's) covered earnings]. [pp. xv-xvi]

DOCUMENT 9.1: U.S. Congress, House, Committee on Ways and Means, *Reports of the Quadrennial Advisory Council on Social Security,* 94th Cong., 1st sess., H.D. 94-75, March 10, 1975 (Washington, D.C.: U.S. Government Printing Office, 1975), pp. xv-xvii and 14.

Although social security covers over 90 percent of workers, the gaps that remain often result in unwarranted duplication of benefits. Social security coverage should be applicable to all gainful employment. [p. xvi]

Further study is needed on three matters: the effects of the social security program on different racial and ethnic groups, ways of simplifying the social security program and its administration, and the frequency of cost-of-living adjustments in benefits. In addition, a general study of social security should be made by a full-time non-Government body, covering such matters as funding vs. pay-as-you-go, possible effects of social security on capital formation, productivity, the proper size of the trust funds, the incidence of payroll taxes, and other basic questions. [p. xvi]

[The financing recommendations because of their complexity are given in greater detail.]

The cash benefits program needs a comparatively small amount of additional financing immediately in order to maintain the trust funds levels. Beginning about 30 years from now, in 2005, the program faces serious deficits. Steps should be taken soon to assure the financial integrity and long-range financial soundness of the program. [p.xvii]

[As OASDI costs increase,] the OASDI tax rate should be gradually increased. . .the increases should be met by reallocating taxes now scheduled in the law for part A (hospital insurance) of the Medicare program. Income lost to the hospital insurance program by this reallocation should be made up from the general funds of the Treasury. Hospital insurance benefits are not related to earnings, so should be phased out of support from the payroll tax.[1] [xvii]

The present 7-percent limitation on the tax rate for the self-employed should be removed. The self-employment OASDI tax rate should be the same multiple of the employee contribution rate as was fixed at the time the self-employed were first covered—150 percent. . . . Although the Council is not recommending an increase in the age of eligibility for social security retirement benefits, the Council does believe that such a change might merit consideration in the next century, when the financial burden of social security taxes on people still working may become excessive. [p. xvii]

The Council therefore recommends that a worker's earnings should be "indexed"—that is, adjusted to reflect increases in average earnings over his working lifetime—up to retirement, and after retirement his benefits should be adjusted according to changes in the cost of living. [p. 14]

---

1. Four members of the Advisory Council dissented from this two-part recommendation [author's note].

Document 9.2   Report of the President's Council of Economic Advisors, January 1976 [excerpt]

Issues have arisen with respect to both the short-run and long-run financial situation of the social security system. The Administration is proposing measures to deal with both of these problems. . . . In response to the decline in the trust fund the Administration is proposing to increase the combined social security tax rate paid by employers and employees by 0.6 percentage point as of 1977. This increase will enable the trust fund to be maintained at a level of at least one-third of outgo for at least the next 5 years.

Projections of the social security system indicate that program costs relative to payroll receipts, under present law, are likely to escalate considerably. The size of the projected shortfall depends on assumptions about the birth rate, the rate of inflation, and the growth rate of real wages. [p. 116]

The Administration will propose a specific plan to modify the system so that benefit levels will rise at the same rate as average wages. The goal is to make a person's benefits rise solely in accordance with wages during his working years in accordance with the CPI [Consumer Price Index] in years after his retirement. [p. 117]

Document 9.3   President Ford's Message to Congress, February 9, 1976 [excerpt]

[*Author's Note.* The following section is in response to the Advisory Council's recommendation.]

The particular vulnerability of the aged to the burdens of inflation, however, requires that specific improvements be made in two major Federal programs, Social Security and Medicare.

We must begin by insuring that the Social Security system is beyond challenge. Maintaining the integrity of the system is a vital obligation each generation has to those who have worked hard and contributed to it all their lives. I strongly reaffirm my commitment to a stable and financially sound Social Security system. My 1977 budget and legislative program include several elements which I believe are essential to protect the solvency and integrity of the system.

First, to help protect our retired and disabled citizens against the hardships of inflation, my budget request to the Congress includes a full cost of living increase in Social Security benefits, to be effective with checks received in July 1976. This will help maintain the purchasing power of 32 million Americans.

DOCUMENT 9.2: *Economic Report of the President: With the Annual Report of the Council of Economic Advisors,* January 1976 (Washington, D.C.: U.S. Government Printing Office, 1976), pp. 116-17.

DOCUMENT 9.3: Gerald R. Ford, *Weekly Compilation of Presidential Documents,* February 16, 1976, vol., 12, no. 7, pp. 168-70.

Second, to insure the financial integrity of the Social Security trust funds, I am proposing legislation to increase payroll taxes by three-tenths of one percent each for employees and employers. This increase will cost no worker more than $1 a week, and most will pay less. These additional revenues are needed to stabilize the trust funds so that current income will be certain to either equal or exceed current outgo.

Third, to avoid serious future financing problems I will submit later this year a change in the Social Security laws to correct a serious flaw in the current system. The current formula which determines benefits for workers who retire in the future does not properly reflect wage and price fluctuations. This is an inadvertent error which could lead to unnecessarily inflated benefits.

The change I am proposing will not affect cost of living increases in benefits after retirement, and will in no way alter the benefit levels of current recipients. On the other hand, it will protect future generations against unnecessary costs and excessive tax increases.

I believe that the prompt enactment of all of these proposals is necessary to maintain a sound Social Security system and to preserve its financial integrity.

Income security is not our only concern. We need to focus also on the special health care needs of our elder citizens. Medicare and other Federal health programs have been successful in improving access to quality medical care for the aged. Before the inception of Medicare and Medicaid in 1966, per capita health expenditures for our aged were $445 per year. Just eight years later, in FY 1974, per capita health expenditures for the elderly had increased to $1218, an increase of 174 percent. [p. 169]

There are weaknesses in the Medicare program which must be corrected. Three particular aspects of the current program concern me: (1) its failure to provide our elderly with protection against catastrophic illness costs, (2) the serious effects that health care cost inflation is having on the Medicare program, and (3) lack of incentives to encourage efficient and economical use of hospital and medical services. My proposal addresses each of these problems.

In my State of the Union Message I proposed protection against catastrophic health expenditures for Medicare beneficiaries. This will be accomplished in two ways. First, I propose extending Medicare benefits by providing coverage for unlimited days of hospital and skilled nursing facility care for beneficiaries. Second, I propose to limit the out-of-pocket expenses of beneficiaries, for covered services, to $500 per year for hospital and skilled nursing services and $250 per year for physician and other noninstitutional medical services.

This will mean that each year over a billion dollars of benefit payments will be targeted for handling the financial burden of prolonged illness. Millions of older persons live in fear of being stricken by an illness that will call for expensive hospital and medical care over a long period of time. Most often they do not have the resources to pay the bills. The members of their families share their fears because they also do not have the resources to pay such large bills. We have been talking about this problem for many years. We have it within our power to act now so that today's older persons will not be forced to live under this kind of a shadow. I urge the Congress to act promptly.

Added steps are needed to slow down the inflation of health costs and to help in the financing of this catastrophic protection. Therefore, I am recommending that the Congress limit increases in Medicare payment rates in 1977 and 1978 to 7% a day [sic] for hospitals and 4% for physician services.

Additional cost-sharing provisions are also needed to encourage economical use of the hospital and medical services included under Medicare. Therefore, I am recommending that patients pay 10% of hospital and nursing home charges after the first day and that the existing deductible for medical services be increased from $60 to $77 annually.

The savings from placing a limit on increases in Medicare payment rates and some of the revenue from increased cost sharing will be used to finance the catastrophic illness program.

I feel that, on balance, these proposals will provide our elder citizens with protection against catastrophic illness costs, promote efficient utilization of services, and moderate the increases in health care costs.

The legislative proposals which I have described are only part of the over-all effort we are making on behalf of older Americans. Current conditions call for continued and intensified action on a broad front.

We have made progress in recent years. We have responded, for example, to recommendations made at the 1971 White House Conference on Aging. A Supplemental Security Income program was enacted. Social Security benefits have been increased in accord with increases in the cost of living. The Social Security retirement test was liberalized. Many inequities in payments to women have been eliminated. The 35 million workers who have earned rights in private pension plans now have increased protection.

Document 9.4   The *Congressional Quarterly* Covers the Debate on Raising the Social Security Tax, February 1976

Democrats on the House Ways and Means Social Security Subcommittee showed little enthusiasm for President Ford's proposal to raise Social Security taxes as the subcommittee began hearings Feb. 2 on that and related Ford proposals.

DOCUMENT 9.4: Martha V. Gottron, "Social Security Tax Hikes: Merits Argued," *Congressional Quarterly*, February 7, 1976, pp. 262-63. © 1976, *Congressional Quarterly*, Inc. Reproduced by permission. All rights reserved.

The hearings represented the second round in the subcommittee's efforts to draft legislation dealing with a projected short-term deficit in the nation's public retirement system. Because inflation had increased benefits and high unemployment had reduced revenues, the system was paying out more in benefits annually than it was collecting in payroll taxes, requiring the Social Security retirement trust fund to make up the difference. It had been predicted that the trust fund could be depleted as early as 1980 if additional revenues were not made available.[2]

Ford's politically unpopular proposal reflected concern over the rapidly diminishing trust fund. It would increase the tax rate paid by employers and employees on covered wages by .3 per cent each, beginning in 1977. Thus employers and employees each would pay 6.15 percent, rather than 5.85 per cent, in Social Security taxes. The tax rate increase would accompany an already scheduled hike in the wage base from the 1976 level of $15,300 to the 1977 level of $16,500.[3]

Tax Increase Arguments

But Democrats on the committee and several witnesses argued that a tax hike would be regressive, placing a heavier burden on the low-income wage earner than it did on high-income workers. Ford's proposal only compounded the already regressive nature of the Social Security payroll tax, said Abner J. Mikva (D.,Ill.). Too many people already paid more in Social Security taxes than they did in income taxes, complained James R. Jones (D., Okla.).

Representing the administration, Health, Education and Welfare Secretary David Mathews acknowledged that, taken in isolation, the tax hike was regressive. "But when one looks at the Social Security system as a whole, it is clear that the very progressive features of the benefit structure for lower wage workers, that is, the minimum benefits and the weighting of the benefit formula, give us an overall system that is progressive," he said.

In addition to its regressive nature, the tax hike proposal also was criticized on grounds that it could exacerbate already high unemployment. According to William Pietz, staff attorney for the Public Citizen Tax Reform Research Group, evidence indicated that an increased payroll tax discouraged employers from hiring new workers and thus adding to their total tax bills.

Subcommittee Democrats implied that the deficit would be taken care of if the Ford administration adopted policies aimed toward a quicker reduction of the unemployment rate, which stood at 8.3 percent in December. Under questioning, Social Security Commissioner Bruce Cardwell acknowledged that there would probably not be a short-term problem if unemployment

---

2. Previous hearings, *1975 Weekly Report,* p. 1,302.

3. Proposal, *Weekly Report,* p.134.

levels were at or about 5 percent. The administration did not expect the
unemployment rate to drop below 5 percent until 1981.

Alternatives

Mathews was adamantly opposed to two other alternatives frequently
proposed to overcome the projected deficit. He contended that an increase in
the taxable wage base would increase future benefit rights and would add to
long-term deficit projections for the program and he opposed the infusion of
general revenues. "Although Social Security trust funds may be in short
supply, general revenues are in even shorter supply," he said.

Representatives of the American Life Insurance Association and the
National Association of Life Underwriters supported Ford's proposal as the
best of the three alternatives. "It should be remembered that the system is
running an actuarial deficit now despite an increase of over 100 per cent in the
wage base since 1969," pointed out Jack E. Bobo of the underwriters'
association.

"The injection of general revenues into the time-tested approach of the
system being wholly self-supporting from payroll taxes would erode the self-
sustaining concept by moving in the direction of a welfare concept," contended Robert J. Myers, formerly chief actuary of the Social Security
Administration, on behalf of the life insurance association. "In turn this could
lead to means testing for benefits."

Former Social Security Commissioner Robert M. Ball opposed the tax
increase, proposing instead a hike in the wage base to $21,300 in 1977. Ball
said that would produce the same revenues as the tax increase and would
affect only the high-income workers while assuring them greater future
benefits. "Under a rate increase everyone pays and no one gets more benefits,"
Ball said.

Subcommittee Chairman James A. Burke (D.,Mass.) continued his support for general revenues, suggesting that one-third of the Social Security
revenues come from employers, one-third from employees and one-third from
general Treasury funds. "I don't know what's so sacrosanct about this [trust]
fund that we can't use general revenues," he said.

Burke may receive powerful support from Senate Finance Committee
Chairman Russell B. Long (D.,La.), who recently said he was ready to
consider putting general revenues into the Social Security trust fund.

Calling Ford's proposal an "ineffective and very temporary remedy,"
Elliott H. Levitas (D.,Ga.) said the tax increase should not be considered
"without an accompanying, comprehensive proposal for reforming, revising
and improving the entire system." Levitas proposed the establishment of a
special advisory committee to recommend reforms in the system. Among
alternatives he would have the committee study would be a substitution of

general revenues for the payroll tax, mandatory participation in a private insurance program and a program offering workers a choice between private and public retirement insurance, or a combination of the two.

Other Proposals

Most of the witnesses agreed with Ford's proposal that the benefit structure be changed so that retirement benefits would bear a stable relationship to pre-retirement earnings. An anomaly in the existing law would allow benefits to far outstrip earnings in future years. Mathews said the administration hoped to propose specific language addressing this problem by March 1.

Witnesses were not so pleased with another Ford recommendation that would end payments to full-time students between 18 and 22 whose parents were eligible for Social Security benefits. Ford said such students could receive educational aid through other student assistance programs.

Speaking in behalf of eight organizations of post-secondary institutions, Charles B. Saunders, Jr. of the American Council on Education pointed out that Ford did not budget additional funds in the student aid programs to absorb the students aided under Social Security.

Furthermore, he said, Social Security educational benefits were frequently used for family maintenance and 20 per cent of the students receiving aid under the government's main student assistance program, which was based on need, were also receiving the Social Security benefits. Elimination of these payments, he said, would deprive many low-income families of a vital source of income and deny many students an opportunity to go to college.

"I think you've got a tough bill to sell on that one," Burke agreed.

Document 9.5   Congressional Budget Office, March 1976

[*Author's Note.* In 1974, Congress passed new controls over federal spending (P.L. 93-344). Revisions were made in the procedures under which congressional committees review federal budget proposals. In addition, the new law created a Congressional Budget Office (CBO) to develop technical data on expenditures by function—data that would match the appropriations requests from the executive branch's Office of Management and the Budget (OMB). The first full year in which the new appropriations procedure took effect was 1976, for the fiscal year beginning October 1, 1977. In response to the president's budget message, CBO provided data to help congressmen decide among the various national

DOCUMENT 9.5: Congressional Budget Office, *Budget Options for Fiscal Year 1977: A Report to the Senate and House Committees on the Budget,* March 15, 1976 (Washington, D.C.: U.S. Government Printing Office, 1976), pp. 133-34.

priorities and to evaluate the budget's fiscal impact. Among the topics
reviewed by Congress were whether total spending exceeded or was equal
to total revenues, and what effect the budget would have on inflation,
production, and employment. On September 16, 1976, Congress set
binding levels for federal spending and revenues for the forthcoming fiscal
year.

Among the functional areas considered by CBO was "income security,"
which included social security. The following excerpts illustrate the way in
which congressmen and their staffs are now able to appraise more readily
appropriation bills that do not necessarily match the OMB's functional
categories.[4]]

The President's budget contains a number of proposed changes in the social
security system that are aimed primarily at eliminating the short-term deficit
in the trust fund. Foremost among these changes is an increase in the social
security (OASDI) tax from 9.9 percent to 10.5 percent. Individuals earning
median wages would pay $36 more in 1977 than they would pay under current
law. This tax increase would add $3.5 billion in income to the funds in 1977,
and $9.9 billion in 1981. Rather than falling to $30 billion or 25 percent of
outlays, the reserves in the OASDI funds would rise from $45 billion in 1976
to $72.7 billion or 60 percent of outlays by 1981.

The President's budget also calls for a prohibition on certain types of
retroactive claims. Under current law, a person may file retroactively for up to
a year's benefits if he would have been eligible for benefits during that period.

The President's proposal would prohibit retroactive claims if they resulted
in reduced monthly benefits. The proposal is directed at persons whose
effective retirement date would be earlier than age 65 thereby giving them a
lump sum payment worth up to a year's benefits while reducing their monthly
benefits up to 7 percent permanently thereafter. This prohibition would save
$400 million in 1977 but in the long run these savings would be offset by higher
future monthly benefits.

The President also has proposed a test of monthly postretirement earnings.
Under current law, benefits can be paid for all months of the year if total
postretirement earnings in the year are less than the prescribed annual limit
($3,000 in 1977). Furthermore, benefits can be paid for *any* month in which
postretirement earnings are less than the monthly limit ($250), even if the
money earned during those months when benefits are not paid exceeds the
annual limit. The intention of the monthly measure was to permit low-income
persons to take seasonal employment, e.g., summer camps, one-time projects,
etc., without significant loss of retirement benefits. It has been abused by

4. In writing this note I drew heavily on appropriate sections of the *Congressional Quarterly*'s
1975 and 1976 Annual Almanac.

certain persons who crowd very large earnings into a single month. The President's proposal would prohibit the payment in any month if the annual earnings exceeded the annual limit. If this proposal were enacted, $200 million would be saved in 1977.

The President also proposes phasing out, over a four-year period, the benefits that since 1965 have been accorded to beneficiaries' children, 18 to 22, who are attending school. Similar provisions of the veterans benefit program, railroad retirement, and other programs would not be affected. This change would affect 581,000 beneficiaries, most of whom would probably increase their reliance on the benefits available under the Basic Educational Opportunities Program. The savings to the trust funds from this change have been estimated by the Administration to be $283 million in the first year rising to $1.4 billion the fourth year. The President's budget message also proposes changing the formula by which benefits are computed to correct overcompensation of future beneficiaries for inflation, but the details of the proposal have not yet been provided.

The budgetary impact of the President's proposals [is summarized in Table 9.1]. [pp. 133-34]

TABLE 9.1
IMPACT OF PRESIDENT'S BUDGETARY PROPOSALS, FISCAL YEAR 1977
(Billions of dollars, fiscal years)

	1977	1978	1979	1980	1981
Additional income from taxes	3.5	5.6	6.9	8.2	9.9
Savings from benefit reductions	0.8	1.5	1.8	2.1	2.6
Increase to funds	4.4	7.1	8.7	10.3	12.5

SOURCE: Congressional Budget Office, *Budget Options . . . 1977*, p. 134.

Document 9.6 Ford Administration's Proposal to Correct Double Indexing, June 1976: A. President's Message

I am today submitting to the Congress a legislative proposal that will correct a serious flaw in the Social Security system. This proposal is one of three components of my 1977 budget and legislative program intended to insure a secure and viable Social Security system. My strong personal commitment to Social Security embraces both a genuine concern for the 32 million persons who currently depend on Social Security benefits for income,

DOCUMENT 9.6: White House Press Release, June 17, 1976 (Washington, D.C.: Office of the White House Press Secretary, 1976).

and an unyielding dedication to protect the financial integrity of the system for the millions of workers who will depend on it in the future.

My program to insure the integrity of the Social Security system, as outlined in January of this year, includes:

First, a full cost-of-living increase for all beneficiaries, scheduled to take effect in checks sent out in July of this year.

Second, an increase in Social Security payroll contributions by three-tenths of one percent for both employees and employers. This increase would remedy the immediate, short-term financing problem facing Social Security. It would stop the drain on the trust funds — which are now expected to pay out about $4 billion more in benefits each year than they take in. This correction would cost no employee more than $1 per week in additional contributions.

Third, legislation to correct a serious flaw in the Social Security benefit structure which, if left unchanged, would undermine the principles of Social Security and create severe long-range financial pressures on the system. My proposal would eliminate this flaw and be a major step towards resolving the long-range financial problem. It would help stabilize the system and permit sufficient time for careful and thorough analysis of the remaining future financial pressures.

What is the status of these items?

I am happy to report that the full cost-of-living increase will be included in July Social Security checks. Unfortunately, the Congress has so far avoided its responsibility to provide a means of paying for the full cost of the system.

The proposal I am submitting today corrects an inadequate method of adjusting benefit payments which, over time, could mean that many new retirees would receive Social Security benefits in excess of the highest earnings they ever received. Such a result was never intended and is clearly undesirable, both from the standpoint of the individual and the excessive costs to the system.

My proposal would correct this defect by insuring that future retirement benefits are a constant share of preretirement earnings. This produces three important improvements:

- It eliminates the long-term financial deficiency associated with the flaw (about half the projected long-range deficit), and moves more closely to the system which Congress intended to create in 1972;
- It helps to stabilize the system despite variations in the economy; and
- It makes individual benefits more predictable than under the current system.

To insure fairness to those approaching retirement as these proposals are implemented, I am suggesting a ten-year phase-in period during which those persons retiring will be assured that their benefits are no lower under the new formula than they would have been under the old formula at the time the law goes into effect.

The correction of the flaw will be a major step toward bringing the system back into financial balance over the long-term. But it is not the complete solution and we should not pretend that it is. The Social Security Trustees estimate that even with this legislation, sizeable long-term financial pressures remain.

There is sufficient time, however, to analyze this situation and to correct it. If action is taken promptly on my proposals the system will not be in jeopardy. But this should not delay our efforts to identify the further steps needed to protect the system's permanent financial integrity.

Over the next few years I intend to work with the Congress in resolving these problems. But the time to begin is now. We must begin immediately to solve both the short and long-range problems. The corrected benefit formula that I am submitting today would eliminate more than half of the estimated long-range financial problem. The .3% increase in employee and employer contributions which I proposed earlier this year would bring the system into current balance.

In order to protect both those who currently receive benefits and those who are contributing to the system towards their future retirement, I urge the Congress to move immediately to enact these two vital proposals into law.

GERALD R. FORD

Document 9.7 Ford Administration's Proposal to Correct Double Indexing, June 1976: B. White House Fact Sheet

The "Flaw" in the Current System

Prior to 1972, all increases in Social Security benefits required Congressional action. The 1972 Social Security Amendments built into the law automatic cost-of-living escalators. For those already receiving benefits, these provisions guarantee that their benefits will keep pace with growth in the Consumer Price Index.

The provisions were also intended to protect current workers against inflation through annual modifications in the formula used to compute initial benefits. Only recently have the full implications of these modifications been recognized. They result in a significant overadjustment for inflation, causing initial benefits to grow over time to the point where a great many new retirees would receive benefits in excess of the highest wages they ever earned.

These inflated benefits would place severe long-term financial pressures on Social Security. Adding to the long-range cost problem is the fact that, as

DOCUMENT 9.7: "Social Security Benefit Indexing Act," White House Fact Sheet, June 17, 1976 (Washington, D.C.: Office of the White House Press Secretary, 1976).

currently estimated, U.S. fertility rates are expected to result in a declining ratio of workers (Social Security contributors) to retirees (Social Security beneficiaries).

The 1976 Social Security Trustees Report estimates that the long-range costs of the current system would exceed projected revenues by an average annual amount of 8% of covered payroll.

The Administration Proposal

The Administration proposal would eliminate half of the estimated long-range financial deficit, and yet continue the system's commitment to increase benefits in accord with inflation. The formula is designed to approximate as closely as possible the benefit amounts payable under present law in January, 1978 (the month the revised formula is expected to go into effect).

Benefits

A useful tool for comparing the proposed formula with current law is "replacement rates" (i.e., initial benefits as a percent of preretirement earnings). [Table 9.2] illustrates how the proposed law stabilizes replacement rates

TABLE 9.2
PROJECTED REPLACEMENT RATES FOR ILLUSTRATIVE CASES OF REGULAR WORKERS WITH EARNINGS AT LOW, AVERAGE, AND MAXIMUM LEVELS

INITIAL BENEFITS AS A PERCENT OF FINAL YEAR EARNINGS

YEAR OF ENTITLEMENT AT AGE 65	Low Earnings PRESENT LAW	PROPOSAL	Average Earnings PRESENT LAW	PROPOSAL	Maximum Earnings PRESENT LAW	PROPOSAL
1976	63%	63%	44%	44%	33%	33%
1980	62	61	44	43	34	33
1990	66	62	47	44	34	33
2000	78	62	51	44	37	34
2010	92	62	55	44	40	35
2020	100	62	59	44	43	36
2030	108	62	62	44	44	36
2040	114	62	64	44	46	36
2050	119%	62%	66%	44%	47%	36%

NOTE: The 1975 earnings levels of $3,400 for low earners, $8,600 for average earners, and $14,100 for maximum earners are adjusted annually according to the intermediate set of assumptions used in the 1976 Annual Report of the Board of Trustees of the Federal OASDI Trust Funds.

SOURCE: White House Fact Sheet, June 17, 1976, p. 3.

at current levels, and prevents the unnecessary escalation caused by the flaw in existing law. For example, a low wage earner would continue through time to receive benefits replacing approximately 62% of preretirement earnings. This compares to benefits under current law which would, if unchecked, grow to 100% of preretirement earnings by 2020 and to 119% by 2050. (See [Table 9.2] for additional comparisons of persons with average and maximum wages).

LONG-RANGE COSTS

The proposed law would eliminate approximately half of the estimated long-range deficit projected for the system under current law. [Tables 9.3 and 9.4] illustrate how this occurs over the next seventy-five years.

ANNUAL COST-OF-LIVING INCREASES

As under present law, all beneficiaries would receive automatic cost-of-living increases in their benefits.

TABLE 9.3
COMPARISON OF OASDI LONG-RANGE COST
PRESENT LAW AND ADMINISTRATION BILL

| YEAR | EXPENDITURES AS PERCENT OF TAXABLE PAYROLL[a] | | |
	PRESENT LAW	BILL	DIFFERENCE
1980	10.68%	10.70%	-.02%
1990	12.06	11.82	.24
2000	13.41	12.38	1.03
2010	15.99	13.41	2.58
2020	21.29	16.46	4.83
2030	26.03	18.92	7.11
2040	27.45	18.87	8.58
2050	28.59%	18.77%	9.82%
25-year average:			
1976-2000	11.81%	11.53%	.28%
2001-2025	17.95	14.60	3.35
2026-2050	27.04%	18.82%	8.22%
75-year average:			
1976-2050	18.93%	14.98%	3.95%

a. Based on the assumptions of alternative II in the 1976 OASDI Trustees Report.

SOURCE: White House Fact Sheet, June 17, 1976, p. 4.

TABLE 9.4
COMPARISON OF OASDI ACTUARIAL BALANCE
PRESENT LAW AND ADMINISTRATION BILL
(PERCENT OF TAXABLE PAYROLL)

ITEM	Average for Period[a]		
	PRESENT LAW	BILL	DIFFER-ENCE
1st 25-year period (1976-2000)			
Expenditures	11.81%	11.53%	.28%
Tax Rate	9.90	9.90	—
Difference	-1.91%	-1.63%	.28%
2nd 25-year period (2001-2025)			
Expenditures	17.95%	14.60%	3.35%
Tax Rate	11.10	11.10	—
Difference	-6.85%	-3.50%	3.35%
3rd 25-year period (2026-2050)			
Expenditures	27.04%	18.82%	8.22%
Tax Rate	11.90	11.90	—
Difference	-15.14%	-6.92%	8.22%
Total 75-year period (1976-2050)			
Expenditures	13.93%	14.98%	3.95%
Tax Rate	10.97	10.97	—
Difference	-7.96%	-4.01%	3.95%

a. Based on the assumptions of alternative II in the 1976 OASDI Trustees Report.

SOURCE: White House, June 17, 1976, p. 5.

REMAINING LONG-RANGE FINANCIAL PRESSURES

Seventy-five year estimates are inherently speculative and quite complex — dependent upon assumptions of inflation, economic growth, the size and makeup of families, etc. Nevertheless, current projections show a sizeable financing problem after the turn of the century even with the Administration proposal (see [Tables 9.3 and 9.4]). The Administration proposal would help stabilize the system against variations in the economy, thus providing sufficient time over the next several years to analyze and correct for the remaining financial pressures on the system's future.

[Figure 9.1] shows the present-law tax rates and the present-law expenditure curve. It also shows the future expenditure curve under the Administration's decoupling proposal, the saving that it would yield in the future, and the

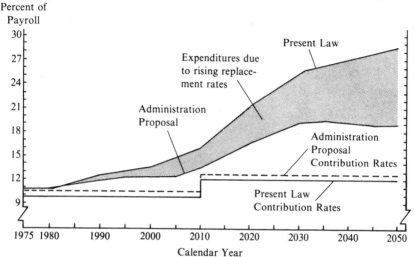

FIGURE 9.1

**EXPENDITURES AND CONTRIBUTION RATES
UNDER PRESENT LAW AND UNDER ADMINISTRATION PROPOSAL**

SOURCE: White House Fact Sheet, June 17, 1976, p. 6.

effect of the Administration's proposed tax rate increase. Under present law the average long-range cost of the OASDI program is 18.93 percent of taxable payroll and the average contribution rate is 10.97 percent. Thus the deficit is 7.96 percent.

The decoupling proposal would reduce the cost to 14.98 percent, which, with present-law contribution rates, would reduce the deficit by nearly one-half—to 4.01 percent of payroll. The President's proposal for a tax rate increase would further reduce the deficit to 3.32 percent of taxable payroll.

Document 9.8.   Report of the Consultant Panel on Social Security, August 1976 [excerpts]

[*Author's Note.* The Consultant Panel would use a price-index method of decoupling that would result in decreasing replacement ratios of retirement benefits to average earnings during periods of inflation and increasing

DOCUMENT 9.8: U.S. Congress, Joint Committee (House Committee on Ways and Means, Senate Committee on Finance), *Report of the Consultant Panel on Social Security to the Congressional Research Service,* 94th Cong., 2d sess., August 1976 (Washington, D.C.: U.S. Government Printing Office, 1976).

ratios during periods of deflation. President Ford's proposal, the same as the Advisory Council's, would maintain constant replacement ratios of retirement benefits to average earnings.]

1. Benefit formula. The Panel recommends that:

(a) as under present law, retirement benefits continue to be increased automatically after retirement in proportion to the Consumer Price Index;
(b) benefits for future retirees be computed using earnings that have been indexed in proportion to the change in price levels during the earnings-averaging period;
(c) the progressively lengthening averaging period of present law be retained. . . . [p. 3]

The effect of these recommendations would be:

— Benefits to workers already retired would be protected against erosion from inflation.
— The purchasing power of benefits for future retirees would tend to increase even without future congressional action and can be further increased by congressional action. [p.3]

2. Financing. The Panel recommends that:

(a) the system continue to be financed by payroll taxes, not from general government revenues;
(b) the ceiling on wages subject to payroll tax be moderately increased, and then maintained at a point at which the entire earnings of approximately 90 percent of all workers are covered. In 1977, the estimated maximum would be $18,900 instead of the $16,500 expected under present law. This maximum would continue to increase automatically in proportion to increases in covered wages, subject to revisions from time to time to maintain the 90 percent benchmark;
(c) the combined employer and employee payroll tax rate be increased by 0.4 percent (i.e. 0.2 percent each); and
(d) the tax rate for the self-employed, for both OASDI and HI, be increased to 75 percent of the combined rate for employees and employers. [p. 4]

The emphasis. . .is upon congressional control rather than upon maintenance of approximately today's tax rate. Even if Congress believes that workers at the turn of the century will be willing to pay a combined payroll tax rate substantially higher than the current tax rate, we consider it undesirable to incorporate that belief into the system at the present time, thereby causing rigidity. As time passes Congress can raise benefit levels and the corresponding taxes at its discretion.

The Panel has concluded that the use of general government revenues to finance the OASDI program is inappropriate. Our reasons are:

— General revenues are more properly used to support needs-related old-age income programs and general tax relief to low-income workers.
— Needs of elderly persons other than for income maintenance—such as housing, long-term care, and social services—appear to have more urgent claims on general revenues.
— General-revenue financing of the OASDI program would weaken the earnings-related nature of the program. It could even jeopardize the long-range stability of the entire social security system, thwarting citizen expectations of retirement income protection. . . .

3. Spouse's benefit. The Panel recommends abandonment of the present schedule of spouse benefits for future retired workers. We recommend instead averaging the earnings of the husband and wife for determining benefits to members of both one-worker and two-worker families. [p. 5]

Further Recommendations

1. Retirement test. Effects created by the retirement test are largely unknown; so are the forces responsible for the present large number of early retirements. The Panel recommends that Congress use OASDI Trust Funds to finance a study of the economic impact of the retirement test. . .[and] supports in the interim the removal of the monthly earnings test as part of the retirement test.

2. Universal coverage. The Panel recommends that social security coverage be made universal. [p. 5]

Document 9.9   Dissent of Gabriel Hauge to Advisory Council's 1971 Report

[*Author's Note.* The Advisory Council recommends wage indexing to correct the 1972 error of counting double any inflation in computing benefits of future retirees. The Consultant Panel recommends using only price indexing. The two sets of recommendations agree that benefits of persons once retired should be automatically increased as the Consumer Price Index increases. A concise objection to this latter procedure was

DOCUMENT 9.9: Quadrennial Advisory Council on Social Security, 1971, *Reports on the Old-Age, Survivors, and Disability Insurance and Medicare Programs* (Washington, D.C.: U.S. Government Printing Office, 1973), pp. 104-5. In addition, Charles A. Siegfried, Robert C. Tyson, and Dwight L. Wilbur concur with this statement.

written by Gabriel Hauge, then an economist and chairman of the board for Manufacturers Hanover Trust, in his dissent to the 1971 Advisory Council's recommendations as follows.]

The Council's recommendation that social security cash benefit levels be automatically adjusted upward to keep pace with the cost of living leaves me with deep concern, because such automatic adjustment would make the control of price inflation even more difficult than it already is.

One-eighth of the total population of the Nation, and fully 21 percent of the voting age population, receive retirement, survivors, or disability insurance benefits. To insulate so large a group from the cost of inflation with respect to their social security benefits would surely undermine the public's willingness to support the self-restraint and sometimes painful policies that are necessary to curb inflation. Of even more importance is the virtual certainty that the adoption of an "escalator clause" for social security benefit payments would give additional support to the already insistent demands for inflation protection through escalation in a whole range of other private contracts. I do not see how we, as a Nation, can wage a successful battle against inflation by automatically adjusting to it.

If the issue were simply that of protecting those who cannot protect themselves from the consequences of inflation, escalation of benefits would be the easy answer. But there are other considerations. First, the record of the past twenty years is that the Congress has not only adjusted benefits to compensate for changes in the cost of living, it has much more than compensated for price increases. There is no reason to believe that the Congress will be less responsible in the future. Second, the ironic fact is that those least able to protect themselves—precisely the groups receiving social security benefits—are the people most hurt by the acceptance of inflation as a fact of life. Approximately four million retired workers are presently getting benefits under private pension plans, equal to about 30 percent of the retired workers receiving social security benefits; many more retired people have supplemental income in the form of fixed income investments; and a very large number of disabled persons and widows and children have similar sources of fixed income. The hardship that inflation imposes upon these people, in my opinion, far outweighs the marginal benefits that automatic adjustment to inflation would confer upon other social security beneficiaries.

But most important is the pervasive effect that acceptance of inflation through income escalation would have upon our society. With the passage of time, more and more of the self-imposed disciplines that have made possible our unique social, political, and economic structure seem to be eroding. I regard it as a great mistake to accelerate that process.

[*Author's Note.* To this, I add that if all social security benefits are increased as the cost of living rises, then the "non-indexed majority" of the labor force bears both a higher inflation and higher social security taxes to support these benefits.

Under the Consultant Panel's proposal (1976) to use a price-index method and not a wage-index method, replacement ratios of retirement benefits to average earnings would tend to decline whenever increases in wage rates are greater than increases in prices or in other words, there is a real wage gain or productivity increases. Under the Council's wage-index proposal, replacement ratios in these circumstances would be constant.

Thus, the Panel's proposal would permit some uncommitted monies to accumulate over several years of growth in the real national income. Congress could then legislate an increase in benefits without having to increase the taxes or Congress could maintain the trust fund at a higher level in anticipation of the demographic squeeze as the birth rate falls. The Panel's proposal lets Congress remain in control of the redistribution of any increase in real national income rather than an automatic redistribution occurring in accordance with the wage-indexing formula to maintain the existing replacement ratios of retirement benefits to earnings at different income levels.

Insofar as the growth rate of the real national income exceeds 2 percent per annum, there would still be some leeway under the Council's proposal *if* its long run assumptions were met. I concur with the more recent proposal of the Panel, primarily for the reason that no one can predict for many years ahead with any reasonable hope of accuracy, the variables involved in the determination of social security benefits and their financing. Therefore, an uncommitted margin of monies is desirable.

The immediate diffusion of the first 2 percent of real growth of national income into maintenance of existing replacement ratios of benefits implies that the existing replacement ratios are by some magic the precise ratios which ought to be sustained and that their maintenance takes precedence over any other use to which the nation's resources might be diverted.

If there were no increases in real wages and this appears likely in some future years, as when price increases may exceed wage increases, then under the Panel's proposal replacement rates would rise, while under the Council's assumptions they, of course, would be maintained. The Panel assumes, and again I concur, that under conditions of successive years of no rise in real income, Congress would legislate changes and that this is preferable to having a rigid replacement-ratio structure of benefits.]

Document 9.10   President's Economic Report, January 1977 [excerpt]

DOCUMENT 9.10: *Economic Report of the President,* January 18, 1977 (Washington, D.C.: U.S. Government Printing Office, 1977), pp. 9-10.

[*Author's Note.*   This was President Ford's last official statement on financing social security.]

The discipline implicit in a prudent fiscal policy is not easy but it offers very considerable and lasting rewards. I am hopeful that the recent creation of the budget committees to serve the Congress will help to provide this necessary discipline. Prudent budget policies are essential if we are to restore stable full-employment conditions and provide the productive jobs which our people need and want. Some part of our present deficit is the result of the recession and will accordingly disappear as full employment is restored. Beyond this, however, we must restrain the growth of Federal expenditures. If we do not, we shall have to resign ourselves to higher taxes or to high employment deficits with their inflationary consequences.

Nowhere are these tradeoffs so evident as in our social security program and our efforts to provide medical insurance for our people. I have emphasized the need to maintain a fiscally sound social security system and repeatedly rejected proposals to fund increased benefits out of what are called general revenues. The purpose of linking social security benefits to specially designated taxes is to balance the benefits to one segment of society with the costs to another segment. Our democratic processes of government work better when the costs of programs are open and visible to those who pay them. Funding our social security benefits through specifically designated payroll taxes strengthens the discipline that should govern these decisions. Benefits are not costless, and we should not allow this fact to be submerged in any general revenue funding of the social security system. [pp. 9-10]

President Carter's Administration

President Carter's message to Congress (January 31, 1977) did not address the immediate financial problems of social security. In fact, the only mention of social security was within the following context.

A $50 payment in 1977 to every beneficiary of Social Security, Supplemental Security Income (SSI), or Railroad Retirement. These payments would be of particular benefit to the aged poor. This will cost $1.8 billions.[5]

During the first two months of the Carter administration, no formal announcement on the social security program had been made. On

5. Jimmy Carter, "Economic Recovery Program," Message to Congress, January 31, 1977, in *Weekly Compilation of Presidential Documents,* vol. 13, no. 6, February 7, 1977, p. 126.

February 16, 1977, an employee of HEW asked the President:
"You have recently given advice against living in sin. Don't you think the present tax laws encourage this?"

The President replied, in part:

> When we have a complete revision of the income tax structure, the study of which will be completed I think by the end of September, that will be one of the basic questions.
>
> I would also like to remove the social security regulations and others that encourage the breaking up of families. . .
>
> . . .We will be ready to recommend to the Congress a complete tax reform package this fall. Our present target date is the 4th or 5th of October.[6]

Although during the two-hour telephone call-in program of March 5, 1977, not a single direct question on any aspect of social security was broadcast, President Carter did respond to an indirectly relevant question as follows:

> We are at least freezing your medicare costs, if the Congress goes along with our proposal, and over a period of years we'll try to expand the coverage of the health care services for all citizens like you.[7]

That the new assistant secretary of Health, Education, and Welfare for legislation was Richard Warden, who until January 1977 was legislative director for the United Auto Workers, gave some clues as to the probable direction of the Carter administration. This, coupled with the Senate Finance Committee's action of March 2 to postpone any increase in social security payroll taxes for at least one year, pointed to general-revenues funding. Also, during March 1977, the U.S. Supreme Court ruled to equalize by sex entitlement rules for secondary benefits to widows and widowers and to retired wives and retired husbands. These rulings were expected to cost about one billion dollars in their first year and successively larger amounts in each succeeding year.

---

6. In *Weekly Compilation of Presidential Documents,* vol. 13, no. 8, February 21, 1977, p. 208.

7. Ibid., no. 11, March 14, 1977, p. 296.

Document 9.11   President Carter's Message to Congress on Social Security, May 1977

The Social Security system affects the lives of more Americans than almost any other function of government. More than 33 million people currently receive benefits. Another 104 million people are making contributions with the expectation that they will receive benefits when they retire or become disabled, or when their survivors need help.

Today, the Board of Trustees of the Social Security Trust Funds is submitting its 1977 report to the Congress. The report tells us that the system critically needs financial support in the short term. The high unemployment of recent years has curtailed Social Security's revenues, while benefits have risen with inflation. Since 1975 expenditures have exceeded income; and existing reserves will soon be exhausted.

Unless we act now, the Disability Insurance (DI) Trust Fund will be exhausted in 1979 and the Old Age and Survivors Insurance (OASI) Trust Fund will run out in 1983.

The Trustees' Report indicates that there are serious longer term problems as well. Under current law the Social Security system will have an estimated deficit of 8.2 percent of taxable payroll over the next seventy-five years. About half of this deficit is due to changes in the projected composition of our population over those years. Higher life expectancy and lower birthrates will make the nation older as a whole. About half is due to a technical flaw in the automatic cost of living formula adopted in 1972.

While campaigning for President, I stressed my commitment to restore the financial integrity of Social Security system. I pledged I would do my best to avoid increases, above those already scheduled, in tax rates which fall most heavily on moderate and lower-income workers. I also promised to correct the technical flaw in the system which exaggerates the adjustment for inflation, and to do so without reducing the relative value of retirement benefits as compared with pre-retirement earnings.

I am announcing today a set of proposals which meet those commitments and which solve both the short-term and long-term problems in the Social Security system through the end of the twentieth century. These proposals are designed to:

— Prevent the default of the trust funds now predicted to occur.

— Bring income and expenses into balance in 1978 and keep them that way through the end of the century.

— Create sufficient reserves to protect the system against sudden declines in revenue caused by unemployment or other economic uncertainties.

— Protect the system's integrity beyond the turn of the century to the

DOCUMENT 9.11: Jimmy Carter, *Weekly Compilation of Presidential Documents,* May 16, 1977, vol. 13, no. 20, pp. 683-85.

extent we can predict what will happen in the next 75 years.

— Provide for an orderly review and examination of the system's basic structure.

My proposals are the result of a number of hard choices. I am convinced that action is needed now, and that these steps will restore the financial integrity of the Social Security system.

I will ask the Congress to take the following specific actions:

1. Compensate the Social Security trust funds from general revenues for a share of revenues lost during severe recessions. General revenues would be used in a countercyclical fashion to replace the payroll tax receipts lost as a result of that portion of unemployment in excess of six percent. General revenues would be used *only* in these carefully limited situations. Because this is an innovative measure, the legislation we submit will provide this feature only through 1982. The next Social Security Advisory Council will be asked to review this countercyclical mechanism to determine whether it should be made permanent.

2. Remove the wage-base ceiling for employers. Under present law employers and employees pay a tax only on the first $16,500 in wages. Under this proposal the employer ceiling would be raised over a three-year period, so that by 1981 the ceiling would be removed. This action will provide a significant source of revenue without increasing long-term benefit liabilities.

3. Increase the wage base subject to the employee tax by $600 in 1979, 1981, 1983, and 1985, beyond the automatic increases in current law. This will provide a progressive source of financing.

4. Shift revenues from the Hospital Insurance Trust Fund to the Old Age, Survivors, and Disability Trust Funds. In part, this shift will be made possible because of substantial savings to the Medicare system from the hospital cost containment legislation that I have proposed.

5. Increase the tax rate on the self-employed from 7 percent to 7.5 percent. This will restore the historical relationship between the OASI and the DI rates paid by the self-employed to one and one-half times that paid by employees.

6. Correct certain technical provisions of the Social Security Act which differentiate on the basis of sex. This will include a new eligibility test for dependent benefits. Recent Supreme Court decisions would result in unfinanced increases in the cost of the system and some inequities without this change.

These six steps, along with measures already contained in existing law, will eliminate the short-term financing problem and improve the overall equity of the Social Security system.

In order to guarantee the financial integrity of the system into the next century, two additional steps must be taken. I will be asking the Congress to:

1. Modify the Social Security benefit formula to eliminate the inflation over-adjustment now in law. This modification, known as "decoupling,"

should be done in a way that maintains the current ratio of retirement benefits to preretirement wages.

2. Adjust the timing of a tax rate increase already contained in current law. The one percent tax rate increase presently scheduled for the year 2011 would be moved forward so that .25 percent would occur in 1985 and the remainder in 1990.

Taken together, the actions I am recommending today will eliminate the Social Security deficit for the remainder of this century. They will reduce the estimated 75-year deficit from the Trustee Report forecast of 8.2 percent of payroll to a manageable 1.9 percent.

Prompt enactment of the measure I have recommended will provide the Social Security system with financial stability. This is an overriding immediate objective.

In addition, I am instructing the Secretary of Health, Education and Welfare to appoint the independent Social Security Advisory Council required by law to meet each four years. I will ask the Council to conduct a thorough reexamination of the structure of the system, the adequacy of its benefits, the effectiveness and equity of disability definitions, and the efficiency and responsiveness of its administration. Their report, which will be issued within the next two years, will provide the basis for further improvements.

I call upon the Congress to act favorably on these major reform initiatives.

JIMMY CARTER

───10───

A PLAN FOR REFORM

A PLAN FOR REFORM

The key problems faced by the social security system have now been discussed. Summarized below are my recommendations on the social security program with regard to: (1) coverage; (2) financing; (3) benefits (balancing social adequacy and individual equity, for both men and women); (4) retirement age and the retirement test; (5) simplification of the system.

Coverage and Entitlement Amount

As soon as possible, all workers should be covered by and required to participate in the social security system.

During 1975, about one hundred million workers had earnings that were taxable and creditable toward benefits. About 10 percent, or 8.8 million, of the regularly employed labor force remained outside the system. For reasons of equity no less than the necessity to alleviate the short-run financing problem, all workers should be covered. In "all workers" I would include ideally government employees at all levels despite the probable legal hurdles.

There are many reasons why universal participation is a desirable goal. The 6 million government workers—federal, state and local—who comprise the bulk of workers not now covered are not contributing their fair share to the redistributive, social adequacy aspects of the system. Some 2.8 million federal-level officials and employees in the legislative, judicial, and executive branches, as well as some state and local government employees, do not contribute any part of their primary salary to the system's redistributive aspects. Worse, they are also taking advantage of work in secondary occupations to qualify for social security benefits—frequently, for those monthly *minimum* benefits that are greater than the monthly average earnings taxed. Forty-three percent of the current federal civil service annuitants also draw benefits under social security. About one-third of these "double dippers" receive social security minimum benefits weighted in such a way as to favor low-income earners. The number of persons who will become eligible for such double-employment benefits appears to be increasing. Proposals in Congress to include coverage of federal employees naturally have been opposed by strong federal employee organizations.

In addition to the 3.5 million state and local government workers not participating in the system, increasing numbers of such workers now covered are considering withdrawing from it. They have a triple incentive: reducing the federal taxes paid by employer and employee; restructuring the benefits package to eliminate some social security benefits; and using the money so retained to pay for higher benefits in private pension systems. (It is recognized that securing mandatory coverage of state workers poses constitutional states' rights questions that will be difficult to resolve.)

The revenues actually lost because of the current nonparticipants and the potential loss from the increasing number of social security dropouts impose an unfair additional cost on those who have no choice but to remain covered and pay taxes. Their nonparticipation creates additional pressure to increase the social security taxes paid by those who remain covered and by future generations of covered employees. Covering all government employees—federal, state, and local—would reduce the short-term cost of the system by 0.70 percent of taxable payroll and the long-term cost by 0.25 percent. Universal coverage would immediately increase OASDI tax revenues by about $8 billion annually.

The nonparticipation of government workers in a government-mandated program is creating more and more dissatisfaction among those participants who have no choice but to participate. Particularly dissatisfied are healthy, younger, unmarried workers in higher-paying occupations who know that they could secure a better annuity under a privately run plan, and who value less than older persons the coverage for permanent disability and anticipated hospitalization benefits when 65 years of age (Part A of Medicare). Also dissatisfied are many working married women and their husbands who believe that the benefits are now being distributed inequitably.

The major argument against inclusion of government workers is that they already have satisfactory pension, disability, and survivor plans. In 1975, federal, state, and local governments paid out $21.6 billion in cash benefits to 3.7 million persons under these plans.[1] Obviously, some way should be found to integrate existing government retirement plans with social security. Almost all employees of large companies also have what they generally believe are satisfactory private pension, disability and survivor plans. Yet they are required to pay social security taxes that in many cases exceed their taxes on income. Under many union-negotiated plans, and increasingly under other private plans, the employer's premium to the private insurance company falls as social security payroll taxes rise. Integration of private plans with social security is already occurring. Other existing government plans need to be integrated with social security so that there is a minimum of "double dipping."

Noncompliance by teen-age employees and their employers and the potential high cost of attempting to enforce such compliance are arguments for not requiring that social security taxes be paid by and for young people under 18 (the legal adult age), especially when they work for small employers.

Earnings before age 21 are not counted in computing benefits. Although a few individuals under 18 in the entertainment world make a great deal of money, they pay the progressive personal income tax on their earnings. Most teen-agers make very little, and the law if enforced would dry up further the odd jobs that are most open to them. The nuisance to the householder in filling out forms for teen-age baby sitters, snow-shovelers, gardeners, etc., results in noncompliance (often they are unaware of the requirement), and fewer such jobs may become available. Knowledgeable and unknowledgeable teen-agers alike resent what they believe is an unfair tax. Young persons are not likely to place a high value on income that they may receive in their old age. The costs of enforcing compliance are probably too high to warrant continuance of social security tax on the earnings of teen-agers under 18. This would be true both of the administrative costs and of the teen-agers' resentment costs.

There should be an increase in the required entitlement amount of $50 total earnings per quarter, which represents earnings of about $3 per week. The amount of earnings required should have some connection with the level of wages in the 1970s. In 1935, $3 a week might have

---

1. U.S. Department of Health, Education, and Welfare, Social Security Administration, Research and Statistics Note No. 17, August 20, 1976.

represented one day's pay; in 1977 it represents one hour's pay. Such an increase could be looked on as alternative or—better—complementary to not imposing the tax on workers under 18. In 1977 the annual tax base was $16,500, or 5½ times the initial base of $3,000. The entitlement amount should become at least $200 a quarter, or four times the initial base; at most, it should be $300 or six times the base. The advantage of this increase is that it would decrease the number of double dippers without hurting the low-income earner. An increase to $300 would require earnings of about $24 a week and one to $200 earnings of about $16 a week. It is not known whether these two measures—increasing the entitlement amount and eliminating the tax on those under 18—would result in an actual dollar gain to the system.

Universal, compulsory coverage would eventually prevent windfall benefits to those whose primary work has been in the past in uncovered employment. It would also increase the overall equity of the system, and help to keep increases in social security taxes lower than they will otherwise be. At the same time, the erosion of popular support for the system might be stemmed by this and the other changes proposed. Admonitions to taxpayers by government officials to "do as I say, not as I do" cannot be said to encourage popular support for any government program!

The Financial Soundness of the System Should Be Restored

By 1977, every recent group studying the current and anticipated levels of OASI revenues, taxes, and interest on trust fund monies, and comparing them with expenditures on administration and benefits, had predicted that, beginning with calendar year 1976, payments would exceed income for both the combined old-age and survivors insurance and the disability insurance systems. Furthermore, the shortage was expected to increase in future years. By 1984, unless legislation was enacted, the OASI trust fund seemed likely to be exhausted.

The "intermediate set of alternative assumptions" in the 1976 trustees' report on the OASI trust fund (see document 5.7) yields estimates of future average annual deficits as follows: 0.82 percent of taxable earnings over the period 1976 to 1981; 1.91 percent over the period 1976 to 2000; 6.85 percent over the period 2001 to 2025; and

15.14 percent over the period 2026 to 2050. Under the same set of assumptions, and without any corrective action, the disability insurance trust fund would be exhausted in 1979 and the assets of the old-age and survivors' insurance trust would be exhausted in 1984. As of early 1976, the latter reserve amounted to 8.5 months of the payout rate.

The reasons for an annual deficit in the old-age and survivors' insurance trust fund have been detailed in previous chapters.[2] The total assets of the OASI trust fund fell by about $2 billion from fiscal year 1975 to the end of fiscal year 1976. The major factors causing the projected gap between outlays and tax income were: *(a)* the inflation-fueled, cost-of-living benefit increases mandated by Congress in 1972; *(b)* the unintended "double counting" of inflation in these benefits, also created by the 1972 amendments; *(c)* the failure to match automatic benefit increases by an increase in the tax rate; and especially *(d)* demographic factors, such as the declining birth rate. The last-mentioned factor deserves further comment. The replacement rate is 16.2 births per 1,000. In the first half of 1976, the rate was 14.2 per 1,000. Even if this rate increases slightly as the economy improves, a severe financial strain on the system will occur as the so-called post-war babies retire and receive benefits from taxes paid in the future by the relatively smaller labor force produced by the first generation to use oral contraceptives.

During 1976 the death rate, according to the provisional data, continued to decline. In 1975 the general decline in the crude death rate was 3.3 percent over 1974—for those 65 years and over, 4.4 percent. For diseases of the heart the decline was 5.2 percent. Because heart disease is the leading cause of death in the United States, it accounts for 44 percent of the 1975 drop. It is difficult to predict advances in medical prevention, diagnosis, and treatment of disease, but 1974 is the first year of decline in the crude death rate since 1941, when antibiotics became commonly prescribed. The decline in the 1970s appears due to a combination of factors including declining infant mortality rates, and a reduction of automobile accident deaths generally ascribed to the 55-mile-per-hour speed limit. However, the decline also reflects reduction in deaths at older ages, and this is more unusual. If life expectancy

---

2. None of the recent study groups had attempted to predict what additional costs might be imposed on the system by the accelerating withdrawals of state and local government groups. The 1976 trustee's report on the trust funds admitted that they could not take account of this new factor.

continues to increase, albeit slowly, at older ages, it will place a greater drain on the trust fund than originally anticipated. In 1975 life expectancy for males at age 65 was 13.7 years and for females 17.9 years.[3] In the 1939-41 period the comparable figures were 12.1 years for males and 13.6 for females.[4] These amount to gains in average life expectancy at age 65 of 1.6 years for men and 4.3 years for women.

The disability trust fund was anticipated to be drawn down because of the higher than forecasted number of disability beneficiaries who increased from 2.5 million in 1969 to 4.4 million in 1975. Among the reasons were liberalization of entitlement requirements for younger persons, more liberal interpretation of the eligibility criteria, greater awareness of the program, and fewer persons leaving the rolls as "recovered."

Decoupling

Inadequate financing of pension and survivor benefits, both in the short and long run, could be remedied in many different ways. For the immediate period, the most important action would be to correct the double counting of inflation—for instance, by "decoupling" or by freezing the benefit-earnings ratios at different earning levels as of a given date. This would, of course, also help the long-run deficit as would other approaches to improve the financial status of the funds.

Correction of the double count is the obvious first step. In 1976, there appeared to be general agreement in this matter, as represented by proposed decoupling legislation (for example in H.R. 14480, 94th Congress). The problem, if uncorrected, "threatens the solvency of the social security system."[5] The average long-run, 75-year expenditure for OASI benefits of the current, uncoupled system is 15.42 percent of taxable payrolls. This is the estimate in the 1976 trustees' report; it is based on assumptions of 5¾ percent increase in average earnings, a 4 percent increase in the Consumer Price Index, and an ultimate fertility rate of 1.9 children per woman. In the 1976 report, these are the intermediate assumptions.

Because the trustees of the OASI and Disability trust funds are the same, data on the two funds are often integrated. Also, an individual's

3. Metropolitan Life Insurance Company, *Statistical Bulletin,* May 1976, p. 4.

4. U.S. Department of Health, Education, and Welfare, *Trends: Part 1, National Trends, 1966-67* (Washington, D.C.: U.S. Government Printing Office, 1976), p. S-16.

5. David Mathews, secretary of Health, Education, and Welfare, letter to Nelson Rockefeller, June 17, 1976, p. 3.

disability benefit is converted to a retirement benefit at age 65. The long-run, 75-year expenditure of taxable payroll for disability is estimated to be 3.51 percent, which when added to the OASI expenditures totals 18.93 percent average expenditure of taxable payrolls. At the same time, the average tax revenues (over the 75-year period) of OASDI, it is estimated, will be only 10.97 percent, yielding a long-term deficit of about 8 percent for the combined OASDI system. The alternative, "low" set of assumptions in the 1976 trustees' report yields OASDI expenditures of 13.83 percent of taxable payroll, while the alternative "high" set increases this amount to 25.47 percent.[6] Obviously, wide ranges may result and 75-year estimates are at best informed guesses.

Decoupling could reduce long-range deficit by one-half

The benefits formula should be adjusted so that persons not yet retired are compensated only once for inflation. Persons retiring now are receiving benefits computed to reflect the inflation twice: once, in their inflation-related wage increases; and again, in a cost-of-living factor that increases the initial level of benefits awarded, which, since it is derived from wages, already reflects the inflation. Once they have retired, their benefits continue to increase when the cost-of-living increases.

"Decoupling" as was proposed by the Advisory Council and President Ford in June, 1976, may freeze the current benefit-earnings ratios.[7] Alternatively, decoupling can be so constructed as to yield changing ratios in a predictable manner, as for example, the decreasing replacement ratios of benefits to earnings over the years under the Jones Bill (H.R. 12334, 94th Congress). This latter would have reduced the estimated long-run deficit by more than one-half.

Decoupling assumes that the agreed-on, scheduled benefit-ratios for different annual income levels are what society wants for a long period. The existing system lets replacement ratios fluctuate over a very wide range in accordance with deflation or inflation. An example of the

6. U.S. Trustees of the Federal Old-Age and Survivors Insurance and Disability Insurance Trust Funds, *1976 Annual Report,* mimeographed (Washington, D.C.: U.S. Government Printing Office, 1976), p. 91.

7. For example, the revised benefit structure of the 1975 recommendations of the Advisory Council embodied in the administration's bill is as follows: 91% of the first $175 average indexed monthly earnings (AIME), plus 33% of AIME over $175 through AIME of $1,050, plus 17% of AIME over $1,050. U.S. Department of Health, Education, and Welfare, "Explanation to Congress of the proposed Social Security Benefit Indexing Act," June 17, 1976, Table A, p. 2.

inflationary impact under the present system was given by Commissioner Cardwell, November 5, 1975, when he stated that, under certain assumptions as to prices and wages, "in the year 2010 it will be possible for a low-income worker and his wife, both 65 years of age, to receive about $1.34 in benefits for each dollar of the worker's final earnings."[8] Since future benefits will be paid by taxation on work-income of future generations, the system implies compliance by future generations with a "social contract" that they took no part in formulating.

The Advisory Council's proposal was to index wage rates by changes in the average of wage rates, and all wage rate credits would be so adjusted. This would eliminate differences because of the uneven timing of wage rate increases in different industries and by different companies within the same industry. Replacement ratios of benefits to earnings would remain constant.

After persons have retired, their benefits would be computed on their indexed wages. Once awarded, these benefits would then, as now, increase as the cost-of-living increases during retirement. Thus retirees would be fully protected from any impact of cost-of-living increases, even from price increases that might reflect decreases in natural resources—for instance, because of a decline in the supply of oil from abroad. It could be argued that general-indexed protection against the latter type of price increases is not in the public interest and should be extended only cautiously, if at all, to selected groups.

The Consultant Panel's proposal would use a price-index method of decoupling so that replacement ratios of recent earnings would tend to decline when real earnings increase. Either method would protect against occurrence of unpredictable ratios of benefits to past earnings. The result of double-counting is magnified when double-digit inflation occurs. The panel's method would permit Congress to remain in control of the distribution of future growth in real income. No longer would increases in real national income be automatically used to maintain the now unduly high benefits to earnings-after-taxes ratios already in effect in 1977. Demographic predictions are unreliable. It therefore seems wise to leave some leeway for congressional discretion in future years.

There are other proposals for decoupling that differ in relatively minor ways. The Consultant Panel's method, which I prefer, was

---

8. James Cardwell, "Remarks," photocopied, (Statement addressed to American business press, Washington Editorial Conference, November 5, 1975), p. 9.

discussed in detail in Chapter 5, on financing. To repeat that discussion and to include other alternate methods—a fairly complex matter— would confuse those who may read only this, the concluding chapter, without adding to their understanding of the problem.

Insofar as the growth in real national income exceeds 2 percent per annum, there would still be some leeway under the Advisory Council's proposal *if* its long-run assumptions were met. I concur with the Consultant Panel's more recent proposal, primarily because no one can predict, with any reasonable hope of accuracy, the relevant variables for many years ahead. Therefore, an uncommitted margin of monies is desirable. The panel's method of decoupling would save more than the council's because slightly less benefits would be awarded in future years under the 1976 trustees' intermediate assumptions. For example, under the same set of assumptions and a somewhat higher tax base (initially $18,900 instead of $16,500 in 1977) there is a 1.3 percent of taxable payroll difference, or about $10 billion less benefits paid under the panel's plan in that year.

Under the council's wage-indexing proposal, the immediate diffusion of the first 2 percent of real growth of national income into maintenance of existing ratios of benefits to average earnings implies that the existing replacement ratios are by some magic precisely the ratios that ought to be sustained, and that maintaining them takes precedence over any other use to which the nation's resources might be applied.

If there were no increase in real wages—and in some future years, as when price increases may exceed wage increases, this appears likely— then under the panel's proposal replacement rates would rise, while under the council's assumptions they would of course be maintained. The panel assumes, and again I agree, that if there were no rise in real income for several years in a row, Congress would legislate changes, and that this would be preferable to a rigid replacement-ratio structure of benefits. The average long-run, 75-year expenditures for OASDI benefits would be only 11 percent of taxable payroll under all of the panel's proposals and 15 percent under President Ford's proposal of June 1976.[9] These yield an actuarial imbalance of -0.7 percent and -3.4 percent, respectively. From this alone, it is obvious that long-run

9. U.S. Congress, Joint Committee (House Committee on Ways and Means, Senate Committee on Finance), *Report of the Consultant Panel on Social Security to the Congressional Research Service,* 94th Cong., 2d sess., August 1976 (Washington, D.C.: U.S. Government Printing Office, 1976), p. 6.

actuarial balance is not unobtainable. It is a political not an economic problem.

The importance of recognizing in each of the succeeding three 25-year periods the different patterns of costs over taxes was made clear by the 1976 Trustees' Report on the funding of OASDI:

> Over the first 25-year period the cost would exceed taxes by an average annual amount equivalent to 1.91 percent of taxable payroll, over the second 25-year period by 6.85 percent, and over the third 25-year period by 15.14 percent. In all cases the underfinancing is more pronounced for the disability insurance program than for the old-age and survivors insurance program when viewed as a proportion of the cost of each program.[10]

Proposals to Increase Revenues

Other proposals, which alone or in combination would help to raise revenues to equal outgo and thus would decrease the short-run and long-run imbalance, are: (1) to extend coverage to include all workers; (2) to increase the rate of payroll tax; (3) to increase the level of base wages to be taxed; (4) to use general revenues from existing income tax or other taxes, as for example, the value-added tax. Inclusion for income tax purposes of OASI retirement benefits upon receipt would not help the OASI trust fund, but would increase the amount of general revenues and, therefore, is relevant.

Because previous sections have discussed in detail the factors in favor of securing universal coverage of all workers and these discussions include the improvement in funding that would result, no further analysis of this will be presented here.

Increase rate of payroll tax

An obvious and simple solution to the short-term deficit is to increase the rate of payroll taxes as recommended by several groups that have reviewed the deficit problem. In the spring and summer of 1976, apparently because it was an election year, Congress delayed consideration of any solutions and rejected President Ford's plan to raise the rate by three-tenths of one percent on employee and employer. It was estimated that such an increase would cost no worker more

10. U.S. Trustees. . . ,1976 Annual Report, p. 93.

TABLE 10.1
COMPARISON OF EXPENDITURES AND TAXES FOR OLD-AGE, SURVIVORS AND DISABILITY INSURANCE SYSTEM AS PERCENT OF TAXABLE PAYROLL UNDER ALTERNATIVE II
(Percent)

ITEM	AVERAGE FOR PERIOD		
	OLD-AGE AND SURVIVORS INSURANCE	DISABILITY INSURANCE	TOTAL
1st 25-yr period (1976-2000):			
Expenditures as percent of taxable payroll	9.79	2.02	11.81
Tax rate in law	8.56	1.34	9.90
Difference	-1.23	-.68	-1.91
2nd 25-yr period (2001-2025):			
Expenditures as percent of taxable payroll	14.00	3.95	17.95
Tax rate in law	9.52	1.58	11.10
Difference	-4.48	-2.37	-6.85
3rd 25-yr period (2026-2050):			
Expenditures as percent of taxable payroll	22.47	4.57	27.04
Tax rate in law	10.20	1.70	11.90
Difference	-12.27	-2.87	-15.14
Total 75-yr period (1976-2050):			
Expenditures as percent of taxable payroll	15.42	3.51	18.93
Tax rate in law	9.43	1.54	10.97
Difference	-5.99	-1.97	-7.96

NOTE: Expenditures and payroll are calculated under the intermediate set of assumptions which incorporates ultimate annual increases of 5¾ percent in average earnings and 4 percent in CPI, an ultimate unemployment rate of 5 percent, and an ultimate fertility rate of 1.9 children per woman. (See the text for further detail). Payroll is adjusted to take into account the lower contribution rates on self-employment income, on tips, and on multiple-employer "excess wages" as compared with the combined employer-employee rate.

SOURCE: U.S. Trustees of the Federal Old-Age and Survivors' Insurance and Disability Insurance Trust Funds, *Annual Report 1976,* mimeographed (Washington, D.C.: U.S. Government Printing Office), p. 95.

than one dollar a week and would raise about $3.5 billion annually. However, if the employer-paid portion was assumed to be ultimately paid by the employee, then the cost to the latter would be about two dollars a week.

President Ford, in repeating his proposal in June 1976, which would have increased the tax rate from 5.85 percent to 6.15 percent, or the combined employer-employee tax rate from 11.7 to 12.3 percent, noted that the anticipated gain in revenues of $3.5 billion annually would virtually eliminate the short-run, yearly deficit of about $4 billion. If his decoupling proposal were also adopted, the tax rate increase would further reduce the 75-year deficit by about an additional 0.7 percent of taxable payroll (including a 0.10 percent increase due to increasing the tax on the self-employed to its original rate), yielding a deficit of 3.32 percent. The Consultant Panel, made up of experts and with no public members or politicians, recommended in August 1976 a combined employer and employee tax rate increase of 0.4 percent. A smaller tax rate increase of 0.1 percent on both employee and employer was discussed in the House Ways and Means Committee during 1976 as a less deflationary alternative to a 0.3 percent increase. The 0.1 percent of tax increase, by itself, is too low to change substantially the inadequate funding status of these programs. Congress appears to agree on no tax rate increase beyond scheduled increases. Although there is apparent agreement that legislation to correct the double count of inflation is needed, no legislation as of March 1977 had been passed.

Practically all economists agree that the final incidence of the payroll tax is on the employee. It is not paid out of profits over any meaningful period of time. That the employer "pays" the matching tax is only the mechanism through which the tax is paid. Those who oppose raising the rate of OASDI taxes argue that the tax considered alone is regressive after the limit of the earnings base is reached, and below that level is proportional to earnings. Although there is substantial but not total agreement that, if the benefits are considered in conjunction with the tax, the social security system is unevenly progressive up to those income levels of the tax base, use of revenues from the personal income tax, which is progressive, would increase that progressiveness and extend it into higher levels of earned income. Income taxes, unlike social security taxes, are levied on what the Internal Revenue Service calls unearned incomes. Persons who oppose increases in the payroll tax rate usually believe in general-revenue financing; they tend to assume that the only source of these additional monies would be from upper-middle and high-income persons. Some, possibly, believe that a small additional amount could come from inheritance tax revenues. Less than 2 percent of taxable returns have annual adjusted gross taxable income of $50,000 or more, and only 7 percent of all total adjusted gross taxable income is in this category.[11] It is obvious, then, that there are insufficient revenues from this tax source to support an ever-growing level of all the benefits now provided and to pay for many other traditional federal government expenditures.

If general revenues become an accepted means of financing a sizable proportion of OASI benefits, additional forms of taxes yielding large revenues are needed. The value-added tax rather than the personal income tax fits this bill in particular. The pros and cons of using general-revenue financing are discussed below.

Earnings base

Another way to increase revenues would be to increase the amount of covered wages that are taxed at a given rate. The wage base that is taxed and on which future benefits are computed already rises under the 1972 amendments with the increase in covered average wages. In 1974 it was $13,200; in 1975, $14,100; in 1976, $15,300; and in 1977, $16,500. During its December 21, 1974 meeting—the Saturday before Christmas—the Quadrennial Advisory Council, with three members absent, voted 7 to 4 to recommend an increase of the tax and benefit base to an arbitrarily chosen amount of $24,000, beginning in 1976.[12] This proposal was supported by J. Van Gorkom, chairman of the Finance Subcommittee, who estimated that it would "save one-half of one percent of the (long-run) cost."[13]

After considerable discussion, the Social Security Administration's acting actuary, Francisco Bayo, stated that "in 1974, 84 percent of all [covered] workers would have had their earnings totally covered by the [1976 base of $15,300]. If we move to. . .$24,000 it would be about 93 percent."[14] Van Gorkom then stated: "So 9 percent lay between 13.3

11. U.S. Internal Revenue Service, *Statistics of Income 1972: Individual Tax Returns*, Public Document No. 79, 1-75 (Washington, D.C.: U.S. Government Printing Office, 1975), p. 6.

12. During all the meetings one member was consistently absent but was represented by another person from the same organization who was permitted by agreement to vote.

13. Quadrennial Advisory Council on Social Security, 1974, Transcript (Van Gorkom), p. 65.

14. Ibid., December 21, 1974, p. 68.

and 24 thousand. That would be about 8 million workers." The Department of Commerce data show that between the level of $15,000 to $25,000 annual income of one-earner families there were in 1974, 21 percent of all U.S. families, and from $10,000 to $15,000, 29 percent. For all families, many having more than one worker, the corresponding figures were 28 percent and 24 percent, respectively.[15] Thus the decision of December 21, 1974, was based on at best impressionistic data. On January 19, 1975, the Advisory Council voted, all members present or represented, to withdraw this recommendation, which might have acted to depress employment; in all likelihood, it would have decreased the disposable income of many persons and imposed an unexpected high increase in labor costs on employers, who would have passed it back to their employees as soon as possible.

In the long run, the rigidity of labor supply associated with trade-union seniority rules and firms' nonunion personnel practices might delay the anticipated sizable deflationary impact on the economy. Eventually, however, such high additional and unforeseen labor costs might induce employers to lay off workers and possibly also to increase prices. Employees would have had less disposable income to spend or save.

Also, to increase revenues in this fashion would create a much higher level of future benefits. Benefits are a function of the level of earnings subject to the payroll tax, and therefore any increase in the base taxed eventually creates higher benefits. That benefit increase would eventually have gone to middle-income workers. Proponents, however, argued that increasing the base rather than the rate would initially redistribute income from middle-income to lower-income persons, as from those covered workers with annual incomes of $15,000 through $24,000 to those below $15,000. They also argued that the tax increase was not a burden on the former but rather forced them to save or buy an annuity that later they would enjoy tax-free. Opponents, as noted above, used the latter part of this statement to argue *against* the proposal: in the *long run* it would tend to favor middle-income, not low-income workers. In the short run, earners below $15,000 would not be receiving the benefits except for the small numbers in this group who would be retiring. Avoidance of permitting a higher tax base to count for a later increase in benefits might be possible, if the employer pays taxes on a higher base than does the employee.

15. U.S. Bureau of Census, *Consumer Income,* January 1976 (Washington, D.C.: U.S. Government Printing Office, 1976), p. 35.

Opponents also argued that the benefits were already heavily weighted to favor low-income persons as compared to middle-income persons and that a $24,000 tax base would place an unfair burden on the latter. Thus it would reduce the disposable income of those younger persons, with families to support, who might as yet have relatively few household assets as compared to a large number of OASI beneficiaries, 62 years and over, many of whom owned homes, household equipment, cars, etc., paid no income or social security taxes, and had no children dependent on them. Some of these latter might additionally have sizable other incomes from rents, interest, and dividends, on which, of course, they would pay income tax but no social security tax.

The major private asset of older persons is their home, often owned free of mortgage. In 1967 (the latest detailed SSA data available), 52 percent of individuals 65 years and older, who were not in institutions, owned their own homes, as did 77 percent of married couples in that age bracket. Moreover, 80 percent of them owned them free of mortgages.[16] It is noted that about 40 percent of single aged persons live with relatives. In 1967, the median value of the aged person's equity in home ownership was $11,000. This value is estimated to have risen by 1973 to $18,000. Few younger workers who pay social security taxes own their own homes; generally, they carry sizable mortgages. Comparison of economic classes solely on the basis of covered earnings, which ignores income outside of earnings, durable household goods, home ownership, and other private assets, may lead to the biased conclusion that earners are necessarily better off than those of retirement age. Assets and income from assets are generally under-reported.[17]

Because of the inflation, the social security earnings base is moving up automatically and rapidly. Increasing the earnings base will not in the long run redistribute income from middle-income to lower-income persons. It will, however, redistribute income from younger working to retired, nonworking persons. It appears, therefore, that specific legislation to increase funding should not be focussed on the earnings base of the payroll tax.

---

16. U.S. Department of Health, Education, and Welfare, *Demographic and Economic Characteristics of the Aged*, Research Report No. 45, SSA 75-11802 (Washington, D.C.: U.S. Government Printing Office, 1975), p. 106.

17. Ibid., p.124.

General-revenue financing

Because of the growing size of the long-run deficit; because demo-graphic factors outside the government's control affect the total dollars paid out in benefits; and because of the large proportion of welfare-type benefits in the system, some argue that general revenues rather than earmarked payroll taxes should support OASI benefits. This is not a new thought. From time to time, however, it has had substantial support from those who believe that OASI should redistribute income from rich to poor by use of personal income tax funding. General-revenue funding also has the support of economist Milton Friedman, but for the opposite reasons: that only in this way will the rapidly expanding expenditures be contained, and the public will realize that it is not an insurance system.

In the mid-1970s, the rate of increase in real growth of the national product was falling. It was argued that it was unfair to burden future workers with the cost of pension-like benefit payments to today's older workers upon their retirement. If both population and real wages continue to fall, pay-as-you-go funding to support the intergeneration-al transfer of funds represented by the OASI system would become even more unpopular.

Many persons believe, and for different reasons, that only general revenues, as from the progressive income tax and the value-added tax (as yet unused in the United States), have tax capability to generate revenues sufficient to cover the increasing liabilities of OASI as the ratio of beneficiaries to workers increases. They argue that this type of taxation, unlike the current social security tax system, would not reduce business and work incentives. Social security, in their view, induces early retirement, reduces private savings, and therefore, by causing loss of monies available for private capital formation, de-presses the size of gross national product.

With the current rates of U.S. personal income taxes and the current frequency distribution of personal income after deductions, any tax that must yield per se a large amount of new revenue cannot be made more progressive unless one wishes to place a limit on allowable annual income after taxes and that limit be set somewhere in the $20,000 to $30,000 range. At these levels, incentives to work are definitely affected. Alternatively, inflation could be permitted so that more persons have earned incomes in the higher brackets. This would yield higher tax revenues if other economic deterrents, such as a much higher price level, were not concomitantly created. Unfortunately,

OASI benefits are tied to the price level. This route, then, is a vicious circle. An across-the-board increase in income tax rates is another alternative supported by economist Joseph Pechman.

General revenues may include other types of taxes—notably, the "value-added" tax which is not used by the United States Government, but is used by many foreign governments. The concept of a value-added tax may be explained as follows. As raw material is processed, semi-finished, and finally converted to an end product for sale, there may be several intermediate points of sale. At each point, the purchaser pays a tax on the "value added" by the previous processor. This acts as a tax on a company's sales minus a credit for the amount of value-added tax paid on the company's purchases. It is estimated that a 1-percent value added tax would raise about $4 to $5 billion. Because of probable exemptions and price increases, however, the amount is difficult to predict.[18]

Other taxes that add to general revenues are inheritance and gift taxes. As inheritance taxes increase, they encourage the wealthy not only to increase their current consumption but to make gifts to their children and others. There is, of course, a tax on gifts above certain amounts. The 1976 changes in the law on gifts and inheritance tax somewhat weakened this incentive. However, the laws still encourage more current consumption by wealthy persons, greater investment in human capital (for instance, through education of their children) and less savings. The latter results in less returns to workers because it reduces capital-goods formation. Thus the returns on capital, which are in smaller supply, would be relatively greater than otherwise.

Inheritance and gift taxes do prevent very high concentrations of wealth from being handed down from one generation to the next. Annual yield from inheritance and gift taxes was only $11.4 billion in 1974. A good case on equity grounds can be made for high inheritance taxes and this usually outweighs any economic arguments against them. Such a verdict rests on a value judgment.

It is also possible to raise general revenues from excise taxes, such as those on tobacco and alcohol. The form of taxation that provides the general revenues determines whether income is redistributed from rich to poor or from smokers to nonsmokers.

Others who oppose general revenue taxes state that the decline in the rate of productivity and real wages is temporary and that sensible

18. Dan Throop Smith, et al., *What You Should Know About the Value Added Tax* (Homewood, Ill.: Dow Jones-Irwin, 1973).

steps taken now to control benefits and costs would permit today's accepted intergenerational transfer of income system to continue. They consider general revenue monies unacceptable financing of an "earned-benefit" system—the concept on which OASI was originally promoted—and fear that, over time, use of general revenues would transform the current system into a relief system with means test. Some argue further that general-revenue financing, because of the amount of revenues needed—$63 billion of OASI benefits were paid out in 1976—would be the beginning in the United States of new forms of general taxes as, for example, the "value-added" tax. Once additional revenues are gained, governments usually spend the money.

There have been proposals to rebate some part of the OASI taxes paid by low-income workers. Such proposals could be in the form of a negative income tax. Since the income tax acts as a means test, it can be argued that all taxation should be administered by the Internal Revenue Service.

The total of all types of income security benefits (including civil service employees and the means-test program, SSI) paid by the federal government to the aged in 1975 were, in cash, $65 billion, and in kind (Medicare, Medicaid, food stamps, etc.) $16 billion—a grand total of $81 billion.

The present social security system is, because of its financial imbalance, at a crossroads. It must either be restructured to conform to the initial dominance of the insurance (individual equity) concept, or on the other hand, be allowed to complete its progression towards a welfare system and be financed out of general revenues.

Because of the great expansion of welfare benefits and their maladministration—for example cash social service grants to the states[19] and the recently exposed provider abuses in the "in-kind" Medicare and Medicaid programs—I select the first option. General-revenue funding would admit on the financing side a type of funding that is generally used to finance welfare or assistance benefits. It would therefore imply to many individuals that persons should meet a means or needs test to receive a social security benefit. I prefer that assistance-type benefits be largely removed from the social security system, and that they be funded as are welfare benefits under the now established Supplemental Security Income (or SSI) program. Even if the present

---

19. Martha Derthick, *Uncontrollable Spending for Social Service Grants* (Washington, D.C.: Brookings Institution, 1975).

system of indexing social security benefits is corrected to count inflation only once and all jobs are covered, the anticipated, long-run demographic changes compel a drastic restructuring to separate out a large portion of the welfare-type benefits, or a substantial increase in payroll taxes, or some other way of finding a new source of monies.

In short, it would be better to return the system to the one originally promised in 1935. This was, in large measure, a system of individual equity in which there was a relationship between the amount of taxes paid by the worker and his or her earned benefit. The government could then make good on those promises rather than dilute the social security benefit structure to cover all types of welfare benefits and, by this, force the use of general-revenue financing. To make up deficits without limit through general revenues, which after all are revenues derived from some other types of taxes paid by individuals, tends, I believe, to hide the true costs of the system. And if this happens, the system will become even more of a political football than it has in the past. Benefits will be increased for whatever groups of persons have the largest number of votes. Because our population is aging, general-revenue funding of so-called earned benefits, when there are likely to be many aged people in need, will absorb funds that, under alternative options could be available for those really in need. Moreover, as the gross national product and employment grow, the long-run funding problem of a payroll-tax-supported program should ease.

Proponents of general-revenue funding usually state that they would use only revenues from the progressive income tax, and thus equity would increase. Every group that proposes a program requiring large amounts of federal government money lays claim to the progressive income tax revenues. An examination of the income structure of the United States and its existing progressive income tax structure indicates that this route has only a very small potential of new funding without so increasing the rate of income taxation on low and especially middle-income persons that they will tend to reduce the labor supply and thus affect negatively the size of the gross national product. This route is the one that Great Britain has been following with such disastrous results in recent years.

There are, of course, other types of taxes that could be earmarked for social security benefits and especially for the Medicare benefits, which are not cash benefits directly paid to the consumer. On January 19, 1975, the day on which the Advisory Council recommended diversion of hospitalization trust fund monies to make up the short-run imbalance of the OASI trust fund, I questioned whether a more relevant tax might be an excise tax on cigarettes. This was considered by other council members to be merely an attempt to insert some humor into an otherwise very tense situation. It was not.

Very early the Advisory Council as a whole had decided not to review the Medicare Programs, either Part A or Part B, and delegated to its Subcommittee on Finance the charge to study the status of the trust funds of Medicare as required by law. However, the Subcommittee on Finance's report on the consultants' meeting of September 4, 1974, stated the following:

> With respect to the long-range actuarial deficit in the OASDI trust funds, the consultants had discussed the use of general revenue contributions and a lowering of the HI contribution rate with a concomitant increase in the OASDI rate. None of the consultants had technical or economic grounds for recommending a general revenue contribution, and some were strongly opposed to it. Because of the uncertainty of rising hospital costs it seemed unwise to recommend that the contribution rates for HI be changed.[20]

After that date, and prior to its meeting on Sunday, January 19, 1975, when the vote to use Medicare funds was taken, the council had not discussed Medicare further during its several meetings, which under the "Sunshine Acts" were open to the public. Members of the council of course had breakfast, lunch, and dinner with whom they pleased during the days of the meetings. The lack of in-depth data about the Medicare trust fund among even members of the Subcommittee on Finance was clearly indicated by Henry Smith (Actuary and Chairman of the Board, Equitable Life) of that subcommittee in his one-sentence dissent in the printed reports as follows:

> I do not believe the Council sufficiently investigated the Medicare program and probable costs thereunder to be justified in making the unequivocal statement that Part A is actuarially sound.[21]

During its September 20 and 21, 1974, meetings the council voted on several matters with the understanding that all votes were "tenta-

---

20. Quadrennial Advisory Council on Social Security, 1974, *Summary of Proceedings,* September 22, 1974.

21. U.S. Congress, House, Committee on Ways and Means, *Report of the Quadrennial Advisory Council on Social Security,* 94th Cong., 1st sess., H.D. 94-75, March 10, 1975 (Washington, D.C: U.S. Government Printing Office, 1975), p. 68, footnote 2.

tive" because the costs or savings of each proposal created interrelationships among all the proposals. The council voted not to discuss
Medicare because Congress had many bills on different forms of
national health insurance before it and abuses under Medicare and
Medicaid were being investigated. As a past member of the Health
Services Industry Committee I knew that, although Phase II controls
had reduced the increase in hospital *charges* to a level somewhat less
than one-half of the rate of increase before the freeze, when the freeze
on medical charges was lifted, hospital costs, which had been rising
faster than their revenues, would act as does the steam in a teakettle
filled with boiling water: the whistling spout would blow off its top and
hospital charges would increase rapidly to make up recent losses.
During that earlier meeting, it became clear to me through questioning
that the 1974 trustees of the Medicare trust fund had assumed price
controls would continue on hospitals when they made their estimates.
Price controls in the health sector were removed in April 1974. At the
January 19, 1975 meeting, I reminded my fellow council members of
this, but the vote was nine to four in favor of diverting Medicare, Part
A, trust fund's monies which were bound to decline.

Taxation of social security benefits upon receipt is supported for
reasons of equity. Low-income aged who have a double exemption
would be unaffected, while middle- and higher-income aged would pay
their share of income taxation. It would be preferable to tax the one-
half of the benefits represented by past payment by the employer and
on which the employee pays no tax when it is received in the same
fashion as private pensions. This would both help younger working
people and encourage older persons to postpone retirement. The
proposal is prospective and does not apply to persons already receiving
benefits.

Proposals to Decrease Expenditures

Another group of proposals to bring revenues and benefits into
long-term actuarial balance are those that would reduce the future
costs. These alone and/or in combination could bring the short-run
and long-run financing of social security into balance. Costs can be
reduced by: (1) reducing types of benefits (for instance, by phasing out
dependency spouse benefits); (2) by encouraging persons to retire at
later ages or even by eliminating the option, now at age 62, of

retirement with a reduced benefit. These measures should increase the size of total payrolls taxed, since they would probably reverse the trend of more persons retiring before age 65.

There have been at least four specific printed proposals made to reduce kinds or levels of benefits. One is my proposal to phase out the spouse's retirement benefit over a 30-year period. This is detailed in my dissenting statements to the reports of the Advisory Council. The proposal was estimated in 1974 to save about 0.4 percent of long-run payrolls.[22] Another proposal, by the Task Force on Women and Social Security, would reduce the spouse's dependent benefit to one-third instead of one-half of the primary benefit. It was criticized by James Cardwell, commissioner of social security, on October 23, 1975, as too costly: 1.9 percent of taxable payroll and $9 billion in the first year. It is costly because, while that specific proposal would reduce the cost of spouses' dependent benefits, it also would simultaneously increase all primary benefits by 12½ percent.

The Consultant Panel would abandon "the present schedule of spouse benefits for future retired workers." Instead, it would average "the earnings of the husband and wife for determining benefits of both one-worker and two-worker families."[23] With the increasing divorce rate, this would create administrative difficulties.

Additionally, President Ford proposed to eliminate monthly secondary benefits to persons aged 18 but under 22 who were in school, and who were either surviving children of deceased, covered workers or dependent "children" of retired covered workers' benefits. The argument for this was that, in a pay-as-you-go system, persons aged 18 to 22 who are working and not in school or college are paying social security taxes that may be used to support others in the same age group who are attending college. The current costs are about $1 billion annually.

Retirement at a later age

The Advisory Council recommended in 1975 that there be a gradual phase-in of an increase from age 65 to 68 for entitlement to OASDI benefits, and an increase from 62 to 65 for entitlement to reduced benefits. However, with unemployment in 1975 at the highest levels—

22. Ibid., p. 146.
23. *Report of the Consultant Panel . . .* 1976, p. 5.

and in 1976 only slightly lower ones—since the depression of the 1930s, while employment was also at its highest levels (about 85 million people), pressure for *earlier* rather than later retirement could build. Both unemployment and employment remain high because in each recent year more women work and are seeking work. Early retirement, that is, before age 65, is increasing. This decreases the potential gross national product, social security tax revenues, and the general tax capacity of the country.

The current financial imbalance of the OASDI program (both the pension and disability trust funds) is a strong economic argument from society's point of view for persons to continue work to 65 and even into their late 60s. Economic incentives should be structured to encourage later retirement by individuals. All the present incentives encourage retirement. Although for each year an individual works in covered employment after 65 his or her OASDI benefit is increased by one percent, the OASDI tax rate paid by the employee over 65 and his employer in 1977 is the same as for any other age group, and thus the amount of taxes paid greatly exceeds this small increment in benefit.

A simple way to create an economic incentive for persons to work beyond 65 would be to eliminate OASDI taxes paid by the employee who is 65 or older while retaining the matching employer-paid tax. The cost of this proposal was estimated to be negative (-0.02 of long-run payroll), if earnings after 65 years were not used to recompute benefits. There would be some loss of revenues from social security taxes not paid by employees over 65. Within the total tax structure, however, there would be a gain from their payment of personal income taxes. The social security system as a whole would enjoy an even larger gain because if persons are working and earning more than the retirement test permits, they will not be drawing social security retirement benefits.

To encourage persons to retire later in life, other financial incentives can be devised. Many early retirees with dependents have net untaxed social security benefits after retirement that are higher than their net after-tax recent earnings prior to retirement. Some persons are dissatisfied with mandatory retirement at age 65 or earlier, as imposed automatically by many firms. They would prefer greater flexibility in individual work-leisure arrangements. The increase in part-time workers at all ages reflects this. A new life style of combining leisure and work in more individualized ways is developing. For example, many men who retire from full-time work at 55 seek part-time work in occupations new to them. Today, there is one part-time worker for every 5½ full-time workers, while 15 years ago it was one for every 10. Among all the unemployed, 20 percent want only part-time work. Although many persons working part time are women, an increasing percentage are men. Tax incentives could be structured to give greater flexibility of individual choice and at the same time reduce costs of the social security system.

If benefits were not awarded until age 64 (reduced benefit) and age 67 (full benefit), the impact of the existing retirement test would be greatly lessened. To encourage work beyond these years, the council's proposal to reduce the penalty of loss of $1 in benefits for every $2 earned beyond the limit to $1 for every $3 might be more favorably received than it has been. Also, if the age of entitlement to benefits is increased, then a gradual phase-out of the retirement test could be considered, as the cost of eliminating it would be lessened.

Recent popularized versions of medical literature claim that, on the average, persons who continue to work live longer. However, I have not seen definitive, controlled studies of observed differences resulting from different ages of retirement by groups of individuals matched at age 62 or 65 years for health status, socio-economic status, and other independent, meaningful variables. Without these kinds of data, no defensible conclusion can be drawn.

Ireland, in 1975, had reduced its age eligibility requirement from 70 to 68, leaving Israel as the only country to have a 70-year requirement. Sweden recently reduced its entitlement age for government pensions from 70 to 67. The recent, more favorable mortality rates for males in the United States and the continued greater life expectancy of females justify a later age of retirement. The initial selections of 65 for full and of 62 for actuarially reduced retirement ages in the United States were both arbitrary decisions. Ideally, individualized retirement ages may be preferable, but large firms may find this difficult to administer.

Manual and assembly-line workers prefer earlier retirement. It is the professional, some service, and white-collar workers who prefer later retirement. Persons who enjoy their work and who remain healthy generally try to continue in their existing or new jobs. The tax system should be structured to favor this choice, not discourage it. The established retirement age for a now-reduced OASI benefit should be looked at within the newly developed benefit pattern of permanent disability benefits. For these there is at least a separate trust fund (admittedly also short of funds and estimated to be exhausted by 1979). Supplemental Security Income, or welfare benefits (SSI), available since January 1974, are also relevant here. To some degree the increase in persons receiving permanent disability benefits reflects a substitution by older persons of these benefits for earlier-than-usual retirement benefits.

In 1975, 59 percent of all retirement benefit awards to men and 72 percent of all retirement benefits to women were to those below 65 years. The trend to retire early is increasing. About 40 percent of men receiving a reduced benefit work part time or intermittently. Data indicate that availability of social security benefits and private pensions influence the decision to retire early as much if not more than a person's state of health. Consideration should be given to increasing gradually the retirement age *(a)* for full entitlement of benefits, at least for non-industrial workers, and *(b)* for reduced benefits for all workers.

Although those persons who do hard physical labor, work on assembly-line jobs, and perform routine work may have started to work at age 18, others, especially those in the professions, may have begun to work at a later age. The latter, if healthy, usually enjoy their work and may be in their more productive years later in life. If one starts to work at age 18, by age 65 he or she has worked 47 years. Persons who have done graduate work in the professions may begin to work at age 24 years or later and those who do postgraduate work may start to work as late as 26 or 28 years. Thus, at age 65, the latter individual (except for possible part-time or summer employment) may have worked less than 40 years.

One approach might be to admit persons who have worked 40 years (or 45 years) to entitlement to a full benefit at age 65. If they have worked less than that amount, they must be age 68, or alternatively receive a reduced benefit.

Consideration should be given to retaining the existing lower ages—65 and 62—for persons in certain hazardous occupations such as mining.

Phase-out of dependency, spouse benefits

In my dissent to the Advisory Council on Social Security, I proposed that the retired spouse's benefit should be phased out over a 30-year period. To this I have now added that a surviving spouse benefit should be phased out over a 50-year period. If this were done, there would be major reductions in the costliness of the recent Supreme Court decision, March 2, 1977, *Goldfarb* v. *Califano,* equalizing entitlement by sex to widows and widowers of covered deceased workers, and of the March 21, 1977, Supreme Court's dismissals of cases resulting in equal entitlement by sex to retirement dependency benefits.

Because the Social Security Act was written initially in 1935, it assumes that married women are generally financially dependent on their husbands. At that time "fewer than 15 percent of married women were in the labor force."[24] The Act, although amended many times, still makes this basic assumption, which no longer is true. Married women who work are discriminated against by the statutory law because their dependents have to prove actual financial dependency, while married men's dependents are *assumed* to be dependent. Recent Supreme Court decisions have ruled in specific cases *(Wiesenfeld* v. *Weinberger,* March 9, 1975, re a surviving male parent, and *Goldfarb* v. *Califano,* March 2, 1977, re a widower) that a difference in treatment of spouses of men and of women is unconstitutional. This interpretation was extended by the Supreme Court, March 21, 1977, to all social security cases involving dependency benefits to retired spouses. The requirement for entitlement for a dependency benefit has to be the same whether it is based on a man's or a woman's earnings record. No ruling re divorced males has been made.

To require wives and widows to prove financial dependency, as husbands and widowers are now required, would emphasize the concept of welfare benefits because then a test of need determines whether a benefit is awarded or not. To eliminate the existing requirement that husbands and widowers prove their financial dependency, as the Supreme Court has ruled, will increase the long-run costs of OASI substantially. The Advisory Council favored elimination of the support test only if, concomitantly, all private pension benefits due to an individual on his or her earnings were automatically offset against any OASI dependency benefits to which the individual might be entitled. Even with this offset, costs would increase, and underreporting of private pensions probably would occur. Moreover, new immediate inequities would exist for those persons who, as does a married woman who works in uncovered employment and whose husband works in

---

24. Ibid., p.2.

covered employment, may plan on both a private pension and the dependency retirement benefit.

Although the Supreme Court rulings in March 1977 eliminated the one-half-support-test requirement for males, Congress can specifically impose this test on both females and males because it would equalize the entitlement rules. This action, however, is very unlikely.

Therefore, I propose that both widows' and widowers' secondary benefits be gradually phased out over a 50-year period, in addition to my 1975 proposal to phase out secondary benefits for retired aged wives and husbands over a 30-year period. The savings of the newer proposal should in the long-run be greater than that gained by phasing out secondary benefits to the aged, retired spouse alone, which was estimated to be about 0.4 percent of long-run payroll.[25] A very rough estimate of 0.6 percent in respect to widows and widowers over the 75-year period of long-run payroll yields a savings from both proposals together of 1.0 percent.

Total Potential Long-Run Savings

Decoupling was estimated by the Social Security Administration in 1975 to save under the Advisory Council's method only 1.1 percent,[26] while in June 1976 the amount saved was expected to average 4 percent of long-run payroll[27] and under the Consultant Panel's about two percent more.[28] Universal coverage will save 0.25 percent of the long-run payroll. Thus a total of 4.25 to 6.25 percent of long-run (75-year) payroll costs could be saved, and additional savings could be found. For example, if benefits to students 18 to 22 years were eliminated and/or retirement benefits were available at only later ages, for example full retirement benefits at age 68 years by 2023, one might find an additional amount up to 1.5 percent of long-run payroll.[29]

However, there are also some equity considerations, especially in respect to two-worker, husband-and-wife, families, that would initially cost money. The council's subcommittee's proposal, which would permit them to combine earnings up to the base, seems to me to be very

25. *Reports of the Quadrennial Advisory Council* . . . 1975, p. 146.

26. Ibid., p. 57.

27. "Social Security Benefit Indexing Act," White House Fact Sheet, June 17, 1976, p.5 ("Intermediate" Assumptions).

28. *Report of the Consultant Panel* . . . 1976, p. 8.

29. *Reports of the Quadrennial Advisory Council* . . . 1975, p. 63.

reasonable in that it would help only the low-income, two-worker families who now receive less upon retirement than the single-worker, usually husband-earner, family and where he, the one worker, earns the same amount. The estimated long-run cost of this modest proposal prospectively was about 0.3 percent of payroll. As spouses' benefits are phased out, so that persons pay and receive as individuals, this cost would not necessarily disappear. In fact, if each individual receives on the basis of a close approximation of an "earned right," costs in this area could rise higher than the total of retirement and survivor benefits paid in 1976. However, they would not be as high as under the Supreme Court decisions of 1977 in future years.

The June 1976, long-run actuarial imbalance of about 8 percent of taxable payroll is undoubtedly considerably higher in 1977 because of the annual increases in benefits as the cost-of-living increases; because total payrolls have not increased as anticipated; and because more benefits will be paid to surviving male parents, widowers, and retired husbands. Primarily, however, the actuarial imbalance will become greater and greater the longer the double count of the inflation continues.

Several combinations of the changes suggested here add up to amounts that are near to an actuarial balance. Such calculations lead to optimism if Congress acts to enact needed reforms. Continuation of the program, supported by the same type of tax that has traditionally supported it, is preferable to adding new types of tax revenues, because the program does not redistribute income to the poor. Moreover, existing welfare programs in the United States, according to testimony of Alice Rivlin, director of the new Congressional Budget Office, have been so successful that only 5 percent of the population have annual cash and noncash incomes below the poverty line, as defined by the U.S. Bureau of the Census.[30] This 5 percent figure is the same as the one predicted by J. Palmer and J. Minarik.[31]

How the Plan Increases Individual Equity

It is the welfare aspects of OASDI that create problems of financing and inequity. The phase-out of spouse benefits is supported by the

---

30. *The National Observer,* February 19, 1977, p. 1. "The CBO study found only 4 percent are [poor]."

31. See their chapter "Income Security Policy," in Henry Owen and Charles Schultze, eds., *Setting National Priorities: The Next Ten Years,* p. 526.

extraordinary increases in the percentage of women in the labor force. In 1976, 60 percent and more of women in all the age groups from 20 through 54 years were in the labor force, with a peak of 75 percent for those 20 to 24 years. If all persons are required to be covered, then it will be a very rare person—disabled, or an exceedingly wealthy person, or a woman with many children—who will not have earned an OASDI primary benefit. The trend of a declining birth rate also substantiates my earlier predictions that increasingly more women will work for pay over a substantial period of their adult life. The ratio of beneficiaries to workers will increase because in the long run fewer persons will be born.

Thus the OASDI system could be gradually transformed to reflect individual equity rather than, increasingly, welfare needs. At the same time, children or minors who are dependents of men and women workers would continue to receive benefits as would the more rare case, aged parents. Nonmarried persons or singles would also gain more equity. The new welfare programs, especially Supplemental Security Income, could care for men and women in need.

It is true that even if OASDI has identical provisions for men and women, these provisions will not, because of factors outside of the Social Security Act, result in equal treatment of men and women. The Advisory Council refused to consider the latter types of "inequity," and turned down its subcommittee's recommendations to give more equity to the married woman who works, pays OASDI taxes, and yet may upon retirement or widowhood collect no more than if she had never worked or paid sizable taxes.

The above proposed phase-out of spouses' benefits would eventually eliminate this problem. It would not, however, help the low-paid women worker (the median wages of full-time women workers are still only 57 percent of that of full-time male workers), nor the woman who leaves the labor force two or three times to bear and raise children and, therefore, works intermittently. Even if, when she works, she has very high monthly earnings, these are greatly diluted when her average monthly earnings over a work lifetime are computed. This is because the divisor that is used includes all months since age 21 or later whenever she began work, minus five years. The computed average of lifetime monthly earnings minus five years is the basis of the OASI primary benefit.

Although it can be argued that higher wages may eventually be paid to women, even this would not solve the latter problem. If national population policy is to encourage a declining birth rate, some argue that the matter might well stand where it is. If national policy is to encourage 2.1 ultimate births per woman—and in 1976 we were at 1.7 or well below this replacement rate—consideration should be given to an additional three or five year dropout period for the birth of each of a woman's first two children.

Early congressional action on decoupling can be expected to restore financial confidence. However, the basic demographic problem of an increasing aged population relative to the working population cannot be assumed away. It is important in formulation of future policy to have a more precise understanding of the effect of the current social security program on savings decisions before basic changes are made. Whether to phase in a later retirement age and/or to phase out welfare-type benefits can be analyzed well only if there is better knowledge as to the effect of the program on savings.

Simplification

Among other recommendations of the various official groups have been proposals to simplify the social security program. The Advisory Council recommended that:

> When future changes in the social security program are considered, the effect of these changes from the standpoint of program simplification should be taken into account. Continuing attention should be given to simplifying the program, subject to considerations of equity and cost.[32]

The council amplified the above with:

> The social security law now has so many ramifications and so many complex provisions that few people covered under social security understand the nature and extent of the protection provided. This lack of understanding can frustrate individual efforts to plan retirement and to work toward building additional protection to supplement social security. The complexities of the program have also made its administration increasingly difficult. . . .

> The Council's recommendation that the monthly measure under the retirement test be eliminated would simplify the administration of the retirement test provisions. The method of computing benefits the

---

32. *Reports of the Quadrennial Advisory Council . . .* 1976, p. 41.

Council is recommending would, over the long run, be a desirable simplification over the present method. Also, in addressing the issue of equal treatment of men and women under the program, the Council has chosen to recommend that the dependency test be eliminated for eligibility for husband's and widower's benefits instead of recommending the addition of a dependency test for wife's and widow's benefits.[33]

The Supreme Court rulings also selected the latter solution to equalize entitlement to men's and women's benefits.

In 1977, there was a thirteen-volume, loose-leaf claims manual that was used by SSA staff to interpret the Social Security Act and the administrative rulings made under it. Although the Consultant Panel also in general indicated the need for greater simplicity in the system, their recommendations, if taken in entirety, would complicate it. This is primarily because they used a concept of family equity rather than individual equity. In 1975 the marriage rate had declined for the third consecutive year, while divorces numbered twice what they were a decade ago. This was the tenth successive year in which the divorce rate had increased. These data emphasized the need for individual rather than family records of earnings.

In 1977, another new government committee was established to simplify the procedures used by the social security system in handling information and computing benefits, and to ensure that it took every advantage of the new advanced technology. Unfortunately, preceding recommendations of this nature have not worked to decrease the complexity of the system, partly because the formula itself to compute benefits is so complex.

In 1976, a revised and up-dated booklet *A Precise Formula for Primary Insurance Amounts* was printed. This booklet has twenty pages and covers only computation of the "primary benefit"! It does not cover the multiplicity of entitlement rules and other formulae. I have included in the following Appendix a table (Document A.3) that gives the precise formula for computing a primary benefit under the benefit tables, and also the computer program (Document A.4), as of June 1975.[34] Additionally, there are several other tables in this publication, but I think the two included in this book are sufficient to indicate the complexity of the computations involved. How one

---

33. Ibid., pp. 41, 42.

34. U.S. Department of Health, Education, and Welfare, *A Precise Formula for Primary Insurance Amounts,* Staff Paper No. 22, mimeographed (Washington, D.C.: 1975).

explains such a complex formula to the average citizen, I do not know. Therefore, one of my major recommendations is that a formula be adopted that is simple enough for the average high school graduate to understand.

In respect to entitlement rules, again simplification would be greatly appreciated. Elimination of all spouse's benefits, as already proposed, would eliminate the complicated definitions of when a divorced person may or may not receive a benefit, but it will do nothing to simplify the complex area of entitlement for children's benefits. The definition of a child who is entitled under the act and under what circumstances he or she might receive a benefit are exceedingly complex. Section 737 of the *Social Security Handbook* (1973) clearly states that a child's insurance benefit will be paid "only on one record. . . ." This would be pertinent for a child whose parents worked in covered employment and who were unfortunately killed simultaneously in an accident.

Section 738 states as follows:

> A child entitled to benefits on one earnings record will automatically be entitled on a second social security record, if: A. the child is eligible for benefits on the second and B. any child eligible for benefits on both records applies for benefits on the second record.[35]

Interpretation of the above depends on knowing that the child under B, section 738, is any child additional to the child mentioned under A, because at no time do the law and its administrative regulations deviate from permitting entitlement to only one benefit, whichever is the larger. In other words, the child under B is probably a sister or brother of the child under A.

The unwieldly, self-conflicting, and incomprehensible body of regulations of the frequently amended law leads the average person to frustration. The individual finds it difficult to understand either the underlying, hopefully logical concepts or, on the practical side, to estimate what his or her retirement benefit five, ten, or more years hence will be. When the best advice that experts can give to persons contemplating retirement is for them to ask, at least one or two years ahead of the intended time of retirement, for a computation of their primary benefit so that the bureaucratic and computation snarls will be worked out in time before they retire, one must grant that more

---

35. U.S. Department of Health, Education, and Welfare, *Social Security Handbook,* fifth edition (Washington, D.C.: U.S. Government Printing Office, 1973), section 738, pp. 140-41.

simplicity would have great virtue. It seems preferable to eliminate gradually the welfare aspects of social security, and thus simplify its requirements and also reduce the number of persons needed to interpret it. This type of simplification would reduce the program's needs for funds and increase equity.

To continue the past policy of tinkering with different aspects, major and minor, in order to correct one inequity by creating another, all for the sake of political compromise, is no longer acceptable to the younger generations who will be paying the bill.

APPENDIX

Federal OASDI Trust Funds

The following excerpt contains long-range cost estimates based on the trustees' "intermediate" set of assumptions about various components of economic growth (see chapter 5, section headed "Should the Program Be Fully Funded?," especially the subsection "Difficulties of Predicting"). These particular estimates assume that the law remains as it was in 1976.

Document A.1   Trustees' Report on OASDI Funds, 1976

Basic to the discussion of the long-range cost estimates is the concept of expenditures as percent of taxable payroll. The expenditures consist of outgo from the trust funds. They include benefit payments; administrative expenses; interchanges between the old-age, survivors, and disability insurance trust funds and the railroad retirement trust fund (including the reflection of net income from that fund); and payments for vocational rehabilitation services for disability beneficiaries. The payroll consists of the total earnings which are subject to social security taxes after adjustment to reflect the lower contribution rates on self-employed income, tips, and multiple-employer "excess wages"; this adjustment is made so as to facilitate both the calculation of tax income (which is thereby the product of the combined employer-employee tax rate and the payroll) and the comparison of expenditure percentages with tax rates.

[Table A.1] contains the projected expenditures of the old-age, survivors, and disability insurance system under present law based on the intermediate set of assumptions.

DOCUMENT A.1: U.S. Trustees of the Federal Old-Age and Survivors Insurance and Disability Insurance Trust Funds, *1976 Annual Report,* May 24, 1976, mimeographed (Washington, D.C.: U.S. Government Printing Office, 1976), pp. 90-92 and 116-18.

TABLE A.1
ESTIMATED EXPENDITURES OF OLD-AGE, SURVIVORS AND DISABILITY INSURANCE SYSTEM AS PERCENT OF TAXABLE PAYROLL FOR SELECTED YEARS 1985-2050 UNDER ALTERNATIVE II
(percent)

| | EXPENDITURES AS PERCENT OF TAXABLE PAYROLL [a] | | | | |
CALENDAR YEAR	OLD-AGE AND SURVIVORS INSURANCE	DISABILITY INSURANCE	TOTAL	TAX RATE IN LAW	DIFFERENCE
1985	9.46	1.70	11.16	9.90	-1.26
1990	9.98	2.08	12.06	9.90	-2.16
1995	10.37	2.52	12.89	9.90	-2.99
2000	10.48	2.93	13.41	9.90	-3.51
2005	10.90	3.43	14.33	9.90	-4.43
2010	12.10	3.89	15.99	9.90	-6.09
2015	14.18	4.22	18.40	11.90	-6.50
2020	16.89	4.40	21.29	11.90	-9.39
2025	19.68	4.41	24.09	11.90	-12.19
2030	21.67	4.36	26.03	11.90	-14.13
2035	22.61	4.43	27.04	11.90	-15.14
2040	22.84	4.61	27.45	11.90	-15.55
2045	23.13	4.79	27.92	11.90	-16.02
2050	23.72	4.87	28.59	11.90	-16.69
25-year averages:					
1976-2000	9.79	2.02	11.81	9.90	-1.91
2001-2025	14.00	3.95	17.95	11.10	-6.85
2026-2050	22.47	4.57	27.04	11.90	-15.14
75-year average:					
1976-2050	15.42	3.51	18.93	10.97	-7.96

a. Expenditures and payroll are calculated under the intermediate set of assumptions (alternative II) which incorporates ultimate annual increases of 5¾ percent in average earnings and 4 percent in CPI, an ultimate unemployment rate of 5 percent, and an ultimate fertility rate of 1.9 children per woman. . . . Payroll is adjusted to take into account the lower contribution rates on self-employment income, on tips, and on multiple-employer "excess wages" as compared with the combined employer-employee rate.

SOURCE: OASDI Trustees' *1976 Annual Report*, p. 91.

Under the intermediate set of assumptions the cost of the old-age and survivors insurance program is projected to increase slowly during the remainder of this century. After the turn of the century two effects combine to cause the expenditures to increase very rapidly. One is that the replacement ratio continues to increase. The second is that workers born during the period of very high birth rates, from post-World-War-II years through the late 1950s and into the 1960s, reach retirement age and begin to receive benefits.

During the last years of the projection period the expenditures continue to increase but at a much slower rate, thereby reflecting both the decelerated increases in the replacement ratios and the low birth rates of the 1970s. [pp. 90-92]

[*Author's Note.* The report concludes that the disability insurance trust funds' assets declined in 1975 and 1976. Under two of the three sets of assumptions, assets will continue to decline in 1980. Indications are that the disability trust fund may be exhausted by 1979 or 1980. Table A.2 is from the Trustees' 1977 *Annual Report* and shows that estimates of the short-run and long-run actuarial imbalances are again higher than the estimates made in the preceeding year.]

The short-range actuarial cost estimates indicate that the assets of the old-age and survivors insurance and disability insurance trust funds will decline during the period 1976-1981, under each of the three alternative sets of assumptions presented in this report. Without legislation to provide additional financing, the assets of the disability insurance trust fund will be exhausted in 1979 under all three alternative sets of assumptions. Similarly, the assets of the old-age and survivors insurance trust fund will be exhausted in 1981 under the most pessimistic set of alternatives, in 1984 under the intermediate set, and sometime after 1984 under the most optimistic set of assumptions.

The Board recommends that prompt action be taken to strengthen the financing of the old-age, survivors, and disability insurance system over the near term by means of appropriate increases in the tax rates. The Board opposes the use of additional general revenue financing for the old-age, survivors, and disability insurance program. The Board recommends against an increase in the taxable earnings base, other than increases which will occur automatically as average wages in covered employment increase, as a means of producing additional income because of the effect this would have on increased benefits and expenditures in future years.

The long-range actuarial cost estimates indicate that for every year in the future, under present law, the estimated expenditures will exceed the estimated income from taxes. This excess increases with time and is estimated to average about 1.9 percent of taxable payroll over the next 25-year period (1976-2000) based upon the intermediate cost estimates. Under more optimistic assumptions this excess of expenditures over income is projected to average 1.0 percent of taxable payroll, and under more pessimistic assumptions this excess is projected to average 2.9 percent of taxable payroll. Therefore, all alternative long-range cost estimates presented in this report

TABLE A.2
ESTIMATED EXPENDITURES OF OLD-AGE, SURVIVORS, AND DISABILITY INSURANCE SYSTEM AS PERCENT OF TAXABLE PAYROLL FOR SELECTED YEARS, 1977-2055 UNDER ALTERNATIVE II
(In percent)

Expenditures as percent of taxable payroll[1]

CALENDAR YEAR	OLD-AGE AND SURVIVORS INSURANCE	DISABILITY INSURANCE	TOTAL	TAX RATE IN LAW	DIFFERENCE
1977	9.40	1.50	10.91	9.90	-1.01
1980	9.21	1.59	10.80	9.90	-0.90
1985	9.64	1.92	11.56	9.90	-1.66
1990	10.12	2.27	12.39	9.90	-2.49
1995	10.50	2.64	13.14	9.90	-3.24
2000	10.79	3.12	13.91	9.90	-4.01
2005	11.30	3.66	14.96	9.90	-5.06
2010	12.46	4.11	16.57	9.90	-6.67
2015	14.47	4.42	18.89	11.90	-6.99
2020	17.05	4.59	21.64	11.90	-9.74
2025	19.75	4.55	24.30	11.90	-12.40
2030	21.57	4.45	26.02	11.90	-14.12
2035	22.26	4.43	26.69	11.90	-14.79
2040	22.12	4.55	26.67	11.90	-14.77
2045	21.83	4.76	26.59	11.90	-14.69
2050	22.02	4.91	26.93	11.90	-15.03
2055	22.53	4.98	27.51	11.90	-15.61
25-yr averages:					
1977-2001	10.00	2.24	12.24	9.90	-2.34
2002-26	14.65	4.20	18.85	11.18	-7.67
2027-51	21.86	4.61	26.47	11.90	-14.57
75-yr average: 1977-2051	15.51	3.68	19.19	10.99	-8.20

1. Expenditures and taxable payroll are calculated under the intermediate set of assumptions (alternative II) which incorporates ultimate annual increases of 5¾ percent in average wages in covered employment and 4 percent in CPI, an ultimate unemployment rate of 5 percent, and an ultimate total fertility rate of 2.1 children per woman. (See the text for further detail.) Taxable payroll is adjusted to take into account the lower contribution rates on self-employment income, on tips, and on multiple-employer "excess wages" as compared with the combined employer-employee rate.

SOURCE: OASDI Trustees' 1977 *Annual Report*, p. 89.

indicate that over the remainder of this century the old-age, survivors, and disability insurance program will require additional revenues.

The long-range cost of the old-age, survivors, and disability insurance program projected to occur after the turn of the century will substantially exceed the taxes scheduled in present law. Although those projected costs are highly sensitive to variations in the demographic and economic assumptions, all reasonable assumptions indicate that there will be significant excesses of expenditures over income. Estimates have been presented in this report under three alternative sets of assumptions indicating a broad range within which actual future experience may fall; however, no assurance can be given that these estimates define the broadest possible range of variation in the long-range cost estimates.

The Board recognized in the 1975 annual report, as it does in this report, that the high cost of the old-age, survivors, and disability insurance program projected to occur after the turn of the century is partially due to unintended results in the automatic benefit adjustment provisions enacted in 1972. These provisions, under the economic assumptions currently being utilized in making projections, cause future projected benefits to increase substantially from the levels of wage replacement established by benefits currently paid under the program, resulting in unreasonably high benefits for persons first becoming eligible for benefits in the next century. Accordingly, the costs which are projected to occur after the turn of the century should be interpreted with caution and in light of the likelihood that legislation will be enacted to prevent these projected benefit levels from materializing. The Board is in full concurrence with the intent of the 1975 Advisory Council on Social Security that the benefit structure be revised in a responsible manner. The Board recommends the adoption of a specific plan as soon as possible in order to improve the predictability of future benefit levels and to reduce the long-range cost of the system.

The Board also recommends that the development of additional plans to further strengthen the long-range financing of the old-age, survivors, and disability insurance program be given high priority. [1976, pp. 116-18]

The Complexity of Benefit Computation

The following three exhibits are intended to illustrate the extreme complexity, unintelligible to the average citizen, of the formulae by which social security benefits are calculated. Document A.2 traces the historical development of the formulae; Document A.3 shows the actual calculations, as of June 1975; and Document A.4 shows those calculations translated into computer language. Now all the reader needs is a computer.

Document A.2   Social Security Benefit Computation, 1939-1973

Act
Average Monthly Wage (AMW)

1939   AMW computed using earnings after 1936 and before year of death
        or retirement divided by months after 1936 and before quarter of
        death or retirement, excluding months before age 22 in quarters not
        QC.
1950   AMW computed using earnings after 1950 (or year aged 21) and
        before year of death, year of retirement or subsequent year, or year
        aged 65 if then insured, divided by number of months in those years.
1954   Earnings and months in 4 years may be excluded in all cases; in 5
        years if worker has 20 QC. Period of disability may be excluded.
1956   Earnings and months in 5 years may be excluded in all cases.
        Computation period may end at age 62 for women then insured.
1960   Earnings may be used for any year after 1950 and before year of
        retirement, with the number of years equal to the years elapsed after
        1955 (or year aged 26) and before year of death or age 65 (62 for
        women).

        Same method may be used for earnings after 1936 and years elapsed
        after 1941.
1972b Number of years for men reaching age 62 after 1972, measured to
        age 62 or to 1975, if later.

Primary Insurance Amount (PIA)[1]

1935   Formula applied to cumulative wages: ½ of 1% of first $3,000 plus
        1/12 of 1% of next $42,000 plus 1/24 of 1% of next $84,000.
        Effective for January 1942 but never applicable.

Based on AMW

1939   Formula applies to AMW (limited to $250) computed for period
        after 1936: 40% of first $50 plus 10% of next $200. Total increased
        by 1% for each year with at least $200 of creditable wages. *Effective
        for January 1940.*

        Modified by *1950 Act* so that increment years may not exceed 14,
        with benefit amount increased under *conversion table* in the law.

DOCUMENT A.2: U.S. Department of Health, Education, and Welfare, Social Security
Administration, *Social Security Bulletin, Annual Statistical Supplement, 1974* (Washington
D.C.: U.S. Government Printing Office, 1974), pp. 18-19.
1. Before 1951, primary insurance benefit (PIB).

Act

Effective for September 1950. Increase of about 77% in benefit level—from 100% at lowest level to 50% at highest level.

Modified by *1967 Act* to distribute wages in years 1937-50 over 9-14 years, with 14 increment years assumed.

1950 Formula applies to AMW computed for period after 1950: 50% of first $100 plus 15% of next $200. *Effective for April 1952.*

1952 55% of first $100 plus 15% of next $200. *Effective for September 1952.* Increase of the lesser of 10% or $5. (Increase of 12½%, but not less than $5 in *current* benefit levels.)

1954 55% of first $110 plus 20% of next $240. *Effective for September 1954.* Increase of at least $5 (*current* benefit levels increased by approximately 13%).

1958 Underlying formula applies to AMW contained in the table in the Act: 58.85% of first $110 plus 21.40% of next $290. *Effective for January 1959.* Increase of the greater of 7% or $3 in benefit level.

1965 62.97% of first $110 plus 22.90% of next $290 plus 21.40% of next $150. *Effective for January 1965.* Increase of the greater of 7% or $4 in benefit level.

1967 71.16% of first $110 plus 25.88% of next $290 plus 24.18% of next $150 plus 28.43% of next $100. *Effective for February 1968.* Increase of at least 13% in benefit level.

1969 81.83% of first $110 plus 29.76% of next $290 plus 27.81% of next $150 plus 32.69% of next $100. *Effective for January 1970.* Increase of at least 15% in benefit level.

1971 90.01% of first $110 plus 32.74% of next $290 plus 30.59% of next $150 plus 35.96% of next $100 plus 20% of next $100. *Effective for January 1971.* Increase of 10% in benefit level.

1972a 108.01% of first $110 plus 39.29% of next $290 plus 36.71% of next $150 plus 43.15% of next $100 plus 24% of next $100 plus 20% of next $250. *Effective for September 1972.* Increase of 20% in benefit level. (Provision for automatic "cost-of-living" increase.)

1973a 114.38% of first $110 plus 41.61% of next $290 plus 38.88% of next $150 plus 45.70% of next $100 plus 25.42% of next $100 plus 21.18% of next $250 plus 20% of next $50. *Effective for June 1974 through December 1974 but never applicable.* Increase of 5.9% in benefit level, eliminated by 1973b legislation.

1973b 119.89% of first $110 plus 43.61% of next $290 plus 40.75% of next $150 plus 47.90% of next $100 plus 26.64% of next $100 plus 22.20% of next $250 plus 20% of next $100. Increase of 11% in 1972a benefit levels, *effective in 2 steps: 7%, for March-May 1974; 4% additional, for June 1974.* (Beginning June 1975, subject to automatic "cost-of-living" increase, under modification of 1972 provision.)

129.48% of the first $110 of AME, plus 47.10% of the next $290 of
AME, plus 44.01% of the next $150 of AME, plus 51.73% of the
next $100 of AME, plus 28.77% of the next $100 of AME, plus
23.98% of the next $250 of AME, plus 21.60% of the next $175 of
AME. *Effective for June 1975.* Increase of 8% in benefit level.

Based on Years of Coverage

1972b Alternative formula: $8.50 per month multiplied by the number of
years of coverage above 10, limited to $170 per month. *Effective
January 1, 1973.* The "number of years of coverage" equals the
number obtained by dividing total creditable wages in 1937-50 by
$900 (but not more than 14) *plus* the number of years after 1950 in
which the worker is credited with at least 25% of the effective annual
maximum taxable earnings.

1973b $9.00 per month, limited to $180 per month. *Effective March 1,
1974.*

Document A.3   A Precise Formula for Primary Insurance Amount under Benefit Table, Effective June 1975

AVERAGE MONTHLY WAGE	FIRST COMPUTATION	ADJUSTMENT	SUCCESSIVE MULTIPLIERS
$76 or less	$101.40		
$77-$94	7.45+.55W	Round	1.13,1.15,1.10,1.20,1.11,1.08
$95-$110	—+.5885W	Round	1.07,1.13,1.15,1.10,1.20, 1.11,1.08
$111-$403	41.195+.214W	Round	1.07,1.13,1.15,1.10,1.20, 1.11,1.08
$404-$552	50.195+.214W	Round	1.13,1.15,1.10,1.20,1.11,1.08
$553	345.90		
$554-$651	33.233+.2843W	Round	1.15,1.10,1.20,1.11,1.08
$652	396.90		
$653-$656	398.10		
$657-$750	145.40+.2W	Round; add $0.40	1.20,1.11,1.08
$751-$1,000	204.40+.2W	Round; add $0.50	1.11,1.08
$1,001-$1,175	249.40+.2W	Round	1.08

NOTE: W = Average monthly wage. "Round" denotes that the preceding value is rounded to the nearest multiple of $1 if it is not a multiple of $1.

The successive multipliers are applied to the adjusted amount (or product of adjusted amount and ratio) in the order shown. Each product is raised, before the next ratio is applied to the next higher multiple of 10 cents if it is not a multiple of 10 cents; for example, $0.105 is raised to $0.20. For AMW of $84, the calculations are as follows:

1. 7.45 + (0.55 x 84.00) = 53.65 rounded to 54.
2. 54.00 x 1.13 = 61.02 raised to 61.10.
3. 61.10 x 1.15 = 70.265 raised to 70.30.
4. 70.30 x 1.10 = 77.330 raised to 77.40.
5. 77.40 x 1.20 = 92.880 raised to 92.90.
6. 92.90 x 1.11 = 103.119 raised to 103.20.
7. 103.20 x 1.08 = 111.456 raised to 111.50.

There is an exception to the above rule. If the fractional parts of the products were .001, .002, .003, or .004, the products were rounded to the next lower multiple of 10 cents prior to the 1973 amendments. Beginning with the 1973 amendments, such products were raised to the next higher multiple of 10 cents.

AUTHOR'S NOTE: Subsequent to the preparation of this publication, the earnings base was increased from $14,000 in 1975 to $15,300 in 1976 as a result of the automatic-adjustment provisions. The AMW was extended by $100: (15,300 - $14,100)/12. Therefore, future benefits will be somewhat larger.

DOCUMENT A.3: U.S. Department of Health, Education, and Welfare, Social Security Administration, Office of Research and Statistics, *A Precise Formula for Primary Insurance Amounts,* Staff Paper No. 22, mimeographed, Oct. 1975, table 1, p. 8.

Document A.4 Fortran V Program of the Precise Formula for Primary Insurance Amount under Benefit Table, Effective June 1975

```
            PARAMETER N1=12,N2=8,N3=1100
            DIMENSION A(N1),X(N1),Z(N1),AMWL(N1),AMWH(N1),
            1AMW(N3),M(N1),SMUL(N2),PIA(N3)
        199 FORMAT(T3,'AMW',T8,'PIA'//)
        200 FORMAT(T2,F5.0.,F7.2)
        C   AMWL REPRESENTS LOWER RANGE OF AVERAGE MONTHLY WAGE.
            . DATA(AMWL(I),I=1,N1)/76.,77.,95.,111.,404.,
            A553.,554.,652.,653.,657.,751.,1001./
        C   AMWH REPRESENTS HIGHER RANGE OF AVERAGE MONTHLY WAGE.
            DATA(AMWH(I),I=1,N1)/76.,94.,110.,403.,552.,553.
            A,651.,652.,656.,750.,1000.,1175./
        C   A REFERS TO A IN FORMULA A+X*W IN FIRST COMPUTATION.
            DATA(A(I),I=1,N1)/101.40,7.45,0.,41.195,50.195,
            A345.90,33.233,396.90,398.10,145.40,204.40,249.40/
        C   X REFERS TO X IN FORMULA A+X*W IN FIRST COMPUTATION.
            DATA(X(I),I=1,N1)/0.,.55,.5885,.214,.214,0.,.2843,0.,0.,3*.2/
        C   Z REPRESENTS ADJUSTMENT.
            DATA(Z(I),I=1,N1)/9*0.,.4,.5,0./
        C   SMUL REPRESENTS ALL THE SUCCESSIVE MULTIPLIERS.
            DATA(SMUL(I),I=1,N2)/1.07,1.13,1.15,1.10,1.20,1.11,1.08,1.00/
        C   M REPRESENTS THE START OF THE ACCUMULATION OF THE SUCCESSIVE MULTIPLIERS.
            DATA(M(I),I=1,N1)/8,2,1,1,2,8,3,8,8,5,6,7/
            AMW(1)=AMWL(1)
            PIA(1)=A(1)
            DO 100 I=2,N3
            AMW(I)=AMW(I-1)+1.
            J=1
        105 IF(AMW(I).LE.AMWH(J))GO TO 110
            J=J+1
            GO TO 105
        110 PIA(I)=A(J)+X(J)*AMW(I)
            IF(AMWL(J)-AMWH(J)),113,
            IF(J.EQ.9)GO TO 113
            IF(AMOD(PIA(I),1.)-.49999)111,112,112
        111 PIA(I)=PIA(I)-AMOD(PIA(I),1.)
            GO TO 113
        112 PIA(I)=PIA(I)+1.-AMOD(PIA(I),1.)
        113 PIA(I)=PIA(I)+Z(J)
            K=M(J)
            CALL SERIES
        100 CONTINUE
            WRITE(6,199)
            WRITE(6,200)(AMW(I),PIA(I),I=1,N3)
            SUBROUTINE SERIES
            DIMENSION P(N3),P100(N3)
            DO 50 L=K,N2
            P(I)=PIA(I)*SMUL(L)
            CALL ROUND (P,P100,PIA,I,L)
        50  CONTINUE
            RETURN
            SUBROUTINE ROUND(X,X100,XB,I,L)
            DIMENSION X(N3),X100(N3),XB(N3)
            IF(L.GE.6) GO TO 4
            Q=.499
            GO TO 5
        4   Q=.01
        5   X100(I)=X(I)*100.
            IF(AMOD(X100(I),10.))3,2,3
        3   IF(AMOD(X100(I),10.)-Q)2,1,1
        2   XB(I)=X(I)
            RETURN
        1   XB(I)=X(I)+.10-AMOD(X100(I),10.)/100.
            RETURN
            END
```

DOCUMENT A.4: Ibid., table 5, p. 12.

Birth Rates

The following table should be used to supplement the discussion in chapter 5 of the Advisory Council's demographic assumptions.

Document A.5   Birth Rates by Live-Birth Order: United States, 1960 and 1965-1974.

| Year | Total | LIVE-BIRTH ORDER | | | | | | |
		1	2	3	4	5	6 and 7	8 and over
1974	68.4	28.9	21.5	9.6	4.2	1.9	1.5	0.8
1973	69.2	28.8	21.1	9.8	4.5	2.2	1.8	0.9
1972	73.4	29.9	21.5	10.7	5.3	2.7	2.2	1.2
1971	81.8	32.1	23.2	12.5	6.4	3.3	2.8	1.5
1970	87.9	34.2	24.2	13.6	7.2	3.8	3.2	1.8
1969	86.5	32.8	23.4	13.4	7.4	4.0	3.5	2.0
1968	85.7	32.1	22.5	13.2	7.5	4.2	3.9	2.3
1967	87.6	30.8	22.6	13.9	8.3	4.8	4.5	2.7
1966	91.3	31.0	22.5	14.8	9.2	5.4	5.2	3.2
1965	96.6	29.8	23.4	16.6	10.7	6.4	6.0	3.7
1960	118.0	31.1	29.2	22.8	14.6	8.3	7.6	4.3

NOTE: Rates are live births per 1,000 women aged 15-44 years, enumerated as of April 1 for 1960 and 1970 and estimated as of July 1 for all other years.

DOCUMENT A.5: U.S. Department of Health, Education, and Welfare, *Monthly Vital Statistics Report 24* (1976) no. 11 (Feb. 13), supplement 2, table 5, p. 8.

BIBLIOGRAPHY

Aaron, Henry. "Benefits Under the American Social Security System." In
Otto Eckstein, ed. *Studies in the Economics of Income Maintenance.*
Washington, D.C.: The Brookings Institution, 1967.

―――. "Social Security: International Comparisons." In Otto Eckstein, ed.,
Studies in the Economics of Income Maintenance, Washington, D.C.:
The Brookings Institution, 1967.

―――. "The Social Insurance Paradox," *Canadian Journal of Economics
and Political Science* 32 (1966).

Alberts, Robert C. "If You're Counting on Social Security for Your Retirement Income One Day, Count Again—Catch 65." *New York Times
Magazine,* August 4, 1974.

Allen, Jodie T. "Social Security: The Largest Welfare Program." *Washington
Post,* April 6, 1976, p. A-15.

Astor, Gerald. "One Family's Unavoidable 'Deficit'." *New York Times,*
March 7, 1976.

Auerbach, Alexander. "Social Security System Faces New Strains." *Los
Angeles Times,* May 25, 1976, part I, pp. 18, 19.

Ball, Robert M. "The Treatment of Women Under Social Security." Testimony before the Joint Economic Committee, 93rd Cong., 1st sess., July
25, 1973.

―――. "Social Security and Private Pension Plans." *National Tax Journal* 27
(1974), no. 3 (September).

Ballentine, J., and I. Eris. "On the General Equilibrium Analysis of Tax
Incidence." *Journal of Political Economy,* June 1975.

Barro, Robert J. "Are Government Bonds Net Wealth?" *Journal of Political
Economy* 82 (1974), no. 6 (November).

Beier, Emerson. "Incidence of Private Pension Plans." *Monthly Labor
Review* 94 (1971).

"Big Apple Bye-Bye, Social Security." *Time,* April 5, 1976, p. 72.

Bilas, Richard. "The Multiple Myths of Social Security." *Bakersfield Californian,* November 29, 1975.

Bixby, Lenore E. "Women and Social Security in the United States," *Social Security Bulletin,* September 1972.

Boskin, Michael. "Recent Econometric Research in Public Finance." *American Economic Review,* May 1976.

———. "Social Security and Retirement Decisions." *Economic Inquiry* 15 (1977), January.

———. "Taxation, Saving and the Rate of Interest." U.S. Treasury Department, 1976.

———, ed. *The Crisis in Social Security: Problems and Prospects.* San Francisco: Institute for Contemporary Studies, 1977.

Bowen, William B., and T.A. Finegan. *The Economic of Labor Force Participation.* Princeton University Press, 1969.

Break, George F. and Joseph A. Pechman. "Federal Tax Reform: The Impossible Dream?" The Brookings Institution, Washington, D.C., 1975.

Brittain, John A. "The Incidence of Social Security Payroll Taxes." *American Economic Review,* March 1971, pp. 110-25.

Brittain, John A. *The Payroll Tax for Social Security.* Washington, D.C.: The Brookings Institution, 1972.

Brown, J. Douglas. *An American Philosophy of Social Security: Evolution and Issues.* Princeton University Press, 1972.

Browning, Edgar K. "Social Insurance and Intergenerational Transfers." *Journal of Law and Economics,* October 1973, pp. 215-37.

Buchanan, James. "Social Insurance in a Growing Economy: A Proposal for Radical Reform," *National Tax Journal* 21 (1968).

Budget of the United States Government. Special analyses: Fiscal Year 1977. Washington, D.C.: U.S. Government Printing Office, 1977.

Burris, C., and B. Clements. "The Private Pension Story, 1." *Women's Lobby Quarterly,* March 1974.

Cagan, Phillip. *The Effect of Pension Plans on Aggregate Saving: Evidence from a Sample Survey.* National Bureau of Economic Research, Occasional Paper No. 95. New York: Columbia University Press, 1965.

Calvert, Geoffrey N. *Pensions and Survival: The Coming Crisis of Money and Retirement.* Toronto, Canada: Maclean-Hunter, 1977.

———. "Will a Trillion Dollars Satisfy the Wolf?" In *Thinking About the Future.* New York: Alexander and Alexander, July 1975.

Campbell, Colin. "Social Insurance in the United States: A Program in Search of an Explanation." *Journal of Law and Economics* 12 (1969).

————, and R.G. Campbell. "Conflicting Views on the Effect of Old-Age and Survivors Insurance on Retirement." *Economic Inquiry* 14 (1976), September.

————. *Over-Indexed Benefits: The Decoupling Proposals for Social Security.* Washington, D.C.: American Enterprise Institute for Public Policy Research, 1976.

————, and Rosemary Campbell. "Conflicting Views on the Effect of Old-Age and Survivors Insurance on Retirement." *Economic Inquiry,* September 1976, pp. 369-88.

"Can Magic Save Social Security?" *New York Times,* March 14, 1976, p. 15.

Carroll, John. *Social Security Financing Revisited.* Washington, D.C., 1966.

Cardwell, James. "Remarks." Photocopied statement addressed to American business press, Washington Editorial Conference, November 5, 1975.

Carter, Jimmy. "Economic Recovery Program." In *Weekly Compilation of Presidential Documents,* vol. 13, no. 6, February 7.

"Census Shock: A Senior Boom," *San Francisco Examiner.* AP dispatch, June 1, 1976.

Citizen's Advisory Council on the Status of Women. *Women in 1975.* Report, March 1976. Washington, D.C.: The Council, 1976.

Cohen, Wilbur J., and Milton Friedman. *Social Security: Universal or Selective?* Washington, D.C.: American Enterprise Institute for Public Policy Research, 1972.

Congressional Quarterly, Annual Almanac.

Congressional Quarterly, Weekly Report.

Cook, David T. "Social Security Woes: No Solutions This Year?" *Christian Science Monitor,* July 2, 1976.

Cowan, Edward. "One Way or the Other, Social Security Will Need Help." *New York Times,* March 7, 1976.

Crowley, Francis J. "Financing the Social Security Program—Then and Now." *Studies in Public Welfare,* Paper No. 18, Joint Economic Committee, 93rd Cong. 2d sess. Washington, D.C.: Superintendent of Documents, 1974.

Deran, Elizabeth. "Changes in Factor Income Shares Under the Social Security Tax." *Review of Economics and Statistics,* November 1967, pp. 627-30.

————. *Economic Aspects of the Social Security Tax.* New York: The Tax Foundation, 1966.

Douglas, Paul H. *Social Security in the United States: An Analysis and Appraisal of the Federal Social Security Act.* New York: McGraw-Hill, 1936.

————. *Social Security in the United States.* New York: McGraw-Hill, 1939.

"Dropouts Seen as Future Problem." Editorial, *St. Louis Globe-Democrat,* July 14, 1976.

Drucker, Peter F. *The Unseen Revolution: How Pension Fund Socialism Came to America.* New York: Harper and Row, 1976.

Economic Report of the President: With the Annual Report of the Council of Economic Advisors. January, 1976. Washington, D.C.: U.S. Government Printing Office, 1976.

Economic Report of the President. January 18, 1977. Washington, D.C.: U.S. Government Printing Office, 1976.

Derthick, Martha. *Uncontrollable Spending for Social Service Grant.* Washington, D.C.: The Brookings Institution, 1975.

Eizenga, W. *Demographic Factors and Savings.* Amsterdam: North-Holland Publishing Company, 1961.

Feldstein, Martin. "Social Insurance." Paper presented at the Conference on Income Distribution, American Enterprise Institute, May 20, 1976.

————. "Social Security and Private Saving: International Evidence in an Extended Life Cycle Model." Discussion paper No. 361, Harvard University, May 1974.

————. "Social Security and Savings: The Extended Life-Cycle Theory." *American Economic Review,* Proceedings, May 1976.

————. "Social Security, Induced Retirement, and Aggregate Capital Accumulation." *Journal of Political Economy,* September-October, 1974, pp. 905-26.

————. "Facing the Social Security Crisis," *Public Interest,* Spring 1977.

————. "The Social Security Fund and National Capital Accumulation." In *Funding Pensions: The Issues and Implications for Financial Markets.* Federal Reserve Bank of Boston, 1977.

————. "Toward a Reform of Social Security," *The Public Interest,* Summer 1975, pp. 75-95.

————, and John Brittain. "The Incidence of the Social Security Tax: Comment and Reply." *American Economic Review,* September 1972.

Fisher, Irving. *The Theory of Interest.* New York: Macmillan, 1930.

Fisher, Paul. "Major Social Issues: Japan, 1972." *Social Security Bulletin,* March 1973, pp. 3-15.

Ford, Gerald R. *Presidential Documents.*

"Ford's Plea on Social Security." *San Francisco Chronicle,* June 18, 1976.

"Fresh Scare Over Social Security." *U.S. News and World Report,* February 16, 1976, pp. 68-70.

Friedman, Milton. *A Theory of the Consumption Function.* Princeton, New Jersey: National Bureau of Economic Research, 1957.

Friend, Irwin, and Charles Lieberman. "Short-Run Asset Effects on House-hold Saving and Consumption: The Cross-Section Evidence." *American Economic Review* 65 (1975), September.

Fullerton, H.N., Jr., and Paul Flaim. "New Labor Force Projections to 1990." *Monthly Labor Review,* December 1976.

Goldsmith, Russell. "Feeding the Kitty: Out-Moded Social Security." *New Republic,* August 30, 1975.

Gottron, Martha V. "Social Security Tax Hike: Merits Argued." *Congressional Quarterly,* February 7, 1976, pp. 262-63.

Grubisich, Thomas. "Fairfax to Cut Social Security." *Washington Post,* April 6, 1976, p. 1.

Haber, William, and Wilbur J. Cohen. *Social Security: Programs, Problems, and Policies.* Homewood, Illinois: Richard D. Irwin, 1960.

Hall, James. "Incidence of Federal Social Security Payroll Taxes." *Quarterly Journal of Economics,* November 1938.

Harberger, A.C. "The Incidence of the Corporation Income Tax." *Journal of Political Economy,* June 1962.

Harris, Louis, and Associates, Inc. *The Myth and Reality of Aging in America.* Washington, D.C., 1975.

Harris, Seymour E. *Economics of Social Security.* New York: McGraw-Hill, 1941.

Hauge, Gabriel. *Advisory Council on Social Security: Reports on the Old-Age, Survivors, and Disability Insurance and Medicare Programs.* Washington, D.C., GPO, 1973.

Haygle, Howard. "Families and the Rise of Working Wives—an Overview." *Monthly Labor Review,* May 1976.

Henle, Peter. "Recent Trends in Retirement Benefits Related to Earnings." Reprint 241, Washington, D.C.: Brookings Institution, 1972.

Hobbs, Charles D. and Stephen L. Powlesland. *Retirement Security Reform: Restructuring the Social Security System.* Concord, Vermont: Institute for Liberty and Community, 1975.

Hoffman, Ronald F. "Factor Shares and the Payroll Tax: A Comment." *Review of Economics and Statistics,* November 1968. pp. 506-08.

Hoskins, Dalmer and Lenore E. Bixby. "Women and Social Security: Law and Policy in Five Countries." U.S. Department of H.E.W. Research Report No. 42, DHEW Pub. No. (SSA) 73-118 (1973).

———. *Women and Social Security: Law and Policy in Five Countries.* Social Security Administration, Office of Research and Statistics Research Report No. 42., Washington, D.C., Government Printing Office, 1973.

———. *Women and Social Security: Law and Policy in Five Countries.* Social Security Administration, Office of Research and Statistics,

Research Report No. 41, Washington, D.C., Government Printing Office, 1973, pp. 53-54.

Hov.ard, H. "Families and the Rise of Working Wives." *Monthly Labor Review,* May 1976.

"How to Rescue Social Security." *The Wall Street Journal,* November 3, 1976.

"In Hock to the Hilt." Editorial, *Wall Street Journal,* July 7, 1976.

Kaplan, Robert S. *Financial Crisis in the Social Security System.* Washington, D.C.: American Enterprise Institute for Public Policy Research, 1976.

Katona, George. *The Powerful Consumer.* McGraw Hill, N.Y., 1960.

———. *Private Pensions and Individual Saving.* Ann Arbor, Michigan: University of Michigan Survey Research Center, Monograph No. 40, 1965.

Keppel, Bruce. "Country Urged to Pull out of Social Security." *Los Angeles Times,* May 14, 1976.

———. "Country to Remain in Social Security." *Los Angeles Times,* June 2, 1976, part 1, page 34.

Kerner, A. *Your Pension: How to Make Sure You Get It.* Chicago: Industrial Gerontology Unit, Mayor's Office for Senior Citizens, 1973.

Keynes, J.M. *The General Theory of Employment, Interest and Money.* Macmillan, 1936.

Klein, Laurence. *An Introduction to Econometrics.* Prentice Hall, 1962.

Kleinkosky, R.C., and D.F. Scott. "Pension Funds: Prevailing Issues." *M.S.U. Business Topics,* Winter 1973.

Kolodrubetz, W.W. "Private Retirement Benefits and Relationship to Earnings: Survey of New Beneficiaries." *Social Security Bulletin,* May 1973.

Korns, Alexander. "The Future of Social Security." *Studies in Public Welfare,* Paper No. 18, 93rd Congress, 2d sess., Joint Economic Committee, Washington, D.C.: Superintendent of Documents, 1974.

Krzyzaniak, Marian, and Richard Musgrave. *The Shifting of the Corporation Income Tax.* Baltimore: Johns Hopkins Press, 1963.

Lauriat, Patience. "Social Security Benefits for Older American Women." Mimeographed. Washington, D.C.: Social Security Administration, Office of Research and Statistics 1972. Prepared for the Research Conference on Women and Social Security, Vienna, Austria, 1972.

Lesnoy, Selig, and John Hambor. "Social Security, Saving and Capital Formation." *Social Security Bulletin,* July 1975.

"Local Government Dropouts Not Hurting Social Security." AP dispatch *San Francisco Examiner,* March 12, 1976, p. 12.

McKinnon, Ronald I. "Wages, Capital Costs, and Employment in Manufacturing: A Model Applied to 1947-58 U.S. Data." *Econometrica,* July 1962, pp. 501-21.

McLure, C.E., and W.R. Thirsk. "A Simplified Exposition of the Harberger Model I: Tax Incidence." *National Tax Journal,* March 1975.

Metropolitan Life Insurance Company. *Statistical Bulletin,* May 1976, p. 4.

Mieszkowski, P.M. "On the Theory of Tax Incidence." *Journal of Political Economy,* June 1967, pp. 250-62.

————. "Tax Incidence Theory: The Effect of Taxes on The Distribution of Income." *Journal of Economic Literature,* December 1969, pp. 1103-24.

Miller, Merton H., and Charles W. Upton. *Macroeconomics: A Neoclassical Introduction.* Homewood, Illinois: Richard D. Irwin, 1974.

Miller, Roger LeRoy. "The Cruelest Tax." *Harpers,* June 1974.

Modigliani, Franco, and Albert Ando. "The Life Cycle Hypothesis of Saving: Aggregate Implications and Tests." *American Economic Review,* March 1963.

————, and Richard Brumberg. "Utility Analysis and the Consumption Function." In Kenneth Kurihara, ed., *Post Keynesian Economics.* New Brunswick, N.J.: Rutgers University Press, 1954.

Morgan, James N. "Saving and Spending as Explained by All the Variables." In Richard F. Kosobud and James N. Morgan, eds., *Consumer Behavior of Individual Familes over Two and Three Years.* Ann Arbor, Michigan: Ann Arbor Press, 1964.

Munnell, Alicia Haydock. *The Effect of Social Security on Personal Saving.* Cambridge, Massachusetts: Ballinger, 1974.

————. "The Impact of Social Security on Personal Savings." *National Tax Journal* 27 (1974), no. 4 (December).

————. "The Impact of Social Security on Personal Savings." *Studies in Public Welfare,* Paper No. 18. Joint Economic Committee, 93rd Cong., 2d sess. Washington, D.C.: Superintendent of Documents, 1974.

Munro, Douglas R. "Welfare Component and Labor Supply Effects of OASDHI Retirement Benefits." Ph.D. dissertation, Ohio State University, 1976.

Musgrave, Richard. *Fiscal Systems.* New Haven: Yale University Press, 1969.

————. *Theory of Public Finance.* New York: McGraw-Hill, 1959.

————, and Carl Shoup, eds. *Readings in the Economics of Taxation.* Homewood, Illinois: Richard Irwin, 1958.

————, and Peggy Musgrave. *Public Finance, the Theory and Practices.* New York: McGraw-Hill, 1973.

Myers, Robert J. "Social Security and Sex Discrimination." *Challenge,* July-August 1975.

Nader, R., and K. Blackwell. *You and Your Pension*. New York: Grossman, 1973.

Okner, Benjamin A. "The Social Security Payroll Tax: Some Alternatives for Reform." *Journal of Finance* 30 (1975), no. 2 (May).

Okonkwo, Ubadigbo. "Individual Equity Under Social Security: Some Black-White Comparisons." University of Rochester, 1974.

"On Balance: What's the Truth Behind All the Reports on Social Security." *American Views*, August 16, 1976.

Owen, Henry, and Charles Schultze, eds. *Setting National Priorities: The Next Ten Years*. Washington, D.C.: The Brookings Institution, 1976.

Patterson, Kathleen. "Feminists Take Aim at Social Security." *Kansas City Times*, April 12, 1973.

Pauly, David, and Tom Joyce. "Social Security: Trouble Ahead." *Newsweek*, March 24, 1975.

Pechman, Joseph A. *Federal Tax Policy*. The Brookings Institution, Washington, D.C. 1971.

———, Henry J. Aaron, and Michael K. Taussig, *Social Security: Perspectives for Reform*. Washington, D.C.: The Brookings Institution, 1968.

Peterson, Ray M. "Misconceptions and Missing Perceptions of Our Social Security System (Actuarial Anesthesia)." *Transactions of the Society of Actuaries* 11 (1959), no. 31 (November).

Pigou, A. C. *Employment and Equilibrium*. London, 1941.

"Plan to Work After You Retire? Better Check Social Security." *U.S. News and World Report*, March 29, 1976.

Porter, Sylvia, "Your Money, 'Stay in Social Security'." *San Francisco Chronicle*, May 6, 1976, p. 60.

"Propping Up Social Security." *Business Week*, July 19, 1976.

Pullen, Emma E., and Paul E. Steiger. "Social Security Inequities Under Attack." *Los Angeles Times*, February 23, 1976, p. 10.

Quadrennial Advisory Council on Social Security, 1974, *Minutes*.

Quigley, Dennis. "Changes in Selected Health Care Plans." *Monthly Labor Review*, December 1975.

Reno, Virginia. "Why Men Stop Working at or before Age 65: Findings from the Survey of New Beneficiaries." *Social Security Bulletin* 34 (1971), June.

———. "Why Men Stop Working Before Age 65." In *Reaching Retirement Age*. U.S. Department of Health, Education, and Welfare, Research Report No. 47.

———. "Women Newly Entitled to Retired Worker Benefits: Survey of New

Beneficiaries." *Social Security Bulletin,* April 1973.

Ruby, Michael, and Jeff B. Copeland. "Social Security: The Dropouts." *Newsweek,* April 26, 1976.

Samuelson, Paul A. "An Exact Consumption-Loan Model of Interest with or without the Social Contrivance of Money." *Journal of Political Economy* 65 (1958), December.

Scheibla, Shirley. "Anti-Social Security: Employees of State and Local Governments are Opting Out." *Barron's,* March 8, 1976.

Schmitt, Raymond. "Integration of Private Pension Plans with Social Security." *Studies in Public Welfare,* U.S. Congress, Joint Economic Committee, Paper No. 18, 93rd Cong., 2d sess. Washington, D.C.: Superintendent of Documents, 1974.

Seidman, Bert. "Future Structure of Social Security System and Interrelation with Private Pension Plans." *National Tax Journal* 27 (1974), no. 3 (September).

Seligman, Edwin. *The Shifting and Incidence of Taxation.* New York: Columbia University Press, 1921.

Shore, Warren. *Social Security: The Fraud in Your Future.* New York: Macmillan, 1975.

Shoup, Carl. *Public Finance.* Chicago: Aldine, 1969.

Shultz, William J. *Social Security and the Economics of Saving.* New York: National Industrial Conference Board, 1948.

Simon, William E. "How to Rescue Social Security," *Wall Street Journal,* November 3, 1976.

Slichter, Sumner. "The Impact of Social Security Legislation Upon Mobility and Enterprise." *American Economic Review,* March 1940.

Smith, Dan Throop, special assistant and deputy to the Secretary of the Treasury, 1953-59. Memo to the author, August 13, 1974.

———, et al. *What You Should Know About the Value Added Tax.* Homewood, Ill.: Dow Jones-Irwin, 1973.

"Social Insecurity." *Forbes,* July 1, 1976.

Social Security Administration, Office of Research and Statistics. *Social Security Programs Throughout the World.* Washington, D.C., 1974.

"Social Security: A Sound and Durable Institution of Great Value." White Paper, By former Secretaries of Health, Education, and Welfare Wilbur Cohen, Robert Finch, Arthur Fleming, John Gardner, and Elliot Richardson, and former Social Security Commissioners Robert Ball, William L. Mitchell, and Charles Schottland. Mimeographed press release, February 10, 1975. Washington, D.C.: U.S. Department of Health, Education, and Welfare, 1975.

"Social Security—Forty Years Later." *Social Security Bulletin,* August 1975, pp. 1-4.

Social Security Bulletin, Statistical Supplement 1974.

Social Security Handbook, 1973.

"Social Security Hearings." *Congressional Quarterly,* May 1976.

"Social Security: How Secure for the Young Worker?" National Federation of Independent Business Public Policy Discussion Series. San Mateo, California: 1976.

"Social Security: No Bankruptcy—but a Need for Money." *Time,* February 1976.

"Social Security Revision." *Washington Report.* Women's Equity Action League, Newsletter, vol. 4 (1975), no. 2 (April).

"Social Security: What Next?" *Forbes,* July 1, 1976.

"Social Security: What Next?" *Newsweek,* January 19, 1976.

Spivak, Jonathan. "Solving the Problems of Public Employee Pullouts." *Wall Street Journal,* July 22, 1976.

"State Should Stay in Social Security, Post Declares." *Los Angeles Times,* July 20, 1976.

Strober, Myra H. "Wives' Labor Force Behavior and Family Consumption Patterns." *American Economic Review* 67 (1977), no. 1 (February), pp. 410-17.

Tax Foundation Incorporated. *Economic Aspects of the Social Security Tax.* Research Publication No. 5. New York: The Tax Foundation, 1966.

———. *Employee Pension Systems in State and Local Government.* Research Publication No. 33. New York: The Tax Foundation, 1976.

Tilove, Robert. *Public Employee Pension Funds.* New York: Columbia University Press, 1976.

Tracy, Martin B. "Payroll Taxes Under Social Security Programs: Cross National Survey." *Social Security Bulletin* 38 (1975), December.

Ture, Norman B. *The Future of Private Pension Plans.* Washington, D.C.: American Enterprise Institute for Public Policy Research, 1976.

U.S. Bureau of Labor Statistics, *Historical Series.*

U.S. Congressional Budget Office. *Budget Options for Fiscal Year 1977: A Report to the Senate and House Committees on the Budget.* March 15, 1976. Washington, D.C.: U.S. Government Printing Office, 1976.

U.S. Congress, Senate. "Compilation of the Social Security Laws," S.D. 27, 82d Cong., 1st sess. Washington, D.C.: U.S. Government Printing Office, 1951.

U.S. Congress, House, Committee on Ways and Means. *Decoupling the Social Security Benefit Structure: Hearings Before the Subcommittee on Social Security on H.R. 14430.* 94th Cong., 2d sess., June 18, July 23, 26, 1976. Washington, D.C.: U.S. Government Printing Office, 1976.

U.S. Congress, House, Committee on Ways and Means, *Reports of the Quadrennial Advisory Council on Social Security.* 94th Cong., 1st sess., H.D. 94-75, March 10, 1975. Washington, D.C.: U.S. Government Printing Office, 1975.

U.S. Congress, House, Committee on Ways and Means. *Social Security After 18 Years.* Staff Report. Washington, D.C.: U.S. Government Printing Office, 1954.

U.S. Congress, House, Committee on Ways and Means. *1976 Annual Report of the Board of Trustees of the Federal Old-Age and Survivors Insurance and Disability Insurance Trust Funds.* 94th Cong., 2d sess., May 25, 1976. Washington, D.C.: U.S. Government Printing Office, 1976.

U.S. Congress, House. "Social Security Amendments of 1965." Public Law 89-97, 89th Cong., H.R. 66-75, July 30, 1965. Washington, D.C.: U.S. Government Printing Office, 1975.

U.S. Congress, House Select Committee on Aging, Subcommittee on Retirement Income and Employment. *Income Security for Older Women: Path to Equality,* 94th Cong., 2d sess., Washington, D.C.: U.S. Government Printing Office, 1975.

U.S. Congress, Joint Committee (House Committee on Ways and Means, Senate Committee on Finance). *Report of the Consultant Panel on Social Security to the Congressional Research Service.* 94th Cong., 2d sess., August 1976. Washington, D.C.: U.S. Government Printing Office, 1976.

U.S. Congress, Senate. Special Committee on Aging. *Women and Social Security: Adapting to a New Era.* A Working Paper Prepared by the Task Force on Women and Social Security. October 1975. Washington, D.C.: U.S. Government Printing Office.

U.S. Department of Health, Education, and Welfare. Social Security Administration. *Earnings Replacement from Social Security Benefits: Newly Entitled Beneficiaries, 1974.* Research and Statistics Note No. 13, June 15, 1976.

———. *History of the Provisions of OASDHI, 1935-1972.* Washington, D.C.: U.S. Government Printing Office, 1973.

———. *Self-Employment and Retirement Age.* Research and Statistics Note No. 15, July 30, 1976.

———. Research and Statistics Note No. 17, August 20, 1976.

———. *State and Local Government Employees Covered Under Social Security, 1972-73.* Research and Statistics Note No. 18, September 30, 1976.

———. *A Precise Formula for Primary Insurance Amounts.* Staff Paper No. 22, 1976.

————. *Demographic and Economic Characteristics of the Aged.* . . .Research Report No. 45, SSA 75-11802, 1975.

————. *Social Security Handbook,* fifth edition. Washington, D.C.: U.S. Government Printing Office, 1973.

————. *Trends: Part 1, National Trends, 1966-67.*

————. *Social Security Programs Throughout the World, 1975.* Research Report No. 48.

————. *Social Security Programs Throughout the World, 1973.*

U.S. Department of Health, Education, and Welfare; U.S. Labor Department; and U.S. Treasury Department. "Coverage and Vesting of Full-time Employees Under Private Retirement Plans." April 1972.

U.S. Department of Labor. Employment Standards Administration, Women's Bureau. *1975 Handbook on Women Workers.* Bulletin 297. Washington, D.C.: U.S. Government Printing Office, 1975.

U.S. Internal Revenue Service. *Statistics of Income 1972: Individual Tax Returns.* Public Document No. 79, 1-75. Washington, D.C.: U.S. Government Printing Office, 1975.

U.S. National Center for Health Statistics. *Monthly Vital Statistics Reports.*

————. *Vital Statistics Reports.*

Van Gorkom, J.W. *Social Security: The Long-Term Deficit.* Washington, D.C.: American Enterprise Institute for Public Policy Research, 1976.

von Mering, Otto. *The Shifting and Incidence of Taxation.* Homewood, Illinois: Richard Irwin, 1942.

Weekly Compilation of Presidential Documents.

"What Am I to Believe About the Social Security System?" *Wall Street Journal.* Editorial. April 20, 1976, p.19.

Witte, Edwin E. *The Development of the Social Security Act.* Madison, Wisconsin: University of Wisconsin Press, 1962.

INDEX

actuarial balance, 272, 312

actuarial imbalance, *see* deficit

Advisory Council on Social Security (1974, 3, 25-31; on financing, 30-31, 135-41, 150-52, 258-59, 281; on coverage, 35-38, 48; on social adequacy, 55-57; on treatment of men and women, 97-108, 258; on retirement test, 209-13, 258, Carter on, 282

AFDC (aid to families with dependent children), 3-4, 65, 69

AFL-CIO, 189,190

aged persons: social insurance for, 1-2, 22-23; numbers receiving benefits, 5-6; social security taxes paid by, 11, 208, 212-15, 222; and poverty, 23, 67-71, 78, 110-11; general revenues for, 275. *See also* Medicare; retirement benefits; widowers; widows

aid to families with dependent children (AFDC), 3-4, 65, 69

AIME, 114

Alaska, 14,43

allowable minimum, of wages, *see* retirement test

amendments, to Social Security Act; for dependents, 5, 71; for cost-of-living increases, 7-8, 79, 269; and pay-as-you-go system, 20-21, 59, 129; complexity of, 177; and retirement test, 201

Amish, Old Order, 41

AMW, *see* average monthly earnings

annual earnings test, for retirement, 209, 212, 221, 258

armed forces, dependency benefits from, 95

Arnold, Stanford D., 26, 194

average monthly earnings (AMW), 7, 12, 36, 57, 103, 112-18, 324-26

average price-indexed monthly earnings (AIME), 113-18

Ball, Robert M., 264

Basic Educational Opportunities Program, 267

Bayo, Francisco, 297

beneficiaries, *see* aged persons; dependency benefits; disabled persons; retired persons; survivors benefits

benefit formulae, 7-8, 60-63, 281, 315-16, 323-26. *See also* price-indexed formula; wage-indexed formula

benefits, *see* dependency benefits; disability benefits; medicare; retirement benefits

Beveridge Plan, 90

birth rate, 6-11 *passim,* 131, 133, 139-45 *passim,* 183-86, 203, 205, 280, 289

Bixby, Lenore E., 86

"black lung" disease, 28

blind persons, 13, 65, 69, 79

Bobo, Jack E., 264

bonds, 136

Boskin, Michael, 222

British National Insurance Scheme, 90-93

Brittain, John A., 235

Browning, Edgar K., 71n, 245

budget: for income assistance programs, 65, 70-71; of President, 163-64

"Budget Options for Fiscal Year 1977," 18

Burke, James, 15, 264, 265

Byrnes, John W., 26, 216

Cagan, Philip, 245

Califano, Joseph, 85

Califano v. *Hau,* 95,121

Califano v. *Webster,* 101

California, 13-14, 43

California State Employees' Association (CSEA), 14, 48

Calvert, Geoffrey N., 130

Campbell, Rita Ricardo, 26, 177

Campbell, Colin, 250

Campbell, Rosemary, 250

Canada, 169, 170

capital formation, 128, 136, 227-53

Cardwell, Bruce, 263

Cardwell, James, 124, 292, 306

Carter, Jimmy, 19, 80,174, 278-82